Language Contact and Grammatical Change

The phenomenon of language contact, and how it affects the structure of languages, has been of great interest to linguists in recent years. This pioneering new study looks at how grammatical forms and structures evolve when speakers of two languages come into contact, and offers an interesting new insight into the mechanism that induces people to transfer grammatical structures from one language to another. Drawing on findings from languages all over the world, *Language Contact and Grammatical Change* shows that the transfer of linguistic material across languages is quite regular and follows universal patterns of grammaticalization – contrary to previous claims that it is a fairly irregular process – and argues that internal and external explanations of language structure and change are in no way mutually exclusive. Engaging and informative, this book will be of great interest to sociolinguists, linguistic anthropologists, and all those working on grammaticalization, language contact, and language change.

BERND HEINE is Professor of African Studies in the Institute for African Studies, University of Cologne, and has taught in universities all over the world. He has carried out fieldwork in Ghana, Togo, Kenya, Tanzania, Uganda and Namibia, and has published 32 books and approximately 120 papers on African linguistics, sociolinguistics, historical linguistics, and grammaticalization theory.

TANIA KUTEVA is Professor of English Linguistics at the Institute for English and American Studies, University of Düsseldorf. She has taught at a variety of universities worldwide and has previously co-authored – also with Bernd Heine – *World Lexicon of Grammaticalization* (Cambridge University Press, 2002). She is the author of approximately thirty articles on grammaticalization, typology, Slavic linguistics, sociolinguistics, and second language acquisition.

Cambridge Approaches to Language Contact

General editor
SALIKOKO S. MUFWENE
University of Chicago

Editorial board
ROBERT CHAUDENSON, *Université d'Aix-en-Provence*
BRAJ KACHRU, *University of Ilinois at Urbana*
LESLEY MILROY, *University of Michigan*
SHANA POPLACK, *University of Ottawa*
MICHAEL SILVERSTEIN, *University of Chicago*

Cambridge Approaches to Language Contact is an interdisciplinary series bringing together work on language contact from a diverse range of research areas. The series focuses on key topics in the study of contact between languages or dialects, including the development of pidgins and creoles, language evolution and change, world Englishes, code-switching and code-mixing, bilingualism and second language acquisition, borrowing, interference, and convergence phenomena.

Published titles
Salikoko Mufwene, *The Ecology of Language Evolution*
Michael Clyne, *The Dynamics of Language Contact*
Bernd Heine and Tania Kuteva, *Language Contact and Grammatical Change*

Further titles planned for the series
Guy Bailey and Patricia Cukor-Avila, *The Development of African-American English*
Maarten Mous, *Controlling Language*
Edgar Schneider, *Post-colonial Englishes*
Clancy Clements, *The Linguistic Legacy of Spanish and Portuguese*

Language Contact and Grammatical Change

Bernd Heine
University of Cologne

Tania Kuteva
University of Düsseldorf

CAMBRIDGE UNIVERSITY PRESS
Cambridge, New York, Melbourne, Madrid, Cape Town, Singapore,
São Paulo, Delhi, Dubai, Tokyo, Mexico City

Cambridge University Press
The Edinburgh Building, Cambridge CB2 8RU, UK

Published in the United States of America by Cambridge University Press, New York

www.cambridge.org
Information on this title: www.cambridge.org/9780521608282

First published 2005
Reprinted 2006

A catalogue record for this publication is available from the British Library

Library of Congress Cataloguing in Publication data
Heine, Bernd, 1939–
Language contact and grammatical change / Bernd Heine, Tania Kuteva.
   p.   cm. – (Cambridge approaches to language contact)
Includes bibliographical references and index.
ISBN 0 521 84574 2 (alk. paper) – ISBN 0 521 60828 7 (pb.: alk. paper)
1. Language in contact.   2. Linguistic change.   3. Grammar, Comparative and
general – Grammaticalization.   4. Typology (Linguistics)   5. Areal linguistics.
I. Kuteva, Tania, 1958–   II. Title.   III. Series.
P130.5.H45   2005
306.44´6 – dc22   2004054601

ISBN 978-0-521-84574-8 Hardback
ISBN 978-0-521-60828-2 Paperback

Contents

Maps

Tables

Series editor's foreword

The series Approaches to Language Contact (ALC) was set up to publish outstanding textbooks and monographs on language contact, especially by authors who approach their specific subject matter from a diachronic or developmental perspective. Our goal is to integrate the ever-growing scholarship on language diversification (including the development of creoles, pidgins, and indigenized varieties of colonial European languages), language convergence, bilingual language development, code-switching, and language endangerment. We hope to provide a select forum to scholars who contribute insightfully to understanding language evolution from an interdisciplinary perspective or by bridging different research areas in linguistics. We favor approaches that highlight the role of the relevant ecology and draw inspiration both from the authors' own fields of specialization and from other disciplines or other research areas in linguistics. Eclecticism is one of our mottos, as we endeavor to comprehend the complexity of evolutionary processes associated with contact.

We are proud to add to the ALC series Bernd Heine and Tania Kuteva's *Language Contact and Grammatical Change*. This is the first comprehensive monograph that bridges research on grammaticalization with scholarship on language contact and in genetic linguistics. It focuses on linguistic areas, where, because of frequent contacts among their speakers, different languages, some of which are not genetically related, have come to share several structures. The authors propose to identify the language from which a particular structure or function has spread as the *model language*, and the language calquing it as the *replica language*. The very process by which the grammatical pattern is calqued is identified as *grammatical replication*. Various cases are discussed from especially European and Native American languages, but also from African and Melanesian ones. Creoles, in relation to which the process of grammaticalization has been questioned, are also well covered in this book, in which the discussions lead to the conclusion that these vernaculars are no exception to the fact that this diachronic phenomenon can be, and often is, contact-induced.

Quite informative also is the authors' discussion of structural and sociological constraints on grammatical replication. They clearly show that this phenomenon is not different from other diachronic processes which have been shown to be ecologically constrained. Moreover, individual speakers, rather than populations, constantly emerge from behind the processes Heine and Kuteva discuss, because they make it obvious that it is the speakers of a language who produce the changes cumulatively through things they do during their communicative acts, under the influence of a model language. They highlight the extent of osmosis in linguistic systems, making obvious that language boundaries are not so rigidly defined and borrowings can affect any component of the language architecture.

Since grammaticalization is the outcome of various processes of language change (for instance, generalization, category reassignment, and structural reanalysis), the book hits the heart of the distinction between contact-induced and internally motivated change. It disputes allegations that grammaticalization can only be internally motivated. And it also highlights the fact that linguistic convergence has taken place more frequently than has been suspected. In addition, it sheds light on the interaction of universal principles with language-specific ones in the process of change. Readers will also be happy to verify Heine and Kuteva's taxonomy of the most common types of replications, as well as several other research questions, such as (1) to what extent has the Europeanization of the world affected structures of other languages? (2) what can the study of contact-induced grammaticalization contribute to the study of geographically defined linguistic areas? (3) how relevant is the notion of "grammaticalization area" to understanding linguistic areas? The reader will not be disappointed by the breadth and depth of this book, which reflects successful cross-pollination between research in grammaticalization, in genetic linguistics, and in language contact.

University of Chicago   SALIKOKO S. MUFWENE

Preface

A number of students of language have pointed out that the way meanings are expressed in the language analyzed by them is exactly the same as that found in some neighboring language or languages, even though the forms used in these expressions are entirely different, and in spite of the fact that the languages concerned are genetically only remotely related or even unrelated. The main goal of this book is, first, to show that such observations are far from being coincidental; rather, that such cross-linguistic similarities are more common than is widely believed. Second, we will argue that there is a principled way to account for such similarities and, third, that these similarities are the result of processes of conceptualization that are the same across cultures.

The book has benefited greatly from discussions with and comments from many colleagues, in particular the following: Sasha Aikhenvald, Peter Bakker, Walter Bisang, Kate Burridge, Bernard Comrie, Andrii Danylenko, Gerrit Dimmendaal, Bob Dixon, Carola Emkow, Nick Evans, Zygmunt Frajzyngier, Victor Friedman, Jost Gippert, Tom Güldemann, John Haiman, Martin Haspelmath, Lars Johanson, Christa Kilian-Hatz, Christa König, Hiroyuki Miyashita, Salikoko Mufwene, Ulrich Obst, Thomas Stolz, Elmar Ternes, Elvira Veselinović, Debra Ziegeler, and many others. We also wish to thank Monika Feinen for the maps presented, Meike Pfaff and Barbara Sevenich for their typographical work, and Ulrike Claudi and two anonymous reviewers for many critical comments.

We are in particular grateful to the participants of the symposium on Language Contact and Replication that took place in Cologne on July 12, 2003. Comments made by Walter Bisang, Eva Csató, Gerrit Dimmendaal, and others turned out to be extremely valuable when reviewing some of the issues discussed in this book.

Our thanks are also due to the *Deutsche Forschungsgemeinschaft* (German Research Society) for having supported part of the work on which this study is based. Finally, we are deeply indebted to the Center for Advanced Study in the Behavioral Sciences, Stanford, and the Institute for Advanced Study, LaTrobe

University, and in particular the Research Centre for Linguistic Typology in Melbourne, which offered us hospitality to work out our field notes; we are grateful to these institutions for their generosity and understanding. Our gratitude also extends to our colleagues Lenore Grenoble and Lindsay Whaley, Dartmouth College, USA, who offered the first-named author academic hospitality and the means to work on this book when he was invited as a visiting professor from March to June, 2002.

Abbreviations

A	subject of transitive clauses
a.n.	authors' note
ABL	ablative
ABSOL	absolutive
ACC	accusative
ADE	adessive
AL	allocutive
ALL	allative
ANIM	animate
AOR	aorist
AP	adverbial particle
ART	article
AUX	auxiliary
BEN	benefactive
CAU	causative verb
COM	comitative
COND	conditional
CONJ	conjugational verb, conjunction
COP	copula
DAT	dative
DEF	definite
DEM	demonstrative
DET	determiner
DIM	diminutive
DIR	directive
DO	direct object
DUR	durative
ELA	elative
F	feminine
GEN	genitive
HAB	habitual
IMP	imperative

INDF	indefinite
INE	inessive
INF	infinitive
INFR	inferred
INSTR	instrumental
INTER	interrogative
INTR	intransitivizer
IRR	irrealis
L1	first language
L2	second language
LOC	locative
M	masculine; model language
MOD	modal
MT	modal time
N	noun
NEG	negation
NF	non-final
NFIN	non-finite
NOM	nominative
NOMIN	nominalizer
NON	non-
NP	noun phrase
O	object
OM	object marker
OPT	optative
Q	question
PART	partitive
PERF	perfect
PFV	perfective
PL	plural
PM	predicate marker
POSS	possessive
PPA	active perfect participle
PPLE	participle
PPP	past passive participle
PREP	preposition
PRES	present
PRET	preterit
PROG	progressive
PRT	preterit
PTCP	participle
PWOc	Proto Western Oceanic

Q	question marker
R	replica language
REFL	reflexive
REL	relative clause marker
REP	reported
REM.P	remote past
S	subject of intransitive clauses; subject
SE	demonstrative determiner *se* in Finnish
SEC	secondhand
SG	singular
TOP	topic
TRN	transnumeral
TRS	transitive suffix
V	verb
VIS	visual
TZ	transitivizer
WOc	Western Oceanic
1, 2, 3	first, second, third person

1   The framework

That language structure is fairly resistant to change in situations of language contact has been widely held among students of linguistics for a long time, presumably rooted in Ferdinand de Saussure's distinction between "internal" and "external" linguistics. In this tradition, Edward Sapir managed to persuade a generation of American linguists that there were no really convincing cases of profound morphological influence by diffusion (Danchev 1988: 38; 1989). While it was conceded that certain parts of language, such as phonology and the lexicon, tend to be affected by pressure from other languages, grammar was considered to be immune to major restructuring. More recent studies have shown that this view is incorrect. As some of these studies have demonstrated, essentially any part of language structure can be transferred from one language to another (see especially Thomason & Kaufman 1988: 14; Harris & Campbell 1995: 149–50; Aikhenvald 2002: 11–13). In fact, there is substantial evidence to support this general claim; still, it would seem that such an "anything-goes hypothesis," as Matras (1998a: 282) refers to it, is in need of modification: There is at least one domain of language use and language structure where a significant constraint on linguistic transfer from one language to another can be observed, namely the domain of grammatical meanings and structures.

The main purpose of this book is to demonstrate that the transfer of grammatical meanings and structures across languages is regular, and that it is shaped by universal processes of grammatical change. Using data from a wide range of languages we will argue that this transfer is essentially in accordance with principles of grammaticalization, and that these principles are the same irrespective of whether or not language contact is involved, and of whether it concerns unilateral or multilateral transfer.

The present chapter provides the reader with the analytic framework used throughout the book. To this end, we discuss the key notions of this framework in section 1.1, and in section 1.2 this framework is related to alternative approaches and terminologies. Section 1.3 presents the theoretical basis for the analysis of contact-induced language change, while section 1.4 discusses the technical and methodological tools that are used for identifying instances of this change. That the perspective adopted in this book differs from that of a number of other

1

authors who have worked on language contact is pointed out in section 1.5, and the final section 1.6 provides an outline of the subject matters discussed in the book.

1.1   Grammatical replication

If one finds similarities in form, meaning or structure between different languages then these may have arisen for a number of different reasons: they may be due to universal principles of linguistic discourse and historical development, to shared genetic relationship, to parallel development or drift, to language contact, or simply to chance. This book deals with cross-linguistic similarity, but it is concerned only with one of these causes, namely with language contact and the effects it has for grammatical structure. Broadly speaking, contact-induced influence manifests itself in the transfer of linguistic material from one language to another, where linguistic material can be of any of the following kinds:

(1) Kinds of linguistic transfer

        a. Form, that is, sounds or combinations of sounds
        b. Meanings (including grammatical meanings or functions) or combinations of meanings
        c. Form–meaning units or combinations of form–meaning units
        d. Syntactic relations, that is, the order of meaningful elements
        e. Any combination of (a) through (d)

Weinreich ([1953] 1964: 30–1) distinguishes three kinds of grammatical transfer (or interference in his terminology). One concerns the transfer of morphemes from what he calls the source language to the recipient language, that is (1c). The second kind of interference relates to grammatical relations, in particlar word order (1d), and the third to functions or meanings of grammatical forms, that is (1b). Situation (1c) involves what Weinreich calls source and recipient languages, while in the case of (1b) and (1d) he uses the terms model and replica languages.

Our interest in this book is with the transfer of grammatical meaning;[1] thus, the kind of transfer discussed here has traditionally been treated under (1b). Accordingly, we will adopt the terms proposed by Weinreich for (1b) and (1d) by distinguishing between model languages (M), providing the model for transfer, and replica languages (R), making use of that model, and we will call the process involving (1b) grammatical replication.

The following example may illustrate the framework used here. The North Arawak language Tariana of northwestern Brazil is in close contact with Portuguese, the official language of Brazil, and has been influenced by the latter in a number of ways (Aikhenvald 2001; 2002). For example, young and innovative speakers of Tariana recognize that in Portuguese interrogative pronouns are also used as relative clause markers, and these speakers also use their interrogative pronouns as markers of relative clauses on the model of Portuguese. In doing so, they graft their interrogative pronoun (e.g. *kwana* 'who?') onto their own relative construction. Accordingly, instead of (2), which is characteristic of traditional speakers, they use (3) in an attempt to replicate the Portuguese construction of (4).

(2) Tariana (North Arawak; Aikhenvald 2002: 183)

ka-yeka-kanihĩ   kayu-na   na-sape.
REL-know- DEM:ANIM thus-REM.P.VIS 3.PL-speak
PAST.REL.PL
'Those who knew used to talk like this.'

(3) Younger Tariana speakers (North Arawak; Aikhenvald 2002: 183)

kwana ka-yeka-kani hĩ   kayu-na   na-sape.
who   REL-know- DEM:ANIM thus-REM.P.VIS 3.PL-speak
            PAST.REL.PL
'Those who knew used to talk like this.'

(4) Portuguese (Aikhenvald 2002: 183)

quem sabia, falava assim.
(who knew spoke like.this)
'Those who knew, spoke like this.'

As we will see in the following chapters, processes of the kind illustrated above are extremely widespread, they can be expected in virtually any situation of intense language contact. What they have in common is, first, that rather than borrowing, i.e. a transfer of linguistic form–meaning units in accordance with (1c), they involve meaning, that is, (1b). Second, they are suggestive of a fairly complex cognitive process: rather than a simple transfer of meaning from one language to another, they presuppose some kind of equivalence relation that is transferred, in that younger Tariana speakers observe that in Portuguese the marker used for interrogative clauses is also used for relative clauses, and they carry out the same process in their own language – extending the use of their interrogative pronouns to also mark relative clauses; we will be able to look at a number of strikingly similar examples of this kind in the course of the book (see, for example, section 3.1.3).

This example may also illustrate the terminology used in this book: We will call Portuguese the model language (M), Tariana the replica language (R), and the transfer pattern from model to replica language will be referred to as replication.

The terms model language and replica language are relative notions, in that a given language can be associated with both roles. For example, the Austronesian language Tigak of the New Ireland island, Papua New Guinea, has served both as a replica and a model language vis-à-vis the lingua franca Tok Pisin, an English-based pidgin/creole (Jenkins 2002), and in the Vaupés region of northwest Amazonia, the North Arawak language Tariana has acted as a replica language vis-à-vis East Tucanoan languages but as both a replica and a model language for the lingua franca Portuguese (Aikhenvald 2002). In a similar fashion, Basque has served as a replica language vis-à-vis its Romance neighbors Spanish, French, and Gascon (Hurch 1989; Haase 1992; 1997), but it has also acted as a model language for Spanish speakers in the Basque Country (Cárdenas 1995), and Turkish served both as a model and as a replica language for Macedonian (Friedman 2003); for more examples, see Soper (1987).

The effects of contact-induced change[2] are referred to as transfer[3] (or areal diffusion) of linguistic material from one language to another. Transfer tends to be based on some kind of interlingual identification (Weinreich [1953] 1964: 7–8, 32), in our case on some way of equating a grammatical concept or structure Mx of language M (= the model language) with a grammatical concept or structure Rx of language R (= the replica language). In situations of intense language contact, speakers tend to develop some mechanism for equating "similar" concepts and categories across languages, something that Keesing (1991) describes as "formulas of equivalence"; we will refer to them as equivalence relations or, in short, as equivalence (or isomorphism). With this term we refer to corresponding structures of different languages (or dialects) that are conceived and/or described as being the same.

This definition is far from specific; as we will see in section 6.1, equivalence is a complex notion that is associated with a number of different uses. For our purposes, at least two of these uses should be distinguished. On the one hand, it is based on the linguist's analysis, relating to the grammatical categorization as proposed by him or her, referring to structural similarities between the grammars of two or more languages. On the other hand, it refers to the speaker's conceptualization of correspondences between languages in contact, as it is manifested, e.g. in translational practices and conventions. Since in many descriptions it does not become entirely clear which of the two is intended, equivalence is used here for both, but the term (structural) isomorphism (Aikhenvald 2002) is preferred in cases where the former use is intended by the author concerned.

Conceptual transfer will be described in terms of two contrasting descriptive notions, which are use patterns and grammatical (or functional) categories. With the former label we refer to recurrent pieces of discourse associated with the same grammatical meaning, while the latter concerns stable, conventionalized form–meaning units serving the expression of grammatical functions. We will deal with the former notion in chapter 2 and with the latter in chapter 3.

Contact-induced language change is a complex process that not infrequently extends over centuries, or even millennia. Not all components and stages of this process are necessarily an immediate product of language contact. It may happen, for example, that language contact provided the trigger for other changes to occur, that is, changes that are independent of language contact. But it may also happen that some linguistic change not involving language contact at some stage is affected by language contact. Most of the data that are at our disposal do not provide any clues as to which of such developments, or of many other conceivable developments, were involved. As long as there is concrete evidence to the effect that contact-induced transfer of linguistic material was involved in some way or other, we will treat such processes as "contact-induced language change." What this means is that this notion includes a wide range of different phenomena and in some of them, language contact may have played at best a marginal role.

A useful classification of grammatical changes is proposed by Tsitsipis (1998: 34) in his study of contact between the Albanian variety Arvanítika and Greek, distinguishing between completed, continuous, and discontinuous changes. Aikhenvald (2002) adopts this classification in her work on language contact in northwestern Amazonia and demonstrates that the distinction is a relevant one. Unfortunately, most of the works that we were able to access do not provide sufficient information on this issue.

The following chapters will be concerned with languages, and we will have little to say about contact between dialects. The reason is that research on transfer of the kind studied here has focused on contact between distinct languages and, accordingly, corresponding data on inter-dialectal contact are hard to come by. On the basis of the evidence that is available, it would seem, however, that what we have to say about languages applies in much the same way also to dialects in contact.

Our work will be concerned with the influence of one language on another or, more precisely, with how people change their linguistic habits when they are exposed to other languages. This subject falls squarely within what is widely referred to as contact linguistics. Contact linguistics is a broad field that has been the subject of diversified academic activity, involving disciplines such as linguistics, psycholinguistics, sociolinguistics, anthropology, and education. Myers-Scotton observes: "While of course contact linguistics has affinities with both psycholinguistics and sociolinguistics, it is something else. It deals specifically with the grammatical structure of the languages of bilinguals" (Myers-Scotton 2002: 5). We could not agree more with Myers-Scotton. What we will have to say relates to linguistic activity and its products, even if we will also be concerned with the cognitive foundations underlying this activity. At the same time, we will not treat contact linguistics as a discipline of its own. Rather, it would seem that the linguistic processes analyzed here are not substantially different from processes to be observed elsewhere in language use and language change.

1.2   Alternative approaches and concepts

Both the perspective and the terminology proposed above differ from those adopted in many other works on language contact. In fact, a number of the terms that students of contact linguistics may be familiar with will not be used here. This does not mean that we question the significance of alternative approaches and terms; rather, they are not immediately relevant to the analytic framework used in this work. Perhaps more than some other domains of linguistics, contact linguistics has developed a wide range of analytic concepts and labels. In the present section we will relate our framework to alternative approaches to language contact.

To start with, there is one label that we will use, even though it is marginal to the present treatment, which is borrowing. We will use this term exclusively with reference to what we defined in section 1.1 as (1a) and (1c), that is, to contact-induced transfer involving phonetic substance of some kind or other. In avoiding this term for other kinds of phenomena to be discussed in this book we deviate from conventions used in a number of other works. In these works, borrowing is used generally for any kind of linguistic influence of one language on another, in accordance with Haugen's (1989: 197) classic definition, according to which borrowing "is the general and traditional word used to describe the adoption into a language of a linguistic feature previously used in another" (see also Aikhenvald 2002: 3). We will use the term "transfer (from one language to another)" corresponding to Haugen's use of borrowing or to Weinreich's ([1953] 1964) term "interference," and we will restrict borrowing to the uses it is most commonly associated with, namely to processes involving the transfer of either forms or form–meaning units.

There is a variety of terminologies that have been proposed for the kind of process discussed in section 1.1. Most commonly, grammatical replication is subsumed under headings such as grammatical calquing, loanshift (Haugen 1950b), indirect (morphosyntactic) diffusion (Heath 1978; Aikhenvald 2002: 4), interference (see Thomason & Kaufman 1988),[4] congruence (Corne 1999; Mufwene 2001), code-switching, convergence, or attrition (Myers-Scotton 2002), structural borrowing (Winford 2003: 12).

Presumably the most refined descriptive framework to deal with contact-induced transfer can be seen in Johanson's (1992; 2002a) work on code copying. An important distinction figuring in the work of Johanson and his associates is that between *Globalkopieren* (global copying) and *Teilstrukturkopieren* (selective copying). The former refers essentially to the joint effects of transfer of the factors enumerated in (1), while the latter relates to a more limited spectrum of components figuring in contact-induced transfer, frequently only to one of them. The phenomena studied here can be analyzed profitably in terms of *Teilstrukturkopieren*, for the following reasons. First, our terms model language and replica language correspond closely to his terms model code and basic code. Second, our notion replication is similar to Johanson's notion copying, in that both imply that the product of the process is not identical with the model. And third, both replication and copying are conceived of as essentially creative acts (see section 1.5 below). Speakers create a new use pattern or category in language R on the model of another language (M), where the outcome of the process is not an exact copy of what exists in M but rather a new structure that is shaped, first, by what is available in R, second, by universal constraints on conceptualization, third, by what speakers of R conceive as being pragmatically most appropriate in the situation in which language contact takes place, and, fourth, by the length and intensity of contact and – accordingly – by the relative degree to which replication is grammaticalized (see section 1.3; chapter 3).

The term interference has been used as a convenient label for all kinds of processes. Still, we will not use it here since it has been associated with different types of linguistic change and, hence, may lead to misunderstandings.[5] For example, while Weinreich ([1953] 1964: 30–1) proposes to use it in a general sense to refer to all kinds of contact-induced phenomena, it is used by Thomason and Kaufman (1988) in a more restricted sense, relating only to one subset of changes that contrasts with structural borrowing, their second cover term (see also Romaine 1989).

Throughout this book we will be confined to replication, that is, we will have nothing to say about borrowing. This means that a number of issues that are central in some other works on language contact are not dicussed here. One such issue concerns code-switching, which is involved when "contact phenomena show surface-level morphemes from two or more languages" or, less technically, when there is an alternation of two languages within the same discourse, sentence, or constituent (Myers-Scotton 1993; 2002: 3, 105; Savić 1995: 476). As this definition suggests, code-switching involves "borrowing" in a wider sense – hence it is not within the scope of this book. Still, code-switching influences linguistic transfer in a number of ways, and it is at least possible that it may facilitate grammatical replication (Myers-Scotton 1993; 2002). On the whole, however, we have not found concrete evidence to the effect that code-switching is a notion that is helpful to understand contact-induced grammaticalization in particular and grammatical replication in general.

What we observed on code-switching applies in much the same way to what has been widely discussed as constraints or implications of borrowing, or as hierarchies of borrowing. Substantial work has been carried out on this issue (e.g., Weinreich [1953] 1964: 35; Moravcsik 1978; Thomason & Kaufman 1988: 74–5; Scotton 2002; see also Winford's [2003: 93ff.] constraints on borrowing), and it has produced a wide range of generalizations on temporal sequencing or preferences in the way linguistic forms and structures are borrowed; however, most of this work has been confined to borrowing, and it remains largely unclear how such generalizations relate to grammatical replication. Some of these generalizations might turn out to also shed light on conceptual transfer and replication. For example, what surfaces from this work is that in situations of contact, linguistic constituents characterized by structural autonomy and/or referential stability are more likely to be affected by contact than structurally dependent and/or referentially less stable constituents (see Matras 1998a). Overall, however, the relationship between borrowing processes and the temporal order in which grammatical use patterns and categories are replicated remains largely unclear.

In his analysis of syntactic change in Pipil, an Aztecan language of El Salvador, Campbell (1987: 277) observes that some of the changes described by him "are so natural that languages easily undergo them independently, and instances of the change are found repeatedly in the world's languages." He refers to these changes with the term naturalness (for a different use of the term "natural change," see section 6.5), but his discussion does not make it clear what this notion stands for, other than that it is a phenomenon that can be observed cross-linguistically and that languages undergo changes via naturalness independently. Still, Campbell provides two examples to illustrate how naturalness was responsible for changing the structure of Pipil as a result of contact with Spanish. One example is the development of third-person plural forms to markers of impersonal verb forms, and the second example concerns the development of a periphrastic future using a verb for 'go,' both developments being hypothesized by him to have been influenced by corresponding Spanish structures.

Both examples in fact relate to processes that are cross-linguistically common and may happen independently in a given language, and both constitute canonical processes of grammaticalization, as we hope to demonstrate in chapter 3. What this means is that they are suggestive of a unidirectional process: There are quite a number of languages where a third-person plural pronoun (e.g. 'They eat fish in Japan') has been grammaticalized to a marker of an impersonal construction ('Fish is eaten in Japan'), but we are not aware of any language where a marker of an impersonal construction developed into a third-person plural pronoun.[6] And the same applies to periphrastic 'go'-futures: many languages, including English, have grammaticalized a periphrastic verb form involving the lexical verb 'go' to a future tense marker, but so far no evidence has been found for a change from future tense to a lexical verb for 'go.'

While Campbell (1987) provides only these two examples to illustrate what he means by naturalness, his paper discusses a range of additional cases where Pipil has undergone morphosyntactic changes under the influence of Spanish. Of the seventeen examples presented in that paper, three relate to the transfer of form–meaning units, that is, to borrowing (see 1.1 (1c)), which is beyond the scope of the present work. But the remaining fourteen examples are instances of grammatical replication, that is, they are central to the present treatment, and all fourteen conform to principles of grammaticalization, as we hope to demonstrate in the following chapters: They involve unidirectional developments from lexical to grammatical and from less to more grammatical forms and constructions, i.e., none is in conflict with the unidirectionality hypothesis, which is central to grammaticalization theory (see section 1.3 below).

What these observations suggest is, first, that naturalness is not really a notion that is specific enough to be helpful for explaining grammatical change; second, if naturalness is taken to stand for universal principles of grammaticalization, as appears to be the case for the most part, then it captures significant properties of grammatical change. And third, and most importantly, these observations also suggest that contact-induced change in the Aztecan language Pipil is in accordance with what can be found in linguistic evolution that does not involve language contact. As we will see in chapter 3, Pipil is not an isolated case; rather, it conforms to what can be observed in many other situations of language contact.

In quite a number of works, grammatical replication is treated as a manifestation of convergence. In fact, in addition to the various meanings the term has received outside contact linguistics, convergence is proposed in many works as a technical term of contact linguistics. It has been applied to a wide range of phenomena, and some of them are relevant to the present discussion. Most conspicuously, this applies to the recent work of Aikhenvald (2002) and Myers-Scotton (2002; for a detailed discussion, see Myers-Scotton 2002: 171–3). Both authors use it for phenomena that include replication. But there are differences. According to Aikhenvald, convergence means that languages in contact "gradually become more like each other" (2002: 1). Myers-Scotton again uses the term in a more restricted sense. In her model of grammatical outcomes of language contact, instances of grammatical replication are subsumed under the rubric of either attrition or convergence (see section 6.4). Attrition, as treated by her, "is a phenomenon of individuals, referring to what happens to an individual's production of a language (usually an L_1), *and* the state of any loss at a point of time" (Myers-Scotton 2002: 179). Convergence is a complex phenomenon in her usage. It is said to be motivated by a situation where "the influence of one language on another reflects generally asymmetrical sociopolitical relations between the native speakers of the languages involved"; as a process it is "a mechanism in the progressive outcomes of attrition, language shift, language death, and creole formation," and its outcome "is a linguistic configuration with all surface morphemes from one language, but part of its abstract lexical structure from another language" (Myers-Scotton 2002: 101).[7]

Apart from the fact that the subject matter analyzed by Myers-Scotton differs in a number of theoretical and empirical aspects from the one looked at here, she uses the term convergence for a range of phenomena most of which are essentially irrelevant to our discussion. First, this applies to the motivation for and the process of convergence, which are described in terms of a set of sociolinguistic parameters. None of these parameters is a requirement for grammatical replication. As we will see in the following chapters, such constraints do not apply to replication, which is neither confined to specific kinds of sociopolitical situations nor does it correlate in any significant way with such notions as attrition, language death, or creole formation.

Second, Myers-Scotton applies the term convergence as an outcome to a number of linguistic manifestations, some of which do but most of which do not concern replication. One manifestation relates to the neutralization of morphological contrasts (cf. also Myers-Scotton's notion of attrition, which we will take up in section 6.4); for example, speakers of Malinche Mexicano (Nahuatl) take masculine as the default gender when using Spanish content morphemes (Myers-Scotton 2002: 102). Another instance concerns what one might be inclined to call an "inappropriate handling" of grammatical categories of another language, illustrated by Myers-Scotton (2002: 166) with a Spanish-speaking child from Colombia, living in the USA and being fluent in English. In this case, for example, convergence is manifested in the fact that the child produces a compound noun on an English pattern, uses inconsistent gender marking, and does not observe the pro-drop convention of Spanish.

The last example illustrates another problem with this term. The fact that the Spanish child does not observe the pro-drop convention of Spanish, producing overt first person pronouns as subjects instead, is discussed by Myers-Scotton as a manifestation of convergence. But essentially the same phenomenon is treated by her as a case of attrition rather than convergence (Myers-Scotton 2002: 201; see section 6.4): In her analysis of attrition hypotheses she discusses the development of pronominal subject marking of five Russian boys living in the USA for whom English is or is becoming the dominant language. She concludes that this development is characterized by what she calls "the decline in the Standard Russian use of the pro-drop parameter." Now, if speakers of a pro-drop language start using overt subject pronouns on the model of another language then this can be viewed as suggesting either that these speakers do not observe the pro-drop convention, or that they experience a decline in the pro-drop parameter, or else, as Savić (1995: 487–8) argues with reference to Serbian immigrants in the USA, that "the pro-drop parameter is being reset in accordance with English syntactic rules." We do not see what justification there should be to treat this general phenomenon as reflecting two different processes or mechanisms (see section 2.3.4).

As we noted above, the term convergence tends to be used to mean that languages become more alike in contact situations and, conversely, this assumption has frequently been used to formulate hypotheses on language change. Accordingly, language contact has been invoked as an explanatory parameter in cases where similarities were found between languages that are known to have been in contact. As Dorian (1993) shows, however, such similarities can be the result of quite a number of different phenomena, many of which are not necessarily contact-related.

To conclude, in spite of the fact that convergence has been employed for some phenomena to be described as or relating to replication, we will avoid the term, first, because its use is likely to give rise to misunderstandings of one kind or other and, second, because it does not contribute significantly to a better understanding of grammatical replication in situations of language contact.

Note finally that there is another problem associated with convergence, in that it has been used in two essentially mutually exclusive senses, which Hock (1986: 492–3) refers to respectively as mutual and unidirectional convergence: On the one hand, it concerns the reciprocal influence of languages on one another (see Thomason 2000: 89), where the languages involved change toward a new common form (Romaine 1988: 79; Salmons 1990: 454). On the other hand, it concerns the unilateral influence of one language on another (Myers-Scotton 2002: 172).

To conclude, the phenomena studied in the present work have been discussed under a variety of different terms and in a number of different theoretical frameworks. It would seem, however, that these terms highlight only certain aspects of the processes concerned and therefore are not entirely satisfactory to capture salient properties of grammatical replication. Thus the notion of convergence creates the impression of two languages becoming more and more alike as a result of similar structures being "laid on top of each other," whereby the parts sticking out are cut off, that is, the languages in contact are viewed as mutually influencing each other; the notion of grammatical replication, on the other hand, implies directionality from the model to the replica language.

Most of the processes discussed in this book cannot be accounted for exclusively with reference to language contact; rather, they are suggestive of an interaction of both language-internal and language-external factors.[8] What they have in common, however, is first, that they happened in situations characterized by intense language contact and, second, that an explanation of these processes remains unsatisfactory unless they are understood to have been triggered or accelerated by the impact of one language on another language (see section 1.4). What Johanson observes with reference to code copying in general also applies to grammatical replication:

Internal factors should probably not be regarded as "reasons" or "forces," but rather as inherent proclivities or tendencies. Linguistic elements possess structural properties which make them more or less "attractive" in change, acquisition and variation [. . .]. Cases in which the data seem to admit both external and internal motivations [. . .] are often instances of externally motivated internal tendencies. (Johanson 2002b: 286)

For good reasons it has been pointed out by various authors that the sociolinguistic history of the speakers should be the starting point in any discussion of language contact and its linguistic outcome (see especially Thomason & Kaufman 1988). It therefore comes as no surprise that many students of contact linguistics have drawn on sociolinguistic concepts to define, describe, and/or understand contact-related language change, which is commonly related to sociolinguistic or psycholinguistic notions such as social status, dominance, prestige, etc. In fact, work on language contact during the last decades has demonstrated in great detail how important social factors are in shaping language change (see especially Thomason & Kaufman 1988; Winford 2003). In this tradition, Johanson (2002a: 43–8) discusses two main parameters influencing what he calls copying, namely social dominance (or pressure) and relative attractiveness of linguistic structures. Each of these may independently lead to contact-induced change, but the two may as well be jointly present. However, strong social pressure can trigger change even if there are highly unattractive linguistic structures, that is, structures that are unlikely to be copied. One may wish also to draw attention to the notion "pragmatically dominant language" (Matras 1998a: 285) or the distinction subordinate vs. superordinate language (Silva-Corvalán 1994: 6). All these notions are of interest to analyze grammatical replication in some way or other.

Furthermore, in pidgin and creole studies, sociolinguistic notions such as substrate, superstrate, adstrate and the like have been invoked as indispensible notions for understanding the genesis, development, and even the present situation of the languages concerned. In a similar fashion, sociolinguistic models have played quite some role in defining terms such as borrowing, interference, or convergence (e.g. Thomason & Kaufman 1988; Silva-Corvalán 1994: 4–5; Aikhenvald 2002; Myers-Scotton 2002; Winford 2003), and accommodation has been proposed as a central parameter to understanding human behavior in bilingual situations (see the literature on communication or speech accommodation theory, e.g., Giles, Taylor, and Bourhis 1973; Giles et al. 1987; Giles, Coupland, and Coupland 1991). Important as these contributions are for understanding linguistic behavior in situations of language contact, their contribution to the present work is limited.

As has been argued by some authors (e.g. Danylenko 2001b; Aikhenvald 2002: 3), there are limits with regard to the role played by sociolinguistic factors. In fact, there is evidence to suggest that social variables are largely irrelevant as determinants of contact-induced language change – at least of the kind studied here. Aikhenvald (2002: 240) observes with reference to the Vaupés region of northwest Amazonia, which offers a case of extreme contact-induced grammatical tranfer, that sociolinguistic notions such as dominance relations were irrelevant for shaping transfer.[9] In a similar fashion, other sociolinguistic variables that might be expected to affect linguistic transfer do not significantly correlate with the way grammatical replication proceeds (see, for example, Soper 1987: 412ff.) – overall we have so far found no significant sociolinguistic parameters that regularly correlate with presence or absence of, or distinctions between, specific types of grammatical replication.[10] In view of such findings, we will avoid these notions unless there are specific reasons to do otherwise. Accordingly, we will have little to say about sociolinguistic factors (but see section 6.2); perhaps the main reason being that grammatical replication is a fairly ubiquitous process that can be observed across all kinds of sociolinguistic settings.

Johanson (1992; 2000: 165–6; 2002: 3) makes a distinction between two kinds of settings and, in accordance with these settings, he proposes to distinguish between adoption and imposition:

In the case of adoption, speakers of a primary code adopt (or "take over") copies from a dominant code. This is traditionally referred to as "borrowing" and "calque". In the case of imposition, speakers of a primary code insert (or "carry over") copies of their own code into their variety of a dominant code. (Johanson 2000: 166)

Broadly speaking, this distinction corresponds to what we will refer to as L2>L1-replication vs. L1>L2-replication. Important as this discrimination is for describing transfer patterns (or code copying), we have not found any noteworthy evidence to the effect that it affects the way grammatical use patterns and categories are replicated (but see Thomason & Kaufman 1988 for an alternative view).

Nevertheless, the kinds of contact-induced processes that we will discuss are by no means independent of the sociolinguistic situations in which they occur. In particular, they can be said to require a certain degree of intensity of language contact, where the latter can be described roughly in the following way (see Thomason 2003: 689): Grammatical replication is most likely to occur if there is a large degree of intensive and extensive bilingualism[11] among the speakers of the replica language and if contact extends over a longer period of time.

1.3   Contact-induced grammaticalization

In an insightful paper on the ways in which earlier speakers of Irish (Gaelic) handled the imported language English, van Hamel (1912: 273) observed: "Gaelic is a very idiomatic language, and it is but natural that the Irish should have begun speaking English by translating Gaelic phrases into English words" (van Hamel 1912: 273). Translation does in fact play an important role in situations of intense language contact; but, as we will see below, it is constrained in a number of ways. In the present work we will highlight one factor constraining grammatical replication that has found only limited attention in previous studies of language contact. This factor is grammaticalization.

Grammaticalization is a process leading from lexical to grammatical and from grammatical to more grammatical forms, and since the development of grammatical forms is shaped by constructions as well as larger context settings, the study of grammaticalization is also concerned with constructions and larger discourse units (Heine, Claudi & Hünnemeyer 1991; Hopper & Traugott 1993; Bybee, Perkins & Pagliuca 1994; Lehmann [1982] 1995; for a critical review of grammaticalization theory, see Newmeyer 1998; Campbell 2001; Campbell & Janda 2001).

A large body of knowledge has been assembled on the evolution of grammatical categories in the languages of the world (e.g. Heine & Kuteva 2002). All this work, however, has focused on language-internal grammatical change. Not only have grammaticalization processes usually been viewed as independent, language-internal changes, but it has even been claimed that the same grammatical category may re-emerge in a given language, and that this persistence or "diachronic stability" is a phenomenon entirely language-internally conditioned. In some cases, the stability over time may involve the very conceptual pattern on which the formal expression of the grammatical category is based.

Contact-induced language change on the other hand is a regionally confined process resulting from specific historical events. What this suggests is that grammaticalization and language change induced by contact constitute quite divergent phenomena and, in fact, in the relevant literature the two tend to be described as mutually exclusive processes.[12] Whether some specific grammatical change is due to the former or the latter has been the subject of some controversies. It has occasionally been argued, though, that language contact and grammaticalization can go together (Heine 1994; Nau 1995; Bisang 1996a; Kuteva 2000; Heine & Kuteva 2001). Dahl (2000b: 317) points out that grammaticalization processes tend to cluster not only genetically but also areally, and the terms areal grammaticalization (Kuteva 2000) and grammaticalization area (Kuteva 1998; Stolz & Stolz 2001: 1549) have been proposed to describe the effects of grammaticalization processes on the areal patterning of linguistic structures (see chapter 5). Still, the question of whether indeed, or how, the two are interrelated has never been addressed in any detail. As we hope to demonstrate in this book, the relationship between the two can be described in a principled way.

1.3.1   Parameters

In accordance with the definition of grammaticalization provided above, grammaticalization theory is concerned with the genesis and development of grammatical forms and constructions. Its primary goal is to describe how grammatical forms and constructions arise and develop through space and time, and to explain why they are structured the way they are (see Heine & Kuteva 2002: 4–5; Heine 2003a).

There is a wide range of formal parameters that have been proposed to describe the grammaticalization of forms and constructions. In the present work we will be largely confined to four mechanisms serving as convenient parameters for identifying instances of grammaticalization (see Heine & Kuteva 2002). These parameters are:

(5) Parameters of grammaticalization

       a. extension, i.e. the rise of novel grammatical meanings when linguistic expressions are extended to new contexts (context-induced reinterpretation)

       b. desemanticization (or "semantic bleaching"), i.e. loss (or generalization) in meaning content

       c. decategorialization, i.e. loss in morphosyntactic properties characteristic of lexical or other less grammaticalized forms, and

       d. erosion (or "phonetic reduction"), i.e. loss in phonetic substance

A prerequisite for grammaticalization is the use of existing forms or constructions in new contexts and, since new contexts tend to invite new semantic interpretations, also the emergence of new (grammatical) meanings (5a). For a more fine-grained analysis of extension, see chapter 2; for specific kinds of extension, see sections 2.2.2, 4.1.5.

While extension is pragmatic in nature, the remaining three parameters are morphosyntactic products of extension. All three involve loss in properties, but there are also gains: In the same way as linguistic items undergoing grammaticalization lose in semantic (5b), morphosyntactic (5c), and phonetic substance (5d), they also gain in properties characteristic of their uses in new contexts.

Most, though not all, works written within the framework of grammaticalization theory use the notion grammatical (or functional) category as the basic unit of description and explanation. As our work on language contact suggests, however, there is yet another notion that appears to be equally relevant in understanding the process leading to new grammatical structures, especially in the initial phases of this process. We will deal with this notion, which we propose to call "use pattern," in more detail in chapter 2.

The following examples may illustrate the nature of the process that will be the central concern of this book. There is a fairly widespread process of grammaticalization whereby, first, nouns and nominal structures develop into adpositions (prepositions or postpositions) and, second, comitative markers ('together with') develop into conjunctions coordinating noun phrases ('and'), and the latter again may develop further into clause-combining conjunctions ('and'; see Stolz 1998; Stassen 2000; Heine & Kuteva 2002). That this process can be triggered by language contact is suggested by the following example (Campbell 1987). Pipil, an Aztecan language of El Salvador on the verge of extinction, has no formal means for coordinating clauses, that is, clause-conjoining ('and') is not formally marked. But there is a "relational noun" *-wan* in Pipil which serves as a comitative marker; it requires a possessive pronominal prefix as a modifier, thus having the appearance of a possessed noun (Campbell 1987: 256). Under the influence of Spanish, Pipil speakers have developed *-wan* into a preposition *wan* 'with,' and *wan* has further developed into a noun phrase-conjoining conjunction 'and,' although it still appears to allow for a comitative interpretation, cf. (6). Eventually, *-wan* has been further grammaticalized to a coordinating conjunction 'and,' i.e. its use has been extended to also conjoin clauses, cf. (7).

(6) Pipil (Aztecan, Uto-Aztecan; Campbell 1987: 257)

> Juan i-   wan Maria
> John her- with Mary
> 'John and Mary' *or* 'John with Mary'

(7) Pipil (Aztecan, Uto-Aztecan; Harris & Campbell 1995: 130)

> ne ta: kat k- itskih ne mich wan ki- kwah.
> the man   it- caught the fish and it- ate
> 'The man caught the fish and ate it.'

This is not an isolated instance of transfer whereby Pipil speakers replicated grammatical categories on the model of Spanish (which has become the primary language of many Pipil speakers). As the description by Campbell suggests, there is a range of additional grammaticalization processes that Pipil grammar underwent as a result of replication of corresponding Spanish categories (Campbell 1987; see also Harris & Campbell 1995); we will return to these processes in the following chapters. That this is a case of grammaticalization is suggested by the fact that it appears to have involved all four of the five mechanisms distinguished above: Desemanticization had the effect that the comitative meaning was bleached out, with the result that the item eventually turned into a semantically largely vacuous linking device of clauses. This process was accompanied on the one hand by extension (see 5a), whereby *-wan* came to be used in new kinds of contexts involving clausal rather than nominal participants, and on the other hand by decategorialization, in that *-wan* lost its nominal properties, such as the ability to take a possessive pronominal prefix, turning from a relational noun into a functional particle. Finally, erosion was also involved in that the item lost its obligatory possessive prefix, thereby being shortened to a monosyllabic marker *wan*.

1.3.2   Unidirectionality

Grammaticalization is a unidirectional process; still, more recent research has shown that there are some examples contradicting the unidirectionality hypothesis (see especially Newmeyer 1998: 260ff; Campbell & Janda 2001); however, as acknowledged by these scholars, such examples are few, accounting for less than one tenth of all cases of grammatical change (Newmeyer 1998: 275–6, 278; Haspelmath 1999; Heine 2003b).

Such generalizations, formulated on the basis of cross-linguistic findings on language-internal evolution, do not seem to be contradicted by what we observe in situations of language contact. In more general terms, the unidirectionality principle appears to hold true in much the same way for contact-induced linguistic change as it does for language-internal development. In other words, processes underlying the parameters proposed in (5) as well as the overall direction which this cluster of processes follows, *lexical-to-grammatical-to-even more grammatical*, are unlikely to be reversed. Accordingly, we would be surprised to find speakers that, unlike the Pipil speakers in El Salvador, react to contact with some other language in such a way that they develop their grammatical/functional forms used for conjoining clauses into lexical items, and markers for clause coordination ('and') are unlikely to turn into comitative adpositions or nouns – in situations of language contact or elsewhere.

There is one parameter of grammaticalization which seems – at first sight at least – to be hard to accommodate in our understanding of the unidirectionality of both language-internal and contact-induced grammaticalization. This process involves the phonological substance of the structures undergoing grammaticalization. As mentioned above, one of the major parameters of grammaticalization involves the process of erosion, that is, loss of phonological substance. A number of our examples show that contact-induced grammaticalization, just like language-internal grammaticalization, does – indeed – lead to phonological reduction. There exist, however, examples where the contact a replica language has with a model language seems to lead to an increase in phonological substance, i.e. phonological accretion, instead of the expected phonological reduction. For instance, grammatical replication may sometimes result in the coexistence of marking from both the model and the replica languages within the same, new structure in the replica language (see our section 4.1.2), the natural result of which is phonological bulking or accretion (on phonological accretion, see also Kuteva forthc.).

At a closer look, it turns out that in many of these cases the phonological accretion is a characteristic of a transitional period only, which occurs when one structure (the already existing structure of the replica language) is replaced by another (the new structure replicated from the model language). After this transitional period, the process of erosion sets in along with the other three processes we discussed above as parameters of grammaticalization. This peculiarity – disturbing as it may seem at first sight – is not an unsurmountable problem for our analysis. On the contrary, it may well be identified as one more parallel between language-internal and contact-induced grammaticalization for the following reason. The transitional, overlapping stage of the coexistence of marking from the model and the replica language within the replica language structure observed in contact-induced grammaticalization is very reminiscent of a process characteristic of language-internal grammaticalization, too, whereby a historically earlier structure occurs in combination with the newly created, historically later structure (see Heine 1993 on the overlap model in grammaticalization).

Or, to use another example, quite a number of times speakers have developed constructions involving lexical verbs meaning 'go to' or 'want' into future tense markers on the model of some other language in situations of language contact (see section 3.3 for examples); but we are not aware of any speech community that has used a future tense marker to develop a lexical verb for 'go to' or 'want' – irrespective of whether or not language contact was involved. As we will see below, there are some cases to be found in situations of language contact that do not seem to conform to the unidirectionality principle (see section 3.4.1); but again, such cases are neither statistically significant nor do they suggest that language use in contact situations differs dramatically from situations that appear to be unaffected by language contact.

1.3.3   Earlier studies

The general process described in this book has not gone unnoticed in previous works. Weinreich ([1953] 1964: 39–42) views it as an instance of the replication of functions for equivalent forms in another language and tends to treat it as grammatical calquing. Similar analyses have been proposed in more recent works, where the process is generally discussed under the rubric of loan translation, calquing (see, for example, Greenberg 1983), syntactic interference (Alanne 1972; Nau 1995: 94), or indirect morphosyntactic diffusion (Heath 1978; see also Aikhenvald 2002). With reference to the contact situation between Eastern Oceanic Austronesian languages and English-based dialects of Melanesian Pidgin, Keesing (1991) suggests that many features of the pidgin can be attributed to the Eastern Austronesian languages "calqued into morphology that looks like English." In a similar fashion, Drinka describes the evolution of the European periphrastic 'have'-perfect in the following way:

[. . .] these languages tend to calque forms, that is, reanalyze the semantic value or morphosyntactic patterns of their own language according to those of the model language [. . .]. They are, in essence, borrowing the concept of the grammatical form rather than the form itself. (Drinka forthc.: 3–4)

In conventional terms, this is about the most appropriate way of describing contact-induced grammaticalization; but what is not highlighted in such descriptions is the fact that transfer does not involve calquing or loan translation but a grammaticalization process in the replica language. That the process described here is not restricted to copying a polysemy pattern (see section 3.2) but in addition requires grammaticalization in the replica language has already been observed by earlier students of the subject. For example, when describing the replication of a process from a reduplicated form of verbs for 'come' and 'go' as markers indicating the passage of time in narratives of northern and central Vanuatu languages in the pidgin Bislama, Keesing concludes:

Note there are two processes involved in the way *kam* and *go* have been incorporated into Pijin, one of which involves lexical equivalences and the other of which involves grammaticalization, at least to some degree. (Keesing 1991: 324)

A somewhat more specific depiction of the process concerned is provided by Matras in his discussion of contact-induced change in Balkan Turkish and Balkan Romani:

Convergence in the Balkan context is a cross-linguistic fusion of techniques for arranging and organizing propositions. It draws on individual properties of the participating languages, leading to language-internal grammaticalization processes. Grammaticalization of the type discussed below is thus motivated by the need to promote functional and configurational compatibility among languages in a linguistic areal. (Matras 1998b: 91)

In a similar fashion, Aikhenvald observes: "Diffusion of structural patterns implies that if a language adopts, say, a system of case marking, evidentiality, or switch-reference from its neighbours, it is likely to develop formal marking for the new grammatical categories from its own resources." (Aikhenvald 2002: 60). She adds, however, that in addition to grammaticalization, this process may also involve reanalysis,[13] another product of indirect diffusion typically leading to the restructuring of an already existing category; we will return to this issue in section 3.4.3.

A more explicit way of relating contact-induced language change to grammaticalization theory is described by Nau (1995); but perhaps the most detailed account of the mechanism has been proposed by Haase (1992). In his analysis of language contact and language change in Basque, he summarizes his findings roughly thus:

(8) Replication in Basque (based on Haase 1992: 111)

   a. Bilinguals aspire to establish equivalence between their two systems of categorization.
   b. This means that wherever there is an obligatory distinction in the model language, they try to develop a corresponding distinction in the replica language.
   c. Grammaticalization is crucially involved in this process.
   d. Categories for which there is no equivalent in the model language are in danger of being lost.
   e. Categories for which there is an equivalent in the model language are retained.

The claims made in (8d) and (8e) are beyond the scope of the present book (but see section 4.1). But (8a) through (8c) capture the main characteristics of the account we gave in section 1.3. For good reasons, the framework proposed by Haase is phrased in terms of functional, more specifically, language-internal factors. His insightful discussion of the Basque situation suggests, however, that there appear to be additional motivating forces, and this is supported by some of the cases to be discussed in the following chapters: For example, in a number of cases that we reviewed, contact-induced grammaticalization led to the rise of grammatical categories for which there already existed equivalent categories (see also Stolz & Stolz 1996). It would seem that there are socio-psychological forces in addition, such as the desire to use the options available in another language in the best way possible for one's own benefit, or simply to talk like one's neighbors. The data available, however, do not allow for any generalizations on this issue.

While most scholars who have analyzed contact-induced grammatical change in terms of notions of grammaticalization have argued in some way or other that grammaticalization theory offers a useful tool for studying this subject matter, there is one partial exception. In an important discussion of linguistic changes in the Balkans, Matras (1998b) concludes that this theory does not provide a fully satisfactory framework to account for the phenomena studied by him. It would seem that there are several reasons that appear to be responsible for this conclusion. The first is that many of the phenomena studied by Matras relate to morphosyntactic changes that so far have not figured prominently in studies on grammaticalization, such phenomena relating to complex sentence formation. Second, he associates with grammaticalization processes some properties that we consider to be neither necessary nor sufficient prerequisites for defining such processes. For example, "the acquisition of regularity in the system" or "the exploitation of inherent semantic properties" (Matras 1998b: 98) are phenomena that are not necessarily specific to grammaticalization but can be observed in a number of other historical processes. And third, he finds it difficult to maintain that the decategorialization ("decategorization" in his rendering) from major to minor category, and especially from lexical to grammatical category, is necessarily involved in the contact-induced changes studied by him. It is widely held – indeed – that grammaticalization concerns, or is restricted to, the development from lexical to grammatical (or functional) categories. However, such an assumption does not appear to be supported by facts; on the basis of the evidence that has become available it would seem that cases involving developments from lexical to grammatical categories are not the most common ones to be observed, that is, developments from categories that already have grammatical/functional status to even more grammatical categories are probably more frequent.

We will take up the data presented by Matras in subsequent chapters (see especially chapters 5 and 6),[14] and we will try to demonstrate that they are compatible with developments covered by grammaticalization theory. In fact, as we will see in section 3.1.3, the notion mutual isomorphism proposed by Matras (1998b: 100) corresponds to quite some extent to what we will refer to as replica grammaticalization.

1.4   On methodology

The main goal of this work is to reconstruct contact-induced grammatical replication. The most appropriate way of achieving this task is to draw on historical data that document this process. Unfortunately, in the vast majority of cases such data are either not available or do not allow for conclusive reconstructions. In many cases we are therefore left with synchronically available evidence. It is usually fairly easy to establish that transfer has taken place when lexical borrowing is concerned. When transfer is confined to meaning, or in our case to grammatical meaning, it turns out to be much more difficult to understand and describe what exactly is transferred; the relevant literature is rife with controversies relating to this issue.

Thomason proposes the following definition for contact-induced language change:

In my view, contact between languages (or dialects) is a source of linguistic change whenever a change occurs that would have been unlikely, or at least less likely, to occur outside a specific contact situation. This definition is broad enough to include both the transfer of linguistic features from one language to another and innovations which, though not direct interference features, nevertheless have their origin in a particular contact situation. (Thomason 2003: 688)

The message of this predication is clear, but as a definition it is not entirely satisfactory. First, it does not become entirely clear what an unlikely or a less likely change is, that is, what the criteria are for defining likelihood; it is therefore hard to assess the scope of possible linguistic changes that are covered by the definition. Second, the definition restricts the range of possible contact-induced linguistic changes to one subset of such changes, namely to those that are unlikely or less likely to occur outside language contact. There is no reason to assume that contact-induced change is restricted to unlikely or less likely linguistic changes. Accordingly, the definition excludes possible changes that are likely to occur to qualify as instances of contact-induced language change; once again, there is no obvious resaon why likely linguistic changes could not be contact-induced.

However, Thomason's predication offers an important way of approaching contact-induced change, and we will take it – not as a definition but – as a diagnostic device, and we will use it as a convenient tool for identifying instances of contact-induced change (see below). There are many cases of linguistic change that, on the basis of cross-linguistic generalizations, are "likely" to occur; still, they need not, and frequently do not, involve language contact. For example, in many languages worldwide a change can be observed whereby a numeral for 'one' has developed, or is developing, into an indefinite article, or a demonstrative attribute into a definite article. This is a likely change in that it can be expected to occur in virtually any language; still, in most cases in which it occurred there is no indication that language contact played any role. Nevertheless, as we will see below, such changes are more likely to arise in situations of language contact than in other kinds of situations.

Plausible cases of transfer of the kind examined here can only be made when the relevant languages are known to have shared a history of contact, in particular when there is evidence to suggest that (at least some groups of) speakers of the replica language were sufficiently exposed to the model language to make transfer possible. Linguistic criteria relate to questions such as the following:

(i) What evidence is there for transfer to have taken place?
(ii) Could that change have taken place without involving language contact?

Question (i) usually presupposes that we have some knowledge of the structure of the language prior to contact. In a number of cases to be discussed, such knowledge can be derived only from comparative evidence. For example, if we discover that some Austronesian language spoken in Papua New Guinea exihibits structural properties not found in fellow Austronesian languages, but that exactly these properties are also found in a neighboring non-Austronesian language of Papua New Guinea that is known to have been in contact with that Austronesian language, then a case can be made for transfer: As we will see below, quite a number of our examples are of this kind.

Question (ii) raises more serious problems. For example, some Slavic languages have developed use patterns that have been described as (definite or indefinite) articles. The fact that it is exactly those Slavic languages known to have had intense contacts with Germanic or Romance languages that have done so more dramatically than other Slavic languages would seem to suggest that this development was due to the influence of neighboring languages having full-fledged articles. However, the development of articles is a universal process that has taken place in a number of languages without there being any evidence that language contact played a role; accordingly, the possibility that these Slavic languages might have developed their articles without the influence from neighboring languages cannot be ruled out. In some cases there is additional evidence to argue that contact was a contributing factor in triggering or accelerating the process; in other cases such evidence is not provided by the author concerned and we decided not to discuss them in this work.

1.4.1   Genetic patterning

As this discussion suggests, genetic patterning not seldom provides the only evidence to decide on the directionality of contact-induced grammatical replication. By genetic patterning we mean here similarities or distinctions due to genetic relationship between the languages in contact. A couple of examples may further illustrate this point.

The Baltic and Finnic languages of northeastern Europe have had a long history of language contacts, resulting in a plethora of linguistic phenomena being transferred in both directions. As we will see in later chapters (especially chapter 5), this has led among others to a number of grammatical transfers where the Baltic language Latvian provided the model and the neighboring Finnic languages Livonian and Estonian the replica languages (see Stolz 1991 for details). The following case, however, does not correspond to this general pattern. Estonian has grammaticalized the verb *tulema* 'to come' to a modal auxiliary for the deontic modality of necessity ('must,' 'have to'), presenting the agent in the stative-locative adessive (ADE), an oblique case form, cf. (9). In a similar fashion, the Baltic language Latvian has grammaticalized the verb for 'come' in its reflexive form to a modal auxiliary (*nākties*) also expressing the deontic modality of necessity, with the agent being encoded by means of an oblique case marker, the dative (DAT), cf. (10)

(9) Estonian (Finnic; Stolz 1991: 80)

> mu- l   tul- i   see   töö
> (I-   ADE come- 3.SG.PRET DEM.NOM.SG work.NOM.SG
> teha.
> make)
> 'I had to do this work.'

(10) Latvian (Baltic; Stolz 1991: 79)

> man   nāc- ā-   s   ilgi gaidī- t.
> (I.DAT come- PRET.3- REFL long wait- INF)
> 'I had to wait for a long time.'

The striking similarity between these two constructions, as well as the fact that a grammaticalization of verbs for 'come' to deontic modals appears to be cross-linguistically rare, can be interpreted meaningfully only by assuming that the constructions are historically related. Estonian and Latvian belong to different genetic phyla, hence genetic relationship can be ruled out; we are therefore left with areal relationship as the most plausible hypothesis. Now, Finnish, a language closely related to Estonian, also uses the verb for 'come' as a modal auxiliary for deontic modality and an oblique case, the genitive, for presenting the agent, while Lithuanian, like Latvian a Baltic language, does not use the verb 'come' for expressing deontic modality (Stolz 1991: 79). In view of this genetic patterning we follow Stolz in concluding, first, that this is a case of contact-related transfer and, second, that the most plausible hypothesis is that this transfer proceeded from a Finnic to a Baltic language, that is, from Estonian to Latvian, rather than the other way round.[15]

   To conclude, the genetic patterning of linguistic properties can provide important clues for the reconstruction of linguistic transfer in general and grammatical replication in particular; we will return to this issue at the end of this section.

1.4.2   Cross-linguistically unusual grammaticalizations

Our concern in this book is with the interaction of two highly contrastive kinds of phenomena. On the one hand, we will deal with language contact and its products; on the other hand, we will be concerned with patterns of grammatical change that can be shown to be based on universals of human conceptualization and grammaticalization, and we will argue that, rather than being mutually exclusive, the two tend to reinforce one another in producing grammatical change.

What this means with reference to linguistic reconstruction can be illustrated with the following example. In a number of genetically unrelated Meso-American languages there is a polysemy pattern where the spatial notion 'behind' is expressed by a linguistic form that also means 'shoulder,' cf. the following examples.

(11) Náhuatl (Aztecan; Stolz & Stolz 2001: 1544)

    tepotz-   no-   tepotz-   taj
    'shoulder' POSS.1.SG- shoulder- LOC
    'behind me'

(12) Ch'ol (Penutian; Stolz & Stolz 2001: 1544)

    pat   t-   i'   pat   mesa
    'shoulder' LOC- POSS.3   shoulder table
    'behind the table'

(13) Zapotec (Oto-Manguean; Stolz & Stolz 2001: 1544)

    cožə'   cozžə'   ya'an
    'shoulder' shoulder mountain
    'behind the mountain'

A pattern of this kind, where one and the same linguistic form is used for both 'behind' and a body part, is cross-linguistically not unusual: Quite a number of languages use the same form e.g. for the body part 'back' and some locative term meaning 'behind,' English *back* being a case in point; thus, there is seemingly nothing special about this Meso-American situation (see Heine & Kuteva 2002). Nevertheless, the present case is noteworthy: While there is a worldwide polysemy between 'behind' and 'back,' in some languages also between 'behind' and 'buttocks,' it is hard to find any other languages where 'shoulder' and 'behind' are conventionally expressed by one and the same linguistic form. The situation found in these Meso-American languages is thus exceptional, and in need of explanation. One possible explanation would be genetic relationship, that is, that this "polysemy" pattern is inherited from some ancestor language shared by the languages concerned. As the evidence available suggests, however, such an explanation can be ruled out since this polysemy pattern is found in what is commonly assumed to be genetically unrelated languages (Campbell, Kaufman & Smith-Stark 1986; Stolz & Stolz 2001). The only reasonable alternative explanation is that this polysemy pattern is the result of language contact, and we will adopt this explanation here.

What this example suggests is that a knowledge of the cross-linguistic patterns of grammaticalization can be useful to reconstruct certain patterns of grammatical change, in that unusual patterns of grammaticalization found in neighboring languages are likely to be suggestive of language change induced by language contact. We may illustrate this with another example concerning varieties of the Indo-Aryan language Romani spoken in the Balkans. In these varieties there is a construction of the kind ['It does itself to X'], where the experiencer is encoded as a dative participant ['X'] and the verb phrase contains a third-person subject referent and a reflexive pronoun, to express the notion of a volitive/desiderative predication ['X wants/desires to do'], cf. (14). The same construction is found in Balkan languages such as Serbian, Bulgarian, and Albanian, cf. (15).

(14) Southern Balkanic Romani (Boretzky & Igla 1999: 722)

> Na   beš- el   pes   man.ge.
> NEG sit- 3.SG REFL to.me
> 'I don't want to sit.' (Lit. 'It doesn't sit itself to me.')

(15) Bulgarian (Boretzky & Igla 1999: 722)

> Ne   mi   se   jade.
> NEG to.me REFL eat.3.SG
> 'I don't want to eat.' (Lit. 'It doesn't eat itself to me.')

Such a kind of grammaticalization is cross-linguistically unusual and, although all languages concerned are genetically related, genetic relationship does not offer a convincing explanation for this similarity. Most likely therefore, this similarity is the result of language contact and, following Boretzky and Igla (1999: 722), we will assume that the Romani construction is due to grammatical replication by Romani speakers on the model of Balkan languages.

1.4.3   Paired grammaticalization

That contact-induced language change is influenced by grammaticalization is particularly obvious in cases where both the model and the replica languages undergo more than one process leading to essentially the same result in both languages. The situation of language contact between Balkanic Romani and the Slavic language Bulgarian may illustrate the relevance of such cases for grammatical reconstruction.

Boretzky and Igla (1999: 719) argue that, as a result of language contact, speakers of Bulgarian varieties of Romani have replicated the future tense construction of Bulgarian, cf. (16), using their own verb *kam* 'want' plus the finite main verb for this purpose on the model of Bulgarian, cf. (17).

(16) Bulgarian (Boretzky & Igla 1999: 719)

> šte   otida.
> want go.1.SG.PRES
> 'I will go.'

(17) Romani varieties influenced by Bulgarian (Boretzky & Igla 1999: 719)

> ka(m) ker- av.
> want do- 1.SG.PRES
> 'I will do.'

Now, the grammaticalization of a verb of volition 'want' to a future tense auxiliary is cross-linguistically widespread (see, e.g., Bybee, Pagliuca & Perkins 1991), the English *will*-future being a case in point; and it is particularly common in the Balkan languages (see section 5.2.3.1). The presence of the same pathway of grammaticalization in Bulgarian Romani and Bulgarian thus may be due exclusively to a universal cognitive strategy; hence, it does not provide compelling evidence for contact-induced grammaticalization. But Boretzky and Igla demonstrate that there is additional evidence to prove that language contact must have been involved in this grammaticalization. For the negative future, Bulgarian speakers use a different construction, namely a possessive construction based on an auxiliary verb meaning 'have,' cf. (18), and this is exactly what is found in Romani varieties of Bulgaria, as illustrated in (19).

(18) Bulgarian (Boretzky & Igla 1999: 719)

> njama da otida.
> not.have to go.1.SG.PRES
> 'I will not go.'

(19) Romani varieties influenced by Bulgarian (Boretzky & Igla 1999: 719)

> naj/nane te ker- av.
> have.not that do- 1.SG.PRES
> 'I will not do.'

That there are two parallel grammaticalization processes leading to the rise of future tense forms in the two neighboring languages, involving exactly the same cognitive schemas and giving rise to the same affirmative/negative split situation of future tense marking, is presumably unique in the languages of the world. Since the languages concerned are known to have had a history of intense contact, and since neither genetic relationship nor chance seem to provide convincing hypotheses to account for the similarity, this case is strongly suggestive of contact-induced change. This hypothesis is further supported by the following observation: The grammaticalization of possessive constructions to future tenses is widespread in European languages but fairly uncommon elsewhere (see, for example, Bybee, Pagliuca & Perkins 1991); it therefore seems plausible that Romani, a language of Indian origin, acquired it from the European language Bulgarian.

1.4.4   Sociolinguistic parameters

In addition to the linguistic and historical parameters mentioned above, sociolinguistic information can also be of help in reconstructing grammatical replication. For example, a number of studies suggest that in contact situations
involving a local language used as the L1 (first language) and a regional lingua
franca as the L2 (second language), urban dwellers are more likely to replicate
use patterns of the L2 than rural populations (see, for example Jenkins 2002:
256ff. on the situation in New Ireland, Papua New Guinea). Accordingly, if one
finds in such contact situations differences in the amount of replication cor-
relating with this parameter, one can hypothesize, *ceteris paribus*, that urban
speakers are more likely to reflect the earlier and/or more advanced state of
grammatical replication.

But perhaps a more salient parameter is age. Situations of language contact
are more likely to involve younger than old people, and male speakers are
overall more likely to participate in such situations than female ones, etc. In
cases of recent language contact one will therefore not be surprised to find
the use patterns of younger generations to have been more strongly affected
by another language than those of older people. Conversely, if in a situation
of language contact one finds a difference in speech along generational lines,
then this might be suggestive of contact-induced language change where the
speech of the younger generations reflects the innovated and that of the older
generations the conservative state of the language.

A plethora of cases illustrating situations of this kind can be found in
Aikhenvald (2002); one example was provided in section 1.1. The following example shows that this was not an isolated case (see Aikhenvald 2002:
153–4).[16] Among the North-Arawak-speaking Tariana of northwestern Brazil
there is a difference in usage between younger and older, traditional, speakers, in
that the latter have no copula in identity and equation clauses, while the former
have a copula *alia* 'be,' at least when contrastive focus is involved. Tariana
has been strongly influenced by East Tucanoan languages such as Tucano and
Desano, and has replicated many use patterns of these two languages. Speakers
of Tucano and Desano obligatorily use a copula in identity and equation clauses.
This suggests that there is a contact-induced change in Tariana leading from a
non-copula structure to a copula structure, rather than the other way round (see
map 1.1).

On the basis of the above observations the copula-less use pattern of traditional Tariana speakers can be assumed to reflect the earlier situation, while
the copula use of the younger generation constitutes an innovation, induced
by contact with East Tucanoan languages. This is in line with the reconstruction proposed by Aikhenvald (2002: 153–4), and it is supported by

Map 1.1 The language contact area in northwestern Amazonia (based on Aikhenvald 2002)

the following piece of evidence: While the majority of North Arawak languages do not have any copula verb, all Tucanoan languages have a copula verb.

Another example relates to the situation on the island New Ireland in Papua New Guinea. The Austronesian language Tigak does not have obligatory plural marking on nouns. However, under the influence of their L2 English,[17] which has obligatory plural marking, educated young Tigak increase the use of their overt plural morpheme. Thus, Jenkins (2002: 260) found in her transcribed Tigak material that these speakers use their plural morpheme with 46 percent of all plural nouns, while traditional, conservative Tigak speakers use the plural marker only with 19 percent of plural nouns.

Note, however, that age as a parameter of linguistic change has to be taken with care; there are a number of studies to suggest that age-related differences in language use may as well be the result of stable variation in different age groups (see, for example, Silva-Corvalán 1994: 5).

1.4.5   Circumstantial evidence

The problem that needs to be examined at this point is the following: What kind of and how much evidence is required to establish that contact-induced change, more specifically grammatical replication, has taken place? Our trivial answer is: The more evidence there is, the stronger a case can be made to substantiate one's hypothesis.

Kuteva (2000: 270–2) discusses an example from two Kenyan languages involving the structure of a verbal proximative aspect ('be just about to,' 'be on the verge of'). One of the languages is Gusii, a Bantu language, and the other Nandi, a dialect of the southern Nilotic language Kalenjin. Proximatives are found in quite a number of languages in Africa and elsewhere, the question therefore is whether the fact that the two languages share the same grammatical category can be accounted for with reference to historical factors. Genetic relationship can be ruled out since the two languages appear to be genetically unrelated: Gusii belongs to the Niger-Congo and Nandi to the Nilo-Saharan phylum. Lexical borrowing can also be excluded since the expressions used in the two languages for the proximative are phonologically entirely different.

Kuteva (2000) nevertheless argues that the two are areally related, for the following reasons. First, Gusii and Kalenjin can be shown to have been in contact in the past.[18] Second, these contacts have resulted in a number of transfers of linguistic material in both directions, leading among others to the rise of new tense categories in Kalenjin (Dimmendaal 1995; 2001b; see section 4.2). Third, the markers used for the proximative in the two languages are structurally alike: both are verbal auxiliaries, and both are used in one particular tense-aspect form, which is the perfect in the case of the Gusii auxiliary -ís- and the past tense form in the case of the Nandi auxiliary *eku*. Fourth, in spite of this tense-aspect restriction of the auxiliary, the use of the proximative is not restricted in time – neither in Gusii nor in Nandi. Fifth, in both constructions the main verb follows the auxiliary in a relative clause form. And sixth, both auxiliaries express 'become' as one of their meanings: Gusii -ís- denotes 'come' but also 'become,' while Nandi *eku* is a third person singular past form of 'become.' Thus, there are reasons to suggest that these similarities can be due neither to genetic relationship nor to borrowing, nor to coincidence.

To conclude, there is reason to argue that the two constructions are areally related. One way in which languages may acquire a proximative aspect is by grammaticalizing a verb 'come to' to an aspect auxiliary (Heine & Kuteva 2002: 78). Gusii speakers appear to have chosen this pathway, and Kalenjin speakers are likely to have replicated this grammaticalization by establishing an equivalence relation between one of the senses of the Gusii verb -ís- with their verb *eku* 'become' and developing a proximative on the model of the

Gusii construction (Kuteva 2000: 272), with the result that they acquired a semantically and morphosyntactically equivalent category.

1.4.6 Problematic cases

Unfortunately, quite a number of cases of possible contact-induced grammaticalization are not backed by conclusive evidence. In the Pennsylvania German variety spoken by Old Order Mennonites in Waterloo County, Canada, there are two emerging future tense categories (Burridge 1995: 61ff.; see also Fuller 1996). One of them is based on the Goal Schema [X goes to Y] involving the verb *geh* 'to go.' That this is a recent innovation is suggested by the fact that it is an immediate future; note that the evolution from goal-oriented motion to future tense is likely to lead via an intermediate stage where the construction is confined to the expression of immediate future events (see Bybee, Pagliuca & Perkins 1991). On the other hand, this Pennsylvania German category is not restricted to human or animate agents, which again suggests that it appears to be a well-established tense category, cf. (20).

(20) Pennsylvania German (Burridge 1995: 61)

       Ich hab   geglaubt – es geht ihm happene.
       (I   have believed   it goes him happen)[19]
       'I thought – it's gonna happen to him [i.e. at any moment]!'

Considering that in English, the major second language spoken by Pennsylvania Germans, there is a well-established future tense also based on the Goal Schema (*be going to*), it would seem plausible that (20) is an instance of contact-induced grammaticalization, that is, that Pennsylvania Germans replicated the English category.[20] That this is not a compelling hypothesis is suggested by the fact that Goal-Schema futures are cross-linguistically quite common (Bybee, Pagliuca & Perkins 1991; Bybee, Perkins & Pagliuca 1994); the possibility that this evolution could have happened without language contact can therefore not be ruled out. Burridge nicely describes the problems associated with the interpretation of cases such as (20) in the following way:

The role of English here is difficult to determine. For example, a calquing of English *gonna* may well have triggered the grammaticalization process moving PG [= Pennsylvania German; a.n.] *geh* towards a future marker. But it is impossible to tell. Patterns of grammaticization are demonstrated time and time again and across the languages of the world. The seeds for this particular change were probably already sown by the very nature of the (universal?) cognitive processes driving language use. It does not mean necessarily that English contact plays no part – but it is probably simply accelerating a tendency already long in existence. (Burridge 1992: 206–7)

To conclude, the presence of the *geh*-future of Pennsylvania German could be accounted for by any of the following hypotheses:

(21) Accounting for the *geh*-future of Pennsylvania German

    a. The construction arose on the basis of a universal strategy of grammaticalization, where contact did not play any role.

    b. There was one language (in this case English) that provided the model for replication in another language.

    c. The construction is due to (b) but it was supported by (a).

    d. The construction is due to (a) but the process was accelerated by (b).

In many cases that we are dealing with in this book, either (21c) or (21d) applies; in the case of (20), however, there is no conclusive evidence. Still, there are pieces of evidence that seem to suggest that a hypothesis based on (21a) is less plausible than any of the other three hypotheses. First, the English *be-going-to* future has turned out to provide quite an attractive model for replication by immigrant communities in the USA; as we will see in section 3.3, it appears to have induced a number of communities speaking languages other than English as their L1 to replicate it in some way or other. Second, while the Goal Schema in fact provides a cross-linguistically very common source for future tenses, it does not appear to have had any significance in the history of German dialects. Accordingly, the fact that it was recruited exactly in this particular case, where English provides a convenient model, is in need of explanation. To conclude, we assume that in the case of (20), English must have played some role. Irrespective of whether that role concerned (21b), (21c), or (21d), we will therefore argue that language contact was involved, either as a trigger or an accelerating device, and we will refer to the process summarily as contact-induced grammaticalization.

    Another kind of problematic case can be illustrated with the following example. Tok Pisin, an English-based pidgin/creole of Papua New Guinea, has been influenced by Austronesian languages, involving e.g. the replication of a number of use patterns and categories of the latter languages (see Keesing 1988; 1991; Jenkins 2002; see also section 3.1.2). These cases include the development from a verb 'to have' to an existential marker 'there is.' Thus, the Austronesian language Tigak of New Ireland, Papua New Guinea, has a verb *togtogan* which means both 'to have' and 'there is,' and the same polysemy is found in the Tok Pisin verb *gat*, e.g. *i gat sevenpela brata* (PM have seven brother) 'there were seven brothers.' Jenkins (2002: 219–20) therefore argues that the Tok Pisin use pattern is based both structurally and semantically on an Austronesian substrate of the kind found in Tigak.

There is a widespread grammaticalization process whereby constructions involving a verb for 'have' as the main verb and a dummy third-person subject pronoun give rise to existential constructions, cf. French *il y a* ('it there has' >) 'there is' (see Heine 1997a), and Tigak and Tok Pisin also appear to have undergone this very process. But the question is whether there is enough evidence to argue that this is indeed a case of substrate influence, or whether the two languages could not have undergone the same process without language contact. The fact that Tok Pisin must have experienced a number of grammatical replications on the model of Tigak suggests that the present case is yet another instance of replication, hence, that language contact must have played some role. On the other hand, the grammaticalization from 'have'- to 'exist'- constructions is particularly widespread in creole languages (Bickerton 1981: 66; Heine & Kuteva 2002), hence the possibility cannot be ruled out that this process in Tok Pisin is due to some specific development that this language shares with other languages, particularly with languages commonly classified as pidgins/creoles.[21] We will therefore not include cases of this kind in our treatment of contact-induced grammaticalization.

Unfortunately, cases like the present ones are not uncommon in the literature on language contact. What this means is, first, that in a number of cases figuring in the relevant literature, the question of whether some linguistic change was contact-induced or not rests on one single piece of evidence and, second, that it remains frequently unclear which of the hypotheses (21b), (21c), or (21d) is most plausible to account for the historical facts concerned.

On the basis of the observations made above we will adopt the following heuristic to identify instances of contact-induced linguistic transfer in the absence of any other evidence:

(22) Identifying instances of contact-induced transfer

If there is a linguistic property x shared by two languages M and R, and these languages are immediate neighbors and/or are known to have been in contact with each other for an extended period of time, and x is also found in languages genetically related to M but not in languages genetically related to R, then we hypothesize that this is an instance of contact-induced transfer, more specifically, that x has been transferred from M to R.

Something on the lines of (22) has been employed in some way or other by many students of contact-induced transfer, perhaps most explicitly by Aikhenvald (2002). In spirit, (22) relates to Emeneau's (1956: 16) classic definition of a linguistic area, by which he understands "an area which includes languages belonging to more than one family but showing traits in common which are found not to belong to the other members of (at least) one of the families."[22] While it is possible to find examples of documented language change that are at variance with (22), it would seem that, in the absence of any further linguistic, sociolinguistic, or historical information, (22) provides an empirically well-founded tool for identifying cases of contact-induced linguistic transfer, being supported by a large corpus of language contact data.

1.5   Grammatical replication as creative activity

In some of the literature on contact-induced change, speakers are portrayed as fairly passive participants in linguistic discourse, exposed to challenges resulting from the presence of another language and being constrained in their linguistic behavior by the kind of sociolinguistic "straightjacket" they are exposed to. The perspective underlying this kind of research is reflected in the terminology employed, characterized by labels such as "interference," "deviation from the norm," "learners' errors," "imperfect learning," "simplification," "overuse," or "overgeneralization." For example, Thomason and Kaufman (1988) make a basic distinction between what they call borrowing and imperfect learning. In the case of borrowing, fluent speakers of the receiving language adopt features from the source language, while in situations of imperfect learning, native speakers of the source language learn the receiving language imperfectly and incorporate their learners' errors into their version of it (see Thomason 2001a: 1640). In both cases, description tends to be biased in favor of one of the languages concerned that is somehow considered to provide the template of analysis for describing language change, and speakers are viewed as reacting to models, either by modifying something they receive from another language, or by failing to meet the norms of that language.

In a related fashion, Silva-Corvalán (1994: 3–6) proposes "simplification" and "overgeneralization" to be major strategies used by bilinguals in contact situations "aimed at lightening the cognitive load of having to remember and use two different linguistic systems." While the processes described by her are no doubt relevant manifestations of contact-induced change, the use of terms such as these overemphasizes the role of one of the languages in contact as a template for describing linguistic variation, and/or the relative contribution of speakers in situations of language contact.

Such frameworks account for a wide range of phenomena that have become known about situations of language contact, especially in situations of pronounced language attrition (see section 6.4). But on the basis of the data that we were able to access on grammatical replication there is another perspective of looking at contact-induced language change that appears to be more important. Rather than viewing replication as leading to a "deviation from the norm" or as a disruption of an existing state, we view it as leading to a new state that is simply different from the earlier state but is not necessarily less coherent, less "systematic," or less complete than the earlier state of the language concerned. And rather than viewing speakers as receivers, imperfect language learners, etc., we find massive evidence for a perspective according to which speakers are more appropriately analyzed as actors and "language builders," as Hagège (1993) proposes (but see section 3.4.4). For example, after a detailed analysis of replication ("loan syntax") from the Turkic language Uzbek to Tajik, the eastern variety of Modern Persian,[23] and from Persian to the Turkic language Qashqay of southern Iran, Soper concludes: "Apparently, loan syntax on this kind of scale involves not merely a few adjustments to the original set of grammatical structures, but rather the creation of a new set of structures, which correspond closely to the structures in the donor language" (Soper 1987: 423; see also Soper 1987: 7). What applies to grammatical replication in particular appears to apply also to code copying in general: "The result of convergent developments due to code copying are innovative and creative structures which must be regarded as integral parts of their respective codes" (Johanson in press. c: 12).

According to the perspective adopted here, there is a range of factors that speakers are confronted with in situations of language contact, in particular the ones listed in (23).

(23) The main variables of grammatical replication

      a. the sociolinguistic setting
      b. the structure of the model language
      c. the structure of the replica language
      d. communicative needs and intentions
      e. cultural values characterizing the communities associated with
         the model and the replica languages, and
      f. creative behavior activated to use the linguistic resources
         available in novel ways

On the basis of such variables, most of all on the basis of (23f), speakers tend to develop new structures of grammatical expression, manipulating the linguistic resources available in ways that are most beneficial to them in the situation concerned. Obviously, these structures are not identical with the corresponding structures provided by the model language, nor are they imperfect or deviant copies of the respective model; rather, they represent new ways in which linguistic discourse is organized. The following example from Bunte and Kendall (1981) may illustrate the process concerned – a process that we will encounter time and again in the following chapters. Speakers of Verde Valley Yavapai and Kaibab Paiute of Arizona have been found to make utterances such as the following when using English, their L2:

(24) English spoken by Verde Valley Yavapai and Kaibab Paiute (Bunte &
      Kendall 1981: 4–5)

      The car's brakes need greasing, they say.
      He's crying, they say.
      He fell off his bike, they say.

Such utterances, characterized by the use of the phrase *they say*, are made even if it is clear from the context that there is nobody saying something, e.g. when the speaker personally witnessed the event concerned. For an L1 speaker of American English, these utterances frequently sound peculiar, being suggestive of an "imperfect" handling of English (see Bunte & Kendall 1981 for a more elaborate discussion). Note that the phrase *they say* is used when the relevant speakers would employ the word *?ikm* in Yavapai or *aik* in Paiute. These words are grammatical markers which are required in many contexts and social settings to indicate what kind of evidence speakers have to make utterances such as (24), e.g. whether they are reporting rumors or inferences – technically speaking, Yavapai and Paiute have a grammatical category of evidentiality (see Aikhenvald & Dixon 2003). English does not have a corresponding category and when speaking English, Yavapai and Paiute speakers make an attempt to create such a category by drawing on the English phrase *they say* to express their notion of evidentiality, thereby creating a new use pattern in their variety of English (see also section 2.2). The result is that for an L1 speaker of English unfamiliar with Yavapai or Paiute, the use of *they say* is peculiar or even aberrant.

Thus, using one of the languages in contact, the model or the replica language, as a basis for describing and understanding linguistic change is likely to lead to an unduly restrictive perspective of what speakers actually do in manipulating the linguistic resources available to them. Accordingly, we will avoid labels such as simplification, overgeneralization, reduction, elimination of alternatives, etc. (see, e.g., Silva-Corvalán 1994; but see 2.2.4 below on "narrowing") – except for specific situations, e.g. situations involving advanced language attrition (see section 6.4). We will deal with a wide range of examples such as the Yavapai/Paiute case just mentioned (for an example strikingly similar to the present one, see section 2.4.1; see also Aikhenvald 2002: 315–16).

The perspective adopted here is that such cases are in no way characteristic of a peculiar or imperfect use of another language; rather, they illustrate how, in situations of language contact, speakers create new structures by drawing on universal strategies of conceptualization – in accordance with (23f). Using constructions involving lexical verbs for 'say' (e.g., 'it is said', 'they say') as conceptual templates for developing a grammatical category of evidentiality is cross-linguistically a not uncommon strategy (see Heine & Kuteva 2002: 265; Aikhenvald & Dixon 2003), and speakers of Yavapai and Paiute also appear to have drawn on this strategy for developing an evidential category in their variety of English. This is a canonical process of grammaticalization, where a construction involving a verb 'say' gradually loses its lexical meaning (= desemanticization; 1.3.1 (5b)) in favor of a grammatical meaning – in the present case that of expressing reported and inferred evidentiality. While being an odd way of saying things in English, for these speakers the phrase *they say* serves as an expression corresponding to the evidential markers of their model languages Yavapai and Paiute, and it can be viewed as constituting an enrichment of the English language, whereby one of its varieties acquired a new dimension of grammatical expression – one that appears to be absent in other varieties of English (see Aikhenvald 2002: 313).

That speakers in situations of language contact are not satisfied with imperfect copying but rather tend to create new grammatical categories in one language on the model of another language has been pointed out time and again in the relevant literature; the following example is representative of a wide range of studies that we will discuss in this book:

> Finally, a third factor may be a tendency on the part of bilinguals to create patterns in one of their languages which are structurally parallel to those found in the other. Thus, since in Spanish, subordinating morphemes occur clause-initially, it would be natural for a Luiseño/Spanish bilingual to use a Spanish subordinator in creating an analogous subordinator-initial adverbial clause in Luiseño. (Thompson & Longacre 1985: 205)

To conclude, what grammatical replication tends to involve is a process where speakers combine a number of different variables, in particular those listed in (23), to create novel forms of expressing grammatical meanings in the replica language. Accordingly, we are dealing – at least to some extent – with a creative process (see Johanson 1992; Hagège 1993 for a similar perspective): speakers are not only receivers and imperfect learners but also creators who use what they find in one language and sociocultural environment to shape another language in novel ways – they do not simply imitate grammatical categories, or produce imperfect copies of such categories; rather, they are likely to develop new use patterns and new categories on the model of other languages.[24]

Accordingly, the notion "imperfect learning" (see Thomason 2001a; 2003 for discussion) does not appear to be very helpful in understanding the mechanism underlying grammatical replication. To be sure, it does play an important role in spontaneous and/or individual situations bilingual language use, as has been pointed out abundantly in the literature on contact linguistics (see also section 3.4.4). But accounting for contact-induced language change, e.g. with reference to how speakers respond to a given norm, either by reproducing that norm imperfectly or by adding some features to the norm (see Thomason 2003: 692), highlights only one aspect of the process concerned and ignores others that are crucial for understanding replication.

However, as we will see in more detail in chapters 2 and 3, creativity is constrained in a number of ways (see (23)). First, it is of a special kind: it involves a gradual process that may extend over centuries; second, it is constrained by universal principles of grammaticalization; third, it is shaped by the nature of the model categories; and fourth, it is also influenced by the structural outfit provided by the replica language.

1.6   The present work

In this book we wish to present a new perspective of analyzing grammatical replication. To this end, we will deal with the initial phases of the process in chapter 2, drawing attention to the role played by use patterns in the emergence of new contact-induced grammatical structures. In chapter 3, we will elaborate on the notion contact-induced grammaticalization and its significance for understanding and describing how grammatical meanings and structures are replicated, using a wide range of examples from all major regions of the world. As we will see in section 3.4.3, however, not all cases of grammatical replication are also instances of grammaticalization, and we will propose the term restructuring[25] for those that are due to processes other than grammaticalization.

The implications grammatical transfer has for the structure of the languages affected are the subject of chapter 4. Most of all, we will deal with the question of how the typological profile, i.e. the overall structure, of a language may change as a result of massive grammatical replication. Chapter 5 relates to a field that is commonly known as areal linguistics, where we introduce the notion grammaticalization area, and we will argue that this notion is relevant for an understanding of all major linguistic areas or sprachbunds that have been proposed. The limits of the approach used in this book are discussed in chapter 6, where we will also look into a number of problems that are in need of further investigation.

The data on which the present treatment is based is constrained in two ways. First, our interest extends only to cases of language change for which there is reasonable information on where and how they took place, that is, where a credible hypothesis on what exactly happened can be proposed. This means that we are limited essentially to historical events that occurred fairly recently, typically within the last five hundred years. Second, we will be concerned with cases involving individual grammatical forms, rather than with overall typological generalizations. Accordingly, rather than studying general processes, such as changes from one basic word order to another or from one morphological type to another, we will look more narrowly at the behavior of specific use patterns and grammatical categories. And third, the perspective adopted here is restricted to but one of the many factors that contribute to grammatical replication. In a number of the cases examined, this allows us to capture salient characteristics of language change; in other cases, however, our analysis highlights some specific manifestation of change but ignores the complex interaction of all the factors that jointly contribute to that change.

There are two issues where we ask for the reader's understanding, both concerning the sociolinguistic dimension of contact-induced grammatical change. One concerns the nature of sociolinguistic situations and their implication for what are possible or impossible changes. Much of the recent literature on language contact maintains that such changes are constrained by the particular social parameters obtaining in situations of language contact. While there is compelling evidence to support this position, we will argue that the conceptual strategies that people use when exposed to different languages do not differ essentially from the ones they use in situations not involving language contact.

The second issue concerns our style of presentation. In the following text we will sometimes use shorthand phrasings that, if taken literally, are incorrect or misleading, or both. For example, if we say that languages are in contact, or that one language has borrowed from another language, then we are aware that languages cannot do such things – rather, that it is the speakers using these languages who do. We hope that such phrasings will not be an undue burden on the reader.

2   On replicating use patterns

Ever since the term grammaticalization was used for the first time in 1912 and even earlier, since the time of the neo-grammarians, grammatical change has been studied from the perspective of "competence" rather than "performance," or even better, of structure or *langue* rather than of *parole*. What has been achieved within the framework of grammaticalization theory is the establishment of a whole pool of cross-linguistically attestable developments. But when it comes to the question of what is the selective mechanism for a particular development to happen in a particular language, the study of grammaticalization has not moved much from where it started over one hundred years ago. More and more linguists have come to realize in recent years that what needs to be done is to show how actual language use feeds into language structure.

The model we propose in this chapter is meant to meet precisely this need. Grammatical replication resulting from language contact is discussed in terms of two descriptive notions, referred to respectively as use patterns and grammatical (or functional) categories. The former, to be discussed in section 2.1, relate to the way linguistic discourses are organized, while grammatical categories, the subject of chapter 3, are described in terms of canonical labels used in grammatical descriptions: they concern stable, conventionalized form–meaning units serving the expression of grammatical functions. By using these contrasting notions for analyzing grammatical replication we aim at capturing two different manifestations of the process concerned. While the notion grammatical category is well established in linguistics, that of grammatical use pattern is not. Yet, most of what happens in grammatical replication across languages, especially in its initial stages, relates to this notion.

Grammatical replication has the effect that the replica language (R) acquires some new structure (Rx) on the model of another language (M). As we will see in this chapter, however, the new structure Rx is in most cases not entirely new; rather, it is built on some structure (Ry) that already existed in the replica language, and what replication then achieves is that it transforms Ry into Rx. Depending on the kind of replication involved, Rx may stand for a number of possible structures and – accordingly – the process leading from Ry to Rx may take various forms. As a rule, however, Ry constitutes what we propose to call a minor use pattern, and the process Ry > Rx can be described as leading from minor to major use pattern, as we will see in section 2.2. What this suggests is that replication does not start from nothing; rather, it requires appropriate discourse patterns in the replica language to take place.

2.1   Grammatical use patterns

By grammatical use patterns (in short: use patterns) we understand linguistic structures having the properties listed in (1).

(1) Properties of use patterns
>   a. They are associated with some specific grammatical meaning.
>   b. They are recurrent pieces of linguistic discourse. Such pieces may consist of a clause, a phrase, or even a single form used in some specific context.
>   c. Their use is optional, that is, they may but need not be employed for the expression of that grammatical meaning.
>   d. They are the primary units figuring in the initial stage of grammatical replication.

Rather than full-fledged grammatical categories, use patterns are frequently variants restricted in their occurrence, e.g. to a particular social layer of speakers, register, or region.

2.1.1   Two kinds of use patterns

The role played by language contact in the rise of new use patterns can be illustrated with the following examples. In German there is what we will call a modal passive, that is, a frequently used collocation consisting of the modal *wollen* 'want' and the auxilary *haben* 'have' in combination with the main verb in the past perfect participle and expressing the grammatical meaning 'want to get something done'; an example is found in (2). The status of this use pattern is not entirely clear. It has been described as being passive-like, referred to variously as a modal passive, a statal passive, or a passive variant (Allard 1975: 26ff.; Leirbukt 1981), although some do not relate the pattern to passives (Reis 1985: 145) or propose a causative rather than a passive analysis (Hole 2002: 173–4).

There is a long history of contact between Germans and speakers of Slavic minority languages spoken around the eastern fringes of the German-speaking territory, such as Upper Sorbian, Lower Sorbian, Kashubian, and Slovincian, the last of these languages spoken until the middle of the twentieth century in the parishes of Schmolsin and Grossgarde of northwestern Poland but now possibly extinct. In the course of this contact, these Slavic languages have been massively influenced by German (see, for example, section 2.4.1), and one effect this influence had was that use patterns such as the German modal passive were replicated in the Slavic languages (Lötzsch 1969; see also Hinze 1969; Lötzsch 1996). Slovincian, for example, has a use pattern modelled on the German pattern, using auxiliaries for 'want' and 'have' and a past perfect participle, and expressing the same grammatical meaning as the corresponding German construction, cf. (3).

(2) German

    Sie wollte ein Huhn   gekocht haben.
    she wanted a   chicken cooked have.INF
    'She wanted to get a chicken cooked.'

(3) Slovincian (Lötzsch 1969: 108)

    . . . na-ca   mjìęc   kùǫkǫsš vu̥ var uǫnễ.
    (she.wanted have.INF chicken ?   cooked)[1]
    '. . . she wanted to get a chicken cooked.'

Our second example concerns language contact in northeastern Italy. In Sauris (Zahre), a village in Carnia, three languages are spoken in a triglossia situation: a variety of German (Sauris was founded by Germans in the thirteenth century), the Rhaeto-Romance language Friulian, being the language of the historical province of Friuli, and Italian, the official language. Of these three languages, German is most restricted in use, being virtually confined to use amongst villagers, and it has been influenced in a number of ways by the two Romance languages. One effect this influence has is that Sauris German speakers tend to add stressed personal pronouns to the already existing unstressed subject prefixal pronouns, either before or after the predicate. Thus, on the model of the Friulian structure, illustrated in (4), Sauris German speakers optionally strengthen the weak subject prefixes by adding the corresponding full, stressed, pronouns, cf. (5). The stressed pronouns may but need not express emphasis. Note that the strengthened structure is used only when there is no nominal subject.

(4) Friulian (Rhaeto-Romance; Denison 1988: 29)

    i-   soi strac, (jo). or (jo), i-soi strac.
    (1: SG- am tired I)[2]
    'I am tired.'

(5) Sauris German (Denison 1988: 29)

    I-   pɪn mɪəde, (iː) *or* (iː), ɪ-pɪn mɪəde.
    (1: SG- am tired   I)[3]
    'I am tired.'

On the basis of the description provided by Denison (1988), it would seem that Friulian has a use pattern of pronominal subject marking where originally stressed subject pronouns are part of the verbal group, gradually losing their pragmatic distinctiveness. The rise of this new use pattern in Friulian is presumably influenced by the fact that the unstressed subject prefixes are no longer fully distinctive (Denison 1988: 29). The use pattern consists of pragmatically marked pronouns, its function is to express case, and its use is optional – there is nothing to suggest that it has attained the status of a distinct category. In the language contact situation of Sauris, this is the segment of Friulian discourse that forms the basis of transfer, in that it is being replicated by German speakers on the model of Friulian.

What the two examples have in common is that there is a recurrent piece of discourse that is used for some specific grammatical function, and neither has the status of a full-fledged grammatical category – neither in the model nor in the replica language. But the two examples differ in one important aspect: Whereas the German-Slovincian case concerns a collocation that includes two form–meaning units, that is, auxiliaries for 'want' and 'have,' the Friulian-German one represents a pattern without any fixed form–meaning units. Most of the use patterns that we will be concerned with are of the first type, but there will also be cases where no form–meaning units are involved.

2.1.2 Formulas and constructions

Use patterns share a number of properties with other kinds of taxonomic structures that have been proposed for linguistic description. One kind tends to be described as speech formulas, which Pawley (1992: 22; 1994: 14, 16) defines as a conventional way of saying something for a conventional purpose, and especially of what he refers to as fully productive formulas or formulaic constructions. The latter consist largely of syntactic categories with variable lexical realizations. For example, English expressions such as *The sooner the better* or *The bigger they are the harder they fall* are described as instances of the comparative formula [*The* ADJ$_i$-*er (X), the* ADJ$_j$-*er (Y)*], where ADJ, X, and Y are treated as variable lexical realizations. Like use patterns, fully productive formulas are recurrent pieces of discourse having some specific meaning, and while they are usually clause-sized, they may as well consist of phrases (e.g. *for want of a better word*) or single forms (e.g. *sorry!*). To conclude, it is not always easy to trace a borderline between these two constructs.

Still, there are also differences. Use patterns are not necessarily conventional-ized structures; they are rather fluid units of discourse that stand out against other parts of discourse on account of their higher frequency of use, and they have a grammatical function rather than any other kind of meaning. Most importantly, however, they need not involve any constant linguistic expression; rather, they may consist of some collocation associated with paradigms of different expres-sions. For example, the use pattern of Sauris German speakers just discussed, consisting of stressed personal pronouns added to the unstressed subject pre-fixal pronouns, does not contain any fixed linguistic expression; rather, it has the whole paradigm of personal pronouns as its variable realization. While most of the use patterns figuring in the following paragraphs do contain some constant elements, this is no requirement for the presence of a use pattern.

But even more similarities exist with what is commonly referred to as con-structions (see, for example, Goldberg 1995: 1–7), and in a number of cases use patterns correspond to what in other theoretical frameworks would be described as constructions. The two are distinguished essentially by the fact that, first, constructions are described primarily in terms of morphosyntactic (or syntactic) parameters while use patterns are grammatical collocations that tend to be described with reference to discourse-pragmatic parameters such as frequency of use and context. Second, the latter may but need not exhibit non-compositional meaning, that is, their meaning may or may not be predictable from their component parts; constructions on the other hand are posited if their meaning and/or their form is not compositionally derived from other construc-tions existing in the language; accordingly, constructions typically exhibit a higher degree of either grammaticalization or lexicalization than use patterns. And third, whereas constructions are defined on the basis of language-internal analysis, use patterns are abstracted from observations on cross-linguistic equiv-alence relations established by speakers in situations of language contact; as we will see below, speakers constantly take structures of the model language to create new use patterns or turn minor patterns into major use patterns in the replica language.

To conclude, a number of the examples discussed in this book may with equal justification be treated as constructions or speech formulas; but as long as they conform to the properties listed in (1) we will describe them in terms of use patterns.

2.2   From minor to major use pattern

Language contact may lead to the rise of entirely new use patterns. But perhaps more commonly there is already some collocation, available for deployment in discourse, even if rarely used; for the purposes of the present work we will refer to such a collocation as minor use pattern, corresponding largely to what Koptjevskaja-Tamm and Wälchli (2001: 626) call latent constructions. In situations of contact, a minor use pattern may develop into a major use pattern on the model of another language, where replication has the following effects in particular:

(6) The rise of a major use pattern in contact-induced replication

    a. An existing use pattern is used more frequently.
    b. It is used in new contexts.
    c. It may become associated with a new grammatical function.

Accordingly, minor use patterns can be distinguished from major use patterns in the following way: While the former are used less frequently and are restricted to one particular context or range of contexts, the latter exhibit higher text frequency and involve a wider range of different contexts. Typically, the former are only marginally associated with the expression of a given grammatical function, and speakers may not even be aware of their existence; the latter on the other hand are more likely to be conceptually distinguished by speakers, being regularly associated with some specific grammatical function. In grammatical descriptions, the former usually go unnoticed, that is, they are ignored by grammarians, while the latter are more likely to be recognized as distinct units of discourse.

The effects in (6) can be taken to reflect the earliest stages in grammaticalization, relating to the pragmatic foundations of the process (see section 1.3, (5)). Increased frequency of use (6a) has been proposed as the driving force in instigating the kind of changes characterizing grammaticalization (see, for example, Bybee & Hopper 2001; Bybee 2003: 602ff.). Adding stressed personal pronouns to the already existing unstressed subject prefixal pronouns appears to have been available to speakers of Sauris German as a minor pattern used for pragmatic highlighting; what contact with Friulian achieved is that this pattern gained in frequency of use and was extended to new contexts. Use in new contexts (6b) may lead to context-induced reinterpretation, where the rise of new grammatical functions (6c) is a product of context extension (see section 1.3, (5a)): being gradually freed of their pragmatic function, the stressed pronouns increasingly assume the function of subject markers.

The exact nature of the interaction between frequency of use, context extension, and functional change is still largely unclear. Still, the order of the effects listed in (6) reflects a chronological sequence frequently observed in contact-induced grammatical change. Major use patterns can arise under all kinds of conditions; our interest here is exclusively with instances of (6) insofar as they are the immediate product of language contact. The way new major use patterns arise in situations of language contact is summarized in table 2.1.

As we observed in the introduction to this chapter, contact-induced new use patterns do not normally emerge *ex nihilo*; rather, they are likely to be the result

Table 2.1 *From minor to major use pattern in the replica language*

Stage	Frequency	Context	Meaning
0	Low frequency	Restricted	Weakly grammaticalized
I	Increase in frequency	Extension to new contexts	An additional, more grammatical meaning may emerge in the new contexts
II	High frequency	Generalized	Generalization of the new grammatical meaning

of a process whereby an existing minor use pattern gives rise to a major use pattern; and this transition from one pattern to another is unlikely to affect the overall structure of grammatical categorization.

This suggests that – superficially – replication is not necessarily a dramatic process, frequently consisting simply of a higher frequency and/or a more extensive use of an existing pattern. Take the following example: In German, nominal compounding is a prominent characteristic of morphology, e.g. *Herbstzeit* (lit. 'autumn time') 'autumn'; still, it is possible to use a possessive ("genitival") use pattern instead: *Zeit des Herbstes* ('time of the autumn'). Nominal compounding is uncommon in Romance languages, and Riehl (2001: 257) observes that German speakers in eastern Belgium and South Tyrol, northern Italy, where the majority languages are French and Italian, respectively, tend to develop the possessive pattern into a major use pattern where in Standard German, compounding would be preferred. Accordingly, in an attempt to replicate the possessive construction of Romance languages, German speakers in eastern Belgium may say *die Zeit des Herbstes* on the model of French *le temps d'automne* ('the time of autumn'), and in northern Italy, Riehl found German speakers using *das Bündel von Trauben* 'the bunch of grapes' instead of *das Traubenbündel* ('the grape bunch') on the model of Italian *il grappolo d'uva*.

As this case illustrates, the transition from one use pattern to another does not affect the grammatical structure of the language concerned, that is, German speakers in eastern Belgium or northern Italy did not develop a new construction or category of marking attributive possession, nor did they drop an existing one. What happened is simply that some existing mode of structuring discourse acquired a higher frequency of use and was extended to contexts that previously were primarily associated with some other use pattern.

This process can also be illustrated with an example that we already discussed in section 1.5, relating to the rise of an evidential use pattern in the English variety of speakers of Verde Valley Yavapai and Kaibab Paiute of Arizona, USA. The Standard English phrase *they say* has some characteristics of a minor use pattern, in that it may express that the speaker wishes to present hearsay evidence or rumor (e.g. *She is pregnant, they say.*). In an attempt to replicate the evidentiality category of their L1 in their L2 English, these Yavapai and Paiute speakers have developed that pattern into a major pattern by using it more frequently and extending its use to contexts where its literal meaning no longer makes sense. In such contexts, a new meaning corresponding to that of the evidential category of the model languages, their L1, is foregrounded. To conclude, the evidential pattern that these speakers of Yavapai and Paiute created in their variety of English has all the properties of a major use pattern that owes its existence to language contact, but it did not arise *ex nihilo*; rather, it constitutes an expansion of an already existing pattern in the replica language English.

We will now deal with the three parameters distinguished in table 2.1 in turn.

2.2.1   Frequency

When a major use pattern arises in the replica language, the starting point is an increase in the frequency of use of an existing pattern as a result of the influence of some model pattern, that is, speakers of the replica language tend to employ a pattern that is marginally or infrequently used, and they use it more frequently, thereby replicating what is conceived of as an equivalent use pattern in another language.

That increased frequency of use is the driving force in establishing new use patterns has been pointed out by a number of authors (cf. the notion frequential copying of Johanson 1992; 2002a; see also Hill & Hill 1980;[4] Riehl 1996). For example, there is substantial evidence to show that immigrants in the USA are likely to activate use patterns that are marginal in their respective L1 by using them more frequently in cases where their L2 English provides a convenient model. A fairly common example is provided by immigrant communities in the USA speaking pro-drop languages. Such languages are likely to have a marginal use pattern where personal pronouns may be used optionally for pragmatic purposes such as presenting given vs. new information, etc. Among immigrants speaking these pro-drop languages, such as Serbian, Russian, or Hungarian, this marginal use pattern tends to gain in frequency of use on the model of English (see Myers-Scotton 2002: 201); we will return to this case in sections 2.3.4 and 3.1.3.

German varieties spoken in the USA offer a variety of examples where a fairly uncommon use pattern is activated, acquiring a distinctly higher frequency of use on account of some English model that German speakers are constantly confronted with. A case in point is the English structure of *do*-support, which appears to have been a common target of replication. The German verb *tun* 'do' occurs in a number of use patterns in the dialects of Germany, in many cases taking the form of low-frequency patterns occurring in specific contexts. As observed independently in a number of studies on language contact, German immigrant communities in the USA tend to use *tun* more widely and in a larger range of contexts. In this way, new use patterns involving *tun* (or its American reflexes) have emerged, gradually acquiring new grammatical functions (see especially Costello 1992 for a range of such functions). In a few cases, English appears to have played some role as a model language.[5] For example, Old Order Mennonite speakers of Canadian Pennsylvania German have increased the use of their verb *duh* 'do' in a pattern which acquired something like a pro-verb or pro-form function much like English *do*, as illustrated in (7).

(7) Canadian Pennsylvania German (Burridge 1995: 69)

> Die Leit   dien net all gleich   gschwind Pneumonia kriege.
> (the people do   not all instantly quickly   pneumonia get)
> 'Not all people (do) immediately get pneumonia.'

As the description by Burridge (1992: 219–20; 1995) suggests, this use pattern in Pennsylvania German, while being used quite frequently, has not attained the generalized stage-II status it has in English (see table 2.1), being more limited than English *do*, and being confined to present tense. Eichhoff concludes with reference to the Low German variety spoken in Sauk, Wisconsin:[6]

Sentences like *Tust du ihn sehen?* instead of *Siehst du ihn?* ['Do you see him?'; a.n.] can be heard in northern Germany, to be sure; but their frequency of usage has increased considerably in Wisconsin under the influence of English. (Eichhoff 1971: 53)

An area that is remarkably sensitive to changes in use patterns concerns the organization of discourse, and in particular the role played by discourse markers. In many discourses of American English, the marker *you know* constitutes a major use pattern, being used frequently and in a variety of different contexts; its role as a discourse marker has been the subject of extensive scholarly analysis (e.g., Östmann 1981; Schourup 1985; Schiffrin 1987). Among Germans living in the United States, *you know* tends to be borrowed as a discourse marker, but it has also given rise to replication. In some varieties of European German, the phrase *weißt du* 'do you know?' constitutes a minor discourse pattern (for some speakers also a major one), being employed, e.g. to signal that the speaker expects that knowledge of the matter talked about is shared by the hearer. Among German L1 speakers in Gillespie County, Texas, and Dubois County, Indiana, the English discourse marker *you know* has been replicated as *weißt du* or *weißte*, that is, it is used more frequently than in European German and serves functions similar to those of English *you know* (Salmons 1990).

It would seem in fact that an increase in the frequency of an existing use pattern constitutes the most common kind of contact-induced grammatical transfer.

As we saw in section 1.4.4, the Austronesian language Tigak of New Ireland in Papua New Guinea does not have obligatory plural marking on nouns. But under the influence of their L2 English, which has obligatory plural marking, educated young Tigak increase the use of their overt plural morpheme: Jenkins (2002: 260) found in her transcribed material that these speakers use their plural morpheme with 46 percent of all plural nouns, while traditional, conservative Tigak speakers use the plural marker only with 19 percent of plural nouns.

In his study of word iteration, Stolz (2002c) found that word iteration of the kind illustrated in (8) is fairly common in languages spoken to the north of the Mediterranean Sea, and he argues that the degree of frequency to which it is found in these languages can be related to areal distribution.

(8) Italian (Stolz 2002c: 26)

> desideravano   ardentemente la   donna- donna.
> desire.PAST.3.PL ardently   DEF.F woman- woman
> 'They were ardently desirous of the real woman.'

That increase in frequency as a result of language contact may be a crucial factor in grammatical change has been observed by a number of authors. Johanson cites one instance from Irano-Turkic contacts, where the model language is Persian and the replica language Tebriz Azerbaijanian (Turkic):

Frequential copying may affect the use of constituent ordering patterns. As in spoken Persian and Kurdish, adverbials of direction and purpose are often postposed [in Tebriz Azerbaijanian; a.n.] [. . .]. (Johanson 1998: 333)

The Finnic language Livonian has been heavily influenced by the Baltic language Latvian, resulting, for example, in massive borrowing. But one effect of this influence concerned replication, in that Livonian speakers use their dative case marker more extensively (Larsson 2001: 250). Kostov (1973: 110–13) discusses one common type of what he calls "interference" phenomena under bilingualism where the receiving language develops what is only occasionally used into a regularly used pattern under the influence of another language. As an example he cites the Lovāri variety of Romani whose speakers use Hungarian as a second mother tongue and who grammaticalized their own locative adverbs to derivational[7] verbal prefixes in an attempt to replicate Hungarian verbal prefixes, thereby introducing a new morphosyntactic pattern for which earlier there was essentially no equivalent in Lovāri.[8] Note that verbal composition was not unknown to Lovāri speakers; what they did under Hungarian influence is simply increase the frequency of use of a rare type of expression, and to extend and elaborate it (Kostov 1973: 113). These strategies had quite some impact on the morphosyntactic profile of the Lovāri variety.

That increased frequency of use is a significant phenomenon to be observed in language contact has been pointed out by a number of authors. Perhaps most conspicuously, it is described by Silva-Corvalán (1994: 3) as being suggestive of both overgeneralization and simplification (the latter at least as far as it happens at the expense of some alternative expression), both being treated by her as key notions of contact-related linguistic processes.

From marked to unmarked pattern
A widely observable process triggered by language contact concerns infrequently occurring, minor use patterns that are activated because there is a model provided by another language. Such patterns tend to be pragmatically and functionally marked, being restricted to specific contexts and associated with some specific function; but under the influence of the other language they come to be used more frequently and their function tends to be desemanticized – with the effect that they may turn into more widely used major use patterns. This is how new word-order structures can arise, in that speakers of the replica language activate one of their minor use patterns that matches the word order of the model language and generalize it to a major, unmarked, pattern. The following example illustrates the process.

Turkish is commonly portrayed as a verb-final language, but there are pragmatically marked structures where the verb precedes its complement. For example, Friedman (2003: 66) notes that a sentence such as *Erol'dur iyi öğrenci*, where the verb occurs in non-final position, would have a meaning like 'It is Erol who is the good student' in Standard Turkish. But in West Rumelian Turkish dialects, spoken in Macedonia, this would be an unmarked sentence equivalent of the English 'Erol is a good student' – corresponding to the unmarked Macedonian sentence *Erol e dobar učenik* 'Erol is a good student.' This suggests that under the influence of Macedonian and perhaps other Balkanic verb-medial (= SVO) languages, speakers of West Rumelian Turkish dialects have developed one of their pragmatically marked minor use patterns into an unmarked pattern – in an attempt to establish syntactic equivalence with the language or languages of their Balkanic neighbors. Consequently, in these Turkish dialects of Macedonia the verb occurs far more frequently in a non-final position than it does in Standard Turkish.

2.2.2   Context extension

The more frequently a use pattern occurs, the more likely it is that it is extended to new contexts. Context is a fairly general notion and, accordingly, context extension relates to a number of different phenomena. In the following we will illustrate a few kinds of extension that are particularly relevant to our discussion.

Extension within a morphosyntactic category

Both German and English have a well-established and frequently used possessive perfect. In the contact situation obtaining among Pennsylvania Germans, the use of the possessive perfect ('have'-perfect) has been extended at the expense of the 'be'-perfect; the former is now used with all transitive and most intransitive verbs on the model of English. A mechanism that appears to have contributed to this context extension is that speakers of Pennsylvania German tend to equate their verbs with corresponding English verbs and to use the possessive perfect whenever the latter is required by the relevant English verb. For example, the verb form *geschehne* 'happened' takes the possessive perfect since the corresponding English verb form *happened* does so, e.g.:

(9) Pennsylvania German (Enninger 1980: 344)

> Nau   hoeret moll ihr liewe Leute, was   geschehne hott zu
> (now listen once you dear people what happened has at
> derre Zeit.
> that time)
> 'Now listen, dear people, what has happened at that time.'

In Sauk County Low German of Wisconsin, context extension appears to have proceeded even further – to the extent that the 'be'-perfect has been given up completely in favor of the possessive perfect (Eichhoff 1971: 53).

Another case of context extension can be seen in the following example from Irish English (Hiberno-English). Sullivan (1980: 201) observes that Irish requires its definite article to be used in certain contexts where it would generally not be used in Standard English: (a) before abstract nouns, (b) before verbals used as nouns, (c) before collective nouns, (d) before qualifying adjectives in singular form, and (e) in environments where possessive adjectives would be used in Standard English. Presumably since the end of the eighteenth century, Irish English speakers appear to have replicated this use pattern of definite reference by extending the use of the definite article to such contexts, where its use was previously excluded.

In Tucano and other East Tucanoan languages of northwest Amazonia, inalienable (kinship) possession is expressed simply by juxtaposition, where the possessor precedes the possessee, e.g. Desano *igo pa-go* (she parent-F) 'her mother.' In the North Arawak language Tariana it is alienable possession that is marked by juxtaposition, e.g. *nuha tʃinu* (I dog) 'my dog,' while inalienably possessed nouns require the indefinite prefix with non-pronominal possessors, e.g. *João i-ka: pi* (John INDF-hand) 'John's hand.' Intense contact between East Tucanoan languages and Tariana has the effect that there is now an ongoing process whereby younger and innovative Tariana speakers occasionally omit the indefinite prefix (e.g. *João ka: pi* 'John's hand'), thereby replicating the East

Tucanoan inalienability pattern of juxtaposition and extending their own pattern of alienable possession to inalienably possessed nouns (Aikhenvald 2002: 80–3). While this process is still in its initial stages, it might have dramatic consequences for the structure of equivalence relations, in that it could lead to a loss of the alienable–inalienable distinction in Tariana – a distinction that is consistently marked in the East Tucanoan model languages; we will return to this example in section 6.1.

Perhaps most commonly, context extension within some word class is tantamount to extension within a given grammatical paradigm, whereby a use pattern spreads across all members of the same paradigm. The following examples illustrate this process, which in some way or other can be observed in many cases of transition from a minor to a major use pattern. Morfill ([1885] 1971: 269) observes that language contact between Slovenian and German speakers in Trieste had *inter alia* the effect that the Slovenian pattern of reflexive marking was replicated to some extent by German speakers. Replication had the effect, first, that the German reflexive pronoun *sich* came to be used in new contexts on the model of the Slavic reflexive marker *se*, e.g. with verbs such as *lernen* 'learn,' which do not take a reflexive pronoun in Standard German, and, second, that the German pronoun, which is restricted to third-person referents, was extended to second and first persons, e.g. *wir waschen sich* (we wash REFL) 'we wash ourselves,' that is, its use spread across all three categories of personal deixis.

The second example concerns language contact between Irish and Irish English (Hiberno-English). Standard English has an imperative that is restricted to second-person referents, e.g. *Stay here till I come back!* Irish on the other hand has an imperative mood inflected for all three persons, both in singular and plural. Now, Bliss (1972: 72–3) suggests that under the influence of Irish, Irish English has replicated the Irish pattern by using the verb *let* (or, especially in Munster, *leave*) as an imperative auxiliary, e.g. *Let you stay here till I come back!* Such a use pattern was available to English speakers, as in *Let him go!*[9] But what language contact appears to have achieved is that, under the influence of Irish, the English use pattern was extended from non-second to second persons in Irish English, thereby matching the structure of the Irish imperative mood paradigm. Note that the morphological means used in Irish English differ drastically from those employed in Irish: whereas the latter language uses inflections, the former uses a lexical item, that is, the verb *let* (or *leave*). That this is in no way unusual is suggested by the fact that lexical verbs meaning 'leave' or 'let' are cross-linguistically a not uncommon source for grammatical markers expressing commands or obligation (see Heine & Kuteva 2002: 190ff.).[10]

Our concern here is with functional rather than with lexical use patterns, but the distinction between the two is gradual rather than discrete, and frequently it is not possible to draw a clear-cut borderline between the two. A fairly common strategy to be observed in situations of language contact is to extend the use of some basic verb by allowing it to take new complements in order to express new concepts. This strategy may have the effect that the semantic content of the relevant verb is generalized, and the verb retains its status as a lexical category. Still, the verb also assumes properties of a functional category, namely that of serving as a pro-verb whose meaning can be determined only with reference to the complement it is associated with. This evolution is in accordance with a universal process of grammaticalization whereby verbs occurring regularly in collocation with some specific type of complement tend to assume functions of auxiliaries.

The following example from the Slavic language Macedonian may illustrate the process concerned. For more than half a millennium, Turkish was the official language in much of the Balkan peninsula, and the penetration of Turkisms into Macedonian reached its height during the nineteenth century (Friedman 2003: 1, 15). One effect of Turkish influence can be seen in the fact that the extension of the Turkish verb for 'to eat' to a larger class of complements appears to have been replicated in Macedonian:

For example, the use of *jade* 'eat' to mean 'be subjected to' as in *jade k'otek* 'get a beating' (literally 'eat a blow') is obviously based on Turkish *kötek yemek* 'ibid.'; and so *jade dožd* 'get soaked' ('eat rain', Trk [= Turkish; a.n.] *yağmur yemek*) or *jade gomno* 'say something stupid/embarrassing' ('eat excrement', Trk *bok yemek*, cf. English *to put one's foot in it*) can likewise be identified as calques. (Friedman 2003: 13–14)

Such contact-induced context extensions appear to have led to an increase in idiomatic expressions involving the Macedonian verb *jade* 'eat,' but very likely they also had the effect that that verb acquired some potential as a pro-verb used with a larger variety of complement nouns, that is, as an incipient functional category (as we will see below, replication also appears to have proceeded in the opposite direction from Maecdonian to Turkish).

Finally, there are some kinds of contact-induced change that can be interpreted as being due to context extension even if they can also be interpreted in other ways. One of these changes concerns a fairly common process that has figured under headings such as "preposition calquing"; one example may suffice to illustrate the process: Swiss French *attendre sur quelqu'un* (lit. 'wait on someone') 'to wait for someone' is said to be a replication of German *auf jemanden warten* ('on someone wait'), where the use of the French preposition *sur* 'on' has been extended to a new context, namely to introduce the patient participant of the verb *attendre* 'to wait' (Danchev 1988: 46).

Another case that arguably qualifies as an instance of extension concerns functional categories that are restricted in their occurrence but that are extended to contexts where they no longer need to cooccur with some other category. Adpositions require noun phrases as complements, but in languages such as English there is "preposition stranding," where adpositions can occur in contexts where they are detached from their complements. In the language-contact situation of Prince Edward Island of Atlantic Canada, the variety of Acadian French spoken on the island has been subjected to heavy borrowing from English, but there are also cases of grammatical replication – "preposition stranding" being one of them (King 2000; Winford 2003: 68–9): In relative and passive clauses, speakers of Acadian French have replicated this strategy from English, as in the following example: *Je cherche une fille à avoir confiance en* (I am-looking-for a girl to to.have confidence in) 'I am looking for a girl to trust.'

Extension across categories

The German preposition *in* (dative definite: *im*) 'in' has a wide range of functions, one of them being to present temporal participants, e.g. *im Mai* 'in May,' *im Jahr 1999* 'in the year 1999.' While such examples of *in* with nominal complements constitute a salient use pattern of High German, *in* is not normally used with numbers such as dates of the year. However, under the influence of English, a new use pattern tends to arise where instead of *im Jahr 1999*, *in* can be used with dates of the year, e.g. *in 1999* 'in 1999,' even if this pattern is still largely restricted, e.g. to written registers such as journalese or certain professional discourses (cf. Nau 1995: 153). In cases of this kind, extension has no dramatic effects on the grammar of the language concerned; still, it affects the existing modes of categorization in some way or other.

   The more a use pattern expands, the more likely it is that it will involve new grammatical structures. The Aztecan language Pipil of El Salvador has been strongly influenced by Spanish and, as a result, has experienced a number of structural changes (Campbell 1987; Harris & Campbell 1995). For example, Pipil has a category of past participial forms, marked by *-tuk*, which formerly functioned only in verbal constructions, as in (10a). Apparently, Pipil speakers established an equivalence relation between their category and the Spanish participle, which functions not only in verb forms (*ha roto* 'has broken') but also often as adjectives (*el vidrio roto* 'the broken glass'). On the basis of the model provided by Spanish, the use of the Pipil past participial forms has been extended to new contexts, "to bear an adjectival function as well," as Campbell puts it (glossed PERF by Campbell 1987: 265), as in (10b).

(10) Pipil (Aztecan, Uto-Aztecan; Campbell 1987: 265)

 a. ki- chiw- tuk.
  it- do- PAST.PARTICIPIAL
  'S/he has done it.'

 b. kabál uksi- tuk ne wahkal.
  exact ripe- PERF the gourd
  'The gourd was just ripe.'

Not uncommonly, context extension involves a grammaticalization process (see section 1.3) whereby the use of an item belonging to some open word class is extended to serve as a modifier of another open-class paradigm. In this way, nouns and verbs may lose their categorial status and become clitics or affixes of other nouns or verbs. The following Finnish example, taken from Nau (1995: 86–7), may illustrate the process concerned. Presumably on the model of English *top* (and Swedish *topp*), speakers of Finnish have extended the use of their noun *huippu* 'top, peak' to act as a modifier of nouns in compounds, thereby assuming a schematic meaning, which is 'an outstanding, very important X,' e.g. *huippuhenkilö* 'an outstanding personality,' *huippuurheilija* 'a top sportsman,' or *huipputekniikka* 'top technology.' This use pattern is found especially in journalese, but it is not the only one of its kind. Nau describes a second one, involving the Finnish noun *avain* 'key,' which also has given rise to a compounding pattern on the model of English 'the key X,' e.g. *avainasema* 'key position,' *avainhahmo* 'key figure,' or *avainkysmys* 'key question.'

We seem to be dealing with the emergence of two contact-induced use patterns in Finnish, though neither of them is suggestive of a major use pattern. Both appear to be patterns of limited productivity, and both have been created on the same model and based on the same strategy, where the first of two nouns in compounds is grammaticalized to a modifying constituent, being extended to a specific context (= extension), losing its lexical semantics in favor of some schematic function (= desemanticization), and losing in nominal properties (= decategorialization; see section 1.3, (5) concerning these mechanisms).

That extension across morphosyntactic classes can give rise to grammatical agreement between different categories is suggested by the following example involving West Rumelian Turkish dialects spoken in Macedonia (WRT). As we saw earlier in this section, the presence of Turkish in Macedonia for more than half a millennium has given rise to transfers from Turkish to Macedonian; but there are also transfers in the opposite direction. For example, Friedman observes that there is evidence to suggest that Turkish children tend to replicate patterns of number agreement between nouns and their modifiers, characteristic of the Indo-European languages Macedonian and Albanian, by extending the plural marker from the noun to the modifier:

A phenomenon not noted in the dialectological literature but implicitly recognized as occurring in WRT in textbooks intended for Turkish schools in Macedonia and Kosovo is the use of the plural suffix on modifiers of plural nouns, e.g. *bunlar çocuklar* instead of *bu çocuklar* [. . .] 'these children' on the model of Macedonian *ovie deca*, Albanian *këta fëmijë*, etc. in which both the modifier and the noun carry morphological markers of plurality. The fact that Turkish children in Macedonia and Kosovo need to be told that such agreeing forms are 'wrong' is an indication that they use them. (Friedman 2003: 61)

Extension from nominal to clausal structures

One widespread pathway of grammaticalization concerns a process whereby the use of markers associated with the noun phrase is extended to mark clause subordination as well. In this way, demonstrative attributes commonly develop into relative clause pronouns, case and nominalization markers into markers for complement and adverbial clauses, etc. (see Heine & Kuteva 2002). The North Arawak language Tariana of northwest Brazil provides an example for such an extension pattern. Tariana speakers form complement clauses (that is, clauses that occupy a core argument slot of the predicate) by means of the subordinator *-ka*. But they have been in close contact with speakers of East Tucanoan languages and as a result have replicated many use patterns of these languages. East Tucanoan languages use nominalizations for complement clauses, and younger and innovative Tariana speakers tend to replicate this structure by extending their nominalization markers to introduce complement clauses on the model of East Tucanoan languages (Aikhenvald 2002: 162). Note that this is an ongoing process that so far has not spread throughout the entire Tariana-speaking community.

Extension across conceptual domains: from complementizer
to polar question marker

One kind of context extension giving rise to new grammatical functions can be seen in cases where the use of a complement clause marker 'if, whether' is extended to present polar (yes–no) questions. There appears to be a strategy whereby the use of a complementizer introducing indirect questions ('if,' 'whether') is extended to mark direct, polar questions as well.[11] Presumably, this is the way in which German *ob* 'if, whether,' exemplified in (11a), gave rise to a use pattern for presenting direct questions, illustrated in (11b), although *ob* is not the only means for marking the question.

(11) German

    a. Ich weiss nicht, ob er kommt.
       I know not   if he comes
       'I don't know if he'll come.'

    b. Ob er wohl   kommt?
       if he perhaps comes
       'Will he perhaps come?'

An instance of how this grammaticalization process is triggered by language contact is provided by interrogative marking in Finland Swedish. Standard Swedish uses verb fronting as its major strategy for presenting direct questions – a property that has been described as an innovation characterizing Standard Average European (van der Auwera 1998b; Haspelmath 1998; see also Koptjevskaja-Tamm & Wälchli 2001: 712), while indirect questions are introduced by the complementizer *om* 'whether.' In the Finland Swedish dialect of Solf, however, the Swedish conjunction *om* (*åm*) 'whether' has been extended from indirect questions to direct questions (cf. (12)). This grammaticalization via context extension is convincingly explained as being due to the replication of a pattern of Finnish, where the enclitic particle *-ko/-kö* is used both for direct questions, cf. (13a), and indirect questions, cf. (13b).

(12) Finland Swedish of Solf (Koptjevskaja-Tamm & Wälchli 2001: 713)

    Åm   dö tał ar engelsk?
    (whether you speak English)
    'Do you speak English?'

(13) Finnish (Koptjevskaja-Tamm & Wälchli 2001: 712)

    a. Tulee-   ko hän?
       come.PRES.3.SG- Q (s)he
       'Does he come?'

    b. En   tiedä,   tulee-   ko hän.
       NEG.PRES.1.SG know.NFIN come.PRES.3.SG- Q (s)he
       'I don't know whether he comes.'

A similar context extension is reported by Stolz (1991: 65–8) for Estonian. Like Finnish, this language uses the same marker as a polar complementizer and for presenting polar questions, cf. (14). But there are dramatic differences between these two Finnic languages: whereas Finnish uses the second-position enclitic *-ko/-kö* (see (13)), Estonian appears to have grammaticalized its marker *kas* ('whether, if') to a sentence-initial polar question marker. Exactly the same situation is found in the neighboring Baltic language Latvian, which has a long history of contact with Estonian: Latvian also uses the complementizer *vai* 'whether, if' to mark polar questions, cf. (15). Note that, unlike the Finnish enclitic, the Estonian and Latvian markers are free words[12] (Stolz 1991: 67); thus, there is equivalence between a Finnic and a Baltic language that contrasts with the marking structure in Finnish.

(14) Estonian (Stolz 1991: 66)

    a. Ma   ei   tea, kas   ta   tule- b
       (I.NOM NEG know whether s/he.NOM come- 3.SG.PRES
       või ei   tule.
       or NEG come)
       'I don't know whether he comes or not.'

    b. kas sin- a   tule- d?
       (Q you- NOM come- 2.SG.PRES)
       'Do you come?'

(15) Latvian (Stolz 1991: 67)

    a. es   ne-   zin-   u   vai   viņ- š
       (I.NOM NEG- know- 1.SG.PRES whether he- NOM.SG
       nāk-   s.
       come- FUT.3)
       'I don't know if he will come.'

    b. vai viņ- š   jau   (ir)   at-   nāc-
       (Q he- NOM.SG already COP.3.PRES here- come-
       is?
       PPA.NOM.SG.M)
       'Has he come here already?'

As the discussion by Stolz (1991) suggests, there is reason to assume that the Estonian situation is the result of replication on the model of Latvian (and perhaps Lithuanian), whereby a complementizer 'if, whether' was grammaticalized to a polar (yes–no) question marker (Estonian *kas*, Latvian *vai*).

It would seem that context extension of the Estonian conjunction *kas* strikingly resembles that of Finland Swedish *om* (*åm*) discussed earlier; what distinguishes the two cases in particular is that in the former case we are dealing with an Indo-European model and a Finnic replica language, while in the latter case there is a Finnic model and an Indo-European replica language.

2.2.3   Emerging new meanings

Context extension may go hand in hand with or trigger the crystallization of new meanings: new contexts tend to invite specific inferences for utterance interpretation and, given that a new context is recurrently associated with a new inference, a use pattern can emerge with its own context-induced meaning (see under extension; section 1.3, (5a)).

That increased frequency of use and context extension correlate with the emergence of new meanings is suggested, for example, by an example already looked at above, relating to *do*-support of American English and its influence on Pennsylvania German. Burridge (1995: 69) observes that in the Pennsylvania German of the Mennonite community of Ontario, Canada, the 'do'-verb *duh* is used for a number of purposes, assuming, for example, "something like a proform function, much like English *do*" (Burridge 1995: 69).

The following example illustrates the emergence of a new meaning in the replica language that largely – though not entirely – coincides with that of the corresponding use pattern in the model language. According to van Hamel (1912), Irish (Gaelic) has a use pattern where an adverbial phrase headed by the locative preposition *ar* is used to present experiencers:

In Gaelic the preposition *ar* (= on) is always used of any kind of emotion felt by a person, both bodily and mental. So it is said that sorrow and joy, fear and courage, thirst, hunger, need and sickness are *on* a person. (van Hamel 1912: 281)

It is especially experiencers related to the domain of sickness that figure in this use pattern. The pattern appears to have been replicated in Irish English (Hiberno-English) in the form of a new use pattern, with the English preposition *on* figuring as the equivalent of Irish *ar*. The pattern can be illustrated with the following examples:

(16) Irish English (van Hamel 1912: 282)

> It is not any common sickness that is on him.
> My hip is asleep on me.
> What is it you think of himself, with the fat legs on him?
> He's after dying on me.

It would seem, however, that the pattern is not confined to situations involving bodily or mental impediments of a person; rather, it can also relate to other situations having a negative effect of some kind; consider the following examples:

(17) Irish English (van Hamel 1912: 282)

> There might be no bad thing on the lad.
> You have the morning lost on us.
> And not be wasting my money on me.

The description provided by van Hamel (1912) suggests that the use pattern that evolved in the Irish English variety studied by him is used primarily for presenting malefactive participants:

the construction with *on* is more used of unpleasant emotions than of pleasant ones. Therefore *on me* will sometimes get the meaning of "to my loss", "to my detriment", or simply of an ethical dative. (van Hamel 1912: 282)

What this suggests is that there is a specific case function emerging in Irish English on the basis of a contact-induced use pattern having the structure [*on* – NP].

The way in which new contexts trigger new meanings, or new meanings suggest new contexts, is still largely unclear. Notions such as conversational implicature, invited inference, context-induced reinterpretation, etc., have been proposed to describe grammatical change involving correlations between meaning and context (see, for example, Heine, Claudi & Hünnemeyer 1991; Hopper & Traugott 1993); still, the question remains whether it is in fact new contexts that invite new meanings, or whether speakers propose new meanings and use appropriate contexts to present these meanings, or else whether meaning and context are inextricably involved in the process, thus making the question of which of the two presupposes the other redundant.

In Standard German, one of the main ways in which purpose clauses are formed is by means of the complex conjunction *um zu* 'in order to, so that.' This conjunction is not normally used to introduce nominal or adjectival modifiers; still, there is a widely accepted use pattern where *um zu* can be used, e.g. *ein Messer um Brot zu schneiden* (a knife for bread to cut) 'a knife for slicing bread.' Among German speakers of South Tyrol (Südtirol), northern Italy, massively exposed to Italian as a model language, Riehl (2001: 255) found that this use pattern has been extended to contexts where a purpose interpretation no longer makes sense, and where a new function appears to be emerging, namely that of introducing infinitival phrases, as in (18). Riehl argues that this context extension has been influenced by Italian, the official language (cf. Italian *ideale per* 'ideal for'); we will return to this example in section 3.1.2.

(18) German as used in South Tyrol (Riehl 2001: 255)

> Deutsch finde ich ideal, um die Einheitssprache in Europa
> (German find I   ideal for the unity.language in Europe
> zu werden.
> to become)
> 'I find German ideal to become the unifying language in Europe.'

In Singapore, Chinese is a prominent model language for the variety of English spoken in this state. In Singaporean English, the adverb *already* is used extensively and tends to be used in contexts where it invites an interpretation in terms of a marker of a completive aspect. Mian-Lian and Platt (1993: 152–3) suggest that underlying this usage there is the Chinese perfective aspect marker *le* which serves as a model for the grammaticalization of *already*, leading from adverb to verbal aspect marker.

That context extension and the emergence of new meanings can happen simultaneously is also suggested by an example of quite a different nature. There are a number of languages where speakers have extended the use of second-person plural pronouns to designate second-person singular address too, and this strategy, called pluralization, is assumed to be the result of a universal strategy to express distinctions of respect and/or social distance (Head 1978: 158) – the history of Western European languages offers a number of examples. It would seem, however, that pluralization can also be influenced by language contact. Evidence for this hypothesis is of two kinds. First, the areal distribution cross-linguistically suggests roughly that there is a statistical correlation of the following kind: Pluralization is more likely to be found in a language where some neighboring language also has it than in a language where there is no adjacent language using pluralization. And second, there are cases of European languages where there is historical evidence to support this hypothesis (see Simon 1997: 271). One of them is Scottish Gaelic, as Mühlhäusler and Harré suggest:

> But in Scotland the influence in the eighteenth century of all things French led to the importation of the custom of using the second person plural [. . .] as an honorific, in which role it persists today in the few remaining Gaelic-speaking areas. (Mühlhäusler and Harré 1990: 141)

Accordingly, we assume that in this case a cross-culturally widespread tendency and language contact interacted in producing pluralization – a situation that we will encounter time and again in the following chapters.

What the process reconstructed for Scottish Gaelic suggests is that with the extension of a second-person plural pronoun to contexts where there was only one addressee, the only possible meaning of the plural pronoun could have been that of marking singular reference. Thus, the creation of a new use pattern, initially serving honorific address, appears to have involved simultaneously context extension and meaning change.

2.2.4   Narrowing

The kind of change in use patterns depicted above is a common one, but it is not the only one that can be observed in language contact. Aikhenvald (2002) provides a wealth of alternative changes, and the reader is referred to that work for more details. One perhaps not uncommon kind of change concerns what may be called narrowing,[13] whereby a pattern associated with a range of different optional uses comes to be restricted to one particular use because that use corresponds immediately to an equivalent use pattern in the model language, which does not offer such options. Narrowing has most frequently been observed in syntax, whereby variability in the arrangement of meaningful elements is narrowed down to one particular arrangement. The following examples may illustrate the central role played by narrowing in the rise of new contact-induced use patterns. Kadiwéu, a Waikurúan language of Brazil, has relatively free word order, attested orders being OVS, VOS, SOV, OSV, VSO, and SVO. But Kadiwéu-Portuguese bilinguals tend to prefer SVO word order, which matches Portuguese[14] (Thomason 2001a: 1642). What this suggests is that it is the word-order arrangement that is prevalent in the model language that bilingual speakers of the replica language tend to select, thereby narrowing down the range of syntactic options available to them.

Another example concerns language contact in the Vaupés region of northwestern Brazil, relating to grammatical replication where East Tucanoan languages provide the model and the North Arawak language Tariana is the replica language. Tariana is characterized by the presence of floating clitics, in that markers for tense, evidentiality, and modality are clausal clitics that are attached to a particular constituent in the clause under specific discourse conditions. In East Tucanoan languages, such markers are attached to the verb. Now, younger and innovative Tariana speakers tend to replicate the East Tucanoan pattern by narrowing down the placement of tense-evidentiality enclitics exclusively to the verb (see Aikhenvald 2002: 146–8 for more details).

For another example of contact-induced narrowing involving East Tucanoan languages and Tariana, see section 3.4.3. Narrowing can be treated as one manifestation of what we discuss in section 4.1.4 as equivalence across languages.

2.3   Case studies

In the preceding section we provided a few sketchy examples to illustrate the transition from one use pattern to another as a result of language contact. In the present section we will look in more detail into the process leading from minor to major use pattern by presenting four examples illustrating this process.

2.3.1   Clefting in Irish English

The following example also illustrates that the rise of new major use patterns on the basis of the scenario sketched in table 2.1 may lead to the emergence of a new grammatical meaning. Standard English shares with Irish (Gaelic) a cleft construction of the form [*it is* X REL Y] in which the first clause contains a focal constituent introduced by a copula and the second clause is introduced by a relative clause marker.[15] But there is a difference between the two languages. In Standard English, the following constituents can be clefted (that is, may figure as X): subject and object noun phrases, complements of prepositions, as well as various kinds of adjuncts. Excluded from clefting are verb phrases and subject complement constituents as well as a number of adjuncts such as manner adverbials (e.g. *It is slowly that he walked in*; Harris 1991: 197). Irish does not show such constraints; only tensed verbs or the predicate of a copula cannot be clefted. Accordingly, while predicates and manner adverbs cannot be clefted in Standard English, they can in Irish, as (19a) and (19b) illustrate.

(19) Irish (Harris 1991: 198)

      a. Is   caochta atá   sé.
         COP drunk   REL: be he
         ('It is drunk he is.')

      b. Ní   go maith a   chonaic sé iad.
         COP: NEG well   REL see.PAST he them
         ('It's not well he saw them.')

In Irish English (Hiberno-English), a sentence-initial copular structure followed by some focused participant is conspicuously more common than in Standard English; the following are a range of examples from Irish playwright John Millington Synge's drama *Deirdre of the Sorrows*:

(20) Irish English (Cotter 1994: 142)

> It is I will be your comrade and will stand between you and the great troubles are foretold.
> It's for this life I'm born, surely.
> It's little I heed for what she was born.

Perhaps more importantly, Irish English exhibits essentially the same type of cleft construction as Irish: the range of constituents that can be clefted is more or less identical in the two varieties but contrasts with the situation found in other varieties of English, including Standard English (Filppula 1986; Harris 1991: 199–201). While Standard English also allows for clefts, the overall frequency of clefts is higher in Irish and Irish English than in spoken Standard English (see Jeffers & Lehiste 1979: 154–5). Second, Irish English, like Irish, uses a wider range of syntactic constituents that can be fronted into the focal position than Standard English. For example, like Irish (cf. (19)), Irish English allows for clefted predicates (21a) and clefted manner adverbs (21b); see also (21c).

(21) Irish English (van Hamel 1912: 277; Harris 1991: 199–201)

> a. It's flat it was.
> b. It's badly she'd do it now.
> c. I do be thinking it was a big fool I was.

In addition to frequency and syntactic scope, there is a third difference among the three varieties concerned. In all of them, the cleft construction has two main discourse functions, referred to respectively as the stressed-focus and the informative-presupposition clefts (Filppula 1986: 92ff.; Harris 1991: 198). In stressed-focus clefts, the clefted constituent is highlighted as presenting new information and the relative clause as presenting given information, while in the latter the relative clause expresses information that is new but is presented as something that is not at issue (for a more detailed description, see Filppula 1986: 92–119). Now, the latter discourse function is common in both Irish and Irish English but much less so in Standard English.

This overall situation can be interpreted as having involved a transfer whereby speakers of Irish English appear to have replicated the use pattern of the model language Irish by gradually adopting pragmatic, syntactic, and semantic characteristics of the latter. Obviously, this evolution towards an increased rate of equivalence and intertranslatability was not shared by other varieties of English. On the basis of the data available, the evolution of the cleft construction

Table 2.2 *A reconstruction of the evolution of the cleft pattern in Irish English*

Stage	Frequency	Context	Meaning
0	Low frequency	The syntactic contexts in which the use pattern can be used are limited; it is not used e.g. with predicates and manner adverbs	The stressed-focus function is common, while the informative-presupposition function is far less common
I	Increase in frequency	Extension of syntactic contexts in which the use pattern can be used	Increase in the use of the informative-presupposition function
II	High frequency	Clefting is used with predicates and manner adverbs	Both the stressed-focus and the informative-presupposition functions are common

in Irish English can be reconstructed as sketched in table 2.2 (cf. table 2.1). Note that there is no information on the intermediate stage I in this evolution, so our evidence is confined to contrasting a hypothetical earlier situation (stage 0) with what is found in modern Irish English (stage II).

The following findings presented by Filppula (1986; see also Harris 1991) suggest that the stages distinguished in table 2.2 correlate with the areal distribution of the relevant characteristics of the cleft construction. He analyzed spoken text samples of Irish English in three communities which he selected on the basis of the assumed relative strength of Irish influence: C. Kerry and C. Clare in the rural west of Ireland, where the impact of Irish is most recent and direct, a rural area of C. Wicklow just south of Dublin, where Irish as a first language has been extinct for at least 150 years, and Dublin city, where the link with Irish is most tenuous. With regard to the two functions of the cleft construction, Filppula's quantitative analysis yielded the relative frequency rates presented in table 2.3. What this analysis shows is that there is a positive correlation between the relative frequency of use of the cleft construction and the three stages distinguished in table 2.2: The situation in Dublin city is most strongly suggestive of stage 0, that of C. Wicklow of stage I, and that of C. Kerry and C. Clare of stage II. In a similar fashion, the use of the informative-presupposition function appears to be least common in the community where Irish influence was most tenuous, and most common in the rural west showing the most direct influence of Irish. In short, the frequency ranking in the use of clefts among different Irish English areas correlates with their relative ranking on the scale of assumed intensity of Irish influence. To conclude, it would seem that synchronic areal distribution immediately reflects the diachronic evolution of the cleft pattern in Irish English: the more speakers were exposed to the Irish

Table 2.3 *Frequency of use of two functions of the cleft pattern in three Irish English-speaking communities*

Community	Corpus size (no. of words)	Stressed-focus function	Informative-presupposition function	Both functions
Dublin city	42,173	0.87	0.40	1.28
Wicklow	41,986	1.31	0.52	1.83
Kerry and Clare	69,747	1.77	0.98	2.75

Based on Filppula 1986: 114; Harris 1991. Figures give the number of occurrences of a function per 1000 words.

model, the more they extended the pattern in the direction of the model, and vice versa.

What this example is also meant to illustrate is that Irish English experienced a grammaticalization process leading from a less to a more grammatical use pattern. Now, grammaticalization need not, and in most cases in fact does not, lead to the rise of a new grammatical category. Rather, what it achieves is first and above all a restructuring of existing use patterns whereby some minor pattern, such as a cleft construction of the type found in Standard English, acquires greater text frequency, is exposed to new contexts and may be applied in new contexts, and eventually may come to be increasingly associated with a new grammatical function.

2.3.2   The progressive in Pennsylvania German

In colloquial German throughout Germany, though not in Standard German, there is a widespread progressive construction based on the Location Schema [X is at doing Y], e.g., *Er ist am Essen* (he is at.the eating) 'he is eating.' This construction is also found in Pennsylvania German, where it takes the form [*sei* 'be' + *am* 'at' + main verb in the infinitive]. The fact that the latter construction is used highly frequently is attributed to the influence of English, that is, the increased frequency of the progressive construction is viewed as an attempt by Pennsylvania German speakers to replicate the use pattern of the corresponding English *be doing*-progressive (see Enninger 1980: 346 for earlier references).[16] That contact with English played at least an accelerating role in this process is suggested by the following observation:

In a very early study of PG [Pennsylvania German; a.n.] aspect carried out in 1941, Reed states "the proportion of progressive forms used is extremely small" (Reed 1947: 9). This is no longer the case – the original construction has increased considerably in frequency and has expanded into a number of new contexts, including a new progressive passive construction [. . .]. (Burridge 1992: 211)

The data provided by Burridge (1992) on Pennsylvania German spoken by Mennonite Anabaptists in Ontario, Canada, allow for a more detailed reconstruction of the development towards a major use pattern in recent Pennsylvania German. At an earlier stage, represented in the work of Reed (1947), the progressive was already available as a grammatical option of limited scope: it was only applied to intransitive verbs or verbs of low transitivity with something like an incorporated object, as, e.g., *Aerbse* 'peas' in (22).

(22) Pennsylvania German (Burridge 1992: 213)

> Sie is am Aerbse blicke.
> (she is at peas   shell.INF)
> 'She is shelling peas.'

Furthermore, the early progressive did not occur with modified objects, pronoun objects, or prepositional phrase complements, and it did not take verbs expressing psychological states as main verbs.

The development towards a major use pattern was in accordance with the effects listed in section 2.2 (6), and it also corresponds to the parameters of grammaticalization distinguished in section 1.3. The progressive acquired a higher frequency of use and was applied to more and more contexts (see also section 4.1.5). Context extension had the following effects: The progressive is no longer restricted to verbs expressing activities but also covers ongoing states, cf. (23), and it can now be used with modified objects (24a) and with pronoun objects (24b).

(23) Pennsylvania German (Burridge 1992: 212)

> Ich bin am Sache besser verschteh.
> (I am at things better understand.INF)
> 'I'm understanding things better.'

(24) Pennsylvania German (Burridge 1992: 214; cited from Huffines 1988: 143)

> a. Der   is am sei Schtuul fixe.
>   (this.one is at his chair   fix.INF)
>   'He is fixing his chair.'
> b. Er is am sich   ready griege.
>   (he is at himself ready get.INF)
>   'He is getting himself ready.'

Use in a wider range of contexts also has the effect that the progressive shows traces of desemanticization (or generalization of meaning; see section 1.3), gradually shifting towards a present tense meaning – in a similar fashion to English (Burridge 1992: 212–13).

2.3.3   Impersonal constructions in Malinche Mexicano

The transition from one kind of use pattern to another without affecting the overall structure of grammatical categorization appears to be a ubiquitous process characterizing language contact. That this may lead to remarkable restructurings in the language concerned can be illustrated with the following example from the Aztecan language Mexicano (Nahuatl) as spoken in the Malinche Volcano towns of Central Mexico. Malinche Mexicano speakers are nearly all bilingual in Mexicano and Spanish, and their language has been shaped by Spanish to the extent that Hill and Hill (1986: 1) call it a "syncretic language." Speakers of Classical Mexicano usually formed passive and impersonal expressions with the so-called "nonactive" stems by means of a catalogue of suffixes, such as -lō, -ō, -lohua, and -ohua. But there also was an impersonal use pattern formed with the third-person reflexive prefix *mo-*, which is said to have been of limited use. An example of the latter is found in (25).

(25) Classical Mexicano (Aztecan; Hill & Hill 1986: 290)

      mo-chīhuaz.
      'It will be done, it will happen.'[17]

As a result of intense contact with Spanish, Malinche Mexicano speakers appear to have increased the frequency of this use pattern and to have extended it to new contexts – a process leading to what Hill and Hill (1986: 290) call a "proliferation of impersonals with *mo-*." Local Spanish, like Spanish in general, makes wide use of reflexive marking by means of *se* for a variety of purposes, e.g. with inherently reflexive verbs and for expressing impersonal meanings. Extension of the *mo*-prefix in Malinche Mexicano affected, first, verbs borrowed from Spanish, where instead of Spanish *se*, the own prefix *mo-* is used. Second, *mo-* was also extended to some etymologically Mexicano verbs that earlier did not take the reflexive marker. For example, *mo-* was extended to the Mexicano verb *cualāni* 'to get angry' on the model of the corresponding Spanish verb *se enojaron*. And third, *mo-* has also been generalized to an impersonal use pattern "precisely equivalent in meaning to Spanish impersonals" (Hill & Hill 1986: 292). The authors illustrate the pattern with examples such as (26).

(26) Malinche Mexicano (Aztecan; Hill & Hill 1986: 292)

      Yō-*mo*-patlaco in tiempo.
      'Times have changed.'[18]

But there is a second use pattern that also appears to have been influenced by contact with Spanish, where the element *cē* 'one' expresses passive and impersonal meanings. While not unknown in earlier Mexicano, Hill and Hill argue that this use pattern as well was greatly extended due to Spanish influence, in that Malinche Mexicano expressions such as the ones presented in (27a) are likely to be "calques" on Spanish *se* (cf. 27b).

(27) Malinche Mexicano and local Spanish (Aztecan; Hill & Hill 1986: 290)

	a. Malinche Mexicano	b. Spanish	Meaning
	cē quīza	uno se sale	'one goes out'
	cē yahui	uno se va	'one goes'

To conclude, speakers of modern Malinche Mexicano activated what appear to have been minor use patterns, making them their primary means of encoding passive and impersonal meanings. With the expansion of the *mo-* and the *cē* patterns, the earlier passive and impersonal structure with "nonactive" stems did not disappear entirely, but it does not seem to be productive in modern Malinche Mexicano – Hill and Hill (1986: 289) encountered only two examples of "nonactive" stems. Thus, superficially, the old categorial structure is still there, but linguistic discourse has experienced massive transformation as a result of contact-induced pattern expansion.

2.3.4   On dropping pro-drop

Our fourth case study on the transition from minor to major use pattern involves a case that has received quite some attention in contact linguistics – we have referred to it already earlier (sections 2.1; 2.2.1); we are concerned here only with those aspects of the process that relate to the topic of the present chapter. There is substantial evidence to show that immigrants in the USA are likely to activate use patterns that are marginal in their respective L1 by using them more frequently and extending them to novel contexts in cases where their L2, English, provides a convenient model. A fairly common example is provided by immigrant communities in the USA speaking pro-drop languages. Such languages are likely to have a marginal use pattern where personal (subject) pronouns may be used optionally for pragmatic purposes such as presenting new vs. given information, marking topic or theme, etc.[19] Among immigrants speaking these pro-drop languages, such as Spanish, Serbian, Russian, or Hungarian, this marginal use pattern tends to acquire properties of a major use pattern on the model of English (see Myers-Scotton 2002: 201 for references).

Consider the following cases.[20] The first concerns an utterance made by a Spanish child from Colombia living in the USA and being fluent in English, which is presented by Myers-Scotton (2002: 166) to illustrate convergence from Spanish to English:

(28) Spanish–English bilingual (Myers-Scotton 2002: 166)

    Mami,   yo   quiero,   yo
    Mommy 1.SG.NOM want.1.SG.PRES 1.SG.NOM
    quiero   manzana jugo.
    want.1.SG.PRES apple.F   juice.M
    'Mommy, I want, I want apple juice.'

This example reveals a number of mechanisms at work in contact-induced language behavior; our interest here is with what Myers-Scotton describes thus: The child does not observe the pro-drop convention of Spanish, producing an overt first-person pronoun (*yo*) as a subject instead. In another example presented by Myers-Scotton (2002: 201), based on Schmitt's (2000; 2001) studies on the development of pronominal subject marking of five Russian boys living in the USA for whom English was or was becoming the dominant language, she concludes that this development is characterized by "the decline in the Standard Russian use of the pro-drop parameter." Schmitt studied these children twice at an interval of two years; during the second recording, the boys showed a significantly higher rate of overt subject marking. Polinsky (1995) found that Russians who had not spoken Russian regularly for an average of seven years, they used resumptive pronouns co-indexed with the subject of the same clause when speaking "American Russian", where the resumptive pronoun occurs as a real subject while the noun phrase with which it is co-indexed is a topic (Myers-Scotton 2002: 201–2).

Another case concerns Serbian immigrants in the USA. In her study of twenty-two Serbian students born in the USA, Savić (1995) found that these students use personal pronouns more frequently than Serbian speakers not influenced by English. In the data from the students' discourse, "the occurrence of semantically and pragmatically non-required overt subject and object NPs was 6%–25% higher than would be expected in NEI [non-English-influenced; a.n.] Serbian speakers" (Savić 1995: 487). Finally, on the basis of a study of six Hungarian children living in the USA, being Hungarian–English bilinguals, Bolonyai (2000) found an "overuse" of personal pronouns, i.e. overt pronouns were used very frequently when the children used Hungarian, another pro-drop language.

The phenomenon just described has received different interpretations. Savić (1995: 487–8) argues with reference to the Serbian immigrants in the USA, that "the pro-drop parameter is being reset in accordance with English syntactic rules" and she treats this as an instance of convergence. And so does Myers-Scotton (2002: 201) with reference to the fact that in our first example the Spanish child from Colombia does not observe the pro-drop convention of Spanish, producing overt first-person pronouns as subjects instead, which she views as a manifestation of convergence. The case of the five Russian boys, however, is treated by her as a case of attrition (concerning language change in situations of attrition, see section 6.4).

Analyzing the "decline of pro-drop" in terms of parameter resetting is a convenient way of describing the process concerned. It would seem, however, that such an analysis does not contribute much to understanding some properties of this process. In particular, it is not really helpful in understanding why speakers in situations of language contact readily give up their pro-drop convention while it is more difficult to find examples of a process in the opposite direction. The position maintained here differs from that of these authors. If speakers of a pro-drop language start using overt subject (and object) pronouns on the model of another language then this is suggestive of a change from minor to major use pattern, in accordance with the criteria proposed in section 2.2 (6):

(a) Frequency: The personal pronouns acquire a higher frequency of use.
(b) Context extension: Their use tends to be generalized, being extended to contexts where the model language but not the replica language would use them.
(c) Change in meaning: Originally serving pragmatically defined functions, such as presenting new or topical participants, the pronouns increasingly lose these functions and assume the syntactic function of presenting pronominal subjects (or objects).

This shift towards a major use pattern on the model of another language appears to be structurally the same as the one we observed in section 2.1 on Sauris German of northeastern Italy, where independent personal pronouns gain in frequency of use, gradually losing their pragmatic significance and turning into regular subject pronouns on the model of the Rhaeto-Romance language Friulian. As we will see in section 3.1.3, this process is suggestive of contact-induced grammaticalization.

2.4   From use pattern to category

Grammatical change in general and grammaticalization in particular start out with pragmatically motivated patterns of discourse that may crystallize in new, conventionalized forms of grammatical structure. Use patterns are discourse-pragmatic units that need not, and frequently do not, affect the structure of grammatical categorization. However, once language contact gives rise to major use patterns, this may lead to a transition from pragmatically motivated to morphosyntactic templates, in particular to the emergence of new grammatical (functional) categories. As the data that we will review in the following chapters suggest, transition is gradual. There is no straightforward replacement of major use patterns by full-fledged grammatical categories; rather, use patterns gradually acquire properties of grammatical categories. The first stage in this development will be referred to as incipient categories.

2.4.1   Incipient categories

Incipient categories arising in situations of language contact have some or all of the formal properties in (29).

(29) Properties of incipient categories

> a. Incipient categories are ambiguous between their earlier (= source) and their present (= target) meanings, that is, an interpretation in terms of the source meaning is generally possible.
> b. Their use is optional in that they may but need not be used. This means that the grammatical meaning expressed by the category is not obligatorily marked.
> c. They are morphosyntactically largely indistinguishable from the source category and their use is confined to the context in which they arose.
> d. They are phonetically indistinguishable from their respective source categories.
> e. They are used less frequently than the corresponding categories of the model languages.
> f. They are not generally recognized by speakers (or grammarians) of the language as distinct entities of grammar. The question of whether they have any existence of their own tends to be a matter of controversy.
> g. Accordingly, "purist" grammarians and language planning organizations are likely to deny their existence, and their use is discouraged in formal education.

We will now look at a couple of examples to illustrate these properties of incipient categories.

The rise of articles

One kind of example concerns the development of definite and indefinite articles in situations of language contact. The following case concerns a number of Slavic languages spoken at the western periphery of the Slavic language area having had a long history of contact with German (see also Heine & Kuteva forthc.). As a result of these contacts, Slavic languages such as Sorbian, Czech, and Slovenian have grammaticalized demonstrative attributes to use patterns serving the expression of definiteness, and Sorbian has grammaticalized its numeral 'one' to a marker of indefinite reference (Lötzsch 1996: 53; see Lötzsch 1969). In all cases we seem to be dealing with use patterns that have acquired properties of incipient grammatical categories, fairly common in spoken discourse but likely to be suppressed in the modern written languages and in formal education (see, for example, Breu 1994: 54): With reference to (29a), these articles are in most cases ambiguous between their demonstrative source meaning and their target meaning as definite markers, or between their numeral meaning ('one') and their meaning as indefinite articles.

In (29b) one salient property of incipient categories is captured, namely that there is no iconicity between meaning and form. First, presence of the form does not imply that it necessarily expresses the target meaning (see (29a)) and, second, absence of the form does not imply absence of the target meaning. With reference to the Slavic languages just mentioned this has the following consequences. When the relevant form is used, this does not necessarily mean that it is used in its definite meaning since it may be that it is the demonstrative meaning that is intended or understood, and absence of that form does not necessarily mean that there is no definiteness involved, since prior to the introduction of the incipient category, unmarked nouns could be either indefinite or definite.

Property (29c). Demonstratives and numerals can as a rule be used both as pronouns and as attributes; when grammaticalized, to incipient articles, however, they occur exclusively in use patterns where they serve as nominal attributes.

Property (29d). As a rule, the article-like elements in these Slavic languages are weakly grammaticalized, and their form is indistinguishable from that of the source category. Nevertheless, there is one exception: the Upper Sorbian item *jedyn* 'one' (masculine singular) is usually replaced by the contracted monosyllabic form *jen* in its article uses (Lötzsch 1996: 53), and the Upper Sorbian demonstrative *tón* (masculine nominative singular) has no stress when expressing the function of a definite article (Lötzsch 1996: 52), that is, Upper Sorbian appears to have undergone erosion (i.e., phonetic reduction; see section 1.3), thereby developing from an incipient to a new, full-fledged grammatical category (see also section 6.3.3).

Property (29e). Lötzsch (1996: 52) observes that the Sorbian definite article is used much less commonly than its model, the definite article of German, and the same applies to all the other Slavic languages mentioned.

Property (29f). That the status of incipient forms as grammatical categories is notoriously controversial has been pointed out by a number of students of contact-induced replication. The reaction of descriptive linguists vis-à-vis incipient categories is ambiguous. On the one hand, they take note of their existence, on the other hand they tend to deny them any status as grammatical categories, especially on account of property (29b). Thus, after a detailed analysis, Berger comes to the conclusion that Czech does not have a definite article since the form *ten* is not used obligatorily as a resumptive anaphoric reference marker, hence it is not a conventionalized marker for the category of definiteness (Berger n.d.: 462; cited from Breu 1994: 54). While innovative speakers are likely to welcome them, traditional speakers tend to condemn them, describing them as "bad" or "corrupted" speech. The following quote by Lötzsch on the incipient definite article in Sorbian is characteristic of such a situation:

Kein Wunder also, daß die Frage des Artikelgebrauchs bereits in den ältesten Grammatiken des Sorbischen kontrovers behandelt wird und daß sich schließlich die puristische Richtung durchsetzte, die in ihm einen verabscheuungswürdigen Germanismus sah.[21] (Lötzsch 1996: 52)

Property (29g). While professional linguists may decide to treat incipient categories as forming part of the inventory of grammatical categories of the language concerned, language teachers are likely to reject the use of incipient categories, discouraging students from using them; the literature on the use of "articles" in Slavic languages having had a history of intense contact with German is rife with discussions on this issue.

This kind of article use in peripheral Slavic languages is not an isolated case. In a similar fashion, a number of Slavic languages have acquired incipient possessive perfects (or 'have'-perfects)[22] presumably on the model of neighboring languages having full-fledged possessive perfects (see Heine & Kuteva forthc. for details). For example, Breu (1994: 55) observes that there is a possessive perfect in Czech, Slovenian, and Serbian/Croatian, but he concludes that in these languages it "scheint aber keine Grammatikalisierung erreicht zu haben" (= it does not appear to have reached any degree of grammaticalization).

The rise of evidential markers

In much the same way as definite and indefinite articles and possessive perfects are part of the grammaticalized structures of Standard Average European languages[23] and have served as models for languages that are in close contact with these languages but lack such articles, there are other grammatical domains in languages outside Europe that are equally grammaticalized and also appear to have provided attractive models for replication. The following example is meant to show that the process sketched above is not an isolated case.

The North Arawak language Tariana of northwest Amazonia has an obligatory paradigm of four clitics marking tense and evidentiality, distinguishing between visual, non-visual, inferred, and reported evidence. Tariana speakers use Portuguese, the official language of Brazil, as an important lingua franca, but Portuguese has no grammaticalized categories marking evidentiality. In using Portuguese, Tariana speakers tend to replicate their evidentiality system by drawing on lexical expresssions of Portuguese, using them more frequently and developing them into what appear to be incipient categories for which there is no equivalent in Standard Portuguese (cf. our discussion in section 1.5). Table 2.4 summarizes the expressions that tend to be employed by Tariana speakers in creating equivalents for their evidential categories.

Table 2.4 *Portuguese expressions used by Tariana speakers corresponding to evidential categories in Tariana*

Tariana evidential category	Corresponding Tariana Portuguese expressions
Visual	eu vi 'I saw',
	eu tenho prova 'I have proof',
	eu tenha experiência 'I have experience'
Nonvisual	eu escutei 'I heard',
	eu senti 'I felt'
Inferred	parece 'it appears, it seems'
Reported	diz que 'it is said that'

From Aikhenvald 2002: 117–27, 315–6.

As the description by Aikhenvald (2002: 315–16) suggests, the Tariana Portuguese use patterns appear to have a number of properties characterizing incipient categories: unlike the corresponding model categories, they do not appear to have acquired categorial status, their use is not obligatory, they seem to be phonologically indistinguishable from the corresponding non-evidential expressions, and they can also be interpreted with reference to their non-grammaticalized source meaning, especially by non-Tariana speakers.

As the examples provided by Aikhenvald (2002: 315–16) show, evidentiality marking is on the way to proceeding from incipient to full categorial status. When this happens, the use pattern concerned is extended to contexts where its literal meaning no longer makes sense, that is, where the pattern is more profitably interpreted with reference to its grammaticalized function. In connection with the reported evidential *diz que*, Aikhenvald observes:

> *diz que* 'it is said' can be extended to cover all non-first-hand evidentiality specifications. Thus, an Indian who has read an announcement, may just as well talk about it using *diz que* (which sounds equally bizarre for speakers of Standard Portuguese; since for them this conveys a tinge of incredulity). (Aikhenvald 2002: 315)

Incipient categories represent intermediate stages of grammaticalization, and as such they are a *sine qua non* in the development of new grammatical categories. Note, however, that they do not necessarily lead to full-fledged new categories since grammaticalization can be discontinued at any stage of its development.

2.4.2   Use pattern vs. category

Whether we are dealing with major use patterns or incipient grammatical categories is largely a matter of the perspective adopted rather than of the facts to be described. While the former are treated here as discourse-pragmatic entities, to

Table 2.5 *Discourse-based vs. categorial structures in grammatical replication*

Stage	0	Ia	Ib	II	III
		minor use pattern	> major use pattern		
			incipient category	> full-fledged category	

be described with reference to such parameters as frequency and context, the latter are the result of an analysis in terms of discrete grammatical categorization, and they tend to be described with reference to their morphosyntactic structure. Thus, the two notions are at the same time mutually exclusive and nevertheless compatible with one another, with each highlighting a different aspect of grammatical replication. Our observations suggest that replication starts out with gradually changing use patterns, leading from minor to major patterns; at the same time, these patterns increasingly acquire properties of distinct categories, and eventually they may turn into conventionalized grammatical categories. On the basis of such observations we will use the scenario depicted in table 2.5 to describe grammatical replication.

Table 2.5 suggests, first, that in its earliest stages, grammatical replication is described most appropriately in terms of use patterns, while grammatical categorization is essentially irrelevant. The more the process advances, the more relevant an account in terms of discrete categorization becomes, while discourse structures such as use patterns lose in significance. Second, the two notions do not correspond to one another in a one-to-one fashion but nevertheless can be related to each other. Minor use patterns tend to exhibit more properties of incipient categories the more they approach major use patterns. Further, major use patterns themselves may correspond to incipient categories, but they may also show characteristics of full-fledged grammatical categories – even if not every major use pattern will necessarily give rise to a new grammatical category.

2.5   Discussion

It would seem in fact that the most common process leading to grammatical replication concerns a change where an existing use pattern simply acquires a higher frequency of use and comes to be used in new contexts. Such a process is hard to identify, especially since it does not affect the conventionalized structure of grammatical categorization; it therefore comes as no surprise that – more often than not – this process tends to go unnoticed in the relevant literature.

One of the main characteristics of the Balkans as a linguistic area can be seen in a process whereby the infinitive is lost, being replaced by finite clauses (for a detailed analysis, see Joseph 1983; see also Banfi 1990). There is wide agreement that this process was contact-induced, that is, that it spread from one Balkan language to another as a result of areal diffusion, even if the exact nature of directionality in the spread is far from clear. But what appears to be suggestive of a discrete development leading to the replacement of one morphosyntactic structure by another can perhaps more profitably be described as a gradual transition from minor to major use patterns. Consider the following characterization of the process by Matras, relating to Balkan Turkish:

It is significant that all languages concerned displayed a finite option at least in some environments in the earlier system (i.e. prior to contact), and that the loss of the infinitive involves a gradual extension and ultimately a generalization of this option. (Matras 1998b: 90)

Matras argues that Balkan Turkish underwent a process similar to other Balkan languages, extending the distribution of a finite option to contexts where it was originally highly marked or even inadmissible (Matras 1998b: 93), thereby turning a minor, contextually restricted, use pattern into a major one via the extension and functionalization of an inherited device, namely the optative/ subjunctive.

The following is an example of a different nature. In Germanic languages, nouns are generally used in their plural form when modified by a numeral other than 'one,' e.g. German *drei Männer* (three man.PL) 'three men.' Frequently, however, there is a minor use pattern in one specific kind of context: nouns expressing weight and/or measure are used in their singular form after numerals, e.g. German *drei Dutzend* (three dozen.SG) 'three dozen,' Swedish *sex fot* (six foot.SG) 'six feet.' Finnic languages such as Finnish or Estonian treat nouns and noun phrases modified by numerals generally as singular entities. Now, Swedish dialects in close contact with Finnic languages appear to have extended their minor use pattern to other contexts on the model of their respective Finnic contact language, thereby giving rise to a major use pattern generally applying to nouns modified by numerals. However, replication by extending the minor use pattern in the direction of the model has not been complete. In Estonian Swedish, masculine and neutral nouns are normally singular after numerals. Thus, Koptjevskaja-Tamm and Wälchli (2001: 701) say that instead of Standard Swedish *tre män* (three man.PL), Estonian Swedish speakers say *tri mann* (three man.SG) 'three men.'[24] But replication does not appear to have affected feminine nouns in Estonian Swedish, e.g. *fem bärkiar* (five birch.PL) 'five birches.' The extension from minor to major use pattern correlates positively with the relative intensity of language contact, as is suggested by the fact that in peripheral Swedish dialects where Estonian influence is significantly higher, the major use pattern has been generalized to include feminine nouns used in the singular after numerals.

As we observed in section 2.1, new contact-induced use patterns tend to be built on already existing patterns. There is, however, also some evidence to suggest that a new use pattern can arise essentially *ex nihilo* without requiring an earlier pattern as a prerequisite. For example, Boretzky (1975: 262–3) observes that in Turkish there is a pattern whereby verbs are formed by using *etmek* 'make' and *olmak* 'become, be' as auxiliaries in combination with borrowed nouns. Albanian has been strongly influenced by Turkish as a result of a history of over five centuries of language contact, and colloquial Albanian is said to have replicated this use pattern by recruiting its own verbs *bëj* and *bëhem*, respectively, in combination with nouns borrowed from Turkish. Boretzky emphasizes that there was nothing in Albanian on which this new use pattern could be built, that is, Albanian speakers replicated the Turkish use pattern without having any structure in their own language to draw on.

Most of the data that we were able to study suggest that frequently used grammatical patterns are likely to have a longer history of grammaticalization, and differences in the relative frequency of corresponding use patterns between languages (or dialects) in contact may therefore reflect the kind of directionality characterizing the transfer of that pattern (see section 3.4.5). Still, this observation must be taken with care, as the following observations by Koptjevskaja-Tamm and Wälchli (2001: 626–7) suggest. As these authors note with reference to the analytic superlative of the type 'better than all' in Latvian, Estonian, and Livonian, a high frequency and/or a generalization of this use pattern is not necessarily suggestive of a longer period of grammaticalization; rather, it can be due to the fact that there was some equivalent pattern that was lost, leading to the generalization and extension of the new use pattern to all contexts where the earlier pattern had been used. In other words, differences in frequency and context extension do not necessarily correlate with the relative age of the use patterns concerned but may be the result of language-internal structural developments that do not relate to language contact.

At the same time, Koptjevskaja-Tamm and Wälchli (2001: 627) emphasize that relative frequency of use nevertheless is a relevant factor for determining directionality in grammatical transfer. In doing so, they draw attention to the use of a verbal compound in Finno-Ugric and Eastern Slavic languages literally meaning 'they lived and were' (Russian *žili-byli*) which was grammaticalized to a use pattern introducing fairy tales (comparable to English *Once upon a time there was*). The highest frequency of this opening marker of fairy tales (between 67 and 74% of occurrence) is found in Central Russian areas that formerly were at least partly Finno-Ugric-speaking, while Russian elsewhere shows a lower percentage (56%), and the lowest percentages are found in Belorussian (8%) and Ukrainian (0.5%) (see also section 3.1.3). Such a geographical distribution indicates that this compound has most likely been transferred from Finno-Ugric to Russian rather than vice versa.

2.6   Conclusions

The main purpose of the present chapter was to demonstrate that contact-induced language change is not an abrupt process, leading straight from one category or structure to another; rather, it involves a gradual transition best described in terms of the discourse-based notion of use patterns. What surfaces from the relevant literature is that speakers in situations of language contact are less centrally concerned with replicating categories of another language; rather, they aim at adjusting their way of structuring discourse, for whatever reasons, to what they find in the other language. This has the effect that conventional patterns of collocating words may be used more frequently, be extended to new contexts, and come to be associated with new grammatical meanings – innovations that are triggered by use patterns and categories of another language serving as a model.

What starts out as individual and subsequently as communal deviation from an established norm may in appropriate circumstances crystallize as a new grammatical category – a process that is the topic of the next chapter.

3 Grammaticalization

Summarizing some of his findings on language contact in the Balkans, Victor Friedman observes that

the structural convergences called Balkanisms, among which grammaticalized status can be counted, must have begun as discourse-bound variations that resulted in part from communicative needs and desires of multilingual speakers and in part from competing grammatical systems. Balkanisms began as variation when speakers of different languages attempted to communicate more effectively and mediated between the languages of their interlocutors and the structures of their native languages. The place of any given Balkanism in the systems of the various languages can be described in terms of a continuum from pragmatically conditioned variation to grammaticalization, which in turn suggests that discourse functions are not merely subject to borrowing but actually serve as entry points for the development of structural change. (Friedman 2003: 110)

Discourse-bound, pragmatically conditioned variation was discussed in chapter 2 in terms of use patterns. The present chapter highlights the second phase of the process leading to fixed grammatical templates: It is concerned with the emergence of new functional categories and constructions (see also Heine & Kuteva 2003).

3.1   The mechanism

As the preceding chapter may have shown, the transfer of grammatical information from one language to another without involving any linguistic forms is perhaps more widespread than has previously been thought. In its initial stages, replication tends to involve pieces of discourse that acquire higher text frequency, are extended to new contexts, and gradually come to be associated with new grammatical functions. We described this development with reference to the gradual transition from minor to major use patterns, and we observed that this development may lead to the crystallization of new grammatical structures. What the observations made seem to suggest is that virtually any minor use pattern can be activated in language contact and give rise to new functional categories – even if most of these use patterns never succeed in acquiring category status. We will now describe the mechanism giving rise to such categories in situations of language contact, which we propose to call contact-induced grammaticalization.

Contact-induced grammaticalization is a grammaticalization process that is due to the influence of one language on another. We will distinguish two main types of contact-induced grammaticalization depending on whether or not there exists already a model source-to-target grammaticalization process to be replicated. If no such model exists we will refer to the process as ordinary (contact-induced) grammaticalization.[1] Replication in this case is confined to creating a category in the replica language that corresponds to the model category – that is, it does not affect the manner in which that category is created (section 3.1.2). If the model language provides a model for both a category and the way that category is replicated, we will refer to it as replica grammaticalization (section 3.1.3).

3.1.1   Grammaticalization theory

In section 1.3 we presented an outline of grammaticalization theory, whose primary goal it is to describe how grammatical forms and constructions arise and develop through space and time, and to explain why they are structured the way they are. To this end, we proposed a catalogue of parameters for describing and understanding the evolution of grammatical use patterns and categories (see section 1.3, (5)):[2]

(1) Parameters of grammaticalization

      a. extension, i.e. the rise of novel grammatical meanings when linguistic expressions are extended to new contexts (context-induced reinterpretation),

      b. desemanticization (or "semantic bleaching"), i.e. loss (or generalization) in meaning content,

      c. decategorialization, i.e. loss in morphosyntactic properties characteristic of lexical or other less grammaticalized forms, and

      d. erosion (or "phonetic reduction"), i.e. loss in phonetic substance.

In the present chapter we will be concerned with data on contact-induced language change from a wide range of languages, with a view to establishing that grammatical replication is a cross-linguistially fairly regular process that can be accounted for within the framework of grammaticalization theory.

3.1.2   Ordinary contact-induced grammaticalization

As observed in Heine and Kuteva (2003: 533), contact-induced grammaticalization rests on a strategy used for transferring some grammatical concept or structure from the model language (M) to the replica language (R), involving the following mechanism:

(2) Ordinary contact-induced grammaticalization

    a. Speakers notice that in language **M** there is a grammatical category **Mx**.

    b. They create an equivalent category **Rx** in language **R** on the basis of the use patterns available in **R**.

    c. To this end, they draw on universal strategies of grammaticalization, using construction **Ry** in order to develop **Rx**.

    d. They grammaticalize **Ry** to **Rx**.

We saw in chapter 2 that contact-induced grammatical replication involves two distinct though interrelated kinds of structures, which are use patterns on the one hand and grammatical categories on the other. The mechanism sketched in (2) is phrased in terms of the latter, but it applies in much the same way to the former. Furthermore, instead of languages, the mechanism may involve different varieties of one and the same language.

The mechanism raises a number of problems, some of which were discussed in Heine and Kuteva (2003). One problem relates to the nature of categories and the more general issue of cross-linguistic equivalence, which we will return to in section 6.1. Another problem concerns the question of whether, or to what extent, the mechanism is based on conscious or unconscious linguistic activity and what the ultimate motivations may be for (2b) to happen. The remaining questions (2c) and (2d) can be answered with reference to grammaticalization theory, and there are at least some ways in which they have been, or can be, dealt with (see especially Heine, Claudi & Hünnemeyer 1991; Hopper & Traugott 1993; Bybee, Perkins & Pagliuca 1994; Lehmann [1982]1995). But there remains a fundamental problem: grammaticalization is a gradual process that may involve generations of speakers and extend over centuries. This implies that there is likely to be an asymmetrical relation between the two languages, in that there is a category (Mx) in the model language corresponding to a process (Ry > Rx) in the replica language. What this means is that equivalence in grammatical replication is a highly complex notion (see section 6.1).

With the term "create" in (2b) we are drawing attention to the fact that the process concerned is essentially a creative act: Speakers of R do not simply produce a copy of material they find in language M; rather, they tend to create new categories using the resources available in R. As we saw in section 1.5, however, creativity is constrained in a number of ways: first, it is shaped in particular by the nature of the model category Mx, second, it is constrained by universal principles of grammaticalization, and third, it is also influenced by the structural outfit of both the model and the replica languages.

The mechanism sketched in (2) can be illustrated with the following example. Eastern Oceanic languages of northern and central Vanuatu (= M, the model languages) commonly distinguish a durative aspect indicating that an act is in progress (= Mx). Apparently in an attempt to find an equivalent for such a category (= Rx) in Bislama, an English-based pidgin of Vanuatu (= R), speakers used an expression commonly recruited cross-linguistically to develop progressive and durative aspect markers (Heine & Kuteva 2002: 127, 198): They chose a use pattern involving their verb *stap* 'stay, be present, exist'[3] (= Ry) to develop a durative aspect marker (= Rx), which appears in the same syntactic slot as the durative markers (Mx) in the model languages[4] (Keesing 1991: 328); cf. the following sentences, where (3) illustrates the replica and (4) the model structure.

(3) Bislama (English-based pidgin; Keesing 1991: 328)

    em i   stap pik- im   yam.
    he he- DUR   dig- TRS   yam
    'He's in the process of digging yams.'

(4) Vetmbao (Malekula, Oceanic; Keesing 1991: 328)

    naji ng- u-   xoel dram.
    he   he- DUR-   dig yam
    'He's in the process of digging yams.'

That speakers of replica languages draw on universal principles of grammaticalization in order to develop a category that is equivalent to the one they find in the model language can be illustrated with another example from Oceanic languages. Kwaio (= M), a Malaita language of Eastern Oceanic, has a grammatical particle *me'e* used before action verbs to express what could be paraphrased in English as 'went ahead and'; Keesing (1988: 217) calls it a narrative discourse marker introducing consecutive, new events (= Mx). Now, one common way this discourse function is expressed cross-linguistically is by using a verb for 'come' or 'go' as an auxiliary (Heine & Kuteva 2002: 68–9), and Kwaio speakers of Solomons Pijin (= R) have grammaticalized the pidgin verb *kam* 'come' (= Ry) to replicate the *me'e*-category, creating a grammatical marker (= Rx), illustrated in (5), that is both morphosyntactically and semantically equivalent to *me'e* (= Mx), cf. (6).

(5) Solomons Pijin (English-based pidgin; Keesing 1988: 217)

    olketa-i kam goap   long loiakeni.
    (they)   AUX ascend LOC   rattan: vine
    'And then they went ahead and climbed that rattan vine.'

(6) Kwaio (Eastern Oceanic; Keesing 1988: 217)
    gila   me'e fane   naa 'ue la'akau.
    (they) AUX ascend LOC vine DEM
    'And then they went ahead and climbed that rattan vine.'

These examples involve cases where contact-induced grammaticalization introduced a verbal category in the replica language for which previously there does not appear to have been any equivalent. A grammatical domain where speakers of pidgin and creole languages appear to have drawn quite often on "substrate" languages as models for new categories is that of personal pronouns. Where distinctions between inclusive and exclusive first-person plural pronouns or of dual pronouns were commonly made in the languages of the people speaking pidgins or emerging creoles as second languages, such distinctions tended to be replicated in the second languages. Tayo is a French-based creole which evolved around 1860 in St. Louis, New Caledonia. Drubéa and Cèmuhî (= M), the two main Melanesian languages spoken in St. Louis at that time, have an obligatory semantic category of dual (= Mx). Presumably in an attempt to replicate this category in Tayo (= R), the speakers recruited the French numeral *deux* 'two' (= Ry) and grammaticalized it to a dual form *-de* (= Rx) (Corne 1995; see Heine & Kuteva 2003: 534 for an example).

Proto-Oceanic, the hypothetical ancestor of the present-day Oceanic languages, is assumed to have distinguished between four categories of number (singular, dual, trial, and plural) as well as between inclusive and exclusive first-person non-singular pronouns. These distinctions have largely been retained in modern Oceanic languages (= Mx) and were apparently replicated by speakers of these pidgin varieties (= Rx) by drawing on common grammaticalization processes (see Heine & Kuteva 2002): The numeral *tu* 'two' was grammaticalized to a dual marker (cf. above for Tayo), the numeral *tri* 'three' to a trial marker (apparently not widely distinguished), the marker *-fala or -pela* (< English *fellow*) to a non-singular marker, and the combination *yu* 'you' plus *mi* 'I' to a first-person inclusive marker (= Ry > Rx).[5] These grammaticalizations have given rise to a system of personal pronouns in Tok Pisin that appears to reflect the corresponding systems of the Austronesian model languages (see, e.g., Keesing 1988: 160–1). Table 3.1 gives a list of personal pronouns of Tigak, an Austronesian language spoken on the island New Ireland of Papua New Guinea, and table 3.2 provides the corresponding Tok Pisin pronouns.[6]

In a number of the languages of the world, it can be observed that universal principles of grammaticalization can be held responsible for the rise of new markers for personal deixis in situations of language contact. A paradigm case can be seen in a process whereby either impersonal pronouns or nouns meaning

Table 3.1 *Independent personal pronouns of Tigak*

Number and person	Singular	Dual	Trial	Plural
1 inclusive		nakarag	nakaratul	nakara
1 exclusive	naniu	nameg	namemtul	namem
2	nanu	namug	namitul	nami
3	nane	nareg	naritul	nari

Source: Austronesian; Jenkins 2002: 216.

Table 3.2 *Tok Pisin personal pronouns*

Number and person	Singular	Dual	Trial	Plural
1 inclusive		yumi(tupela)	yumitripela	yumipela
1 exclusive	mi	mitupela	mitripela	mipela
2	yu	yutupela	yutripela	yupela
3	em	ol(tupela)	ol(tripela)	ol

Source: Jenkins 2002: 216.

'person' or 'people' are grammaticalized to first-person plural pronouns (Heine & Kuteva 2002: 233–4). This process can be contact-induced, as demonstrated, for example, by Aikhenvald (2003: 18) with an example from the North Arawak language Tariana. In an attempt to accord with the structures of Tucanoan model languages, Tariana speakers are grammaticalizing their impersonal prefix and pronoun to a first-person inclusive marker ('we, including you').

On the rise of adpositions

Rather than to specific grammatical forms, contact-induced grammaticalization may also lead to the rise of new morphological classes. The following two examples illustrate the development concerned.

The first example concerns Pipil, an Aztecan language of El Salvador which is now nearing extinction, being replaced by Spanish. Traditionally, Pipil (= R), like most other Meso-American languages, has neither prepositions nor postpositions, but it has relational nouns instead (Campbell 1987; Harris & Campbell 1995: 126–7; see also Heine & Kuteva 2003: 535). Under the influence of the model language Spanish (= M), Pipil speakers have more recently drawn on these relational nouns (Ry) to develop a set of Spanish-type prepositions (= Rx). Consequently, they used a cross-linguistically common process

Table 3.3 *The grammaticalization of relational nouns to prepositions in Pipil*

Relational noun	Meaning	Preposition	Meaning
-(i)hpak	'on, upon, over, on top of'	pak	'on'
-pal	'possession'	pal	'of'
-wan	'with'	wan	'with'

Source: Aztecan, Uto-Aztecan; based on Harris & Campbell 1995: 126–7.

whereby relational nouns are grammaticalized to adpositions (Heine, Claudi & Hünnemeyer 1991). As table 3.3 suggests, the process shows all the effects of the three main mechanisms involved in grammaticalization (see section 1.3): desemanticization, e.g. the loss of nominal meaning ('possession') in favor of grammatical meaning ('of'), decategorialization, leading to the loss of categorial properties of nouns, such as taking modifiers and affixes, and erosion, i.e. loss of phonetic substance (*-(i)hpak* > *pak* 'on').

Pipil is not an isolated example of a Central American language having redefined its structure of adpositions as a result of contact with Spanish. Another example is provided by Mexicano as spoken in the Malinche Volcano towns of Central Mexico: Malinche Mexicano speakers are nearly all bilingual in Mexicano and Spanish, and their language has been shaped by Spanish to the extent that Hill and Hill (1986: 1) call it a "syncretic language." These authors observe that Classical Mexicano (Aztec, Nahuatl) had postpositions marking locatives, although the repertoire of true postpositional elements was somewhat limited (Hill & Hill 1986: 247–8). What happened under Spanish influence is, first, that Malinche Mexicano speakers borrowed the Spanish possessive/genitive particle *de*, second, that they replicated the prepositional structure of Spanish by turning what appear to be relational nouns having a possessive prefix coreferential with the possessor into preposition-like entities and, third, that they replaced that possessive prefix with the indefinite element *tla-*.

What distinguishes the Malinche Mexicano example from the Pipil one is most conspicuously that, in addition to replication, it also involved borrowing. Furthermore, contact-induced change appears to have been one from minor to major use pattern (see section 2.2), rather than from one categorial structure to another: there was already a preposition-like use pattern in Classical Mexicano, e.g. *ī-pan in cama* (its-on *in* bed) 'on the bed,' which under Spanish influence turned into what Hill and Hill (1986: 248) call the absolutely "preferred way to render prepositional relationships in Malinche usage." And whereas in Pipil the possessive prefix was eliminated on the way from relational noun to preposition, it was replaced by an indefinite marker in Malinche Mexicano, e.g. *tla-cuitlapan den cárcel* (*tla*-behind *de.in* prison) 'behind the prison.' Finally, Malinche Mexicano and Pipil also appear to differ from one another in the fact that the old postpositions of Classical Mexicano, while having "largely given way to a more Hispanicized way of speaking," have not disappeared in modern Malinche Mexicano, even if they are rarely used.

That the same kind of contact-induced grammaticalization process can occur anywhere is suggested by the following example from Papua New Guinea. Ross (1996; 2001) describes a situation where two genetically unrelated languages spoken on Karkar Island off the north coast of Papua New Guinea have become semantically and syntactically largely intertranslatable while each of the two has retained its own lexical material. The model language (= M) is Waskia, a Papuan language of the Trans New Guinea type, and the replica language Takia (= R), a Western Oceanic language of the Bel family of the North New Guinea cluster.[7] Among the properties discussed by Ross there is a set of postpositions exhibiting a similar semantic patterning in the two languages. Western Oceanic languages commonly have prepositions but Takia speakers have lost the prepositions, or no longer use them productively. In an attempt to replicate the postpositions of Waskia (= Mx), Takia speakers developed postpositions (= Rx) by grammaticalizing inalienably possessed relational nouns (Ry).[8] In this way, a Proto-Western Oceanic construction illustrated in (7) turned into a postpositional construction (8) in Takia (note that Takia has given up the possessee-possessor order of Western Oceanic and adopted the possessor-possessee order of Waskia).[9] In accordance with the parameters of grammaticalization, the prepositional phrase **i lalo-ña* lost its nominal structure, turned into an adposition (decategorialization), and was phonetically reduced to *lo* (erosion). Thus, speakers of the replica language Takia took recourse to a grammaticalization process; using relational nouns for 'inside' and developing them into locative (inessive) adpositions, for example, is a cross-linguistically widespread strategy (Heine & Kuteva 2002; see also Heine & Kuteva 2003: 536).

(7) Proto-Western Oceanic (Ross 1996: 189; 2001: 143)

       *i   lalo- ña a   Rumaq
       PREP inside- its ART house
       'inside the house'

(8) Takia (Western Oceanic; Ross 1996: 190; Ross 2001: 143)

       ab   lo
       house in
       'in the house'

Another example illustrating the same grammaticalization process in Takia suggests that this is not an isolated case.

(9) Proto-Western Oceanic (Ross 1996: 189)

> *i   papo- ña a   Rumaq
> PREP top-   its ART house
> 'on the top of the house'

(10) Takia (Western Oceanic; Ross 1996: 190)

> ab   [fu]fo
> house on
> 'on top of the house'

Once again, a prepositional phrase with a possessive noun phrase as its modifier, cf. (9), turned into a postposition, as can be seen in (10), involving the decategorialization of a nominal construction and the erosion of a complex form to a postposition *fufo* or *fo*.

The data provided by Ross (1996: 188–90) make it possible to reconstruct this grammaticalization process in more detail. First, they show that, predictably, the process did not lead straight, e.g. from a prepositional phrase *i lalo-ña* to a monosyllabic postposition *lo*, but rather involved a number of intermediate stages. One such stage is reflected in the Takia form *i-lo-n*, where the erstwhile preposition *i-* is fossilized. In Gedaged, another Bel language closely related to Takia, the form has been further eroded, the postposition for 'in' being *lon*. The final-stage form *lo* is not only found in Takia but also in the other western Bel languages. To summarize, the development from prepositional phrase to postposition in the Bel languages appears to have involved a series of decategorializations and erosions of the following kind:

(11) Takia and other Bel languages (Ross 1996: 189–90)

> From prepositional phrase to postposition
> *i lalo-ña > i-lo-n > lon > lo

Note that two of these stages of grammaticalization have been retained in Takia, and the two can cooccur in one and the same phrase: when a Takia speaker wishes to be precise about the location, s/he can say the following:

(12) Takia (Western Oceanic; Ross 1996: 190)

> ab   ilo-   n lo
> house inside- its in
> 'in the house's inside'

Second, these data also allow us to understand why Takia underwent a change from preposition to postposition.[10] One cross-linguistically fairly widespread conceptual schema leading to the rise of new possessive constructions is referred to by Heine (1997a: 144) as the Topic Schema, taking the form [(As for) X, X's Y] (e.g. something like *John, his car*), where the possessee follows the possessor and agrees with the latter in the form of a possessive attribute. Predictably, in languages using this schema the possessee follows, rather than precedes, the possessor – irrespective of any word-order constraints that may characterize the language concerned.[11] It would seem that Takia speakers have drawn on this schema, with the effect that the possessee follows the possessor. Now, when the possessee phrase **i lalo-ña* was grammaticalized, the expected result was a postposition on the erstwhile possessor rather than a preposition. This suggests that Takia's history from prepositions to postpositions did not involve any word-order change; rather, the prepositions were lost and the postpositions arose via the creation of a new possessive construction. While this was seemingly a language-internal process, we concur with Ross that it was at the same time contact-induced, in that the choice of the Topic Schema provided Takia speakers (or their ancestors) with a strategy to match the postpositional structure of the model language Waskia.

That this hypothesis is correct is also suggested by the following. It would seem that this process is not an instance of ordinary grammaticalization but rather of replica grammaticalization (see below), in that there is evidence to the effect that Takia speakers replicated a grammaticalization process that they observed in Waskia. Ross reconstructs the corresponding process in Waskia thus:

In a Waskia phrase like *kar kuali* 'on the fence', *kuali* 'on' is derived from **k<u>al* + *i*, where the infix *<u>* marks a third person possessor (corresponding to PWOc **-ña*, Takia *-n*), *-i* is the location postposition (corresponding functionally to the PWOc preposition **i* – the formal correspondence is chance), and **kal* was a now-lost part noun meaning 'top' (corresponding to PWOc **papo-*).[12] (Ross 1996: 190)

Accordingly, a Waskia phrase such as (13b) is hypothesized to be historically derived from a structure as sketched in (13a).

(13) Waskia (Trans Guinea Type; Ross 1996: 190)

    a. **X* — k<u>al-i
       '**X* on its top'

    b. *X* — kuali
       'on top of X'

This analysis suggests that Waskia speakers also used the Topic Schema or, more precisely, Takia speakers appear to have replicated the grammaticalization from Topic Schema to postposition on the model of Waskia.

To conclude, Takia and Pipil underwent the same process from relational nouns to adpositions in the creation of a new word class; what distinguishes the two cases essentially is that this new class appears to have replaced an earlier class of prepositions in Takia, while in Pipil there was no earlier equivalent class, hence no replacement.

Extension

Ideally, grammaticalization – whether contact-induced or not – involves all of the four parameters listed in (1). As a matter of fact, however, this is not always so; in quite a number of cases it is confined to desemanticization. But there are also cases where it appears to be restricted to one of the other parameters. We will now illustrate the effect of the other three parameters.

A number of examples were provided in section 2.2.2 exhibiting the effects of extension. That extension tends to go hand in hand with desemanticization is suggested by cases such as the following. In Standard German, one of the main ways in which purpose clauses are formed is by means of the complex conjunction *um zu* 'in order to, so that.' This conjunction is not normally used to introduce nominal or adjectival modifiers; still, there is a widely accepted use pattern where *um zu* can be used, e.g. *ein Messer um Brot zu schneiden* (a knife for bread to cut) 'a knife for slicing bread.' Among German speakers of South Tyrol (Südtirol) in northern Italy, Riehl (2001: 255) found that, under the influence of Italian, this use pattern has been extended to contexts where a purpose interpretation no longer makes sense, and where a new function appears to be emerging, namely that of presenting infinitival phrases as modifiers of nouns and adjectives (see section 2.2.3). Thus, the Tyrol German expression *Schwierigkeiten, um Freundschaften zu knüpfen* (difficulties for friendships to knot) 'difficulties to form friendships,' which is not well-formed in Standard German, is modelled on Italian *difficoltà a farsi delle amicizie*. This process is in accordance with a cross-linguistically widespread grammaticalization of markers for purpose clauses to infinitive markers (see Haspelmath 1989). In this way, the German marker *um zu* was extended to new contexts, at the same time acquiring a more general function, namely presenting both purposive and infinitival participants.

To conclude, context extension is one of the most salient forces characterizing contact-induced grammaticalization, and it is inextricably associated with semantic generalization. But there remains a problem that is still unresolved: there is no conclusive evidence to determine which of the two forces, extension and desemanticization, provides the primary motivation for grammatical change.

Decategorialization

The following example suggests that contact-induced grammaticalization can be confined to decategorialization. Contact between Bantu and Nilotic languages in Kenya resulted in a number of grammatical changes, which have been described in detail by Dimmendaal (2001b). Our example concerns another case where Bantu languages appear to have acted as model languages. Bantu languages are known for their rich paradigms of verbal derivational extensions marked by suffixes. There is nothing comparable in the Nilotic language Luo or its closest relatives, the Southern Lwoo languages of Uganda and the Sudan: verbal derivation is limited, mainly involving internal morphology in the verb root. Now, apparently on the model of neighboring Bantu languages (= M), Luo (= R) speakers have developed a set of what look like verbal suffixes (= Rx), resembling structurally the Bantu verbal suffixes (Mx), expressing functions typically encoded by the Bantu derivational applied suffix *-id- ('for, to, with reference to, on behalf of'). This typological innovation has been described by Heine and Reh (1984: 50–3) as "verbal attraction," a grammaticalization process whereby adpositions lose their independent status and turn into verbal derivational clitics and affixes. Luo speakers used the prepositions *ne* (or *nI*) benefactive, *e* locative, and *gi* instrumental (= Ry) in order to develop verbal enclitics or suffixes (= Rx); the following example is confined to the benefactive preposition *ne*, where (14a) illustrates the prepositional use and (14b), where *Juma* is topicalized, the use as a verbal suffix (see also Dimmendaal 2001b: 101–2).

(14) Luo (Western Nilotic, Nilo-Saharan; Heine & Reh 1984: 51)

    a. jon   nego   diel ne juma.
       John is.killing goat for Juma
       'John is killing a goat for Juma.'

    b. juma jon   nego-   ne diel.
       Juma John is.killing- for goat
       'John is killing a goat for *Juma*.'

These examples might suggest the following: Among all the various possible ways of adapting their language to the model language, speakers of the replica language appear to select what seemingly is a fairly complex solution. Rather than simply borrowing grammatical forms from the model language, they draw on structures that correspond neither in their morphosyntactic form nor in their meaning to the model, and in order to achieve equivalence they have to go through a complex process whereby lexical structures are developed into grammatical markers, adpositional phrases are gradually transformed into adpositions, free forms are grammaticalized to clitics and affixes, etc.

Erosion

That contact-induced grammaticalization can be restricted to erosion is suggested by the following example. The Austronesian language Tigak of New Ireland, Papua New Guinea, has replicated a number of structures from Tok Pisin, spoken by the Tigak as their primary L2 (Jenkins 2002: 243–55). Tigak speakers have developed the phrase *lo tang gaan* 'at the time' into a temporal subordinating conjunction 'when.' Whereas traditional, conservative Tigak speakers use this full phrase, as in (15a), younger Tigak have reduced the phrase to the noun *gaan* 'time,' cf. (15b). As Jenkins (2002: 254–5) argues, this reduction process is suggestive of contact-induced influence by Tok Pisin, which uses the noun *taim* 'time' as an equivalent subordinating conjunction, as can be seen in (16).

(15) Tigak (Austronesian; Jenkins 2002: 254–5)

    a. lo   tang gaan tang vuul gi   me sang vo
      (LOC ART time ART canoe 3.SG.S MT arrive IRR
      nag   kos.
      1.SG.S board)
      'When the canoe arrives I will get on.' (Lit.: 'at the time . . .')

    b. gaan tang vuul gi   me sang vo nag   kos.
      (time ART canoe 3.SG.S MT arrive IRR 1.SG.S board)
      'When the canoe arrives I will get on.'

(16) Tok Pisin (English-based pidgin/creole; Jenkins 2002: 255)

    taim mun i   kam bai mi   kis- im.
    time canoe PM come FUT 1.SG get- TRS
    'When the canoe arrives I will get on.'

When an adpositional phrase, like Tigak *lo tang gaan*, is grammaticalized to an adposition or clause subordinator this is likely to trigger erosion, whereby that phrase is phonologically and/or morphologically reduced (cf. English *by cause of* > *because* (> *coz*)). This process need not, and most often is not, induced by language contact. In the case of Tigak, however, it seems plausible that reduction was triggered or accelerated by the model provided by Tok Pisin. Note that this case involves morphological rather than phonetic erosion (see

Heine & Reh 1984), in that reduction led to a loss of morphological items rather than of phonetic substance of morphemes.

In the examples presented in this section, speakers of the replica languages had a model category (= Mx), but the model language (= M) apparently did not provide any guidance as to how to replicate Mx. The situation is different in another type of contact-induced grammaticalization that we will now turn to, where the model language provides not only a model category (Mx) but also a way of how to replicate that category (My).

3.1.3   *Replica grammaticalization*

As was observed in Heine and Kuteva (2003: 539), there is a second type of process that appears to be even more common than the one described in section 3.1.2. In this process, it is not a grammatical concept but rather a grammaticalization process that is transferred from the model (M) to the replica language (R)[13] (see also Nau 1995: 96 for an insightful discussion). The mechanism underlying this process, which they call replica grammaticalization, differs from the one sketched in (2) only in the fact that (17c) replaces (2c).

(17) Replica grammaticalization

    a. Speakers notice that in language **M** there is a grammatical category **Mx**.

    b. They create an equivalent category **Rx** in language **R**, using material available in **R**.

    c. To this end, they replicate a grammaticalization process they assume to have taken place in language **M**, using an analogical formula of the kind [**My** > **Mx**]: [**Ry** > **Rx**].

    d. They grammaticalize **Ry** to **Rx**.

This mechanism corresponds to some extent to what Matras proposes to call mutual isomorphism in his discussion of contact-induced changes in Balkan Turkish and Romani:[14]

Mutual isomorphism taken in the metaphorical sense suggested here is the tendency of languages in an areal to syncretize their operational procedures in such a way that would enable a corresponding structure to initiate a corresponding processing operation. [. . .] individual languages select suitable candidates among their inherited stock of grammatical items, to which the necessary functions can be assigned most naturally. As a result, language internal form: function correlation is extended, leading ultimately to functional scope-enhancement. (Matras 1998b: 100–1)

There is virtually no information on what conceptual clues speakers may have to reconstruct a process presumed to have taken place in the model language, and it is not always possible on the basis of the evidence available to distinguish neatly between ordinary and replica grammaticalization. Nevertheless, as we will see below, there are frequently clues that make it possible to discriminate between the two (see, e.g., our discussion in 3.3 on the future tense in varieties of Pennsylvania German and Yiddish).

The mechanism sketched in (17) is different from the one discussed in section 3.1.2, as can be illustrated with an example reported by Weinreich ([1953] 1953: 40). In German, the third-person plural pronoun *sie* 'they' is formally the same as the polite/formal second-person singular pronoun *Sie* 'you,' and the same situation is found in the local Polish dialect of Silesia, a contact region between German and Polish speakers. This example appears to be a typical case of (17): the model language German (= M) has undergone a grammaticalization process whereby the third-person plural pronoun (= My) was grammaticalized to a second-person singular pronoun to be used for polite/formal reference (= Mx). Polish (= R) speakers in Silesia replicated this process by extending the use of their third-person plural pronoun (= Ry) to a new function (= Rx). Most likely, those Polish speakers were unfamiliar with the historical factors that were responsible for that grammaticalization in German; still, from the sociolinguistic, pragmatic, and grammatical information that was accessible to them they had enough information for replication. Obviously, replication did not mean that the Polish speakers repeated the history of the German *Sie*-construction; however, replication was not confined to simply copying a polysemy pattern (see section 3.2) that they found in the model language but rather involved a process that was structurally not unlike the one speakers of the model language had undergone centuries earlier.

Verbs expressing predicative possession ('have') are cross-linguistically a not uncommon source for existential copulas, where an expression of the form 'it there has' is grammaticalized to an existential copula ('there is;' for details, see Heine & Kuteva 2002: 241–2), cf. French *il y a* (lit. 'it there has' >) 'there is.' Apparently on the basis of this pathway of grammaticalization, speakers of the colloquial variety of Singaporean English (= R) are using possession verbs (= Ry) to denote existence (= Rx). In doing so, they rely on the model provided by their L1 Chinese (= M), thereby replicating the grammaticalization process from possession verb to existential marker (= My > Mx) (Ho & Platt 1993: 18; Ziegeler 2000: 90).

It is fairly easy to discover cases of replica grammaticalization when the model language has developed a grammatical category by using a conceptual source that is rarely encountered cross-linguistically and where exactly the same source is used by speakers of the replica language. The Irish "hot-news" perfect[15] (= Mx) is based on what appears to be an instance of a spatial or temporal schema of the kind [X is after Y], where the aspectual notion of a hot-news perfect is encoded by means of a locative (or temporal) preposition 'after' (= My). Presumably around the late seventeenth century (Sullivan 1980: 205), the same grammaticalization took place in Irish English (= Ry > Rx; Boretzky 1986: 25; Filppula 1986; Harris 1991: 201ff.), e.g. *She's after selling the boat* 'She has just sold the boat.' The development of a prepositional structure with 'after' into a perfect structure is a very rare process in the languages of the world. The only other example of such a development we are aware of is found in Czech, where it seems to be possible to come across a use of 'after' as a perfect marker, e.g. *Jana je po promoci* (lit. 'Jana is after graduation') 'Jana has graduated,' or *Dedecek je po infarktu* (lit. 'Grandpa is after heart.attack') 'Grandpa has had a heart attack' (Tommola 2000: 474–5). We therefore assume that the Irish English example is another instance of replica grammaticalization.

Clause subordination in Konkani
Most of the above examples concern cases where a new grammatical category was developed for which there existed no equivalent in the replica language. We will now see that this is by no means a requirement for replica grammaticalization to happen since the replica language already had an equivalent category. The use of interrogative pronouns (e.g. English *who*?) as relative clause markers (English *who*) is cross-linguistically widespread, but most instances of it are to be found within Europe (Heine & Kuteva 2002) and in Indo-European languages in general. A similar process has happened at the southeastern end of Europe's periphery: In Turkish varieties spoken on the Balkans, interrogative markers have been grammaticalized to relativizing and coordinating conjunctions on the model of neighboring Indo-European languages. For example, in West Rumelian Turkish dialects spoken in Macedonia the interrogative *ne* 'what' has been grammaticalized to a relativizer modeled on Macedonian *što*, and in a similar fashion the use of Turkish *ne zaman* 'when?' also turned into a relativizer on the model of Macedonian *koga* and Albanian *kur* 'when,' thereby eliminating participial constructions (Friedman 2003: 64; see also Matras 1998b: 94–6).

Balkan Turkish is by no means the only language spoken at the periphery of the Standard Average European area that has replicated the European strategy of using interrogatives as relative and/or complement clause markers. Other examples concern Basque, Nahuatl, and Tariana (Heine & Kuteva 2003: 541–2; see sections 1.1, 4.1.2). In addition to the spread of European languages in the Americas there is another direction of diffusion of the interrogative-to-relative strategy, based on the spread of Russian to other languages of the former USSR: on the model of Russian, some of these languages have recently extended or are in the process of extending the use of interrogative pronouns to mark relative clauses as well, either by borrowing or by replication (Comrie 1981: 12–3, 85).

But essentially the same process has also occurred in the Indo-Aryan language Konkani, as we will now demonstrate. What makes this case, documented by Nadkarni (1975), a particularly interesting one is that it illustrates in some detail the effects of replica grammaticalization and its implications for the typological profile of the language concerned (see also 4.3.3.4). Konkani as spoken by the Saraswat Brahmins (abbreviated KSKo. by Nadkarni) in the coastal districts of North and South Kanara in the Indian State of Karnataka has been deeply influenced by the Dravidian language Kannada as a result of at least four centuries of intense language contact resulting in non-reciprocal bilingualism: These Konkani are fluent speakers of Kannada, while Kannada speakers hardly ever learn Konkani. In the course of this contact, Konkani speakers have replicated a relative construction of Kannada, as can be seen in (18), where (18a) provides a Kannada sentence and (18b) the corresponding Konkani (KSKo.) sentence (the relative clauses are printed in square brackets).[16] Note that (18b) would be ungrammatical in other Konkani dialects, i.e. dialects that have not been influenced by Kannada.

(18) Kannada (Dravidian) and KSKo. (Indo-Aryan; Nadkarni 1975: 674, 675)

    a. [yāva   mudukanu pēpar ōdutta iddān- ō] avanu ḍākṭaranu iddāne.

    b. [khanco mhāntāro pepar vāccat āssa- ki] to   ḍākṭaru   āssa.
       which old.man   paper reading is   that   doctor   is
       'The old man who is reading a newspaper is a doctor.'

The Kannada relative construction is the result of the grammaticalization of two interrogative constructions: The interrogative *yāva* 'which?' turned into a relative adjective, and the element *ō* is a marker of polar (yes–no) questions which turned into a relative clause-final element. Accordingly, if the relative clause in (18a) is uttered without *yāva*, a polar question results: 'Is the old man reading a newspaper?', and if the polar question marker *ō* is omitted, the result is a word question (or WH-question): 'Which old man is reading a newspaper?' Thus, Kannada speakers appear to have combined two interrogative strategies to create this relative clause construction.

Exactly this process was replicated in the Konkani dialect (KSKo.) influenced by Kannada. Accordingly, Nadkarni concludes with reference to (18b) (= (4f) in his counting):

Thus the relative clause in 4f also begins like a WH-question and ends like a yes–no question. If we leave out the interrogative *khanco* from this clause, it becomes a yes–no question: "Is the old man reading a newspaper?" If we leave out *ki*, it becomes a WH-question: "Which old man is reading a newspaper?" – exactly like the relative clause in Kannada sentence 4a [= our (18a); a.n.]. (Nadkarni 1975: 676)

To conclude, replica grammaticalization has resulted in total structural iso-morphism (see section 6.1) in the expression of this construction between two genetically unrelated languages; neither any other dialect of Konkani nor any of the other Indo-Aryan languages of India has such a construction. As Nadkarni (1975: 677, 679) suggests, there was no structural motivation for this replication:[17] Konkani already had a well-functioning relative construction of the Indo-Aryan type, described as a phrasal relative structure using a relative participle instead of a finite verb. This old category, which is also found in Kannada, differs from the replicated category in being more versatile than the new one, in that it allows for extraposition while the new category is restricted to occurrence before the main clause, nor did the new category add any desirable stylistic variant to the already existing situation. Nevertheless, there are indications that the new category is expanding at the expense of the old one – a process that Nadkarni refers to as the Dravidianization of this Konkani dialect. For another effect this contact situation had, see section 4.3.3.4.

From adverb to clause subordinator
A not uncommon grammaticalization concerns the extension of adverbial mod-ifiers to introduce subordinate clauses; for example, locative adverbs may turn into subordinators of locative, temporal, causal, or other adverbial clauses (see Heine & Kuteva 2002). Such a process can also be observed in contact-induced replication. Jenkins (2002: 269) observes that the Austronesian lan-guage Tigak of New Ireland, Papua New Guinea, and the English-based Tok Pisin have a form that functions both as a restrictive modifier ('only/just') and as an adversative ("contrastive") conjunction ('but'), the forms being *kisang* in Tigak and *tasol* (< English *that's all*) in Tok Pisin. Jenkins argues that this functional equivalence is due to substrate influence of Austrone-sian languages on Tok Pisin; we interpret this as a case of replication where Austronesian languages such as Tigak provided the model that was replicated in Tok Pisin. It would seem that underlying this equivalence relation there appears to be a grammaticalization process, so far undocumented, whereby the use of restrictive adverbs (or nominal modifiers) is extended to serve as adversative clause markers. For example, the German particle *nur* 'only/just' serves as a restrictive adverb in (19a) but as an adversative conjunction 'but' in (19b):

(19) German

    a. Er arbeitet nur.
       he works   only
       'He does nothing but work.'

b. Er arbeitet, nur kriegt er kaum Geld   dafür.
   he works   but gets   he hardly money there.for
   'He is working but he gets hardly any money for it.'

In a similar fashion, Tok Pisin *tasol* occurs as a clause-final adverb in (20a) but as a clause-initial subordinator in (20b) – exactly like Tigak *kisang* does, cf. (21).

(20) Tok-Pisin (English-based pidgin/creole; Jenkins 2002: 269)

    a. ol   i   pilai tasol.
       3.PL PM play only
       'They're only playing.'

    b. em   i   gat mani tasol em i   no   givim pe
       3.SG PM have money but   3.SG PM NEG give pay
       long mi.
       to   1.SG
       'He has money, but he did not pay me.'

(21) Tigak (Austronesian; Jenkins 2002: 269)

    a. nari rig   karau kisang.
       3.PL 3.PL.S.AGR play   only
       'They're only playing.'

    b. nane   gi   togani ta   mani kisang
       3.SG.PRN 3.SG.S.AGR have   ART money but
       gi   veko lisani ta   pulpul su- gug.
       3.SG.S.AGR NEG give ART pay   to- 1.SG
       'He has money, but he did not pay me.'

Since Tigak provides both the source and the target uses of the relevant marker, there is reason to assume that this is an instance of replica grammaticalization.

Creating text markers

Contact-induced grammaticalization manifests itself perhaps most frequently in text structure. Unfortunately, this area has not yet been studied in great detail; still, there are a few findings that suggest that the way texts, in particular narrative texts, are organized is determined to some extent by grammaticalization. Paradigm cases concern markers of boundaries, in particular the beginning and the end of a text, significant units within the text such as paragraphs and topic change, but also of continuity of narrative discourse. There is a not uncommon pattern whereby transparent expressions such as clausal propositions are grammaticalized to markers of text organization. As a result of this process, they tend to lose their erstwhile semantic content in favor of some discourse function, to be decategorialized to unanalyzable markers, and to undergo erosion, that is, to be reduced in their morphophonological shape. Almost invariably, the process involved is replica grammaticalization.

Further examples of replica grammaticalization serving the creation of boundary markers in spoken discourse come from the contact situation in the Vaupés area of northwest Amazonia, as a result of which the North Arawak language Tariana has replicated a wide range of grammatical structures from East Tucanoan languages in general and Tucano in particular (Aikhenvald 2002). Among these structures there is a recapitulating clause meaning 'so s/he did' (where 's/he' refers to the subject of the previous clause). This clause, which is *di-ni* 'he did' in Tariana and *wee* '(he) did' in Tucano, appears to have been grammaticalized to a discourse marker introducing new paragraphs. Another example of a boundary marker stemming from this contact situation concerns speeches held in a centre house at gatherings such as religious or political meetings. In Tariana there is an expression *matfa* 'good, OK' which corresponds to Tucano *ayũ* 'good, OK.' In both languages, this expression has given rise to a marker signaling the end of a speech held in such meetings (Aikhenvald 2002: 169–71).

For another discourse marker, replicated in the English-based pidgin Bislama of Vanuatu on the model of Oceanic languages, see section 3.2.1 below.

From optional to obligatory category

One salient characteristic of grammaticalization concerns what Lehmann ([1982] 1995) describes as obligatorification, whereby categories whose use is optional come to be used more frequently and may turn into obligatory parts of words or word groups. Not infrequently, this process concerns pragmatically determined categories gradually losing their pragmatic functions and acquiring the properties of automatic syntactic constituents.

Language contact provides a not uncommon trigger for obligatorification. We mentioned two cases in the preceding chapter, both involving independent personal pronouns which gradually develop into pragmatically non-required subject (and object) pronouns on the model of another language. One example concerned language contact in Sauris, northeastern Italy, between speakers of German and the Rhaeto-Romance language Friulian (section 2.1); the second example dealt with immigrant communities in the USA speaking pro-drop languages such as Spanish, Serbian, Russian, or Hungarian, who tend to redefine their pro-drop convention on the model of English (section 2.3.4).

The following observations suggest that this case of pro-drop "resetting" or "decline," as it has been called, constitutes a canonical process of grammaticalization. As we pointed out above (section 3.1.1), grammaticalization involves four basic mechanisms, and three of these mechanisms can be said to be at work when a language changes from a pro-drop to a non-pro-drop structure. One of these mechanisms is desemanticization, whereby linguistic expressions lose in semantic content. In our case, loss concerns the fact that pronouns that are said to be used for pragmatic purposes such as presenting given vs. new information, marking topic or theme, or expressing "emphasis" lose their pragmatic meaning. Context generalization can be seen in the fact that in pro-drop languages the use of independent personal pronouns is severely restricted, being determined by pragmatic variables. As a result of language contact, the use of these pronouns is generalized, being extended to contexts where the pronouns were not normally used previously. Finally, decategorialization has the effect that the personal pronouns lose their categorial status as independent constituents, turning into largely predictable subject (or object) markers.

To conclude, "pro-drop resetting" among these immigrant communities in the USA has the characteristics of a process leading from minor to major use pattern (see section 2.3.4), and from optional to obligatorily marked category. That one of the mechanisms associated with grammaticalization, namely erosion (or phonetic reduction), does not appear to have been involved is probably due to the following: Erosion is usually, even if not always, the last process to come in grammaticalization, and it may take quite some time before its effects can be observed. All the cases discussed here concern periods of contact that were simply too short to have had a distinct effect on the phonetic substance of the pronouns undergoing grammaticalization.

Extending lexical use patterns

Replica grammaticalization is also involved in a number of cases which tend to be described as instances of lexical polysemy but which, nevertheless, appear to involve a development from lexical to grammatical uses of linguistic items.

The following example concerns the verb *(la)schar* of the Rhaeto-Romance language Surselvian (see section 4.1.2): The German verb *lassen* 'let' has a number of grammatical uses; in particular, it is used as a causative auxiliary ('cause to do') and as a permissive auxiliary ('allow someone to do'). Romance languages express these two functions by using different verbs, e.g. French *faire* vs. *laisser*, Italian *fare* vs. *lasciare*, Spanish *hacer* vs. *dejar*. Similarly, the Rhaeto-Romance languages traditionally make such a distinction: *far* vs. *(la)schar*. Under German influence, however, Stimm (1984) argues, Surselvian tends to generalize *(la)schar* to express both a causative and a permissive meaning – with the effect that there now appear to be two alternative ways of expressing causativity. In this way, the Surselvian verb has undergone replica grammaticalization on the model of the German development from lexical verb to causative auxiliary.

A similar example can be seen in the Swedish verb *ha* 'have': Some Swedish long-term immigrants to the USA who left Sweden in the 1920s were found in the 1980s using this Swedish verb in ways parallel to English *have*, which has developed a grammatical use pattern as a causative auxiliary. This pattern was replicated by the Swedish immigrants, grammaticalizing *ha* to a causative use pattern on the model of English *have* in contexts where in Standard Swedish the verb *få* 'cause' would be required (see Myers-Scotton 2002: 104).

3.2   Polysemy copying

We noted earlier in this chapter that one might argue that there is an alternative analysis to the one proposed here, namely that, instead of a grammaticalization process, we are dealing with the replication of a polysemy pattern, or of calquing or loan translation. In fact, there are cases of grammatical transfer where an analysis in terms of polysemy copying (or grammatical calquing) provides the most plausible hypothesis.[18]

Such an analysis offers itself, for example, in cases where, rather than the meaning of the basic form, it is that of a derived form that is replicated, as in the following example, where Oceanic languages serve as models and Bislama, the English-based pidgin of Vanuatu, as the replica language (Keesing 1991). Many northern and central Vanuatu languages (as well as other Oceanic languages; = M) have grammaticalized a reduplicated form of the verb for 'go' to a marker indicating the passage of time in a narrative (= Mx). Thus, in Epi, the reduplicated form *bababa* of the verb of motion *ba* 'go' expresses the passage of time in a narrative. This situation appears to have been replicated in Bislama (= R), where the corresponding verb of motion *go* (< English *go*) was reduplicated as *go-go-go* and used as a discourse marker also expressing the passage of time in narratives (= Rx).[19]

This is not an isolated example, as suggested by the following case, which also involves reduplication: Serbian/Croatian has developed a productive pattern of forming absolute superlatives on the model of Turkish, e.g. *beli* 'truly' > *bezbeli* 'quite truly,' *ravno* 'even' > *ravravno* 'entirely horizontal' (Weinreich [1953] 1964: 42). As in the preceding example, replication in this case appears to have concerned the semantic relation between the simple and the reduplicated form, rather than a gradual process from less to more grammatical forms.

While such cases suggest that polysemy copying constitutes an alternative to grammaticalization for transferring grammatical categories from the model language to the replica language, most cases of grammatical replication that have been reported cannot be described appropriately in terms of notions such as polysemy copying, calquing, or loan translation. The reader is referred to Heine and Kuteva (2003: 555–9) for detailed discussion; we are confined here to the main points substantiating this position.

One point concerns the observation that most cases that are seemingly instances of polysemy copying can also be interpreted as grammaticalization processes. First, they are unidirectional, leading from less to more grammatical use patterns, and we are not aware of any case of reversed directionality. For example, a number of languages that have been in contact with Standard Average European languages such as French and German have grammaticalized question words to markers of relative and complement clauses; but we are not aware of any example suggesting that any language in Europe, or elsewhere, has undergone a development from relative or complement clause marker to question word.

Second, wherever there is sufficient evidence, it turns out that the replica construction is less grammaticalized than the corresponding model construction[20] (see section 3.4.5 below). For example, in the initial stage of grammaticalization, the new category tends to be ambiguous between its literal and its grammaticalized meaning, it tends to be confined to few contexts, and its use is optional – a situation that has not seldom led to controversies among grammarians on whether or not the relevant category really exists in the language concerned. Such properties are commonly encountered in replicated categories. For example, both the definite article in Sorbian, replicated on the model of German (see section 2.4.1), and the indefinite article of Basque, replicated on the model of Romance languages, exhibit properties of categories in the early stages of grammaticalization, as is suggested, for example, by the fact that their use is contextually restricted and optional to some extent. They thus differ from the corresponding categories in the model languages, which both are fully grammaticalized articles (Heine & Kuteva 2003: 556–7).

Another example is provided by the evolution of the possessive perfect (or 'have'-perfect) [X has done Y] based on the grammaticalization of a possessive schema [X has Y] in Romance, Germanic, and some other European languages, that is, in what Haspelmath (1998; 2001) calls Standard Average European. Some languages spoken at the periphery of the Standard Average European area have replicated this construction; almost invariably, however, the replica constructions have not reached the same advanced stage of grammaticalization characterizing that of Standard Average European languages. Slavic languages such as Sorbian, Czech, and Slovenian, which have a long history of contact with German, are cases in point; Breu summarizes the situation in these languages thus:

Einige slavische Sprachen an der Peripherie haben unter Kontakteinfluß ein analyti-
sches HABEN-Perfekt entwickelt, das allerdings in den Adstratsituationen nicht den
grammatischen Status der Gebersprachen erreicht hat. Der Aufbau hat aber durch die
Nachbildung der periphrastischen Konstruktion begonnen. [Some Slavic languages at
the periphery have developed an analytic 'have'-perfect under contact influence, but in
these adstrate situations it has not reached the grammatical status it has in the donor
languages. Nevertheless, the construction has been initiated via the imitation of the
periphrastic construction.] (Breu 1996: 31)

Third, what distinguishes polysemy copying from canonical instances of grammaticalization is that the former does not appear to involve intermediate stages
of evolution. Frequently it is not possible to reconstruct the grammaticalization
process in every detail since the data available are for the most part not sufficient
to do so. But in a few cases it is possible, and such cases suggest that there is in
fact an intermediate stage between the initial and the final stage of grammaticalization. Several examples are presented in Heine and Kuteva (2003: 555–9);
the Irish "hot-news" perfect provides an additional example. As we mentioned
in section 3.1.3, this category is based on what appears to be an instance of a
spatial or temporal schema [X is after Y], where the aspectual notion of a perfect
is encoded by means of a locative (or temporal) preposition 'after' (Filppula
1986; Boretzky 1986: 25; Harris 1991: 201ff.). The same grammaticalization
process, modeled on the Irish perfect, can be assumed to have taken place in
Irish English presumably around the late seventeenth century (Sullivan 1980:
205), cf. (22).

(22) Irish English (Harris 1991: 205)

>   She's after selling the boat.
>   'She has just sold the boat.'

That replication did not involve polysemy copying is suggested by the following
observation. When the Location Schema is grammaticalized to a construction
for verbal aspect, as illustrated in (22), this involves an intermediate step where
the schema has a nominal complement [X *is after* NP], before the construction is extended to non-finite verbal complements [X *is after* VP]. Such an
intermediate stage appears to exist in the present case of Irish English, where
instead of a verbal complement the preposition *after* has a nominal complement,
cf. (23).

(23) Irish English (Sullivan 1980: 205)

>   He's after the flu.
>   'He just had the flu.'

And finally, replicated categories tend to exhibit properties that bear witness to their grammaticalization history, such as decategorialization (loss of morphosyntactic properties) and erosion (phonetic reduction or simplification; see section 3.1.1 (1)).

To conclude, while the data available in the relevant literature are in most cases too scanty to reconstruct the exact process of replication, there appears to be sufficient evidence to suggest that conceptual transfer of grammatical meanings tends to require grammaticalization; for similar observations, see Nau (1995: 114–22). This is most obvious in the case of ordinary contact-induced grammaticalization (section 3.1.2), where the model language (= M) provides a model for a category (= Mx) but not for how to develop an equivalent category (= Rx) in the replica language (= R). In other words, there is no possible polysemy that could be copied, and the only way of acquiring Rx is via grammaticalization of some other category (= Ry).

3.3   Future tenses

In the preceding sections we have been dealing with a range of different grammatical meanings. We will now try to explore how one particular grammatical meaning may be affected by language contact; to this end, we will be restricted in this section to a cross-linguistic survey of future tense categories (for some examples, see Heine & Kuteva 2003: 551–5). The reason for dealing with this grammatical meaning is that among all grammatical categories it is future tense that appears to be the most likely to be replicated in situations of language contact – hence, it provides quite some information on how contact-induced grammatical categories arise.

The main source for the grammaticalization of future tenses is provided by motion schemas involving goal-directed verbs for 'come to' [X comes to Y] or 'go to' [X goes to Y], or a volition schema [X wants Y] using a verb for 'want' (Bybee, Pagliuca & Perkins 1991; 1994). We will refer to these schemas, respectively, as the de-venitive, de-allative, and de-volitive schemas or constructions (cf. Dahl 2000b: 319ff.; Heine & Kuteva 2003: 552). Other sources for future tenses are cross-linguistically clearly less common.

Europe

All these main sources have been recruited in European languages and are each suggestive of areal spread across neighboring European languages (Dahl 2000b). De-venitive futures are confined to two areas, each having a documented history of language contact. One area is mainland Scandinavia, including Danish, Norwegian, Swedish, and marginally Finnish. The second area is Switzerland, where Romansh dialects and Schwyzertütsch (Swiss German) share the grammaticalization from a verb for 'come' ($\nu\varepsilon\text{ɲ}$ 'come' and $k^g un$ 'come', respectively) to future tense marker (Weinreich [1953] 1964: 41; see Dahl 2000b: 320–1 for details).

A case of a de-allative future has been reported from Luxembourgeois, where speakers of this German dialect are said to have replicated the French de-allative construction *aller faire* ('go to') by developing their verb *goen* 'go' into a future auxiliary (Alanne 1972).

Contact-induced futures derived from modal use patterns are reported from Molisean, a variety of the Slavic Croatian minority in Molise, southern Italy (Breu 1996: 26–7; Heine & Kuteva 2003: 552–3) and from early written Finnish (appr. 1540–1820), where Bible translators are said to have developed weakly grammaticalized futures (based on the modal verbs *pitää* 'should, must' and *tahtoa* 'want, intend') using German and Swedish modals as models. These future tense use patterns were discontinued around or after 1820 (Nau 1995: 99–104).

An instance of a de-volitive future is found, for example, in the Balkan languages[21] – in fact it is among the uncontroversial morphological features that have been adduced to define the Balkan sprachbund (see 5.2.3.1). Joseph describes the situation thus: "A future tense based on a reduced, often invariant, form of the verb 'want' is found in Greek, Tosk Albanian, Rumanian, Macedonian, Bulgarian, Serbo-Croatian, and Romani" (Joseph 1992: 154). That the relevant markers have a "reduced" and/or "invariant" form is a predictable result of grammaticalization: in the process of developing into a tense marker, the erstwhile verb 'want' loses in verbal properties, eventually turning into an invariable marker (decategorialization), and also tends to be phonetically reduced (erosion).[22] As is common with sprachbund situations, there is no reliable evidence on which Balkan language provided the ultimate model for grammaticalization but, again, there can be hardly any doubt that language contact played some role in the spread of the process.

Romani

The role played by areal pressure on shaping equivalence relations and grammaticalization can be demonstrated perhaps most clearly by using the Indo-Aryan language Romani as an example.

Romani offers a perhaps extreme case of how speakers can adapt their modes of grammatical categorization to those of their neighbors. In the Balkans, adaptation had the effect that Romani speakers developed a de-volitive future (see above); elsewhere in Europe they found other models and, accordingly, developed different kinds of future categories. In the dialect of Wales they developed a de-allative future on the model of English *be going to* (Boretzky 1989: 368), cf. (24).

(24) Romani of Wales (Boretzky 1989: 369)

      brišindo džala te del.
      (rain   goes to give)
      'It is going to rain.'

In Russian Romani dialects there is a future tense using the verb *l-av* 'take' as an auxiliary (e.g. *l-av te xav* 'I am going to eat') – a grammaticalization that is cross-linguistically quite unusual. Now, Ukrainian has two future tenses, and one of them also uses the verb 'take' as a future auxiliary. Boretzky (1989: 369) suggests that Vlach Romani speakers acquired their 'take'-future when they crossed Ukrainian territory. Quite a different situation is found in the Sinti variety that was influenced by German: There is no formal future expression in this variety; rather, the present tense is also used to refer to events in the future. This is exactly the situation found in colloquial German, where the present tense is also used in appropriate contexts for future events; conceivably, what this suggests is that absence of a salient model prevented grammaticalization from taking place.[23]

That de-volitive futures found in Balkan languages are in fact due to language contact is suggested, for example, by the fact that the Romani varieties spoken in the Balkans have developed a future category marked with *ka(m)-*, which is derived from the verb *kam-av* 'want, love'[24] (Boretzky 1989: 368). Still, in view of the cross-linguistically widespread distribution of de-volitive futures, a development based exclusively on universal principles of grammaticalization, unaffected by language contact, can never be entirely ruled out. There is, however, additional evidence to suggest that this grammaticalization was contact-induced: while the various Romani varieties developed a number of different future tenses, it is only the varieties spoken in the Balkans that acquired a de-volitive future (Boretzky & Igla 1999: 729); note that the presence of a de-volitive future is widely assumed to be a salient property of the Balkan linguistic area (see section 6.2.3.1).

But the Balkan varieties of Romani provide further evidence that the rise of new future tenses has been shaped primarily by contact. We observed above that there is a less common source for future tense markers based on the grammaticalization of obligation markers typically involving a possession schema, i.e. a possessive verb 'have' plus a non-finite main verb – French and other Romance languages providing paradigm examples of this pathway of evolution. The Geg dialect of Albanian and varieties of Macedonian and Bulgarian have drawn on this pathway to develop future tenses, and Romani speakers in contact with these Balkan languages appear to have replicated this pathway. Now, the Romani equivalent of a 'have'-verb is a construction literally meaning 'is me' (*si man*) to designate 'I have'; accordingly, Romani speakers replicated the possession schema to create a future tense, illustrated in (25).

(25) Romani, Prizren dialect (Boretzky & Igla 1999: 719)

> Hi ma te džav   lesa.
> is me that go.1.SG he.INSTR
> 'I will go with him.'

This kind of replication of grammaticalization processes is perhaps most pronounced in Bulgarian varieties of Romani. Bulgarian has a system of future tense marking where the positive future has a de-volitive source (using a verb meaning 'want') and the negative future using the possession schema (using a verb meaning 'have'). Exactly this split structure of future marking was replicated by Romani speakers influenced by Bulgarian, as we saw in section 1.3.

What this situation suggests is that a future tense exists in Romani essentially only to the extent that it is replicated from languages with which Romani speakers came into contact.[25]

English-induced de-allative futures

English is presumably the most widespread contact language of the world, and wherever speakers of other languages have been in close contact with English, it is probable that they would replicate the English de-allative future in some way or other. A case in point are some immigrant communities in the USA and Canada, which used the English *be-going-to* future as a model for developing a use pattern involving goal-oriented motion as a conceptual source.

One example is provided by Old Order Mennonites in Waterloo County, Canada. In their variety of Pennsylvania German there is an emerging de-allative immediate future tense involving the verb *geh* 'to go' (Burridge 1995: 61ff.), very likely the result of intense language contact with surrounding English-speaking communities (but see section 1.4.6). Another example can be seen in the speech of a community of Yiddish speakers in Venice along the coast next to Los Angeles, which is strongly bilingual in English although Yiddish predominates in everyday conversations (Rayfield 1970). As a result of intensive contact with English, Yiddish speakers have created a future tense on the model of the English *be-going-to* future, illustrated in (26).

(26) Yiddish of Venice, California (Rayfield 1970: 69; quoted from
    Myers-Scotton 2002: 216–7)

> All right, ge ikh   kum- en   bald.
> all right go 1.SG come- INF soon
> 'All right, I'm going to come in a minute.'

The last two examples, both taken from German-based varieties, are remarkable in one respect. What they have in common is that they are instances of
replica grammaticalization rather than of ordinary grammaticalization. In the
latter case we would have expected that the relevant speakers of Pennsylvania
German and Yiddish had drawn on the pattern provided universally for
de-allative futures, taking the format [X goes to Y] (see above). Since both
examples lack an allative marker (encoded in the corresponding English construction by the erstwhile preposition *to*), it would seem that these speakers
conceived English *to* of *be going to* as an infinitive rather than an allative (or
purpose) marker,[26] and that they drew on an isomorphic use pattern existing
in German, whereby the verb *gehen* 'to go' takes infinitival verbal complements without an allative (or purpose) marker, e.g. in Standard German *Ich
gehe schlafen* (I go sleep.INF) 'I go to sleep.' Accordingly, the basis for grammaticalization was not the universally prescribed de-allative pattern, but rather
a language-specific use pattern of the form ['go' + VERB.INF] that these
speakers appear to have treated as an immediate equivalent of the English
model.

Conclusions

What we observed on the situation in Europe also applies to other parts of the
world: New future tenses are constantly arising in language contact situations
on the basis of the principles sketched at the beginning of this section (for
more examples, see Heine & Kuteva 2003: 551–5; see also section 6.1 for an
example from Pipil). And it is essentially the entire range of options that are
universally available for developing categories of future tense that has been
exploited in situations of language contact. However, which particular option is
chosen is determined by the particular circumstances surrounding the contact
situation, such as the use patterns characterizing the replica language and the
kind of category provided by the model language. For example, speakers in
southeastern Europe can be predicted with a certain degree of probability to
develop a new future tense by using a verb for 'want' since the de-volitive
schema offers the primary conceptual choice for speakers in the Balkans, while
immigrants in the USA are most likely to draw on the de-allative schema to
create a new future construction in their L1 because the English *be-going-to*
future provides the most immediately available model for replication. However,

the data available are not sufficient to determine what exactly it is that makes a certain conceptual model more attractive than alternative models in a given situation.

3.4   Some general issues

The analysis proposed above raises a number of questions, such as the following:

a. Is contact-induced grammaticalization unidirectional?
b. Are the conceptual sources used in contact-induced grammaticalization different from the ones to be found elsewhere?

There is yet another question that the preceding discussion raises but that does not seem to require further treatment, namely: Are there any limits as to which kinds of grammatical structures can be replicated? Our data provide no basis for saying that there are limits; contact-induced grammaticalization affects in the same way verbal, nominal, and clausal morphosyntax, including clause combining, it affects ideational, textual, as well as interpersonal functions, and it affects derivational and inflectional forms, as well as free forms. It may well be, however, that on the basis of a larger corpus of data this observation needs to be modified.

In the present section we will deal with the two questions raised above in more detail.

3.4.1   Directionality

Grammaticalization is essentially unidirectional: At least 90 per cent of all instances of grammatical change can be assumed to be in accordance with principles of grammaticalization (Heine 2003b). And the same applies to grammaticalization occurring in, or being triggered by, language contact (Heine & Kuteva 2003: 560). For example, we saw in section 3.3 that language contact may give rise to new future tense categories via the grammaticalization of a verb meaning 'want,' while we are not aware of any example suggesting a reversed directionality, whereby language contact induced speakers to turn a future tense marker into a verb meaning 'want.'

But, as shown in Heine and Kuteva (2003: 560–1), there are possible exceptions, such as the following case concerning post-verbal perfect markers of the Malaita Oceanic languages. As Keesing (1991: 331) argues, these markers have been further grammaticalized to topicalizing particles.[27] In the following examples from the model language Kwaio, (27a) illustrates the perfect use of *no'o*, while (27b) is an example of the use of the same marker as a topicalizing particle.

(27) Kwaio (Eastern Oceanic; Keesing 1991: 330–1)

    a. e   'akwa   no'o.
       he run.away PERF
       'He has run away.'

    b. gila   no'o la   age- a.
       them TOP they do- it
       'They're the ones who did it.'

This process appears to have been replicated in Solomons Pijin:[28] As (28) suggests, the replica language exhibits the same structure as the model language Kwaio or other Oceanic languages of Malaita:

(28) Solomons Pijin (English-based pidgin; Keesing 1991: 330–1)

    a. hem- i   ranawe   nao.
       (him- he run.away PERF)[29]
       'He has run away.'

    b. hem nao i   save.
       him TOP he know
       'He's the one who knows.'

The development from a verbal aspect marker to a topic (or focus) marker has so far not been documented, nor does it seem conceptually plausible – hence we might be dealing with a counterexample to the unidirectionality of grammaticalization. Still, such examples are rare; on the whole, contact-induced language change is in accordance with principles of grammatical change to be observed elsewhere, even if there may be specific circumstances triggering a violation of the unidirectionality principle.

3.4.2   Conceptual sources

Finally, we raised the question of whether the conceptual sources used in contact-induced grammaticalization differ from those to be found elsewhere. The answer is essentially in the negative; most cases of grammaticalization discussed in the previous sections were canonical instances also to be observed in situations where no language contact has been claimed. Thus, we witnessed common processes such as the following (see Heine & Kuteva 2002 for cross-linguistic evidence):

(i) Concrete nouns are grammaticalized to markers expressing case relations. Perhaps one of the most widespread developments concerns concrete nouns, such as nouns for body parts and other relational nouns, that are recruited to express locative, temporal, and other grammatical relations, and language contact provides a number of examples for this grammaticalization.

A different kind of this overall process can be illustrated with an example from Southeast Asia. A number of languages spoken in various parts of the world have grammaticalized a noun for 'thing' to a possessive marker linking two noun phrases. The construction that is used for this process takes the form [possessee, thing(-of) possessor] (Heine 1997a; Heine & Kuteva 2002). Instances of this schema can be found in Vietnamese, Khmer, Thai, and Lao, where a noun meaning 'thing, object, stuff' has been used with this schema and was grammaticalized to a possessive marker; note that the nouns employed appear to be etymologically unrelated. While there is no information on which language provided the model, there can be hardly any doubt that the spread of this grammaticalization was contact-induced (Matisoff 1991: 391; Enfield 2001: 260).

(ii) Verbs give rise to a wide range of grammatical functions, relating to case marking, clause embedding, tense, aspect, and modality, etc. Examples will be given, e.g. in section 6.2.2 involving the Southeast Asian languages Chinese, Hmong, Vietnamese, Thai, and Cambodian, where verbs for 'give' and 'get' have undergone a number of contact-induced grammaticalizations.

(iii) Allative and benefactive markers are commonly grammaticalized to indirect object markers, which again may turn into direct object markers. We will have examples in section 4.3.1 from Turkish-Laz contact, where the use of an allative/goal marker was extended to marking indirect objects, and in the Indian village Kupwar, Kannada speakers appear to have grammaticalized their dative postposition to also mark human direct objects.

(iv) Comitatives are a common source for other case functions including clause combining. One common line of grammaticalization concerns the extension of comitative markers to express instruments too; Basque provides an example of such a development: Its comitative case suffix -*ekin* is derived from an earlier postpositional phrase meaning 'in the company of' (Trask 1998: 318) and as a result of language contact acquired an instrumental function. Another line of development leads from comitatives to noun phrase-conjoining markers ('and') and eventually to clause-combining markers (Stolz 1998; Stassen 2000; Heine & Kuteva 2002). That this line has been exploited in a language-contact situation is suggested by the following example. The Aztecan language Pipil has no formal means for coordinating clauses, that is, clause-conjoining ('and') is not formally marked. Under the influence of Spanish, Pipil is said to have grammaticalized the relational noun -*wan* 'with' to a preposition *wan* 'with,' and *wan* has further developed into a noun phrase-conjoining conjunction 'and.' Finally, the use of *wan* has been extended to conjoin clauses as well (Harris & Campbell 1995: 130). Thus, we seem to be dealing with an entire chain of development from relational noun to preposition (see section 3.1.2), from comitative 'with' to nominal conjunction, and finally to a clause-combining conjunction. Note that, if Harris and Campbell are right, this extended development must have happened within a fairly short time period, that is, only after the introduction of Spanish in the Americas (Harris & Campbell 1995: 127, 129–30, 147).

(v) Independent words turn into clitics and affixes. This process relates to the morphosyntactic component of grammaticalization (decategorialization), of which some examples were presented earlier (see especially section 3.1.2). A widely discussed example concerns the development of the English singular pronoun *him* into a transitive/causative marker in Melanesian Pidgin varieties (Sankoff & Brown 1976; Keesing 1991: 318–19). This process might have been triggered by the fact that in many of the substrate languages, that is, languages spoken by people using these pidgin varieties as a second language (e.g. Eastern Oceanic languages), there was a verbal suffix used for transitivizing or causativizing verbs (Keesing 1991: 318–19), and the speakers of these languages replicated this category in the pidgin varieties by grammaticalizing the personal pronoun *him*. The result of the process was that a self-standing pronoun assumed the grammatical function of a derivational marker and, consequently, lost its status as an independent word, turning into a verbal clitic and affix or, alternatively, becoming a lexicalized appendix of the verb. As we will see in chapter 4, contact-induced decategorialization may have more drastic results, giving rise to a new typological profile in the replica language.

To summarize, the kinds of conceptual sources that people select for grammaticalization in situations of language contact do not normally differ from those found elsewhere. A question that arises in this connection is the following: To what extent are the developments sketched here the result of language contact as opposed to universal principles of grammaticalization? On the basis of the scanty data that are available we can say no more than that there must be some "conspiracy" of both factors, but what exactly this means is open to further research.

3.4.3   Restructuring

Grammaticalization accounts for much of what happens in grammatical replication leading to what is commonly described as increased "isomorphism" among languages, but it does not cover everything. For want of a better term, we will refer to processes of grammatical replication that cannot be accounted for with reference to grammaticalization as restructuring. This term has been discussed in various schools of linguistics;[30] especially in pidgin and creole studies where it has received extensive treatment and has been related to a number of different phenomena (see especially Neumann-Holzschuh & Schneider 2000 and the contributions therein). The reader is referred to Aikhenvald (2002) for a wealth of examples suggesting that grammatical replication may lead to structural changes in the replica language without involving principles of grammatical-ization.

A paradigm case of restructuring concerns word order, where people rear-range the order of meaningful units in one language on the model of another language. The literature on language contact abounds with examples, hence there is no need to illustrate this process. Note, however, that many cases of presumed contact-induced word-order change are not really cases of restructur-ing but rather the by-product of grammaticalization; we saw examples of such cases in preceding sections (e.g. section 3.1.3).

Aikhenvald's (2002: 60) detailed analysis suggests that on the one hand, restructuring neither corroborates nor contradicts principles of grammaticaliza-tion; on the other hand, it also suggests that some cases that have been treated as instances of restructuring can perhaps more profitably be reinterpreted as epiphenomenal effects of grammaticalization. The following examples may illustrate this. Aikhenvald (2002) discusses a wide range of data illustrating how East Tucanoan languages of the Vaupés basin in northwestern Brazil served as models of replication for Tariana, an Arawak language (Aikhenvald 2002: 98–9). For example, East Tucanoan languages have a morpheme meaning 'also' (e.g. Tucano *ke'ra*) which also marks the plural of some kinship terms and serves as an associative plural marker with other kinship terms and personal names. In Tariana there is a structurally similar morpheme (*-sini*) which also means 'also'; at the same time it marks the plural of a few kinship terms and has uses as an associative plural marker on proper nouns and kinship terms. There is reason to assume that this isomorphism is due to a replication process from East Tucanoan languages to Tariana, and there is also reason to main-tain that this is an instance of replica grammaticalization (see section 3.1.3) whereby Tariana speakers created a new number category by grammaticalizing a nominal modifier 'also' to a plural marker on the model of East Tucanoan languages. Assuming that this reconstruction is correct, we would be deal-ing with a restructuring process in Tariana resulting from grammaticalization. This hypothesis is supported by the fact that, first, no Arawak language other than Tariana has an associative plural and, second, that the associative plural in the replica language Tariana does not appear to have been grammaticalized to the extent that it has been in East Tucanoan languages (Aikhenvald 2002: 98–9); on the basis of many other cases of contact-induced change, replica cat-egories are likely to be less grammaticalized than their model categories (see section 3.4.5 below).

Another example adduced by Aikhenvald to illustrate restructuring concerns plural agreement with numerals. In the Arawak language Baniwa, nominal plu-ral marking is confined to human nouns. Speakers of the fellow North Arawak language Tariana have a more complex structure of number marking, but one that exactly corresponds to that of their East Tucanoan-speaking neighbors: while Tariana basically retains the distinction between human and inanimate number marking, there nevertheless appears to be a gradual extension from human to non-human referents: The use of the plural form is optional when there is a numeral attribute for '2' or '3' but obligatory for numerals above '3.' Assuming that this is another case where Tariana speakers have replicated use patterns of East Tucanoan languages, this suggests that Tariana speakers have extended plural marking from human to non-human referents. As is to be expected in this process, extension was gradual, affecting first higher numerals, before spreading to the lower numerals '2' and '3,' where plural marking is optional, that is, where it has not been conventionalized. Such a development is in line with an overall extension pattern of grammaticalization according to which the use of markers for human referents tends to be extended to denote inanimate referents; it is suggestive of context extension (see section 2.2.2, 3.1.2).

Not seldom, contact-induced grammaticalization entails restructuring. Grammaticalization involves first and above form–meaning units that are put to new, i.e. to more grammatical uses. But these units are part and parcel of phrasal, clausal, or even larger use patterns which are also affected by grammaticalization. Accordingly, contact-induced grammaticalization is not confined to morphology but tends to include larger discourse structures too. For example, Tariana speakers of northwestern Brazil use their interrogative pronouns, such as *kwana* 'who?', to mark relative and complement clauses on the model of Portuguese (Aikhenvald 2002: 182). But replica grammaticalization from interrogative to subordinating marker is not restricted to these markers. Complement clauses precede the predicate of the main clause in Tariana, but in the case of this grammaticalization, Tariana speakers replicated the Portuguese use pattern, where the complement clause follows the main clause predicate. Accordingly, (29a) reflects the Portuguese structure of (29b). Thus, the extension from interrogative to relative/complement marking appears to have triggered restructuring, that is, the introduction of a new arrangement of meaningful units.

(29) Tariana (North Arawak) and Portuguese (Aikhenvald 2002: 182–3)

    a. Tariana
       di-   sata dhima-   pidana kwana-   sika
       3.SG.NF- ask 3.SG.NF+ hear-   REM.P.REP who-
       ketemi.
       INFR.INTER rest
       'He asked who remained.'

b. Portuguese
ele perguntou quem restou.
he asked   who   remained
'He asked who remained.'

In a number of other cases, what appears to be suggestive of restructuring can equally well be interpreted as being suggestive of grammaticalization. In one type of restructuring, the replica language exhibits two (or more) structural options (say, A and B) to express one and the same grammatical function. When the model language has only one structure (A) for that function, restructuring may have the effect that speakers of the replica language narrow down these options to A, thereby establishing a one-to-one equivalence relation with the model language; we proposed the term narrowing for this process in section 2.2.4. Now, a common grammaticalization process involves context generalization (see 1.3), whereby the use of some form or construction (A) is extended, and this process can be at the expense of another form or construction (B), which subsequently may be lost. In such cases, restructuring can be induced by grammaticalization.

The following example illustrates this process. Not uncommonly in the Arawak languages of northwest Amazonia, word order is pragmatically based, where, for example, the order of words in adpositional or possessive constructions depends on whether the possessee or the argument of the adposition is focused or not. Thus, in the Arawak language Baniwa, (30a) and (30b) have the same meaning, but in (30b), *João* is in focus. East Tucanoan languages on the other hand have a fixed word order [dependent – head], that is, the possessee invariably follows the possessor and the adposition its complement. Now, the North Arawak language Tariana, which has been heavily influenced by East Tucanoan languages, appears to have replicated the structure found in these languages by generalizing (30a), which is identical in Baniwa and Tariana – with the result that (30b) is an ungrammatical structure in Tariana: there is no variation in word-order, that is, there is now only one word-order arrangement that is isomorphic with that of East Tucanoan languages (Aikhenvald 2002: 167).

(30) Baniwa (North Arawak; Aikhenvald 2002: 167)

a. João i-   siu
   John INDF- to

b. ɾi-   siu João
   3.SG.NF to John
   'to John'

Overall, the relationship between restructuring and grammaticalization remains unclear. While there are examples to show that the former is an outcome of the latter, there are also examples to suggest that restructuring constitutes a mechanism that may trigger grammaticalization. Once again, language contact between East Tucanoan languages and the North Arawak language Tariana in northwest Amazonia provides an example (see also section 4.1.4). Most Arawak langages of the Upper Rio Negro area have a number of locative case markers, distinguishing between locative/directional, directional/allative, ablative, and perlative ('along') case marking. East Tucanoan languages on the other hand have only one multifunctional locative case, expressing location, direction to and from, as well as temporal functions. As the description by Aikhenvald (2003: 8–10) suggests, Tariana has given up the locative case distinctions characterizing its fellow Arawak languages by replicating the East Tucanoan model: being strongly influenced by East Tucanoan languages, Tariana speakers have generalized one of their case suffixes, the allative case suffix -se, to a catch-all locative case used for static location, ablative, and allative functions, thereby matching the locative case polysemy of East Tucanoan languages.[31]

On the surface, this is a straightforward instance of restructuring not involving grammaticalization;[32] as a matter of fact, however, even this case has been shaped by grammaticalization. What appears to have happened in Tariana is that the allative case suffix -se was extended to contexts previously reserved for other case functions, such as locative, directional, and ablative functions, thereby assuming a wider range of functions. This process involved two main parameters of grammaticalization (see section 1.3, (5)): extension and desemanticization, in that – with the extension to more contexts – the erstwhile case marker -se lost its specific function as an allative marker in favor of a more general locative function. On the basis of the description provided by Aikhenvald (2003: 7–10) it would seem, however, that in this case grammaticalization was an epiphenomenal product of restructuring in that, rather than aiming at changing the functional and contextual structure of a case marker, Tariana speakers are likely to have been primarily concerned with establishing an equivalence relation (or structural isomorphism; see section 6.1) with the corresponding locative case marker of East Tucanoan languages.

To conclude, restructuring is an important mechanism of contact-induced replication, but not infrequently it appears to be shaped or influenced by grammaticalization; but, alternatively, it may also be a force that determines what can or cannot be grammaticalized.

3.4.4   On spontaneous replication

As the preceding discussion may have shown, contact-induced grammaticalization is a ubiquitous process. Still, not all processes of grammatical replication do correspond to the definition proposed in section 1.3, and in the present section we will look at some of these processes.

One kind of process concerns cases where speakers simply replicate, or copy, a grammatical category of the model language in the replica language without invoking principles of grammaticalization. This means typically that they adapt a grammatical category of the replica language to the structure of a corresponding category in the model language; we will discuss this process in section 4.1.4. Another kind of process, to be discussed in section 4.4.3, concerns renewal, whereby an existing mode of grammatical expression is replaced by a new, that is, less grammaticalized mode, thereby initiating a new cycle of grammaticalization.

Finally, there is what may be loosely called spontaneous replication. What this term is meant to refer to is that speakers of an L1 having an imperfect knowledge of another language, L2, notice that there is a grammatical category in an L2 for which there is no equivalent category in the L1. In such a situation they may apply principles of replication, including grammaticalization, to guide them in their use of the L2. Having only an imperfect knowledge of the L2, they may apply principles of grammaticalization either less extensively or more extensively than is done by L1 speakers of that language. The result is either an undergeneralization or an overgeneralization of these principles (Deborah Ziegeler, p.c.).

The following example may illustrate the notion spontaneous replication. Perhaps the majority of the world's languages do not have definite or indefinite articles. Now, when speakers of such languages (= L1) acquire Western European languages as L2s, which are characterized by the presence of strongly grammaticalized articles, it is likely to happen that such speakers do not use articles where L1 speakers of the relevant Western European language would use them (undergeneralization), or else use them also in contexts where they are not used by L1 speakers (overgeneralization). The literature on language contact between Slavic languages on the one hand and Germanic and Romance languages on the other offers a wealth of examples of this case of spontaneous replication, as already pointed out by Schuchardt (1884: 112) with reference to Slavic L1 speakers in contact with German and Italian.

While spontaneous replication is no doubt relevant for understanding the mechanism giving rise to new use patterns and grammatical categories in contact situations, we have little to say about it since our concern is not with idiosyncratic or temporally restricted language use but primarily with use patterns and categories that have acquired some stability of expression across space, time, and social interaction. Accordingly, when speakers of languages having no articles are in contact with languages such as English, they tend either to undergeneralize or overgeneralize articles in their use of English in spontaneous speech, and vice versa. But once such idiosyncractic usage is conventionalized we predict that there will be directionality, in that speakers of replica languages having no articles are likely to create articles on the model of a language having articles, while speakers of languages having articles are unlikely to lose their articles when in contact with a language lacking articles, since such a development would contradict principles of grammaticalization.

3.4.5   Space, time, and degree of grammaticalization

One observation that surfaces in studies of contact-induced grammatical replication is that, as a rule, replicated grammatical categories are less elaborated, i.e. less grammaticalized, than the corresponding model categories. In fact, what characterizes areas of intense language contact is that there tend to be continua of grammaticalization that correlate with space and time. Such continua may range from use patterns that are optional, i.e. determined by discourse-pragmatic factors at one end of the area to obligatory, fully grammaticalized use patterns at the other end.

As the findings made by Friedman (1976; 1994) show, this is the situation not uncommonly encountered in the Balkan sprachbund. He demonstrates that there is a synchronic continuum extending from discourse-based variation in Bulgarian to fully grammaticalized structures in Macedonian and Albanian (Friedman 1994). The following example illustrates this situation.

One of the properties characterizing Balkan languages is what is technically known as object reduplication, which means that the direct or indirect object noun or pronoun is cross-referenced in the verb phrase by a clitic pronoun agreeing with the object in gender, number, and case or case function (see section 5.2.3.1 (b)). Example (31) from Macedonian illustrates this structure.

(31) Macedonian (Friedman 1994: 102)

> Na momčeto mu   ja   davam   knigata.
> to boy.DEF him.DAT it.ACC.F give.1.SG.PRES book.DEF.F
> 'I give the boy the book.'

In Macedonian and Albanian, object reduplication is obligatory with indirect objects as well as in some other contexts; in other contexts again it correlates positively with definiteness, specificity, or discourse prominence (see Friedman 1994: 102–4). In Bulgarian on the other hand, object reduplication is entirely facultative, being subject to discourse-bound variation. Thus, (32) would be a normal equivalent of the Macedonian sentence in (31), even though (31) could also occur in Bulgarian in specific pragmatically marked contexts. Object reduplication in Bulgarian does not correlate significantly with such parameters as definiteness, specificity, word order, or disambiguation of case functions but is associated with topicality, and indirect objects are reduplicated 2.5 times more than direct objects.

(32) Bulgarian (Friedman 1994: 104)

  Na momčeto davam   knigata.
  to boy.DEF give.1.SG.PRES book.DEF.F
  'I give the boy the book.'

To summarize, object reduplication has been conventionalized to categorial status in Albanian and Macedonian with indirect objects and to some extent with definite direct objects, whereas in Bulgarian it has remained a use pattern whose occurrence is determined not by morphosyntactic but entirely by discourse-pragmatic variables. This difference correlates with the history of object reduplication:

> The dialects reflect in synchronic spatial terms the diachronic development. Just as earlier Slavic documents that show reduplication began first with pronouns and earliest in southwest Macedonia and latest in northeast Bulgaria, so too in the modern northern and eastern Macedonian dialects that are transitional to Serbo-Croatian and Bulgarian, e.g. in Kumanovo and Kukuš/Kilkis, object reduplication occurs with less consistency than in the west-central dialects [. . .]. (Friedman 1994: 105)

What these findings suggest is that there is a significant correlation between space, time, and degree of grammaticalization: Southwest Macedonia represents the earliest stage, where object reduplication has developed characteristics of an obligatory, full-fledged category, while northeast Bulgaria at the other end of the continuum represents the youngest stage, where grammaticalization is still in its earliest stages, in that object reduplication is still "a discourse-bound pragmatic device characteristic of colloquial style" (Friedman 1994: 105).

The label "Macedonian" refers to a number of varieties differing from one another in substantial typological properties. These differences clearly exhibit an areally defined pattern (Friedman 1976). The Macedonian possessive perfect ('have'-perfect) uses *ima* 'have' as an auxiliary and the main verb in the past passive participle (PPP). The structure of the possessive perfect in Macedonian can be described most appropriately in terms of a correlation of linguistic and areal parameters: There is a continuum extending from northeastern Macedonia, where there is essentially no possessive perfect, to southwestern Macedonia, where there is a fully grammaticalized possessive perfect, while intermediate varieties of Macedonian exhibit intermediate forms of grammaticalization. This areal patterning also correlates with diachronic development: As the data presented by Friedman (1976; see also Drinka forthc.) suggest, there was a wave of innovation giving rise to a fully grammaticalized possessive perfect in southwest Macedonia, gradually diffusing northeast, and the farther it diffused the fewer properties of a perfect category it acquired. The extreme northeast of Macedonia has not been affected by this wave, hence there is (as yet) no genuine possessive perfect.

What these data suggest is that the hypothesis proposed at the beginning of the present section is well-founded: replica categories differ in a principled way from their corresponding models in that they tend to exhibit properties such as the ones listed in (33).

(33) Properties of replica categories, distinguishing them from model categories

    a. They are used less frequently.
    b. They are associated with a smaller range of contexts.
    c. They are less clearly associated with the grammatical meaning.
    d. Their use is more likely to be determined by discourse-pragmatic than by morphosyntactic parameters.
    e. Their use is more likely to be optional than obligatory (see chapter 2 for more details).

A number of authors (see, for example, Soper 1996: 287; Aikhenvald 2002: 7) have pointed out in some way or other that replica categories frequently differ from model categories on the lines sketched in (33); we will discuss a number of examples illustrating this point in section 4.4. Within the framework of code copying, which also includes replication, Johanson (e.g. 1992; 2002a) observes that a copy can always be distinguished from its original; note, however, that the evidence adduced by Johanson is of a different nature from the one used here: rather than grammaticalization, Johanson invokes adaptation (or accommodation) to the structure of the replica language (= the base code in his terminology) that accounts for the fact that the copy (or imitation) differs from the model (= the model code).

The following is a canonical example illustrating the rise and structure of a replica category. Most North Arawak languages of northeastern Brazil do not have any copula verb, while all Tucanoan languages have one. A notable exception is Tariana, which has a locative-existential copula *alia*; note that Tariana has been deeply influenced by East Tucanoan languages, which have copulas corresponding to Tariana *alia*. But unlike East Tucanoan languages, Tariana has no conventionalized copula for identity and equation clauses. But younger people may extend the use of the locative-existential copula *alia* to express such clauses. In doing so, they establish structural isomorphism with East Tucanoan model languages such as Tucano. The model and the replica categories differ, however, in the following way: While the former is an obligatory category, i.e. one which must be used, the replica category is not – it is strongly pragmatically marked, being used only when contrastive focus is expressed.

There is a cross-linguistic grammaticalization path according to which the use of a locative-existential marker (e.g., *X is at Y*) may be extended to identifying (*The X is Y*) and/or classifying copula uses (*Y is an X*). Initially, this extension is optional and tends to be confined to pragmatically marked contexts (stage I). It is only at a more advanced stage that the marker loses its pragmatic function and becomes an obligatory copula (stage II). This suggests that young Tariana speakers have replicated the East Tucanoan stage II copulas by grammaticalizing their locative-existential copula *alia*, but that grammaticalization has not proceeded beyond stage I.[33]

To conclude, Tariana *alia* as an identity/equation copula of younger speakers has most of the properties of a replica category listed in (33), differing from the East Tucanoan model categories in the following way: Being restricted to one pragmatic function, it is used less frequently, is associated with a smaller range of contexts, its use is optional, and since its primary function appears to be pragmatic, expressing a copular relation is not its primary function.

On the basis of (33) it seems possible to determine in a situation where no diachronic information is available which is the model and which is the replica category. Accordingly, if we find a case which does not support this hypothesis then such a case is in need of explanation. One factor that may be considered to constitute a problem to the hypothesis is time. In the early stages of language contact, replica categories tend to exhibit a larger range of the properties listed in (33), but the longer and the more intense the contact is, the more of the properties tend to be lost, and in the end, the two categories may become structurally indistinguishable. Obviously, in such cases, (33) will no longer apply.

3.5   Conclusions

Our main concern in the present chapter was to relate grammaticalization theory to contact-induced language change; in doing so, we were building on the foundation laid by Haase (1992) and Nau (1995). While there are examples that appear to be at variance with the unidirectionality hypothesis (section 3.4.1), overall grammatical replication was found to be in line with principles of grammaticalization. We were dealing with cases where in connection with language contact verbs meaning 'want' or 'go to' developed into future tense markers, relational nouns into adpositions, or nouns for 'thing' into possessive/genitive markers; but we are not aware of any language where language contact was responsible for a development in the opposite direction, i.e. from future marker to verbs for 'want' or 'go to,' etc.

These observations furthermore suggest that contact-induced change as studied here is gradual rather than abrupt, involving a process roughly of the following kind: In order to develop a structure that is equivalent to the one in the model language, speakers choose among the use patterns that are available in the replica language the one that corresponds most closely to the model, frequently one that until then was more peripheral and of low frequency of use, and they activate it – with the effect that a peripheral pattern gradually turns into the regular equivalent of the model, acquires a high frequency of use, and eventually may emerge as a full-fledged grammatical category.

Still, the chapter raises a number of questions that we are unable to answer, such as the following: To what extent are the developments sketched here the result of universal principles of grammaticalization and to what extent are they due to the specific factors obtaining in situations of language contact, including the structures of the model and the replica languages? What the observations made seem to suggest is that in addition to the kinds of motivation that have been defined so far (see, for example, Heine, Claudi & Hünnemeyer 1991; Hopper & Traugott 1993) there are others that have to be taken into account in the study of grammaticalization. They relate to communicative goals, such as making the categories existing in the languages in contact mutually compatible and more readily intertranslatable, or to social goals, inducing speakers, for example, to talk like their neighbors, or in a way that is socioeconomically or otherwise profitable.

Another question is how the various processes of contact-induced grammaticalization to be observed in a given language are related to one another: do they interact with or presuppose one another? For example, how are the different processes to be observed in one and the same replica language, e.g. in Pipil (Campbell 1987), Basque (Haase 1992), or Tariana (Aikhenvald 2002), interrelated? There is no conclusive answer to this question – nor has this question ever been addressed in any systematic way in grammaticalization studies.

There is one question where we are able to propose at least a partial answer, namely the question of whether there are certain functional categories that are more likely to arise in situations of language contact than others. As we saw in the course of this chapter, certain kinds of categories are fairly likely to evolve, such as new tense and aspect markers, adpositions, case markers, conjunctions, discourse markers, definite and indefinite articles, etc., while there is little evidence for some other categories arising as a result of language contact,

such categories relating to personal deixis or negation. We have not been able
to detect any more general principle underlying this differential behavior – one
that would be able to account, for example, for the fact that future tense markers
are highly likely to grammaticalize (see section 3.3) while past tense markers
are considerably less so.

It has been a common practice to classify instances of language change in
terms of whether they are the result of language-internal and/or historically
definable factors or else whether they are due to universal cognitive, communicative, or other constraints. What the discussion in this chapter may have
shown is that these are in no way mutually exclusive alternatives;[34] on the basis
of our data on contact-induced grammaticalization both can be expected to be
potentially present in virtually any given case of language change.

4   Typological change

We saw in the preceding chapter that what happens in situations of language
contact is not coincidental: there are certain grammatical changes that can be expected to happen while others are unlikely to happen. Furthermore, there are
changes that have a strong impact on the existing modes of categorization while
others affect categorization only to a minor extent. For good reasons therefore,
Aikhenvald (2003: 2) distinguishes between system-altering changes, which
involve the introduction of new categories, and system-preserving changes,
where no new categories arise.[1] It would seem that any kind of grammatical
replication leads to a modification of the existing system or grammatical structure. In the present chapter we wish to highlight what appear to be the most
salient effects replication may have on the structure of the replica language, and
we will look into the question of whether replication may lead to a change of
what is widely referred to as the typological profile of a given language.

Each of the processes that we described in chapter 3 has specific implications
for the structure of the languages concerned. By introducing new use patterns
and new grammatical categories, the existing structures of arranging discourses
and grammatical categories change in some way or other. The question that we
are concerned with in the present chapter is what these changes mean with
reference to the grammatical structure of the languages concerned. To this end,
we will propose a taxonomy of the most common kinds of changes in section 4.1.
More dramatic changes affecting the overall typological orientation of replica
languages are discussed in 4.2 and 4.3, while in section 4.4 some general lines
of structural evolution are sketched.

4.1   Types of changes

Contact-induced grammaticalization is a fairly uniform process, leading from
less grammatical to more grammatical forms and constructions. But the effects
this process may have on the structure of the replica language are remarkable. We will now look into the main effects that we observed on the basis
of a survey of a larger sample of contact-induced grammaticalizations and
restructurings. The following is a rough classification of the different ways in

which the introduction of a new, contact-induced use pattern or category affects the existing structure of grammatical categorization (see also Johanson 1992; Aikhenvald 2002: 4ff.):

(1) Structural effects of contact-induced grammaticalization on the replica language

    i There is now a new category for which previously there was no equivalent category. We will refer to this situation for want of a better term as gap filling.

    ii There has been some equivalent grammatical category and the new and the old structures encoding this category coexist side by side (coexistence).

    iii The new and the old categories coexist side by side, but the structure of the old category is redefined as a result of the presence of the new category (differentiation).

    iv Some category of the replica language is restructured to be equivalent to a corresponding category of the model language whereby the grammatical categorization of the replica language is affected (equivalence).

    v The new use pattern is assigned to some old category, with the effect that the latter acquires a larger range of uses, that is, the internal structure of the category is changed (category extension).

    vi The new category replaces the old category (category replacement).

Note that these effects are by no means mutually exclusive; as we will see below, several effects may be involved in a given instance of grammaticalization. All possibilities listed in (1) are documented in the relevant literature and will now be treated in more detail.

4.1.1   "Gap filling"

With the replication of a category on the model of another language, the replica language may acquire a new category for which previously there was no or no appropriate equivalent. This process, which tends to be portrayed in the relevant literature as leading to the filling of a gap in the existing system of the replica language, is discussed by Aikhenvald (2002: 4) under the rubric of system-altering changes, and she provides a wide range of examples for it. That gaps in the morphological inventory of a language facilitate the importation of new categories from another language has in fact been claimed by a number of authors (e.g. Winford 2003: 96–7).

We had a number of instances of gap filling in chapter 3. One concerned the introduction of a durative aspect in Bislama, an English-based pidgin/creole of Vanuatu, on the model of Eastern Oceanic languages of northern and central Vanuatu (New Hebrides): speakers of Bislama chose their verb *stap* 'stay, be present, exist' (historically derived from English *stop*) to develop a durative aspect marker in the same syntactic slot as the durative marker occurs in the model languages (Keesing 1991: 328), thereby creating a new category for which there does not appear to have been any conventionalized equivalent (see section 3.1.2). Another case of gap filling is provided by the French-based creole Tayo, which evolved around 1860 in St. Louis, New Caledonia. On the model of the Melanesian languages Drubéa and Cèmuhî, which have an obligatory semantic category of dual, speakers of Tayo developed a new category by grammaticalizing the French numeral *deux* 'two' to a dual form -*de* (section 3.1.2; see Corne 1995).

Gap filling is particularly common in cases where there is a lingua franca,[2] sometimes pidginized, that is widely used as an L2 (second language), and where speakers draw on grammatical distinctions of their L1 (first language) and replicate them via grammaticalization in their L2. The Tayo example just mentioned is suggestive of such a situation, where the number category dual of the languages serving as the L1 was replicated in the French variety spoken as the L2 in St. Louis. Another example was discussed in section 2.4.1, relating to the use of Portuguese as a lingua franca among Tariana speakers in northwest Amazonia: there is no conventionalized form for expressing evidentiality in Portuguese, while the L1 Tariana has four grammaticalized evidential categories. All of them were replicated by means of lexical-verbal constructions in the L2. In this way, Tariana Portuguese gained four new grammatical expressions for which there is no equivalent in Standard Portuguese (Aikhenvald 2002: 315).

A strikingly similar case has been reported from the Verde Valley Yavapai and Kaibab Paiute groups of Arizona (Bunte & Kendall 1981), as we saw in section 1.5 (see also 2.2). Once again, there are grammatical distinctions of evidentiality in these languages, and bilingual Yavapai and Kaibab people are replicating such distinctions in their use of the L2 English, drawing on what appears to be regarded as the nearest equivalent in English for their categories of reported and inferred evidentiality, using *they say* as such an equivalent. In this way, the English variety of these people has been enriched by a grammatical use pattern that does not exist in this form in other varieties of English.

Languages having a fully grammaticalized system of evidentiality are not really common (see Aikhenvald & Dixon 2003), and quite a number of cases of gap filling that are available concern languages acquiring evidential categories on the model of languages characterized by the presence of evidentiality systems. Two cases are particularly noteworthy. One concerns a number of

South American languages that served as models for the European languages Portuguese and Spanish, the contact situation between Tariana and Portuguese that we just mentioned being a case in point. Other examples are provided, for example, by Quechuan languages such as Aymara and Quechua, which have enriched Andean varieties of Spanish with evidential use patterns. Aymara, like Quechua, has an obligatory marker that distinguishes the source of information, i.e. one must mark whether one has been a direct witness to an event or has received information about it indirectly. Now, the pluperfect indicative tense of Spanish is used by bilingual speakers to indicate that one has been an eyewitness to an event (Klee & Ocampo 1995: 52) – that is, a Spanish aspect category appears to have been grammaticalized to an evidential category on the model of a Quechuan language, thereby enriching that Spanish variety with an additional grammatical category.

The second paradigm case of gap filling via the introduction of evidential structures can be seen in a vast area extending from southeastern Europe to central Asia, where Turkic languages have provided the model of transfer. Evidentials in these languages are of a special type, referred to as "indirectives," where the speaker has not witnessed the narrated event directly and the source of information is mostly unspecified. Johanson concludes:

> Features of Turkic evidential systems have proven highly attractive in contact situations and have exerted considerable influence on non-Turkic contact languages of Asia and Europe, e.g. the Balkans, Anatolia, the Caucasus region, the Volga region and Central Asia. (Johanson in press: 3)

One common, though not the only, way of transfer appears to have involved replica grammaticalization (see section 3.1.3), whereby speakers extended the use of perfect and resultative constructions to also encode indirective functions. In this way, languages geographically as far apart as Bulgarian and Tajik appear to have acquired systems of indirective evidentiality of the Turkic type (Johanson in press b: 4); for a detailed description, see Soper (1987) on language contact between the Turkic language Uzbek and the Iranian language Tajik, the eastern variety of Modern Persian.[3]

Another domain where gap filling appears to be not uncommon is tense marking. There are some languages whose verbal system is characterized by an aspectual distinction imperfective vs. perfective and where tense is not a significant notion, being marked perhaps in the form of minor use patterns but not by means of distinct categories. Now, when such languages are in contact with languages having a clear-cut system of tense categorization it may happen that speakers of the former (aspect) languages replicate tense distinctions of the latter. We will discuss two examples of this kind in section 4.2, involving the Nilotic languages Luo and Kalenjin (Kipsikiis) which appear to have acquired tense distinctions on the model of neighboring Bantu languages.

Another example is provided by the Saharan languages of Chad and Nigeria, like the Nilotic languages commonly classified as belonging to the Nilo-Saharan family. Saharan languages are traditionally characterized by an aspectual distinction imperfective/perfective, but the Saharan languages Kanuri and Teda-Daza also have a future tense formed by means of an auxiliary based on the verb 'go' (see section 3.3). Cyffer (2000: 162ff.) suggests that this tense category is the result of language contact. This hypothesis is supported, first, by the fact that, for example, the Chadic language Hausa, the western neighbor of Kanuri and Teda-Daza, has a future tense (*âa*, Future II) that denotes the same kind of (indefinite, uncertain) future that the tense of these Saharan languages does and, second, that Zaghawa, a Saharan language spoken outside this general area farther to the east, does not have a future tense.

In the same way as there may be "gaps" in the system of marking tense, there are also examples where the replica language lacked an aspectual or aktionsart category characterizing the model language and, accordingly, where grammatical replication was used as a strategy to "fill the gap." For example, we saw above (see section 3.1.2 for more details), that the English-based pidgin Bislama of Vanuatu acquired a durative aspect category via replication of a corresponding category in Eastern Oceanic languages of northern and central Vanuatu (New Hebrides). More examples are provided by Aikhenvald (2003: 11–12; see also Aikhenvald 2002) from northwest Amazonia, where speakers of the North Arawak language Tariana acquired aspect categories via replication from East Tucanoan languages, e.g. by grammaticalizing their verb -*sita* 'finish' to a perfective aspect marker on the model of East Tucanoan languages. Aikhenvald concludes: "That is, grammaticalization of lexical items (verbal roots) is a way of developing new morphology for which no pre-existing structural slot was available in Tariana. Grammaticalization involves changing the verbal structure by introducing an additional slot for a new grammatical category" (Aikhenvald 2003: 12). All languages that we know of appear to have some conventionalized structure for expressing reflexivity, but not many have a reflexive possessive. The Baltic languages Latvian and Lithuanian have one: the reflexive possessive pronoun is used for all persons when the subject and the possessor are identical, cf. (2). Finnish does not have one, but the fellow Finnic language Estonian has developed a reflexive possessive pronoun that is structurally the same as those found in the neighboring Baltic languages, cf. (3), and Larsson (2001: 250) argues that the Estonian reflexive possessive pronoun *oma* is the result of Latvian influence on southern Finnic languages. In fact, the evidence available suggests that speakers of Estonian grammaticalized the possessive word *oma* 'own' to a reflexive pronoun on the model of the Baltic category (Nilsson 1988; Stolz 1991: 56–8; Larsson 2001: 250–1).

(2) Latvian (Baltic, Indo-European; Stolz 1991: 58)

> Es lasu *savu* grāmatu. 'I read *my* book.'
> Tu lasi *savu* grāmatu. 'You read *your* book.'

(3) Estonian (Finnic, Finno-Ugric; Larsson 2001: 250)

> Ma loen *oma* raamatut. 'I read *my* book.'
> Sina loed *oma* raamatut. 'You read *your* book.'

Under the rubric of gap filling one may also include cases where there was already a corresponding category but where the new category expresses some particular meaning or range of meanings not covered by the old category. For example, Maltese (Malti) has various ways of expressing passive-like functions; nevertheless, it has replicated the [*venire* + past participle]-passive of the model language Italian (e.g. *viene usato* 'is being used') by grammaticalizing the imperfective form *jiġi* of its lexical verb *ġie* 'come' to a passive auxiliary, with the main verb appearing in the participle form (e.g. *jiġi uża-t* 'being used').[4] Like its Italian model, the new Maltese category is a dynamic passive, thus expressing a function not covered by the already existing Maltese categories (Drewes 1994: 95–6; Stolz 2003) – hence one might argue that there was no equivalent category in Maltese. In a similar fashion, Czech speakers replicated the German possessive perfect by using its verb for 'have, own' with the passive participle, even though there was already a perfect formed with the auxiliary 'to be' plus past participle. But the new construction differs from the already existing one by "differentiating what in English would be the contrast of 'I've got it done' and 'I've done it'" (Garvin 1949: 84).

Gap filling may simply mean that the replica language acquires another item enriching an existing grammatical paradigm; but it may also have more dramatic consequences for the typological profile of the language concerned. One example will be discussed below (section 4.3.3; see also 1.3), relating to clause combining in the Aztecan language Pipil, which appears to have replicated a Spanish pattern of coordination by grammaticalizing the relational noun *-wan* to a coordinating conjunction *wan*. In this way, Pipil can be said to have filled a gap, changing from a language of limited coordination with no true coordinate conjunctions to one having a conventionalized structure of clause coordination (Harris & Campbell 1995: 129–30).

Another example is provided by the North Arawak language Tariana of northwestern Brazil. While the majority of North Arawak languages do not have any copula verb, all Tucanoan languages have one, and so does Tariana, which has been deeply influenced by these languages. The Tariana copula *alia* shows the same structure of marking locative-existential clauses as the corresponding East Tucanoan categories, and its use is expanding to also mark identity and equation clauses on the model of East Tucanoan languages (Aikhenvald 2002: 153–4;

see section 3.4.5 for more details). In this way, Tariana appears to be drifting from the copula-less North Arawak profile towards a copula language akin to East Tucanoan languages.

These examples raise a general question associated with the notion gap filling. One may wonder whether indeed there was a gap to be filled e.g. in Estonian, considering that other Finnic languages do not seem to need a reflexive possessive pronoun, or whether the creation of evidential categories in many situations of language contact really involved gap filling – in light of the fact that presumably the majority of the languages of the world do not have fully grammaticalized categories of evidentiality. In fact, in a number of examples of presumed gap filling it can be demonstrated that the replica languages concerned were used quite effectively prior to acquiring a new category as a result of language contact, that is, there is no evidence to suggest that there was any gap in these languages.

We will not look into this issue here; rather, we will maintain that if the term "gap filling" can be said to be meaningful at all then it is only with reference to a typological contrast between the model and the replica languages. For example, Estonian speakers using Baltic languages found that their Baltic-speaking neighbors had a category for which there was no immediate equivalent in their own language. In this interpretation, a gap can be said to arise when speakers relate the structure of the model language to the replica language and try to establish an equivalence between the two.

In fact, gap filling of this kind can be a driving force when speakers are confronted with some grammatical category or distinction in the model language for which there is no conventionalized equivalent in the replica language. For example, L1 speakers of German exposed to English as an L2 may feel that in certain contexts where English would require the use of the progressive aspect (*be doing*) there is no conventionalized equivalent in German. They are therefore likely to activate minor progressive use patterns available in German to replicate the English aspect category, and they tend to fill the gap by using that minor use pattern more frequently and in more contexts – with the effect that the minor pattern will turn into a major one. The use pattern almost invariably recruited for this purpose is based on the Location Schema (*am Tun sein* 'be at doing'), which in some way or other is available as a colloquial pattern in most varieties of German. This may be an idiosyncratic process, restricted to one person or a small group of persons; but it can as well be shared by a larger community of speakers, as appears to have happened among Mennonite Anabaptist speakers of Pennsylvania German in Ontario (see section 2.3.2).

In a number of accounts of language contact, gap filling is viewed as providing an important motivation for grammatical replication (see Campbell 1987: 277–8; Harris & Campbell 1995: 128–30 for references). Such a view is not without problems. First, it frequently remains unclear whether or not there really

was a gap that needed to be filled. Second, an overall survey of the data concerned suggests that the number of cases that appear to be fairly uncontroversial
instances of gap filling is fairly small. And third, it remains unclear why there
are so many cases where the model language has a grammatical category for
which there is no equivalent in the replica language but where – nevertheless –
no gap filling took place. We therefore side with Harris and Campbell (1995:
130) who suspect that the general notion of filling "structural gaps" requires
much further investigation.

4.1.2   Coexistence

Coexistence may take two different forms: either the new and the old category
are combined and cooccur in the same construction, thus resulting in double
marking; or the two coexist as alternative constructions available to speakers
of the replica language.

An example of the former type is provided, for example, by the grammaticalization from interrogative pronoun to relative clause marker in a number of
languages that have been in contact with Standard Average European languages
(see also section 5.2.3.1). In Basque, a finite relative clause precedes its head;
there is no relative pronoun, but the verb takes a suffix marking it as subordinate. However, for some generations now, a new relativization strategy has been
used in certain parts of the Basque-speaking area ($= R$) under the influence of
Spanish ($= M$). What happened is that the question marker *zein* 'which?' (also
'who?' in places) was used as an equivalent ($= Ry$) of the Spanish interrogative
pronouns ($= My$) and *zein* was grammaticalized to a relative clause marker
($= Rx$) (Trask 1998: 320). Relative clauses introduced by *zein* are documented
in texts since the seventeenth century but as a rule only in translations (Hurch
1989: 21). As we noted above, the new form does not replace the earlier structure; rather, *zein* is added to the existing relative construction (but see also Trask
1998: 320) – with the result that there is now double marking on post-nominal
relative clauses.

A strikingly similar case is found in the North Arawak language Tariana
of northwestern Brazil, which is in close contact with Portuguese, the official language of Brazil, and has been influenced by the latter in various ways
(Aikhenvald 2002). As we saw in section 1.1, young and innovative speakers
of Tariana recognize that in Portuguese interrogative pronouns are also used as
relative clause markers, and these speakers also use their interrogative pronouns
as markers of relative clauses on the pattern of the model language Portuguese;
in doing so, they retain their own relative construction and simply add their
interrogative pronoun (e.g. *kwana* 'who?') – exactly the way Basque speakers do. Similar processes have occurred in the Aztecan languages Pipil of El
Salvador (Campbell 1985; 1987) and Nahuatl of Mexico (Karttunen 1976),

where Spanish, rather than Portuguese, provided the model: in all these cases, an interrogative pronoun was added to the existing relative clause construction.

The following are examples of the second type of coexistence, where the inherited and the innovated forms provide the speaker with functionally largely equivalent alternatives of expression. One example concerns the replication of Spanish interrogative markers in the Aztecan language Nahuatl (Langacker 1975; Karttunen 1976). What were interrogative pronouns serving as indefinite pronouns of main clauses in Nahuatl appear to have "come to be identified with the interrogative-looking relative pronouns of Spanish and reanalyzed into the subordinate clause" (Karttunen 1976: 151). In this way, the Nahuatl interrogative particles *tlen* 'which,' *aquin* 'who,' and *canin* 'where' were used as equivalents of the Spanish pronoun *que, que,* and *donde,* respectively. Thus, the Nahuatl sentence (4a) appears to have been influenced by a corresponding Spanish structure illustrated in (4b).[5]

(4a) Nahuatl (Aztecan, Uto-Aztecan; Karttunen 1976: 151)

> In   cizhuanton aquin ocualhuicac atl   omocuep ichan.
> the girl   who it.brought   water returned her.home
> 'The girl who brought (us) water went home.'

(4b) Spanish (Karttunen 1976: 151)

> La   muchacha que nos trajo   agua volvió   a casa.
> (the girl   who us   brought water returned to home)
> 'The girl who brought us water went home.'

Karttunen interprets the resulting situation thus: "What we have here, I believe, is a situation in which a Spanish relative clause type has been added to but has not supplanted the surface manifestation of an earlier Na. [Nahuatl; a.n.] relative clause structure [. . .]. The result is three distinct surface realizations of relative clauses" (Karttunen 1976: 153).

4.1.3   Differentiation

Differentiation, whereby an existing category is redefined with the emergence of a new category, can be viewed as a special instance of coexistence (section 4.1.2). An example of differentiation was mentioned in section 3.3, involving a variety of the Croatian minority in Molise, southern Italy. This Molisean example suggests that with the rise of a new category, the old category can become functionally redefined. While the new Molisean future based on the auxiliary *imat* 'have' expresses both necessity and future, in the same way as the Italian model construction does, the old de-volitive future (using a verb for 'want') acquired a probability meaning as a result of the rise of the new future (Breu 1996: 30).

Note, however, that coexistence does not entail differentiation; in a number of examples that we have come across there is no indication that the presence of an old and a functionally equivalent new category necessarily leads to functional specialization of the two categories.

While in the last case it is the meaning of the old category that is redefined, differentiation may also affect the morphosyntax of that category. As we observed in section 2.4.1, the Slavic language Sorbian has introduced an optional definite article on the model of the German definite article. Now, with the grammaticalization of the Sorbian demonstrative *tón* (M) / *ta* (F)/*te, to* (N)[6] to a definite article, the erstwhile demonstrative was "strengthened" by adding, for example, the element *tu-* 'here' to develop a proximal demonstrative and to distinguish the demonstrative from the definite marker (Lötzsch 1996: 52).

A different kind of situation is provided by the North Arawak language Tariana of northwestern Brazil, which has been heavily influenced by East Tucanoan languages. Whereas the latter have a distinction between first-person plural inclusive pronouns ('we including you') and exclusive pronouns ('we excluding you'), such a distinction is absent in Arawak languages. As a result of intense contacts with East Tucanoan languages, however, Tariana speakers appear to be developing a similar distinction, as the description by Aikhenvald (2002: 62–3) suggests. Presumably the most common way in which first-person plural pronouns arise is via the grammaticalization of nouns for 'people' or impersonal pronouns 'one' (cf. colloquial French, where the impersonal pronoun *on* has been grammaticalized to a first-person plural marker; see Heine & Kuteva 2002). It is the latter option that Tariana speakers have chosen, using their impersonal pronoun *paha, pha* 'one' (the inherited first person plural pronoun is *waha, wha*):

The Tariana impersonal pronoun may be used in the meaning of inclusive "we". A construction *pha nawiki* (we:incl people) "us (all the) people" is often used in general statements about what everyone does, while *wha nawiki* (we:excl people) "us the people" may refer to the group that includes just the speakers, not the addressee (for instance, in dialogues between people and evil spirits). (Aikhenvald 2002: 64)

This suggests that Tariana speakers are developing an inclusive–exclusive distinction corresponding to that of East Tucanoan languages. This distinction is only weakly grammaticalized, that is, it is not conventionalized to the extent it is in East Tucanoan languages. Grammaticalization appears to have triggered restructuring (see section 3.4.3) in general and differentiation in particuar, in that, with the emergence of a new first-person inclusive use pattern, an existing category was redefined: The general first-person plural pronoun *waha, wha* was restricted to exclusive reference marking.

As is not uncommon in such kinds of contact-induced change, there are several effects on the structure of the replica language: while the change from general first-person to exclusive pronoun would be an instance of differentiation, the rise of a new inclusive marker can be viewed as being suggestive of gap filling (section 4.1.1), and the overall process as one leading to equivalence (section 4.1.4), whereby Tariana acquired a grammatical distinction that immediately matches that of the East Tucanoan model languages.

4.1.4   Equivalence

Another kind of contact-induced change has the effect that a given category of the replica language can most profitably be described and understood with reference to the model rather than with reference to structures characterizing the replica language. It has been documented in many studies cited in this work that an existing category is restructured to be equivalent to a corresponding category of the model language. With the term equivalence (or isomorphism) we refer to corresponding structures of different languages (or dialects) that are conceived and/or described as being the same (see section 6.1 for discussion). The term must not be confused with metatypy, to be discussed in section 5.1.2, which is reserved for cases of wholesale restructuring of a language's semantic and syntactic structures on the model of another language; "equivalence" is used here exclusively for individual instances of structures.

One area where equivalence appears to be not uncommon concerns the categorization of nominal number marking. The Ilwana are a Bantu-speaking people living along the river Tana south of Garissa in eastern Kenya. They have a history of over three centuries of contact with the Orma, who speak a dialect of the East Cushitic Oromo language. Ilwana's closest relatives, as well as Bantu languages in general, have a robust number distinction singular vs. plural, supported by the noun class system, where there is a singular marker regularly corresponding to a plural marker. Orma on the other hand has a prevailing pattern distinguishing three number categories: singulative vs. transnumeral (unmarked) vs. plural/collective. For example, ethnonyms tend to be used in the unmarked transnumeral form and a singular is formed by adding the singulative suffix. Ilwana speakers appear to have replicated this structure with ethnonyms, whereby the Bantu singular (noun class 1) prefix *mo-* was reinterpreted as a singulative prefix while the Bantu plural noun class 2 was replaced by noun class 10, which is unmarked for number – thereby giving rise to an unmarked plural resembling the transnumeral category of Orma (see Nurse 2000: 125). Thus, a Bantu structure illustrated in (5) was replaced in Ilwana by the structure shown in (6). That the earlier plural category tends to be assimilated to the transnumeral category of Oromo might be suggested, for example, by the fact that in Ilwana nouns, "plural is sometimes marked, sometimes not" (Nurse 2000: 130).

(5) Swahili (Sabaki, Bantu)

   M-pokomo *sg* Wa-pokomo *pl* 'Pokomo person'

(6) Ilwana (Sabaki, Bantu; Nurse 2000: 125)

   mo-bokomo *sg* bokomo *pl* 'Pokomo person'

A similar example, where an existing number category was restructured on the basis of the corresponding model category is reported by Johanson (1992: 248). Turkish nouns unmarked for number have properties of a transnumeral category (referred to as *numerus indefinitus*), in that they can have either singular or plural referents; thus, *at* can mean either 'horse' or 'horses.' When the plural marker is added to count nouns it has an individualizing function, e.g. *at-lar* '(individual) horses.' Johanson argues that this structure of marking number has influenced Modern Persian to develop a similar structure, e.g. *asb* 'horse' or 'horses.' Restructuring was, however, not nearly as dramatic in Persian as it was in Ilwana since speakers of Old and Early Modern Persian already appear to have used a transnumeral form with non-human referents too. What replication achieved in Modern Persian is simply that this use pattern was generalized to include human referents too.

A third example is provided by the situation of language contact between Chinese and English in Singapore (Deborah Ziegeler, p.c.). In Chinese, nouns are typically used transnumerally, that is, they are not marked for plural, though determiners and quantifiers may be used to individuate noun phrases. Now, L2 speakers of English tend to replicate this category on the model of Chinese by treating English nouns as a transnumeral category. This strategy has entered the written use of Singaporean English, where one finds nouns without a plural marker where Standard English would use the plural form, e.g. on shop signs (e.g. *Bargain* instead of *Bargains*), in advertising items on display (e.g. *oran*ge instead of *oranges*), or on the snake enclosure at the Singapore Zoo, which has a sign board *Snake* referring to the snake population of the zoo.[7]

In much the same ways as nouns, verbs can also be restructured to match the corresponding model category. Jenkins (2002: 222–3) says that in Tok Pisin, an English-based pidgin/creole, a passive is most often formed by omitting the transitive suffix *-im* from transitive verbs, and she argues that this usage is based on an Austronesian substrate: in the Austronesian language Tigak of New Ireland, Papua New Guinea, omitting the transitive suffix *-i* from transitive verbs results in a stative (or passive-like) meaning. In a related fashion, Aikhenvald (2002: 316–17) reports that Tariana speakers in the Vaupés region of northwest Brazil tend to replicate the verbal structure of their own language by using many intransitive verbs transitively in their variety of Portuguese. Thus, in their use of Portuguese, the verb *cahir* can mean both 'fall' and 'fell,' or *arder* can mean 'burn (intr.)' and 'cause to burn.'

Verb serialization provides a prominent model for equivalence when the replica language is a lingua franca used as L2 by speakers of verb-serializing model languages. This can be illustrated with the two cases of language contact just mentioned. The L2 Tok Pisin has serialization structures similar to what Jenkins (2002: 223) assumes to be its Austronesian substrate languages, including object–subject switching, whereby the object of the first verb is the subject of the second verb. The following example shows the extent to which this seems to have led to equivalence between Tok Pisin (7) and one of the Austronesian languages that may have served as a model (8).

(7) Tok Pisin (English-based pidgin/creole; Jenkins 2002: 223)

>   em   i   lukim   simok   i   go   antap.
>   3.SG PM see/saw smoke   PM   go   up
>   'He saw smoke rising.'

(8) Tigak (Austronesian; Jenkins 2002: 223)

>   (ne) ga   tarei tang buan   ga
>   3.SG 3.SG.S.AGR.PAST   see   ART   smoke 3.SG.S.AGR.PAST
>   aolong.
>   rise
>   'He saw the smoke rising.'

In a similar fashion, the Tariana language of northwest Amazonia has a productive pattern of verb serialization, and in their use of Portuguese, Tariana speakers use series of juxtaposed verbs without any linking conjunction (Aikhenvald 2002: 316), thereby replicating the serializing structure of their L1 in their L2, the replica language Portuguese.

Another domain of equivalence concerns the semantic organization of lexical and grammatical categories. Languages in contact tend to develop similar polysemies, where speakers restructure the range of meanings or functions associated with a given form or construction in one language on the model of another language. For example, the possessive/genitive particle *bilong* of the English-based pidgin/creole Tok Pisin exhibits the same range of functions as the genitive marker *ina* of the Austronesian language Tigak, being used for encoding possession, part–whole relations, the place of origin, attributes, purpose and function, and Jenkins (2002: 231) argues that this is suggestive of substrate influence from Austronesian languages.

Tariana offers another example where equivalence resulted in the rise of case polysemy (see also 3.4.3). Most Arawak languages of the Upper Rio Negro area have a number of locative case markers, formally distinguishing between locative/directional, directional/allative, ablative, and perlative ('along') case marking. The neighboring East Tucanoan languages on the other hand have only one locative case, expressing location, direction to and from, as well temporal functions. As the description by Aikhenvald (2003: 8–10) suggests, Tariana speakers appear to have given up the locative case distinctions of the fellow Arawak languages by replicating the East Tucanoan model. Being strongly influenced by East Tucanoan languages, Tariana speakers have generalized one of the case suffixes, the allative case suffix *-se*, to a catch-all locative case used for static location, ablative, and allative functions, thereby matching the case polysemy of East Tucanoan languages.[8] Thus, as in the case of Tok Pisin *bilong*, equivalence consists in the presence of a similar kind of case polysemy characterizing the model and the replica languages; and in both cases, category extension appears to have been involved (see section 4.1.5 below).

Equivalence may affect virtually any category of the replica language. In the metatypy situation characterizing contact between the Western Oceanic language Takia and the Papuan language Waskia in Papua New Guinea, establishing equivalence had *inter alia* the effect that Takia speakers appear to have given up their Oceanic prepositions and to develop seven postpositions on the model of Waskia and, with one exception (the Waskia ablative) the categories of Takia postpositions match those of Waskia (Ross 1996: 189; see section 3.1.2).

Finally, Campbell (1987: 266–7) remarks that Spanish has a grammatical category "subjunctive" while Pipil, an Aztecan language of El Salvador which is gradually being replaced by Spanish, lacks such a category, but that Pipil speakers are aiming at replicating the Spanish category. In doing so, they use two of their own categories for this purpose: the conditional (*-skiya*) and the imperative (*x(i)-*, 2.SG, and *ma:*). The data provided do not make it entirely clear to what extent Pipil speakers were successful; what the data suggest, however, is that there appears to be an attempt in establishing an equivalence relation with the Spanish category, which is used for both deontic and epistemic notions of modality.

While equivalence may be confined to restructuring without grammaticalization, the latter is likely to be involved as well, as we will now demonstrate. Consider the following example that is hypothesized to be the result of influence from Baltic languages on Finnic languages:

(10) Partitive/genitive as case of the object (Larsson 2001: 245)

     a. Finnish (Finnic; Finno-Ugric)
       Juon   vettä.
       drink.1.SG.PRES water.PART.SG
       'I drink water.'

     b. Lithuanian (Baltic; Indo-European)
       Geriu   vandens.
       drink.1.SG.PRES water.GEN.SG
       'I drink water.'

What this example is meant to illustrate is an equivalence relation between Finnish and Lithuanian, where the Finnish partitive (PART) case corresponds to the Lithuanian genitive (GEN) case in encoding an object (patient) or a subject participant. As Larsson (2001: 244–7) argues, this is the result of early contacts, perhaps 3,000 to 4,000 years old, whereby "Proto-Finnic has made its case syntax more similar to that of Baltic languages," i.e. Proto-Finnic speakers appear to have changed parts of the case system of their language on the model of Baltic, leading to partial equivalence where the subject is encoded either by the nominative and the object by the acccusative case or else where the subject or the object appear in the partitive (Finnic) and the genitive (Baltic) in specific contexts. On the basis of cross-linguistic observations on the grammaticalization of case marking there is reason to assume that this is another example where the use of case markers (partitive, genitive) originally serving the introduction of peripheral participants was extended to include core participants in addition (see section 4.3.1 below; see also section 6.4) – that is, where equivalence is the result of contact-induced grammaticalization.

Note that the process just sketched has had a number of additional effects, leading also to the coexistence (4.1.2) of two case markers for one case function and category extension (4.1.5), whereby Finnic partitive markers were extended to mark subjects and objects too.

Three more examples of equivalence based on grammaticalization can be found in the North Arawak language Tariana of northwest Amazonia, which has been heavily influenced by East Tucanoan languages. One example relates to the rise of an inclusive/exclusive distinction on personal pronouns and has been discussed in section 4.1.3. The second example concerns core case marking. Aikhenvald (2002: 101ff.; 2003: 7–8) observes that all East Tucanoan languages display a typologically uncommon category, marked by *-re*, which is a non-subject case category. The marking of this category is obligatory on personal pronouns, proper names, and on topical and specific non-subjects, including direct objects. Arawak languages do not have any case marking for core participants – with the exception of Tariana, which has a case marker *-naku/-nuku* that is functionally identical with *-re* in East Tucanoan languages. It is used for topical and specific referents in a non-subject function, also including direct objects. On the basis of Aikhenvald's description, this case of equivalence can be accounted for in the following way. Tariana speakers grammaticalized a locative case marker, still represented as *-naku* in the fellow Arawak language Baniwa,[9] to a marker of specific or definite non-subject reference, being an exact replica of the East Tucanoan model. Grammaticalization led to an extension of the locative marker to a range of case functions similar to that characterizing the *-re*-category in East Tucanoan languages, such as beneficiary, source, and direct object. Note that the development from locative (peripheral) case marker to core participant marker is cross-linguistically a not uncommon grammaticalization process (see section 6.4).

The result of this process is equivalence between Tariana and East Tucanoan languages, whereby Tariana acquired a distinction between a subject and a non-subject category echoing that of the East Tucanoan model languages. Once again, this case of contact-induced change had several different effects on the structure of the replica language: The emergence of a new core-participant marker is suggestive not only of category matching but also of gap filling (section 4.1.1).

The third example involves Tariana not used as a replica language but as a model language. Tariana people have Brazil's official language Portuguese as an L2, and in their use of the lingua franca they tend to replicate use patterns of their L1 Tariana, thereby enriching the structure of their L2. One of these patterns involves the use of stance verbs to specify the posture of a referent, distinguishing, for example, whether an action is carried out while standing or sitting. To this end, Tariana speakers employ specifying expressions in their use of Portuguese, thereby creating a use pattern that is unusual in both Standard Portuguese and Vernacular Brazilian Portuguese, e.g.:

(10) Portuguese spoken by Tariana in northwest Brazil (Aikhenvald 2002: 314, 316–17)

> Tava   pescando mad   sentado.
> be.PAST.3.SG fishing   madi.fish sitting
> '(He) was sitting fishing for madi fish.'

Tariana is not the only case exhibiting large-scale equivalence on the model of other languages; other cases will be discussed in chapter 5 under the heading metatypy, they also include the English-based Melanesian Pidgin and its varieties, such as Solomons Pijin (Keesing 1988; 1991) and Tok Pisin (Jenkins (2002), where Austronesian languages served as the primary model languages.[10]

Equivalence across languages tends to involve a wide range of additional phenomena, among them being what we referred to in section 2.2.4 as narrowing.

4.1.5   Category extension

Category extension is a fairly ubiquitous process associated with contact-induced grammaticalization and is discussed in various parts of this work (see especially section 2.2.2; see also section 1.3, (5a) on extension). Several examples were treated in section 4.1.4, relating to the extension of case functions and leading to the rise of polysemy. For example, Kannada speakers in the

Indian village Kupwar have been in contact with speakers of the Indo-European languages Urdu and Marathi, which both have only a dative postposition for human objects, and as a result of these contacts, Kannada speakers appear to have replicated this situation by extending the use of their dative postposition to also mark human direct objects (Gumperz & Wilson 1971: 158). In this way, the dative case marker of Kupwar Kannada has become polysemous between recipient (indirect object) and patient (direct object) marking. In a similar fashion, with the extension of a comitative marker to be used for instrumental participants as well, a polysemous comitative-instrumental category arose in Basque, Sorbian, and other European languages (Heine & Kuteva forthc.).

Another kind of extension can be illustrated with the following example from English-based Solomons Pijin. The Malaita Oceanic language Kwaio has an aspect particle *bi'i*, translatable by 'just' and denoting that an action has just taken place. This aspect has been replicated in Solomons Pijin by using the particle *das* (or *des, tes*; presumably derived from English *just*), occurring in the same syntactic slot where Kwaio *bi'i* occurs. But *bi'i* is polysemous in that it appears to express an immediate future tense ('an action will take place in a short time') too when combined with the future marker *ta-*, and Solomons Pijin has replicated this polysemy by extending the use of the particle *das* to future situations. Thus, the Solomons Pijin sentence in (11) constitutes an equivalent replica, both in morphosyntax and meaning, of the corresponding Kwaio sentence in (12).

(11) Solomons Pijin (English-based pidgin; Keesing 1988: 215)

        bae   iumi   das luk- im.
        FUT we: INCL just see- TRS
        'We'll see it in a while.'

(12) Kwaio (Eastern Oceanic; Keesing 1988: 214)

        ta-   goru   bi'i aga- si-   a.
        FUT- we: INCL just see- TRS- it
        'We'll see it in a while.'

Maltese is historically a western Arabic dialect which has been influenced by a number of different languages, in particular by Italian and more recently also by English. One effect of Italian influence was that the Maltese preposition *ta'*, expressing the periphrastic genitive, has received new uses on the model of the use patterns of the Italian preposition *da*. For example, like Italian *da*, it can be used without a possessor noun phrase before proper names, e.g. *Ta' Kolina* 'At Kolina's (restaurant),' or with verbal nouns (where Italian speakers would use an infinitive), e.g. *tal-biza'* ('of-fright') 'frightfully' (for more examples, see Drewes 1994: 101). In this way, the Maltese genitive marker has become a grammatical category with a considerably extended range of functions.

In a similar way, the Maltese preposition *fuq* 'on top of, upon' appears to acquire additional functions by replicating the English preposition *on* in phrasal constructions, e.g. *fuq it-tv* 'on television', *fuq btala* 'on holiday,' *fuq parir ta'* 'on the advice of,' *fuq talba ta'* 'on the request of' (Drewes 1994: 101). The result is an extension of the Maltese category on the model of English.

When category extension occurs this leaves the grammatical categorization of the replica language essentially unaffected; what changes is the internal structure of categories. The following example from Irish English may illustrate the process concerned. One of the four main functions expressed by the present perfect of Standard English is an "extended-now" function, denoting a situation initiated in the past and persisting into the moment of speaking (e.g. *I've known Sam for some time*; Harris 1991: 201). Irish uses a simple or periphrastic form of the non-past for this function, cf. (13), and speakers of Irish English appear to have replicated this usage by drawing on their simple or progressive non-past forms, as illustrated in (14) (see Harris 1991). Assuming that, at some earlier stage, Irish English had a system of tense-aspect categorization not unlike that of Standard English, expression of the extended-now function can be assumed to have shifted in Irish English from one category (present perfect) to another (non-past or progressive) without affecting the overall structure of categorization.

(13) Irish (Harris 1991: 206)

Tá   sé marbh le   fada   riamh.
be.NON-PAST   he dead   with long.time ever
'He has been dead for a long time.'

(14) Irish English (Harris 1991: 202)

I know his family all me life.

Category extension of the kind looked at here is a morphological process; but not infrequently it is the epiphenomenal product of other kinds of processes, such as contact-induced changes in the lexicon. When speakers of the replica language establish equivalence relations between their nouns and verbs with corresponding categories of the model language, this may have the effect that they also replicate the grammatical properties associated with these lexical categories. In such cases, lexical replication may entail grammatical category extension. Both English and German have a possessive perfect (or 'have'-perfect), but the two languages differ with regard to the range of verbs this perfect is associated with. For example, in English the use of the possessive perfect has been extended to intransitive verbs where etymologically related German verbs require the 'be'-perfect. As a result of their contact with English, speakers of Pennsylvania German appear to have extended the use of their possessive perfect at the expense of the 'be'-perfect; the former is now used with all transitive and most intransitive verbs (see section 2.2.2 for more details).

One possible explanation of this fact could involve a category extension of the possessive perfect in the replica language as a result of the catalytic force of the English possessive perfect, which is more grammaticalized (i.e. used with more contexts of applicability) than the German possessive perfect. According to an alternative explanation, however, there is a mechanism whereby the speakers of Pennsylvania German tend to equate their verbs with corresponding English verbs and to use the possessive perfect whenever the latter is required by the relevant English verb (Enninger 1980: 344). The fact that the possessive perfect structure in Pennsylvania German is used as a past narrative tense – that is, with an adverbial phrase specifying a point of time in the past – indicates that we are dealing not with a replication of the grammatical category possessive perfect (or the 'have'-to-perfect grammaticalization process as a whole), but rather with establishing equivalences between verbs, which entails also the replication of the morphosyntactic distribution of the model verbs in the replica language.

To conclude, speakers of Pennsylvania German have further grammaticalized their possessive perfect by extending its use to new contexts, as a result of replicating lexical properties characterizing corresponding verbs of the model language English.

4.1.6   Category replacement

As we saw in the preceding sections, the emergence of a new category as a result of language contact need not lead to dramatic changes in the existing modes of grammatical categorization. It may happen, however, that the new category will spread at the expense of an existing category and eventually replace the latter.

An example of replacement can be seen in the diffusion of the possessive perfect (or 'have'-perfect) in the southwest of the Macedonian-speaking area. The Macedonian possessive perfect, using the auxiliary *ima* 'have' plus the main verb in the past passive participle, originated no earlier than the seventeenth century and gradually diffused from southwest to northeast Macedonia. The more it was grammaticalized, the more did it replace the old 'be'-perfect, which uses 'be' plus resultative participle. In northeast Macedonia, this process is still in its early stages; in southwest Macedonia, however, the possessive perfect has largely replaced the 'be'-perfect, and Friedman observes:

In the extreme southwest of Madecondian-speaking territory, i.e. in southeastern Albania (around Korča/Korçë) and adjacent parts of northwestern Greece (around Kostur/ Kastoria), the past indefinite (the old perfect using "be" + resultative participle in -*l*) has been completely replaced by the new perfect in "have". (Friedman 1994: 107)

Replacement of the old category by the new one usually takes some time, and a number of examples that we have come across concern transitional cases where the old category survives e.g. in certain contexts or among older and/or more conservative speakers. The development of a new passive construction in Pennsylvania German spoken by Mennonite Anabaptists in Ontario, Canada, illustrates the latter case (Burridge 1992: 221–2). This construction, illustrated in (15a), differs remarkably from the corresponding passive construction of European German but is structurally almost identical with the English passive construction, as the glosses in (15a) indicate: (a) Instead of *waerre/warre* 'to become' (= Standard German *werden*) it uses *sei* 'to be' as a passive auxiliary, (b) it uses the locative preposition *bei* 'at, with,' which is phonologically similar to English *by* (see section 6.3.1 for a discussion), instead of *vun* (= Standard German *von*), (c) the agent phrase of the passive typically appears outside the verbal brace, in the same way as in English but unlike Standard German, and (d) both the Pennsylvania German and the English passives exhibit the same kind of ambiguity between a passive and a stative reading.

We take this nearly total equivalence to be compelling evidence to hypothesize that this Pennsylvania German *sei*-passive has been replicated on the model of the English passive. This new passive is replacing the original one, illustrated in (15b), which is a more conservative version of (15a). Examples such as (15b) are still heard, although they are becoming less frequent. Thus, replacement has not been concluded.

(15) Pennsylvania German spoken in Ontario, Canada (Burridge 1992: 221, 222)

    a. De Schtrump is geschtoppt bei der Maem.
       the stocking is darned   by the mother
       'The stocking is darned by mother.'

    b. De Schtrump waert   vun der Maem geschtoppt.
       (the stocking   becomes by   the mother darned)
       'The stocking is darned by mother.'

Some of the examples of category extension (section 4.1.5) also illustrate replacement, in that, for example, with the extension of a case marker to a new case function, that marker tends to replace the old marker that had previously been used for this function.

In concluding, one kind of category loss resulting from restructuring (section 3.4.3) should be mentioned – one that does not involve replacement. In situations where language M lacks some specific category that exists in language R, speakers may replicate the situation found in M by eliminating that category from R, thereby establishing a (negative) equivalent relation; in his discussion of borrowing, Winford (2003: 96) hypothesizes: "The lack of a functional category in a source language may lead to loss of a similar category in a recipient category."

With reference to grammatical replication, evidence supporting this hypothesis is scarce; still, there are some pieces of evidence. For example, German has an elaborate paradigm of discourse markers, including *ja*, *denn*, *doch*, *mal*, *schon*, etc., commonly called focus particles. English does not have any equivalents for these particles, and Salmons (1990: 461ff.) observes that German–English bilinguals in the USA (e.g. in Texas and Indiana) have almost entirely given up the use of these particles, thereby replicating the situation characterizing their model language English.[11] Replication in this case involved restructuring, leading to the loss of a conceptual domain that arguably constitutes a central component of the typological profile of the discourse structure in European German.

4.1.7   Conclusions

As we observed in the introduction to this section, the structural processes sketched in section 4.1.1 through 4.1.6 are not necessarily incompatible with one another; frequently they simply highlight different aspects of one and the same general process. This can be illustrated perhaps most clearly with reference to the distinction between coexistence (section 4.1.2) and category replacement (section 4.1.6). A factor that we ignored in this section has to do with the relative time depth involved in language contact. For example, category replacement is a kind of change that normally requires an extended period of time to take place, and it is likely that a process suggestive of coexistence between an inherited and an innovated structure in its earlier phases may eventually end up in category replacement, where the former gives way to the latter.

In some of the cases discussed above, such structural changes had no major impact on the typological shape of the languages concerned; in others again they had, roughly as summarized by Weinreich:

Taking its cue from the speech of bilinguals, a language community can, by systematically extending the functions of morphemes in its language, not only change the use of individual forms, but also develop a full new paradigm of obligatory categories on the model of another language. (Weinreich [1953] 1964: 40–1)

We will now turn to some more dramatic changes in the typological profile of languages.

4.2   Introducing a new conceptual domain

The vast majority of instances of grammatical replication discussed here concern individual use patterns and categories that have no major impact on the overall structure of the replica languages. But there are also examples that involve entire domains of grammar, such as tense, aspect, or modality. In the present section we look at some cases where language contact had the effect that a conceptual domain for which there existed virtually no grammatical distinctions came to be associated with a detailed system of grammatical categorization. We will be confined to a couple of examples; the reader is referred to Aikhenvald (2002) for a wider range of additional examples from the languages of northwestern Amazonia.

Tense in some Nilotic languages

East Africa is an area marked by massive contact between languages belonging to different genetic stocks. Some of the linguistic effects of this contact have been described more recently (Dimmendaal 1995; 2001b; Kuteva 2000). Kenya and Uganda in particular are areas where Nilotic languages (belonging to the Nilo-Saharan family) have been in contact with Bantu languages (belonging to the Niger-Congo family), and this contact led to substantial and mutual transfers (see map 4.1). We are confined here to transfer leading to grammaticalization, and to cases where two Nilotic languages, Kalenjin (Southern Nilotic) and Luo (Western Nilotic), spoken, respectively, in south-central and southwestern Kenya, were the replica languages. Nilotic languages may be called aspect-prominent, in that they commonly distinguish, for example, between a perfective and an imperfective aspect in verbs, mainly by way of tonal inflection. Bantu languages on the other hand are well known for their richness in tense distinctions, and the languages with which Kalenjin and Luo came into close contact are no exception to this rule. For example, the Bantu language Luhya (Luyia), which has been in contact with both Kalenjin and Luo, has among others the following tense categories expressed by verbal prefixes (Bukusu dialect of Luhya): Immediate Past, Near Past, Intermediate Past, Remote Past; Immediate Future, Intermediate Future, and Remote Future (Dimmendaal 2001b: 92). While in Nilotic languages there are hardly any tense categories, the two languages for which there is an attested history of close contact with Bantu languages, namely Kalenjin and Luo, have an array of tense distinctions comparable to that found among their Bantu neighbors. However, none of the tense markers in Kalenjin and Luo is etymologically related to corresponding tense markers in any of the Bantu languages concerned. Note further that tense markers precede the verbal subject prefix in Kalenjin and Luo but follow the verbal subject prefix in the Bantu languages (Dimmendaal 2001b: 93), and they have normally clearly affixal status in the Bantu languages but vary between clitic and affix status in Kalenjin and Luo.

Assuming that these two Nilotic languages replicated their tense categories from Bantu languages, the question arises as to what accounts for the structural difference between the two kinds of languages. Dimmendaal provides a cogent

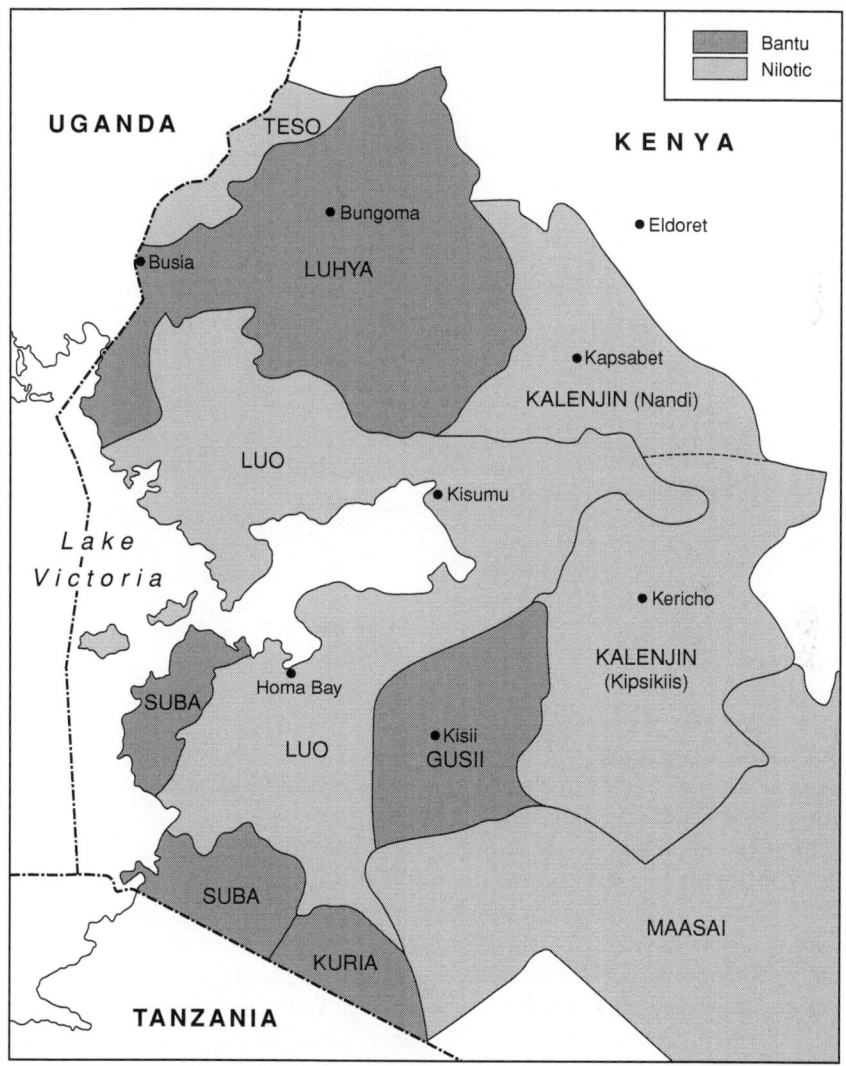

Map 4.1 The Bantu-Nilotic contact area in western Kenya

answer: the Nilotic languages received from their Bantu neighbors a range of tense concepts but neither the corresponding forms nor the morphosyntactic structures. Nilotic languages commonly use adverbs of time clause-initially (or clause-finally) to mark distinctions in time, and transfer had the effect that a set of such adverbs were grammaticalized to tense markers in clause-initial

Table 4.1 *Tense markers in Kipsikiis*

Adverb of time	Verbal proclitic or prefix	Tense meaning
k*aa*n	k*a*-/k*a*-	'today in the past' (hodiernal)
k*oo*n	kɔɔ-/koo-	'yesterday's past' (hesternal)
k*ii*n	kɪɪ-/kii-	'before yesterday past' (remote)
kor	kor	'today (future)'
tuun	tuun	'tomorrow and a few days after'
ka	ka	'a few days from now'

Dimmendaal 2001b: 90–1; based on Toweett 1979.

Table 4.2 *Past tense markers in Luo*

Adverb of time	Verbal proclitic or prefix	Tense meaning
nénde	née, n-	'today in the past' (hodiernal)
nyóro	nyóo, ny-	'yesterday's past' (hesternal)
nyóca	nyóc(a), nyóc-	'the day before yesterday'
yandέ	yand(ê), yand-	'a few days ago'

Dimmendaal 2001b: 101; based on Tucker 1994.

position. Not surprisingly therefore, these tense markers appear before the subject prefixes; in contrast to the model Bantu languages, which commonly have tense markers after the subject prefixes.

Note further that in the two Nilotic languages this appears to be an ongoing grammaticalization process that has not (yet) been carried to completion, as is suggested by the following observations on the Kalenjin dialect Kipsikiis; table 4.1 lists the paradigm of markers found in this dialect. As this table shows, the various markers have attained a different stage of grammaticalization: whereas the future markers have retained their full form and word status, the past tense markers have reached a more advanced stage of grammaticalization, in that they were reduced in form (erosion), assimilated to the following verb stem in vowel harmony, and lost their status as independent words (decategorialization). Essentially the same process has occurred in Luo, as table 4.2 suggests. This process happened independently from that to be observed in Kalenjin. The forms used in the two languages are not cognate (nor are they etymologically related to corresponding forms in the Bantu languages). There is one slight difference between the two Nilotic languages: while the grammaticalized tense markers have been adapted to the vowel harmony pattern of the verb stem in Kalenjin, they have not been affected by vowel harmony in Luo

(Dimmendaal 2001b: 101). To conclude, transfer had the effect that Kalenjin and Luo acquired a new functional domain (tense) via the grammaticalization of adverbs of time. Since the Bantu languages did not provide a model for grammaticalization, both are instances of ordinary grammaticalization (section 3.1.2). The main stages of this grammaticalization process from independent word to affix (decategorialization), and from full form to phonetically reduced form (erosion) are still recoverable in the synchronic state of tense marking (see tables 4.1, 4.2).

That this is not an isolated example of typological change is suggested by the fact that language contact has also been held responsible for Chinookan dialects of northwestern America which have adopted their tense-aspect systems from neighboring languages (Silverstein 1974).

Evidentiality in Tariana

Evidentiality, that is, the grammatical expression of how a piece of information was acquired by the speaker, is not really a salient domain in the North Arawak languages of northwestern Amazonia; there is only one evidential (REPORTED) that is grammatically distinguished. In this respect, these languages contrast with the neighboring East Tucanoan languages, which have an unusually rich system of evidential distinctions. But there is one language, Tariana, which differs from fellow North Arawak languages in having a system of evidential marking as rich as and nearly identical with that of East Tucanoan languages in general and Tucano in particular. Tariana has had a history of intense contact with East Tucanoan languages, resulting in numerous grammatical transfers from the latter to the former, and having the effect that Tariana developed a typological profile resembling that of East Tucanoan languages in many ways (see Aikhenvald 1996; 2002; 2003 for details). Apparently, replication of the evidential system was part of this overall drift towards a new typological orientation:

The four-term system of visual, nonvisual, inferred, and reported evidentials was developed in Tariana, out of its own resources, to match the Tucano patterns [. . .]. Tariana also developed a three-term tense distinction in visual and nonvisual evidentials, and a two-term distinction in inferred evidentials. There are striking similarities in semantics and epistemic extensions of evidentials in Tariana and Tucano, and in the way they are used depending on whether the subject is the first person or not. (Aikhenvald 2002: 127)

While the evidence available is not entirely conclusive, it suggests that the introduction of an evidentiality domain in Tariana is, at least in part, the result of grammaticalization of erstwhile verbs. Note that in spite of all the conceptual similarities between the two languages, there are remarkable morphophonemic differences: evidentials in East Tucanoan languages are for the most part expressed by way of highly grammaticalized portmanteau morphs occurring as suffixes, whereas in Tariana they are clitics that occur with a certain degree of freedom of positioning in the sentence, that is, they are less grammaticalized in the replica language (see section 3.4.5 for an account of this fact).

4.3   Typological changes

As we saw in section 4.1, contact-induced grammaticalization may affect the status of a grammatical category in a number of ways. But it may also have more dramatic effects, leading to changes in the overall typological profile of a language. It has been argued, for example, that it was one of the factors contributing to the partial "Indo-Europeanization" of Hebrew (see Weinreich [1953] 1964: 42), or to a new typological orientation of Basque (Hurch 1989: 28–9; Haase 1992),[12] and the discussion in Heine and Kuteva (forthc.) provides partial evidence in support of the latter claim. The overall typological implications that grammatical replication may have are discussed in a number of works on language contact; suffice it to cite two cases of language contact between Turkic and Iranian languages, documented in great detail by Soper (1987). In the course of these contacts, the Iranian language Tajik has replicated the simplex verb paradigm and the mechanism of verb serialization of the Turkic language Uzbek, while the Turkic language Qashqay has lost the Turkic mechanism of verb serialization but acquired a simplex verb paradigm on the model of the Iranian language Persian (Soper 1987: 409).

These are fairly general examples. In the remainder of this section we will be concerned with a few more specific cases to illustrate the kind of typological implications grammaticalization can have for the languages concerned.

4.3.1   Case syncretism

That in the history of a given language two different cases merge, thereby giving rise to case polysemy, where one and the same form expresses two (or even more) case functions, is widely attested and has been discussed in a number of different frameworks; we will refer to this process as case syncretism. Case syncretism may have a number of different causes, in particular the following:

(16) Some causes of case syncretism

       a. Owing to phonetic processes, different case forms become
          formally indistinguishable.
       b. One case category C_1 extends its functional domain and takes over
          the function of another category C_2, eventually replacing the latter.
       c. One of the case markers disappears and its functions are taken
          over by the other case marker.

Causes (16b) and (16c) are not necessarily alternatives; rather, they may represent different aspects of one and the same general process.

Case syncretism can be described as a morphological, a syntactic, or a semantic process. Our interest here is with the last of these processes, that is, with the way in which case functions associated with different case categories come to be conflated within one category. One common way in which this happens is via grammaticalization in accordance with (16b) and (16c), whereby case marker C_1 is grammaticalized to express in addition the function of C_2, and C_1 replaces C_2, with the latter either disappearing or surviving in specific uses. This process can be induced by language contact. Since grammaticalization is a unidirectional process, we hypothesize that even in contact situations case syncretism is essentially unidirectional.

From comitative to instrumental

In his recent work on Standard Average European, Martin Haspelmath (1998; 2001) proposes a catalog of eleven structural features defining Europe as a sprachbund or linguistic area. It would seem that in addition to the properties proposed by Haspelmath there is another property that might also qualify as a property of the area, namely the fact that one and the same marker is used to present both comitative and instrumental participants, that is, the presence of comitative-instrumental polysemy.

According to a survey of 323 languages carried out by Stolz (1996), the majority of the world's languages (64.70 percent) use separate markers for comitative and instrumental participants, and only about one fourth (24.46 percent) of the languages examined use the same marker, that is, they have a comitative-instrumental polysemy. In Europe, the opposite situation is found: the vast majority of Standard Average European languages have polysemy, while only a minority distinguish comitative and instrumental markers.

Now, a process characterizing the history of European languages of the past millennium can be seen in the fact that languages lacking a comitative-instrumental polysemy are gradually acquiring one on the model of other European languages, especially of Romance and Germanic languages.

We may illustrate this with an example from Basque, a language having a rich morphological paradigm of cases, distinguishing at least fourteen case suffixes. This paradigm includes both a comitative and an instrumental suffix. The languages with which Basque is or has been in contact, that is, Spanish, Gascon and French (= M), like most other European languages (see Stolz 1996), have a comitative-instrumental polysemy, that is, Spanish *con*, Gascon *dab*, *dambe* and French *avec* are used for both comitative and instrumental participants (My = Mx). As a result of these contacts, Basque is in a process of giving up this distinction: wherever in the model languages[13] the comitative-instrumental preposition is used to present instrumental participants (= Mx), Basque uses its comitative case suffix *-ekin* (or *-ekilan*) (= My) for instrumentals (= Mx). The instrumental case suffix *-(e)z* can still be used to some extent to present instruments or means, but in most contexts it tends to be replaced by the comitative case since the model language would use the comitative-instrumental preposition in this context, as Spanish does. In other words, the instrumental case is gradually being replaced in these Basque varieties by the comitative suffix – that is, in an attempt to establish equivalence with the model languages, the comitative-instrumental polysemy of the model languages is replicated in Basque by grammaticalizing the comitative to also present instrumental participants.[14]

Basque is spoken at the western periphery of Standard Average European, but essentially the same process can be observed at the eastern periphery, where languages distinguishing morphologically between comitative and instrumental case marking give this distinction up by extending the comitative to express, in addition, the instrumental (for more details on this process, see Heine & Kuteva forthc.).

From goal/indirect object to direct object

There is a fairly common process of grammaticalization whereby the use of markers for indirect objects is extended to also present direct objects. The following examples show that this process can be observed in situations of language contact.

Speakers of the Dravidian language Kannada in the Indian village Kupwar have been in contact with speakers of the Indo-Aryan languages Urdu and Marathi, which both have only a dative postposition for human objects, and as a result of these contacts, Kannada speakers appear to have replicated this situation by grammaticalizing their dative postposition to mark, in addition, human direct objects (Gumperz & Wilson 1971: 158). In this way, the dative case marker of Kupwar Kannada has become polysemous between recipient (indirect object) and patient (direct object) marking (see 5.2.4).

A related example can be found among speakers of the North Arawak language Tariana in the Vaupés region of northwest Amazonia (Aikhenvald 2002: 314). When using Portuguese as their second language (L2), they employ the preposition *pra*, derived from Standard Portuguese *para* 'to, towards, for' to mark definite and referential objects, as in the following example:

(17) Portuguese as spoken by Tariana speakers (Aikhenvald 2002: 314)

        Quando chegou   o   filho xingou pra o   pai.
        (when   he.arrived the son   scolded to   the father)
        'When (the father) arrived, the son scolded him.'
        (Lit.: 'scolded to the father')

Indefinite or non-referential direct objects tend to be unmarked, that is, no *pra* is used. Thus, we seem to be dealing with another case where the use of an allative/goal preposition is being grammaticalized to a marker of topical direct objects.

In Maltese, human definite direct objects are generally marked with the indirect object marker (cf. (18a)), human indefinite ones rarely so, while inanimate direct objects, whether definite or indefinite, do not receive the direct object marker (OM = object marker) (cf. (18b)); see Borg and Mifsud 2002: 34–6 for more details.

(18) Maltese (Semitic; Borg & Mifsud 2002: 34)

    a. Il-   tifel ra   lil   Marija.
       DEF- boy saw.3.SG OM Mary
       'The boy saw Mary.'

    b. Marija qabdet   il-   ballun.
       Mary   caught.3.SG.F DEF- ball
       'Mary caught the ball.'

Spanish Arabic exhibits the same kind of direct object marking; however, marking is not confined to human or animate objects but extends to inanimate direct objects.

A similar situation is found in Romance languages: In a vast area stretching from Portuguese and Spanish through popular French to southern Italian, instances of direct object marking can be found, involving the preposition 'to' and being generally associated with animate and definite participants (Borg & Mifsud 2002: 42). In all cases concerned, the direct object marker resembles the allative/dative preposition, which is *lil* 'to' in Maltese, *li* 'to' in Spanish Arabic, and *a* 'to' in the Romance languages, and we hypothesize that the object marker is historically derived via grammaticalization from the allative/dative preposition. This is suggested, first, by cross-linguistic evidence, according to which allative or dative markers can give rise to patient markers and, second, by the fact that, wherever the two differ in their phonological shape, the direct object marker is likely to exhibit a phonetically reduced form. For example, grammaticalization tends to involve phonetic erosion, and in Maltese the allative/dative preposition has the shape *lil* whereas the direct object marker *lil* tends to be reduced to *'il* or *l*.

This type of object marking is absent in Western Arabic dialects but is found in Eastern Arabic dialects (e.g. Lebanese, the dialects of Galilee, or Cypriot Arabic) and in Aramaic, and one hypothesis has it that Eastern Arabic or Aramaic influence contributed to the rise of the marker in Maltese, while the Spanish Arabic direct object marking tends to be attributed to a Romance substratum. Borg and Mifsud (2002: 44) suggest that the marking in Maltese may also well be due to Romance influence. In Maltese it is attested from the six-teenth century onwards, while in Italian there are already attestations in Old Sicilian and Old Neapolitan, e.g.,

(19) Old Sicilian (Borg & Mifsud 2002: 42)

truvau   a   Micheli.
found.3.SG OM Michael
'(He) found Michael.'

However well-founded such hypotheses may be, there is so far no convinc-ing evidence to establish that replication of an Eastern Arabic/Aramaic or a Romance use pattern can be held responsible for the grammaticalization of an allative/dative preposition to a direct object particle in either Maltese or Spanish Arabic. Nevertheless, we consider it likely that areal diffusion has played a role in triggering a strikingly similar grammaticalization process across genetic boundaries in these two Arabic varieties and in southern Romance: both Maltese and Spanish Arabic share a long history of intense language contact with Romance languages.

One point that deserves further attention in future work on this issue is the following. As far as the evidence available suggests, the evolution from alla-tive or dative to direct object marker affects first human or animate participants before it spreads to inanimate participants. The fact that among all the languages concerned, only Spanish Arabic uses the direct object marker also with inan-imate participants suggests that it exhibits the most strongly grammaticalized situation, where a subsequent process from human to inanimate objects has taken place. This might be indicative of a relatively old grammaticalization in this language, but more evidence is required to substantiate such a hypothesis.

From allative/goal to indirect object

Another common pathway of grammaticalization leading to case syncretism concerns the development from allative, benefactive, and goal markers to recip-ient/indirect object markers. An example concerning language contact between Turkish and the Kartvelian language Laz in East Anatolia has been described by Haig (2001: 214–16; see also Heine & Kuteva 2003: 544–5). Ardeşen Laz, belonging to the Pazar dialect group of Laz, has drastically restructured its nominal case system as a result of heavy Turkish influence. The indirect object in particular takes a suffix -(y)A in Turkish but is zero-marked in Ardeşen Laz. Now, Haig found that the young urban Turkish/Laz bilinguals he consulted (now living in Ankara) consistently used the goal marker -şa for indirect objects when speaking Laz, suggesting that these Laz speakers have gone one step further in matching the Turkish system of nominal core argument marking. In doing so, they drew on a common grammaticalization process whereby the use of their allative/goal marker was extended to also mark indirect objects, and obviously this process was triggered by the situation in Turkish, where the goal marker -*(Y)a* is also used for indirect objects. While the process can be described as being morphological in nature, its effect is that the core case system of these Ardeşen Laz speakers is now structurally almost identical with that of their model language Turkish.

Case variation

While case syncretism is a fairly common product of contact-induced grammaticalization, the latter may also have other consequences for the structure of the replica language, leading, for example to coexistence (section 4.12). For example, when the use of a case marker is extended to a new case function x then that marker may compete with another marker traditionally used for x, the result being that there are now two different markers for function x. An example was provided in section 4.14, involving early contacts between Baltic and Finnic languages, having *inter alia* the effect that speakers of Finnic languages appear to have replicated the Baltic pattern of encoding certain subject and object (patient) participants by means of the genitive case marker, by recruiting Finnic partitive case markers as an equivalent for the Baltic genitive marker. The result is that subjects and objects have not only the canonical nominative and accusative as case markers but in some contexts also the partitive marker (see Larsson 2001: 244–7 for details).

4.3.2   New morphological profiles

Grammaticalization involves on the one hand a change from one linguistic meaning M to another meaning M'; on the other hand it also involves a change from construction C, to which M belongs, to another construction C', associated with M'. Accordingly, grammaticalization is a semantic process on the one hand, on the other hand it leads to the rise of new morphosyntactic structures, and contact-induced grammaticalization therefore constitutes a not unimportant driving force for morphosyntactic change.

One kind of example was provided in previous sections with examples from Pipil, Takia, and Basque: With the use of items having concrete meanings for expressing grammatical relations, e.g. nominal meanings to express spatial relations, the result may be that new word classes and syntactic categories evolve, that is, that new paradigms of adpositions and new adverbial structures arise. Furthermore, we saw in section 3.1.2 how the replication of verbal derivational extensions of Bantu languages is leading to the emergence of a new morphological class of verbal suffixes in Luo; on the basis of such processes, Luo appears to be drifting typologically away from its Western Nilotic relatives, becoming structurally more similar to Gusii, Luhya, Suba, and other Bantu languages, that is, to languages belonging to a different genetic stock (see Dimmendaal 2001b).

Table 4.3 *The grammaticalization of some Latvian prepositions involving Proto-Baltic *pusē 'side, half' as a head noun*

Preposition	Meaning	Source noun	Meaning
ârpus	'outside'	*âra-*	'air, weather, the outside'
kalβnpus	'above'	*kalβns*	'mountain'
lejpus	'below'	*leja*	'valley'
vìrspus	'above'	*vìrsus*	'top, peak'

Forssman 2000: 127.

Such do not seem to be isolated cases. In a similar fashion, Kostov (1973: 110–13) reports that the Lovári variety of Romani spoken in Hungary has been drifting typologically towards Hungarian in that Lovári speakers, using Hungarian as a second mother tongue, grammaticalized their own locative adverbs to derivational[15] verbal prefixes in an attempt to replicate Hungarian verbal prefixes, thereby introducing equivalence and a new morphosyntactic pattern for which earlier there was essentially no equivalent in Lovári.[16] That this is a fairly productive pattern is suggested by the fact that the use of the new prefixes is not confined to their own verbs; rather, Lovári speakers also apply them to verbs borrowed from Hungarian.

That language contact can trigger new morphological mechanisms is also argued for by Forssman (2000), referring to the results of language contact that took place between the fifth and the seventh century AD when Baltic peoples proceeded to the Baltic Sea and entered territories inhabited by Finnic-speaking people. Forssman observes that in the Baltic languages Latvian and Lithuanian nominal compounding is virtually unknown, that is, it is not a productive means of word formation. In this respect, the two Baltic languages differ from the neighboring Finnic languages Estonian and Livonian, where nominal compounding constitutes a common mechanism. Now, whereas Lithuanian has largely retained the earlier Baltic structure, Forssman suggests that Latvian has introduced productive compounding structures on the model of neighboring Finnic languages. Furthermore, Latvian is said to have replicated a productive process leading to the rise of compound prepositions where the first constituent is a noun, cf. table 4.3.

Forssman (2000: 128) hypothesizes that this Latvian pattern, not found in the fellow Baltic language Lithuanian, is a replication of the grammaticalization leading from nominal compounding involving Proto-Baltic Finnic *pōle 'side, half' as a head noun to locative adverbials, and eventually to postpositions in Finnic languages, e.g. Finnish *al(l)a* 'the one below' + *puoli* 'side, half' + -*lla* adessive case > *alapuolella* 'below,' cf. *sillan alapuolella* 'under the bridge.'[17]

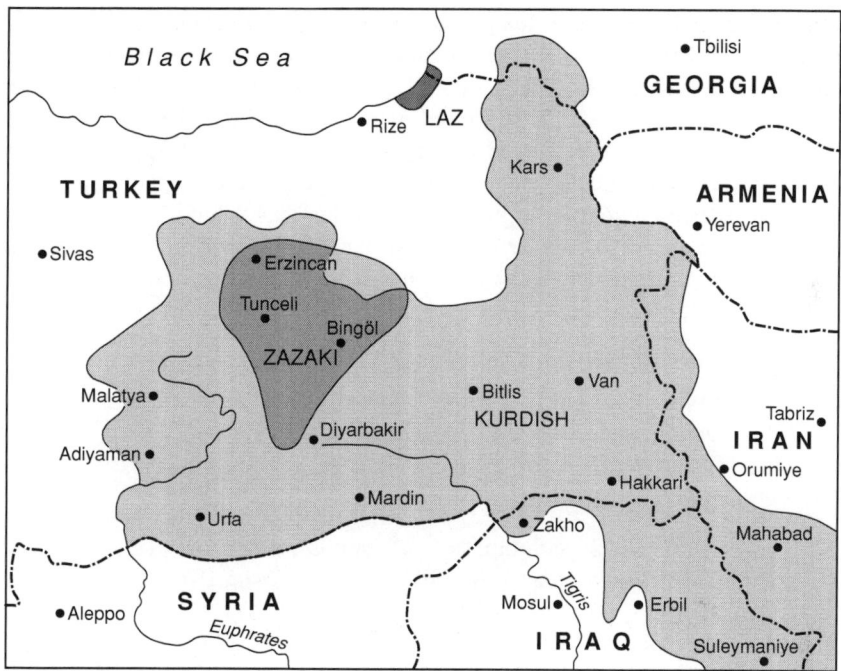

Map 4.2 The language-contact area in East Anatolia (based on Haig 2001)

To conclude, language contact appears to have been responsible for the rise of a new and productive type of preposition in Latvian. But replication did not exactly create an entirely new pattern; rather, it appears to constitute a canonical shift from minor to major use pattern (see section 2.2), having the effect that an existing pattern was extended to new contexts (involving nominal compounding), acquiring a higher frequency of use, and gaining in productivity. Complex prepositions based on *-pus* also exist in Lithuanian but – unlike in Latvian and Finnic languages – they do not seem to be used with nouns as first constituents, and they are used less frequently and less productively than in Latvian.

By exactly the same mechanism, new syntactic means of combining clauses can evolve. Thus, in the languages of East Anatolia, grammaticalization induced by contact has given rise to some new types of clause linkage. Genetically speaking, East Anatolia is a linguistically heterogeneous area which includes languages from four different families (see map 4.2): Turkish (Turkic), Laz (Kartvelian), Zazaki and Kurmanjî Kurdish (Iranian), and Aramaic and Arabic (Semitic). Nevertheless, as the analysis by Haig (2001) shows, this region has a number of properties to suggest that it constitutes a linguistic area. Three languages of the area, Turkish, Laz, and Zazaki, exhibit the same type of

linking sequences of clauses temporally, where a form meaning 'after' appears
to have been grammaticalized to something like a consecutive clause marker
added to the first clause (Haig 2001: 203–4). Accordingly, what in English
would be expressed with [X happened then Y happened] takes the structure
[[X happened]-after [Y happened]] in these languages. Turkish appears to have
provided the model but, in accordance with contact-induced grammaticalization, the replica languages do not use the Turkish form but rather their own
forms, which are: Turkish *sonra* (postposition using a non-finite verb form in
the ablative), Laz *şuk′ule* ('after'; genitive suffix + postposition), and Zazaki
tepeyā ('after'; postposition). The relevant structures are illustrated in (20).

(20)   a. Turkish (Turkic; Haig 2001: 203)

   giyin-   dik-   ten   sonra gitti.
   get.dressed- NOMIN-   ABL   after go.PAST.3.SG
   'After (he) had got dressed he left.'

   b. Laz (Kartvelian; Haig 2001: 204)

   ham   çitaabi golobioni=   suk'ule omçiru-   sa
   DEM   book   read.1.SG.PFV=   after   swim.INF- LOC
   bidi.
   go.1.SG.PFV
   'After I had read this book I went swimming.'

   c. Zazaki (Iranian; Haig 2001: 204)

   ti   merdī   tepeyā, ez   se   kerā?
   2.SG   die.PAST.2.SG after   1.SG what do.MOD.1.SG
   'After you have died, what should I do?'

In a similar fashion, Turkish, Laz, Zazaki, and Kurmanjî have grammaticalized
the word 'again' plus their enclitic topic-switch marker to a marker introducing
the second of two clauses, "where the second clause expresses something that
runs contrary to the expectations raised in the first clause" (Haig 2001: 204–5),
that is, to a concessive marker (translated by Haig as 'nevertheless,' 'although,'
'but'), the markers being Turkish *yine de*, Laz *xolo ti*, Kurmanjî Kurdish *dîsa
jî*, and Zazaki *finā žī*. While Haig does not mention which of the languages
provided the model, there can be hardly any doubt that with the grammaticalization of the item 'again' in a specific construction, language contact led to the
emergence of a uniform syntactic structure uniting four languages belonging to
three different language families (Turkic, Kartvelian, and Iranian).

The rise of verb compounding in Tariana
The following example illustrating a change in morphosyntactic profile concerns language contact in the Vaupés region of northwestern Amazonia, and

in particular grammatical replication by speakers of the North Arawak language Tariana on the model of East Tucanoan languages (Aikhenvald 2002). Tariana, like other North Arawak languages spoken in the area, has productive verb serialization and incipient verb compounding. Verb serialization is almost nonexistent in East Tucanoan languages while verb compounding is very productive. As Aikhenvald (2002: 136ff.) demonstrates, Tariana speakers are acquiring new patterns of verb compounding on the influence of East Tucanoan languages by grammaticalizing verbs to verbal enclitics. For example, the Tariana verb *kawhi* 'wake up, be early in the morning' occurs as a lexical verb in (21a) but as a verbal enclitic in (21b) – a situation that is suggestive of replica grammaticalization, since the East Tucanoan language Tucano exhibits exactly the same structure and can be hypothesized to have undergone the same grammaticalization process.

(21) Tariana (North Arawak; Aikhenvald 2002: 138)

    a. Kawhi-   tha phia.
       be.awake- VIS.PAST.INTER
       'Are you awake?' (A morning greeting)

    b. Pethe   du-   wheta- kawhi-   naka.
       manioc.bread 3.SG.F put-   BE.EARLY- PRES.VIS
       'She makes (i.e. puts on the oven) manioc bread early.'

This is but one example showing how, via the grammaticalization of lexical verbs to second components of verb compounds, Tariana is in the process of replicating the verb-compounding structure of the East Tucanoan model languages:

The creation and gradual expansion of verb compounding in Tariana does not result in making serial verb constructions less productive. Verb compounding in Tariana is expanding, involving more and more verbs as a result of grammatical calquing – or loan translation[18] – from East Tucanoan languages. Verb roots are spontaneously used as second components of verb compounds where they follow the fully inflected verb; they subsequently acquire Aktionsart meanings. (Aikhenvald 2002: 139)

What emerges from this development is that Tariana is acquiring a cross-linguistically uncommon typological profile where serial verb constructions and verb compounding are combined – each involving different grammaticalization patterns (Aikhenvald 2002: 144).

4.3.3   New syntactic profiles

Throughout the history of contact linguistics there has been a mainstream assumption to the effect that syntax is largely immune to replication. Accordingly, in a recent textbook on this subject matter, Winford concludes (note that his term "borrowing" includes replication): "Throughout this chapter, we have suggested that syntactic structure very rarely, if ever, gets borrowed. In stable bilingual situations, there are very strong constraints against such a change, even in languages subjected to intense pressure from a dominant external source" (Winford 2003: 97). On the basis of the evidence that we have presented, such a generalization seems to be of doubtful value. We have seen a wide range of replications that in some way or other resulted in syntactic change. In the present section we will be concerned with some more dramatic cases of syntactic change, and some of them clearly relate to situations of stable bilingualism.

4.3.3.1 Word-order change – Takia/Waskia

Grammaticalization is primarily a semantic process but, as we saw above, it can also have remarkable morphosyntactic consequences. Once there is a pattern of grammaticalizing items having a nominal meaning to, for example, locative markers, this may lead to a development from relational nouns to a morphosyntactic category of adpostions, as the Pipil and Takia examples in section 3.1.2 show.

One common effect language contact has is to induce people to transfer arrangements of meaningful elements from one language to another – a process referred to as restructuring in section 3.4.3. In many cases, however, a new word order arises without actually involving word-order change. This is the case, for example, when in the process of grammaticalization some structure is reinterpreted as some other structure, with the result that a seemingly new word order arises. The following is an example of such a word-order change without word-order change, again relating to the Takia-Waskia situation of metatypy on Karkar Island, Papua New Guinea (Ross 1996; 2001; see section 3.1.2). In an attempt to assimilate their language to Waskia, speakers of the Western Oceanic language Takia largely adopted the syntax of the Papuan language Waskia. For example, whereas Proto-Western Oceanic is reconstructed as having had SVO (subject–verb–object) as its unmarked clause order, Takia has adopted the SOV order of Waskia, and while in Proto-Western Oceanic the determiner (article) preceded the head noun, cf. (22a), it follows the head noun in both Takia (22b) and Waskia (22c).

(22) Determiner – noun order (Ross 2001: 142)

a. Proto-Western Oceanic	*a	tam^{w}ata	'the man'
	DET	man	
b. Takia	tamol	an	'the man'
	man	DET	
c. Waskia	kadi	mu	'the man'
	man	DET	

The way Takia changed from preposed to postposed determiner is the following: Proto-Western Oceanic had a set of three deictic morphemes, one of them being *a ('that,' near speaker). When one of these was used attributively, it followed the Proto-Western Oceanic adjective syntax, taking a pronominal suffix agreeing in person and number with the head noun, the result being a structure as in (23a). This structure underwent a canonical grammaticalization process (which we encountered earlier in our Sorbian example in section 2.4.1) from demonstrative to definite determiner, resulting in the Takia structure (23b) (= (22b)). In this process, the construction was subject to the usual mechanisms of grammaticalization, that is, desemanticization: loss of deictic force; decategorialization: loss of its status as an inflectable constituent, and erosion: loss of the preposed article *a and reduction of the postposed determiner *a-nā > an.

(23) Grammaticalization (Ross 2001: 142)

      a. Proto-Western Oceanic *a tam^{w}ata a- nā   'that man'
                                     DET man that- 3.SG
      b. Takia   tamol an   'the man'
                                      man DET

To conclude, as the description by Ross suggests, the change in Takia from preposed to postposed determiner did not involve any change in the order of constituents;[19] rather, in order to adapt to the postposed determiner order (= Mx) of the model language Waskia (= M), Takia (= R) speakers drew on a construction that was available to them, namely a postposed deictic determiner (Ry), and they grammaticalized it to Rx.

It would seem that this example illustrates a process that appears to be fairly common in language contact. Following a pattern in the model language, speakers draw on some existing use pattern in the replica language that corresponds most closely to the model, frequently one that until then was more peripheral and of low frequency, and they activate it – with the effect that that peripheral pattern turns into the regular equivalent of the model, acquires a high frequency of use, and eventually may emerge as a fully grammaticalized category, equivalent to the model category (see chapter 2).

Winford (2003: 97) hypothesizes that extensive syntactic diffusion appears to be due to mechanisms of change associated with language shift. The present example is an instance of massive syntactic diffusion – still, there is no evidence for language shift.

4.3.3.2 *From nominal syntax to clause combining in Pipil*

Another line of development leads from comitatives to noun phrase-conjoining markers ('and') and eventually to clause-combining markers (Stolz 1998;

Stassen 2000). That this line has been exploited in a language-contact situation is suggested by the following example, already presented in section 1.3 (see also 3.1.2). Pipil, an Aztecan language of El Salvador on the verge of extinction, has no formal means for coordinating clauses, that is, clause-conjoining ('and') is not formally marked. Pipil has a "relational noun" -*wan* which requires a possessive pronominal prefix as a modifier, thus having the appearance of a possessed noun (Campbell 1987: 256). Under the influence of Spanish it is said to have grammaticalized the relational noun -*wan* 'with,' to a preposition *wan* 'with,' and *wan* has further developed into a noun phrase-conjoining conjunction 'and,' although it still appears to allow for a comitative interpretation. Eventually, -*wan* has been further grammaticalized to a coordinating conjunction 'and,' i.e. its use has been extended so that it also conjoins clauses. In this capacity, -*wan* has been decategorialized to the effect that it lost the relational noun requirement of occurring only with possessive pronominal prefixes, turning into an invariable particle *wan*.

Thus, we seem to be dealing with an entire chain of development from relational noun to preposition, from comitative 'with' to nominal conjunction, and finally to a clause-combining conjunction. Campbell summarizes the overall development underlying this process thus:

This change from what formerly could occur only as a relational noun to a coordinate conjunction, coupled with borrowed Spanish conjunctions, has altered the general nature of Pipil. From a language of limited coordination with no true coordinate conjunctions (where both parataxis and hypotaxis were much more restricted), Pipil has become, in essence, very similar to Spanish. (Campbell 1987: 258)

Note that, if Harris and Campbell are right, this extended development must have happened within a fairly short timespan, that is, only after the introduction of Spanish in the Americas (Harris & Campbell 1995: 127, 129–30, 147).

4.3.3.3 Word order in Breton

There is an abundance of information on how in situations of contact one language may adopt syntactic properties of another language; our interest here is with processes that in some way or other involve grammaticalization – more precisely with replication processes that have some effects on the syntactic structures concerned, leading, for example, to the rise of new syntactic relations and new arrangements of meaningful elements.

Breton differs from fellow Celtic languages in a number of respects. Geographically, it is the only modern Celtic language spoken in mainland Europe. Linguistically, it has some properties that also set it apart from all Insular Celtic languages. One of these properties is the presence of a fully grammaticalized possessive perfect akin to what is commonly found in mainland western Europe. Another property concerns word-order syntax: while the Celtic languages Irish, Scottish Gaelic, and Welsh are characterized by a verb-initial (VSO) syntax,

Breton is not. For Breton, a number of different descriptive taxonomies have been proposed, ranging from one in terms of an underlying VSO-syntax with surface SVO-structures, to one in terms of a basic SVO-syntax with relics of VSO-structures (see Ternes 1999). Irrespective of how one wishes to categorize the overall structure of Breton clauses, it seems fairly uncontroversial to say, first, that Breton has salient SVO-structures that are absent in its closest relative Welsh in particular and in the Celtic languages of Britain in general. The following example illustrates this difference.

(24) Celtic languages (Ternes 1999: 238)

    a. Welsh
       Mae 'r tywydd yn braf.
       (is   the weather AP nice)
       'The weather is nice.'

    b. Breton
       An amzer   a   zo brav.
       (the weather that is   nice)[20]
       'The weather is nice.'

Second, it also appears uncontroversial to say that this difference is the result of more recent developments whereby Breton became typologically dissimilar from the Celtic languages of Britain, increasingly replacing its earlier VSO-syntax by SVO-structures. While this is seemingly an instance of syntactic change from one kind of word order to another, thereby making Breton syntactically similar to the majority language French, as a matter of fact it is not; rather, it is the result of a pragmatic process whereby a focus construction, having the structure of a (bi-clausal) cleft construction, is grammaticalized to a new (mono-clausal) syntactic pattern where the (focalized) subject is placed sentence-initially (see Harris & Campbell 1995: 155–7; Ternes 1999 for details). Thus, a sentence of the form (24b) is diachronically derived from a cleft construction of the type (25).

(25) [It is X [that Y]], where [It is X] = copular matrix clause, and [that Y]
    = relative clause.

This reconstruction is supported by the fact that the verb phrase in sentences such as (24b) appears to be historically a relative clause: Throughout the history of Breton, the particle *a* has been used in relative clauses in which the subject or direct object is relativized, and *zo* (or *so*) is a special third-person singular form of the verb 'be,' which originated in relative clauses (Harris & Campbell 1995: 155).

Thus, colloquial Breton has replaced its earlier verb-initial clause structure with a cleft construction where the subject noun phrase is focalized ([*It is* X]) and the rest of the sentence takes the form of a relative clause ([*that* Y]). This process has all the characteristics of a grammaticalization process:

(a) Desemanticization: A pragmatic function (focus) loses its meaning and turns into a syntactic function (subject). Thus, the phrase *An amzer* 'the weather' has lost its pragmatic content and has no more function other than presenting the sentence subject (Ternes 1999: 242).

(b) Decategorialization: A bi-clausal cleft construction is condensed to a mono-clausal construction, whereby the matrix (focus) clause is reinterpreted as the subject noun phrase and the erstwhile relative clause as the verb phrase.

(c) Erosion: Morphological exponents of the earlier cleft construction tend to be lost. There is no (more) copula in the matrix clause, and the relativizer *a* can be omitted under certain circumstances (Harris & Campbell 1995: 157).

While this grammaticalization process is still in its intermediate stages in written Breton, colloquial (dialectal) varieties of Breton are described as presenting the final stages of the process (Ternes 1999: 248).

But this process does not appear to have happened in a vacuum; rather, it also happened in the general area of Romance languages where Breton is spoken, specifically in colloquial varieties of French and in Gascon. In Gascon it has reached a stage of grammaticalization that is not unlike that found in Breton (Haase 1997; Ternes 1999: 248–9). Thus, the grammaticalized Breton structure has its equivalents in these Romance languages (Wehr 1984: 86f.; Haase 1997: 218), as the following examples illustrate, where the subject and the verb phrase are connected by what is diachronically a relative clause marker (the asterisk in the glosses indicates that the forms *que* and *qui* are hypothesized to be historically relative clause markers):

(26) a. Colloquial French (Wehr 1984: 79; cited from Ternes 1999: 250)

> Ton   nez   qui   coule.
> (your nose *REL run)
> 'Your nose is running.'

   b. Gascon (Haase 1997: 218f.; cited from Ternes 1999: 249)

> Lo   monde que   van tribalhar.
> (the world *REL go   work)
> 'The people go to work.'

Given the fact that Breton has been strongly influenced by the varieties spoken by its Romance-speaking neighbors there is reason to adopt the hypothesis proposed by Ternes (1999) according to which Breton speakers replicated a grammaticalization process that they observed in colloquial French and perhaps other Romance varieties.[21] This hypothesis is based on the following facts (see under section 1.4):

(a) Breton shares a grammaticalization process with its immediate Romance neighbors.

(b) This process did not take place in languages genetically closely related to Breton, that is, in the Celtic languages of Britain.

(c) Since Breton is known to have had an extended period of language contact with its Romance neighbors, resulting in massive linguistic transfers, it appears plausible that we are dealing with yet another instance of contact-induced transfer.

(d) The grammaticalization of bi-clausal focus (cleft) constructions to mono-clausal constructions is cross-linguistically not entirely uncommon (see, for example, Heine & Reh 1984; Harris & Campbell 1995: 152–62); still, if it is found in neighboring languages then language contact offers the most plausible hypothesis to account for this fact.

One may wonder why such a process does not appear to have happened anywhere in Great Britain, considering the fact that, like French, English is an SVO-language and has exerted some influence on Celtic languages. Conceivably, the answer has to do with the fact that French shares with Celtic languages a basic structural similarity. As Wehr (1998) argues, both lack a word accent and fully autonomous word units, and both therefore use clefting as their primary means of focus marking. In this respect, French and Celtic languages contrast with English, which has a pronounced word accent and uses it productively for focus marking. It may be this structural similarity that contributed to the generalization of clefting in some varieties of French and in Breton.

To conclude, Breton is experiencing a change that makes it typologically more similar to French, the major second language of the general region where Breton is spoken, bringing it in line with the SVO word order of French. But rather than a syntactic process, i.e. a change of word order, it was a shared grammaticalization process that appears to have been responsible for this typological alignment.

4.3.3.4 A new profile of clause subordination in Konkani

What the preceding cases were meant to demonstrate is that a process starting out with the grammaticalization of a specific construction can have more general implications for the syntactic organization of the language concerned. An example of language contact in the coastal districts of North and South Kanara in the Indian State of Karnataka will illustrate that this process can extend beyond its original domain. As we will see in the next chapter (section 5.2.3.3), there was a process extending over more than three millennia, described as the Indo-Aryanization of Dravidian languages; here we are concerned with the reverse development leading to what Nadkarni (1975) calls the Dravidianization of an Indo-Aryan language, resulting in a new typological orientation of this language.

We saw in section 3.1.3 that, in the course of at least four centuries of intense language contact, speakers of the Saraswat Brahmins dialect of the Indo-Aryan language Konkani (abbreviated by the author as KSKo.) have been deeply influenced by the Dravidian language Kannada. The result was that KSKo. speakers replicated a grammaticalization process that had taken place earlier in Kannada, whereby a complex interrogative construction consisting of both a word question (WH-question) and a polar (yes–no) question turned into a relative clause construction – a grammaticalization process that has happened also in a number of European languages. In this way, KSKo. and Kannada acquired an equivalent relative construction, differing only in the fact that instead of the Kannada question word *yāva* 'which?', KSKo. speakers use their own question word *khanco*, and instead of the Kannada polar question marker *ō* they use the Konkani polar question marker *ki* (see section 3.1.3 for an example).

There is a second relative clause construction in Konkani which Nadkarni (1975) calls the inherited Indo-Aryan type since Konkani shares it with other Indo-Aryan languages (but also with Kannada). Whereas the replicated new construction has a finite verb, the old inherited one has a relative participle, and the clause is introduced by the relative pronoun *jo* inflected for case. But the old construction is also undergoing a process of Dravidianization, in that the two question structures that led to the grammaticalization of the new construction are also grafted onto the old construction, as can be seen in (27a), where the interrogative pronoun *koṇ*, inflected for the accusative/dative case, and the polar question marker *ki* are used. Neither of these markings is found in other Konkani dialects. Example (27b) is taken from the Saraswat Konkani dialect of Goa, which has not participated in the language contact with Kannada and, hence, does not have the Dravidian structure in its relative clause syntax.

(27) Saraswat Brahmins (a) and Saraswat Goan Konkani (b) (Indo-Aryan; Nadkarni 1975: 678)

    a. [hāvē koṇāk āpayllē- ki] to   yeni.
    b. [hāve jyākkā āpaylle   ] to   āylo nā.
    I   whom called   that came not
    'He whom I had called didn't come.'

Note that the KSKo. sentence in (27a) contains the erstwhile polar question marker *ki*, which is absent in the old Indo-Aryan structure illustrated in (27b). The element *jyākkā* in the Goan Saraswat Konkani example (27b) is the accusative/dative form of the relative pronoun *jo*, which has been replaced in KSKo. by the interrogative pronoun *koṇ*, constructed in the accusative/dative case (*koṇāk*) since it refers to an object participant. In a similar fashion, KSKo.

speakers construct the interrogative *kon* in the genitive or locative case when referring to genitive or locative participants, respectively. But the spread of the interrogative structure in KSKo. did not extend to the nominative case – that is, when the noun phrase heading the relative clause is coreferential with the subject of the relative clause; in this case, the old Indo-Aryan construction was fully retained.

Now, the Dravidian-type relative construction of Kannada does not allow for an extraposition of the relative clause whereas the Indo-Aryan type does, that is, in the latter the relative clause can be moved from its position before the main clause to the position after the main clause. KSKo. speakers have replicated this Dravidian syntactic constraint: Whenever an interrogative-derived relative clause marking is used in this Konkani dialect, no extraposition is possible. This means that neither the new KSKo. relative construction of (27a) nor the inherited construction of the type illustrated in (27b) allow for extraposition. The only exception again is when the inherited relative construction uses the nominative case for the participant that is coreferential with the head noun phrase: since in this case there is no interrogative structure, extraposition is possible, that is, this context has not been affected by the extension of extraposition loss.

To conclude, the syntax of relative clause marking in KSKo. has been largely Dravidianized: it has changed from an earlier Indo-Aryan type, where extraposition was generally possible, to a situation where extraposition is now marginalized, being restricted to one specific context. Accordingly, Nadkarni (1975: 677) finds that the old Indo-Aryan relative construction is rarely used in modern KSKo. narrative texts.

4.4   The morphological cycle

While grammaticalization concerns primarily the development of meanings, it also has a morphosyntactic component (decategorialization), and context-induced decategorialization may be responsible for overall changes in the morphological profile of a language. Decategorialization has been described in terms of a morphological cycle leading from free syntactic structures and lexical forms to clitics and further to affixes, theoretically ending in the loss of grammatical forms. Towards the end of this development, "worn-out" or lost grammatical forms may be replaced by new forms, thereby giving rise to a new chain of development (Hodge 1970; Givón 1971; Heine & Reh 1984). While there is strong empirical evidence to support the hypothesis of a cyclic development, there are a couple of caveats. First, this development can be discontinued at any stage – hence it need not be carried through to completion, and second, worn-out or lost grammatical forms need not be replaced by new forms.[22] Thus, cyclic developments may but need not occur.

All three types of change characterizing a morphological cycle, from free word to clitic, from clitic to affix, and the renewal of "worn-out" affixal morphology, can be observed in situations of language contact, and are briefly illustrated below.

4.4.1   *From free word to clitic: incomplete replication*

In a seminal work on language contact in Arnhem Land, northern Australia, Heath (1978) studied four languages in some detail. One of them, Ritharngu, belongs to the Yuulngu family of Pama-Nyungan, while the other three, Ngandi, Nunggubuyu, and Warndarang belong to a family that Heath calls the Prefixing languages. An overall result of language contact was that Ritharngu has developed a new morphosyntactic profile that sets it off from fellow Yuulngu languages but links it with the Prefixing languages Ngandi and Nunggubuyu. Heath summarizes the relevant development thus:

Ri [Ritharngu; a.n.] has borrowed a functional principle – the obligatory presence of pronominals in most clause types – and concomitantly a kind of choppy discourse organisation involving 'afterthought' constructions. (Heath 1978: 127)

In Yuulngu languages, personal pronouns behave like other noun phrases, that is, they are independent words that can occur in various positions in the clause, and they can be omitted. The Prefixing languages Ngandi and Nunggubuyu on the other hand use obligatory pronominal subject- and object-marking verbal prefixes. Apparently under the influence of these Prefixing languages, Ritharngu speakers have developed their free personal pronouns into sentence enclitics occurring after the first constituent in the clause. Thus, in accordance with the Prefixing model languages, Ritharngu has changed by producing a situation where personal pronouns are generally obligatory for subject and object even when a full subject or object noun phrase is present in the same clause, leading to a nuclear clause structure consisting of a verb plus personal pronouns. This structure can be expanded by adding noun phrases providing fuller specification of the subject and the object, giving rise to an afterthought construction similar to the one in Prefixing languages. Accordingly, the Ritharngu structure in (28) exhibits the same general structure as (29), taken from the Prefixing language Ngandi:

(28) Ritharngu (Yuulngu; Heath 1978: 127)

wa: ni- na   ŋai, ḍaramu ya.
(go-   PAST he   the man)[23]
'He went, the man.'

(29) Ngandi (Prefixing; Heath 1978: 127)

ṇi- ṇid- i,   ṇi-yul-yuṇ.
(he- go- PAST the man)
'He went, the man.'

In more general terms, we seem to be dealing with an instance of incomplete replication. As we observed above, decategorialization may involve the development from free word to clitic and finally to affix, that is, if a self-standing personal pronoun develops into an affix then we will expect that there is an intermediate stage where the pronoun has the status of a clitic. On the basis of the description by Heath (1978) there is reason to assume that Ritharngu speakers aimed at replicating the affixal structure of the Prefixing languages but did not proceed beyond the first stage, that is, the intermediate clitic stage.

A similar case is provided by an example that we discussed in section 3.1.2, relating to the contact between Bantu and Nilotic languages in Kenya. Bantu languages are known for their rich paradigms of verbal derivational extensions marked by suffixes. There is nothing comparable in the Nilotic language Luo or its closest relatives, the Southern Lwo languages of Uganda and the Sudan: verbal derivation is limited, mainly involving internal morphology in the verb root. Now, apparently on the model of neighboring Bantu languages (= M), Luo (= R) speakers have developed a set of what look like verbal suffixes (= Rx), resembling structurally the Bantu verbal suffixes (= Mx), expressing functions typically encoded by the Bantu derivational applied suffix *-id- ('for, to, with reference to, on behalf of'). Luo speakers used the prepositions *ne* (or *ni*) benefactive, *e* locative, and *gi* instrumental (= Ry) in order to develop a new grammatical paradigm that has properties of both verbal enclitics and suffixes. Note that the Bantu model category is unambiguously a suffix.

Possibly a third case of incomplete replication can be seen in the following example from Estonian (Stolz 1991: 70–3). The fellow Finnic language Finnish expresses verbal negation periphrastically by means of a separate verb inflected for person using the present tense personal affixes, cf. (30a). In the Baltic languages Latvian and Lithuanian, verbal negation is expressed by means of the affix *ne-*, prefixed to the finite verb, cf. (30c). Now, Estonian has a long history of contact with Baltic languages in general and Latvian in particular and has been strongly influenced by Latvian (Stolz 1991). It would seem that Estonian has adapted its earlier Finnic structure of negation to that of the Baltic languages: It has grammaticalized the third-person singular form of the Finnic negation verb to an invariable negation marker *ei* which may not be separated from the following main verb by any other element, thus having acquired nearly prefixal status, cf. (30b). However, it has not gained all the properties of a prefix (Stolz 1991: 71).

(30) The structure of negation in Finnic and Baltic languages (Stolz 1991: 70–2)

    a. Finnish e-   n   lue.
             NEG- 1.SG read
             'I don't read.'

    b. Estonian mina   ei   loe.
             (I.NOM) (NEG) (read)
             'I don't read.'

    c. Latvian es   ne-   gribu.
             (I.NOM) (NEG-) (want.1.SG)
             'I don't want.'

To conclude, Estonian has developed a structure of verbal negation that contrasts sharply with that of the fellow Finnic language Finnish and is nearly identical with that of the Baltic languages; but, in a similar fashion to what we saw in the two earlier examples, the grammaticalization of a free form did not quite reach the affixal status characterizing the corresponding structure of the model language – a situation that is predictable to some extent (see 3.4.5).

4.4.2   From clitic to affix

Weinreich ([1953] 1964: 42) gives the example of the Iranian language Tajik (Tadzhik), which is said to have an isolating conjugation pattern, cf. (31), and Uzbek, which has an agglutinative one, cf. (33). The Tajik dialect spoken in the north of Tajikistan around Khodzhent and Samarkand, where contact with Uzbek is particularly strong, has been evolving on the Uzbek model from an isolating toward a more agglutinative form, where the auxiliary (*istoda-*) has been phonologically reduced (*-sod-*) and decategorialized to a verbal suffix, as can be seen in (32).

(31) Standard Tajik (Iranian, Indo-European; Weinreich [1953] 1964: 42)

        man xurda istoda- am.
        I   eating am-   I
        'I am eating.'

(32) Uzbek-influenced Tajik (Weinreich [1953] 1964: 42)

        man xur(d)- sod- am.
        I   eating- am-   I
        'I am eating.'

(33) Uzbek (Weinreich [1953] 1964: 42)

        kel-   vat- man.
        coming- am- I
        'I am coming.'

The development that the Uzbek-influenced dialect of Tajik experienced has taken place in many other languages presumably without involving language contact – it is somehow to be expected in the grammaticalization of tense-aspect categories. What the present case may illustrate, however, is that such "natural" developments, leading from an isolating-analytic to an agglutinative profile, may be triggered or accelerated by language contact.

4.4.3   Renewal

Worn-out morphological devices may be replaced by new lexical or grammatical forms, where "worn-out" refers to grammatical forms, typically inflectional affixes, that have lost most of their meaning, categorial distinctiveness, and/or phonetic substance, no longer being able, for example, to carry stress or distinctive tones. Renewal means, for example, that old tense or case affixes are replaced by new periphrastic modes of expressing tense, case, etc. Technically speaking, renewal is not an instance of grammaticalization, which is defined as leading from less grammatial to more grammatical forms and constructions (see section 1.3). Thus, it involves etymological continuity, while renewal concerns etymological discontinuity, leading to the replacement of one form of grammatical expression by another. Nevertheless, renewal is a common part of many grammaticalization processes, constituting the initial stage of the process, and introducing a new cycle of grammatial evolution (see Heine & Reh 1984).

In the domain of case marking, renewal tends to be described as leading from synthetic to analytic modes of case expression, whereby existing case suffixes are strengthened, and eventually replaced, by adpositions. An example is provided by Molisean, a variety of the Slavic Croatian minority in Molise, southern Italy. As Breu (1990b: 54; 1996: 26–7) observes, speakers of this minority language tend to add prepositions having functional equivalents in corresponding Italian prepositions to nouns marked by case suffixes. In this way, the instrumental case suffix is strenghtened by the comitative preposition *z* 'with' to present instrumental participants on the model of Italian *con*, and in attributive possession, a new construction [possessee *do* possessor.GEN] was created on the pattern of Italian [possessee *di* possessor], where the Croatian allative preposition *do* 'to, toward' (governing the genitive case) was selected as an equivalent of the Italian possessive marker *di*, cf. (34):

(34) Italian vs. Molisean Croatian (Breu 1990b: 54; 1996: 26)

      a. Italian   la   casa   di quella donna
      b. Molisean Slavic   hiža do one   žene
                    (the house of that   woman.GEN)[24]
                    'the house of that woman'

Another area of renewal concerns personal pronouns, where affixal personal pronouns are strengthened by adding free personal pronouns. The following case, discussed already in 2.1, illustrates this process (Denison 1988: 29–30). In Sauris (Zahre), a village in Carnia, northeastern Italy, three languages are spoken in a triglossia situation: a variety of German, Friulian of Rhaeto-Romance, being the language of the historical province of Friuli, and Italian, the official language. Of these three languages, German is most limited in use, being virtually restricted to use amongst villagers, and it has been influenced in a number of ways by the two Romance languages. One effect this influence had is that Sauris German speakers tend to add stressed personal pronouns to the already existing unstressed subject prefixal pronouns, either before or after the predicate. Thus, on the model of the Friulian structure, Sauris German speakers optionally strenghten the weak subject prefixes by adding the corresponding full, stressed, pronouns. The stressed pronouns may but need not express emphasis. Note that the strengthened structure is used only when there is no nominal subject. What this appears to suggest is that Friulian is developing a new, analytic use pattern of pronominal subject marking, presumably influenced by the fact that the unstressed subject prefixes are no longer fully distinctive (Denison 1988: 29), and Sauris German speakers have replicated this use pattern.

Another instance of renewal is provided by cases where synthetic, irregular, and/or non-transparent morphosyntactic structures are replaced by analytic, regular, and transparent structures. The contact-induced replacement of inflectional by analytic modes of expressing the comparative of inequality ('more than') is a case in point. For example, speakers of Luxembourgian German (Letzebuergesch) are said to have replicated the analytic French comparative construction by using their own equivalent of French *plus* 'more' (Alanne 1972), and the rise of analytic adjectival comparative constructions in the Balkan sprachbund appear to offer a similar example: Presumably as a result of language contact there was a gradual transition from synthetic suppletive forms to analytic constructions in Bulgarian (*pó-*), Albanian (*më-*), Rumanian (*mai-*), and Modern Greek (*πιό-*) by means of preposed markers (see, for example, Schaller 1975: 149; Solta 1980: 229); we will return to this case in 5.2.3.1.

4.5   Conclusions

In this chapter we have surveyed a number of cases where grammatical replication had some marked implications for the typological shape of the languages concerned – in some cases leading to what may be called a new "typological profile," that is, a new overall typological structure. But in none of these cases did this have the effect that the replica and the model languages became completely equivalent or isomorphic, e.g. to the extent that all their use patterns and grammatical categories regularly correspond to one another in a one-to-one fashion. As Aikhenvald (2002) shows, the North Arawak language Tariana of the Vaupés region in northwestern Amazonia has been massively influenced by East Tucanoan languages, leading to large-scale equivalence with the Tucanoan model languages. Still, this case of what may be dubbed extreme replication has not led to a situation where the model and the replica languages now have the same typological profile. And the same appears to hold true for many of the cases that have been described as instances of metatypy (see sections 5.1.2, 5.2.4): As the evidence available suggests, such cases have resulted in changing an existing profile, or in adding a "foreign" profile to the existing one (Aikhenvald 2002: 6–7), but none of these cases has given rise to total equivalence or typological identity.

A related question that has figured in a number of studies of language contact is the following: Does replication in general and contact-induced grammaticalization in particular make the grammar of the languages concerned simpler? Since these processes appear to be motivated at least to some extent by the goal of making the use patterns and categories of the languages concerned more readily compatible and intertranslatable by establishing equivalence relations between them, one might conclude that this will lead to a "simplification" or "regularization" of the language or languages involved (see Heath 1978: 137–8). As a matter of fact, however, the opposite appears to be the case. As Aikhenvald (2002) has aptly demonstrated, grammars are likely to become more complex as a result of language contact. This is also suggested by the fact that among the six major effects of contact-induced grammaticalization that we distinguished in section 4.1, none is really suggestive of a "simplification" of grammar, while the majority of them is likely to make linguistic categorization more complex.

5   On linguistic areas

The purpose of the present chapter is twofold. On the one hand, we wish to explore how the processes discussed in the preceding chapters relate to what one may wish to refer to summarily as sprachbund linguistics; on the other hand, we will be concerned with the question of what the study of contact-induced grammaticalization can contribute to a better understanding of geographically defined linguistic areas. To this end, we will attempt a review of some main works on areal relationship in section 5.1, at least as far as these works relate to the subject matter of this book, and in section 5.2 we will discuss the term "grammaticalization area" and its relevance for understanding some properties of linguistic areas.

5.1   Types of linguistic areas

A number of terms have been proposed to define classes of languages that, as a result of language contact, have come to share a number of features; we will refer to such classes summarily as linguistic areas. There are many kinds of conceivable linguistic areas; prototypically, three main types may be distinguished. First, there are linguistic areas defined by the presence of a limited set of linguistic properties; we will refer to such areas as sprachbunds (see section 5.1.1). Second, there are areas that are characterized by the fact that the languages concerned exhibit a high degree of mutual intertranslatability, discussed below under the label of metatypy (section 5.1.2). And finally, there are areas that are the result of one and the same historical process, more specifically, of the same process of grammaticalization, even if there may be other properties in addition; we will refer to this type as grammaticalization areas (section 5.2).

As we will see below, these types are by no means mutually exclusive; there are many kinds of regional clusterings of languages that can be defined simultaneously with reference to more than one of the types distinguished above.

5.1.1   Sprachbunds

A variety of different terms have been proposed to refer to sprachbunds, such as linguistic areas, convergence areas, diffusion areas, *union linguistique, Sprachbund*, etc. (see Campbell, Kaufman & Smith-Stark 1986: 530). Perhaps the most frequently discussed sprachbunds are the Balkans (for convenient summaries, see, for example, Joseph 1992; Feuillet 2001),[1] Meso-America (Campbell, Kaufman & Smith-Stark 1986; Stolz & Stolz 2001), Ethiopia (Ferguson 1976; for a critical review, see Tosco 2000), South Asia (Masica 1976; Emeneau 1980; Ebert 2001), the East Arnhem Land (Heath 1978; 1981), the Amerindian Pacific Northwest Coast (Jacobs 1954; Sherzer 1973; Beck 2000), the Vaupés basin of northwest Amazonia (Aikhenvald 1996; 2002; 2003), Standard Average European (Haspelmath 1998; 2001; see also, e.g., Thomas 1975; Hock 1986: 505–9; Thomason and Kaufman 1988: 315–25), and the Daly River area of Australia (Dixon 2002: 674–9). Furthermore, there are quite a number of less widely recognized sprachbunds, such as the Circum-Baltic (Nau 1996; Koptjevskaja-Tamm & Wälchli 2001), the Middle Volga region (Johanson 2000), the Circum-Mediterranean area (Stolz 2002b), and Sri Lanka (Bakker 2000).[2]

Substantial work has been done to define sprachbunds, with the result that there now are a few regions in all major macro-regions of the world that can be described in terms of language contact. With regard to defining sprachbunds, two different stances can be distinguished. On the one hand it is argued that a definition of sprachbunds should highlight the fact that they are the result of language contact, that is, of historical processes; the following is representative of this view:[3]

A *linguistic* area is defined . . . as an area in which *several* linguistic traits are shared by languages of the area and furthermore, there is evidence (linguistic and non-linguistic) that contact between speakers of the languages contributed to the spread and/or retention of these traits and thereby to a certain degree of linguistic uniformity within the area. (Sherzer 1973: 760)

On the other hand, sprachbunds are defined exclusively in terms of linguistic parameters without reference to the historical forces that gave rise to them. Emeneau's classic definition is an example;[4] a more recent version is the following (see also Aikhenvald 2002: 7–8):

A linguistic area can be recognized when a number of geographically contiguous languages share structural features which cannot be due to retention from a common proto-language and which give these languages a profile that makes them stand out among the surrounding languages. (Haspelmath 2001: 1492)

In the present work we will be confined to the second kind of definitions, and we will assume that there is a sprachbund whenever the following situation obtains:

(a) There are a number of languages spoken in one and the same general area.
(b) The languages share a set of linguistic features whose presence cannot be explained with reference to genetic relationship, drift, universal constraints on language structure and language development, or chance.
(c) This set of features is not found in languages outside the area.
(d) On account of (b), the presence of these features must be the result of language contact.

This characterization is fairly general, it is not meant to be a definition; rather, we use it as a convenient heuristic for identifying possible instances of sprachbunds. Note that this characterization does not address crucial problems that have been raised in the relevant literature, e.g. how many languages and how many features (or properties or traits) are minimally required, whether these features should be shared by all languages, whether the features should not occur in languages outside the sprachbund, whether the languages should really be geographically contiguous, whether the languages should belong to different genetic groupings, to what extent isoglosses of features need to bundle, how factors such as the ones just mentioned influence the strength of a sprachbund hypothesis, or whether sprachbunds have any historical reality beyond the linguistic generalizations proposed by the researchers concerned.

Goals

In most treatments of linguistic areas it does not become entirely clear what the ultimate goal of study should be. Nevertheless, there appear to be three main goals that need to be distinguished; we will refer to them in short as the historical, the typological, and the descriptive goals.

(a) The historical goal. Sprachbunds are suggestive of language contact and hence may shed light on earlier interactions of peoples and their cultures. If a language belongs to a certain sprachbund then it can be hypothesized to share some kind of historical relationship with other languages belonging to the same sprachbund. The basic assumption underlying this goal is that a linguistic area is a group of languages that, as a result of historical processes, have influenced one another to the extent that they have come to share a number of structural properties. Accordingly, Campbell, Kaufman, and Smith-Stark (1986: 534) consider "real areal features to be those resulting from diffusion."[5] What characterizes work based on the historical goal is that typological similarity is essentially immaterial; rather, it aims at eliminating any kind of linguistic similarity that does not relate to the diffusion of linguistic properties across languages.

(b) The typological goal. Sprachbunds can be, and have been, viewed as providing generalizations on the geographical distribution of linguistic properties. Accordingly, they can be of use for typological comparisons. For example, if a language has been identified as belonging to a certain sprachbund then it follows that it has a number of linguistic properties characterizing this sprachbund. Consequently, areal linguistics can also contribute to understanding why certain language types and/or typological properties correlate significantly with geographical distribution.

(c) The descriptive goal. In addition, sprachbunds have been viewed as complex linguistic systems characterized, for example, by a set of rules applying to all languages of the sprachbund, that is, as structures that can be analyzed by means of methods commonly used in language description. Accordingly, sprachbund linguistics allows us to proceed from the description of individual languages to that of groups of areally related languages. A paradigm example is provided by Kazazis (1965; 1967), who proposed a contrastive sentence model for Balkan languages,[6] setting up Pan-Balkan rules that allow for language-specific lexical insertion. While the viability of this model is demonstrated with a highly restricted corpus of linguistic structures only, it suggests that it is theoretically possible to extend methods used for describing an individual language to a set of languages that, as a result of language contact, share a large number of isomorphic structures.

Obviously, each of the three goals should be pursued in its own right, requiring its own set of definitional properties and methodology. Most students of sprachbunds subscribe – at least implicitly – to (a) and tend to consider (b) and (c) not to be central goals of areal linguistics. For example, Campbell, Kaufman, and Smith-Stark (1986: 534) remark on what they call the "circumstantialist approach":

One group's approach has been merely to catalog the similiarities found in a particular area – allowing these similarities to suggest diffusion, but without carrying out the research necessary to demonstrate the actual borrowing. This "circumstantialist" approach, as we will call it, can be useful – particularly in the preliminary stages of investigation, or in LA's [linguistic areas; a.n.] where reliable historical facts are difficult to obtain. Even so, one would like to be able ultimately to separate real areal features – those resulting from diffusion – from historical accidents, which may result from undiscovered genetic relationships, universals, onomatopoeia, parallel or independent development, sheer chance, etc. Unfortunately, many circumstantialists have made no attempt to carry out the historical program [. . .]. (Campbell, Kaufman & Smith-Stark 1986: 534)

Nevertheless, if one is concerned with (b) or (c), a "circumstantialist approach" may be useful. For example, attempts have been made to propose convergence models for languages in contact. Even if such work has not been entirely successful so far, using findings on contact-induced structural similarities between languages as a basis for typological or descriptive generalizations appears to be a legitimate goal of areal linguistics.

Sprachbunds as historical entities

With regard to the historical goal, the following question arises: To what extent does work on sprachbunds contribute to reconstructing history? Obviously, students working on sprachbunds generally search for criteria that are most appropriate for reconstructing history, more specifically, for reconstructing the historical effects of language contact. But there is a basic problem associated with many works on sprachbunds. Let us take the following hypothetical example: (i) There are three languages, A, B, and C sharing a bundle of linguistic properties. (ii) The presence of these properties in the three languages can be hypothesized to be the result of areal diffusion, that is, of language contact. The three languages can therefore be assumed to share contact-induced relationship. (iii) Accordingly, A, B, and C can be defined as belonging to the same sprachbund. (iv) Since areal diffusion is a historical process, sprachbunds are historically defined units, and areal linguistics provides a tool for reconstructing history.

The question that arises is the following: In which way can the presence of (i) through (iv) really be of help for reconstructing history? Consider the following possibility: Languages A and B had a period of contact a thousand years ago, leading to areal diffusion of some kind. Five hundred years later, B (though not A) came into contact with C, again leading to areal diffusion. In this way, C acquired some properties from B that B had acquired earlier from A. What this means is, first, that A and C, while belonging to the same sprachbund, have never been in contact with each other. Second, the presence of a sprachbund does not tell us much about how many instances of language contact were responsible for its rise; third, it does not tell us much on the time depth involved in language contact, nor on the directionality of diffusion.

While this is a hypothetical case, such a case could well have been involved in the history of sprachbunds such as the Balkans, South Asia, Ethiopia, or Meso-America. Accordingly, one is led to conclude that, as a tool for reconstructing history, the potential of areal linguistics is limited.

It is generally agreed that the more properties the languages of a given area share, the stronger a case can be made for areal relationship:

That is, we can think of a continuum of LA's [linguistic areas; a.n.] from those weakly defined, on the basis of a single shared feature, to much stronger areas based on many diffused elements. This approach to defining LA's also implies a means of evaluating their strength . . . (Campbell, Kaufman & Smith-Stark 1986: 533; see also p. 558)

The question one might wish to raise is the following: Are "stronger areas" more useful for historical reconstruction than areas defined on the basis of few properties? Obviously, the more evidence there is to support one's hypothesis, the more plausible that hypothesis is. However, if the purpose of defining a sprachbund is to reconstruct history then the number of shared properties is essentially irrelevant: in order to prove that languages A, B, and C share a history of language contact, one property may be as good as ten properties, as long as that single property can be shown to allow for meaningful hypotheses on historical events.

To conclude, defining a sprachbund as a historical unit does not necessarily tell us much about the history of the languages concerned, other than suggesting that language contact of some kind must have been involved, and even less about the history of the people speaking these languages. The situation is different if one's goal is typological or descriptive (see above): the more properties the relevant languages share, the more weight an areally defined typological or descriptive generalization has.

Macro-areas vs. micro-areas

As already observed by Thomason and Kaufman (1988: 95), macro-areas such as Meso-America, the Balkans, Ethiopia, or South Asia are notoriously messy, in most cases being the result of multilateral bi- and multilingualism. In order to describe the internal structure of macro-areas, van der Auwera (1998a) uses isopleth maps which enable him to determine the status of a given language on the basis of the number of features that a language exhibits. This technique, which he applied to the Balkans and Meso-America, makes it possible to establish a quantitative ranking of the languages making up an area but again, it does not tell us much about historical relationship patterns characterizing the area. For example, the fact that Bulgarian turns out to be on top of the ranking, exhibiting all ten Balkan features distinguished, does not tell us much about the role played by Bulgarian in shaping the area; note also that other authors consider Macedonian (Hamp 1977: 281) or Romanian (Campbell, Kaufman & Smith-Stark 1986: 561) rather than Bulgarian to be the most Balkan languages (see van der Auwera 1998a: 262–3).

On account of such problems, some linguists question the historical significance of macro-areas and argue that such areas should be reanalyzed more profitably with reference to smaller units of languages which are more immediately susceptible to historical reconstruction. To this end, Hamp (1979), for example, suggests that rather than being concerned with a macro-area such as Meso-America, a more appropriate approach would be one where such a macro-area is looked at as being composed of several autonomous, regionally defined smaller areas. In a similar fashion, Tosco (2000) questions the validity of Ethiopia as a linguistic macro-area and draws attention to the fact that there are a number of smaller, historically more immediately accessible areal groupings that can tell us more about the linguistic history of the macro-region concerned. A related case concerns the Circum-Baltic area, which includes Baltic, Slavic, Germanic, and Finnic languages. The status of this area as a distinct sprachbund is controversial; Nau (1996), for example, observes that this is a linguistically highly complex area characterized by many layers of micro- and macro-contacts and various kinds of mutual influences stretching over a long period of time (see also Koptjevskaja-Tamm & Wälchli 2001: 627).

Further problems

There are a number of other problems characterizing work on sprachbunds. One concerns directionality: the main problem associated especially with macro-areas is that the directionality of linguistic influence remains in most cases unclear, in that these areas are usually what Thomason and Kaufman (1988: 95–7) describe as multilateral sprachbund situations. In fact, in a number of works the assumption is, implicitly or explicitly, that linguistic influence leading to the rise of the sprachbund was in some way reciprocal, and most of the sociolinguistic processes that contributed to the growth of macro-areas are no longer accessible to the historian.

Another problem may be dubbed the isogloss mismatch: It concerns the fact that, perhaps more often than not, isoglosses of linguistic features do not coincide with the boundaries of sprachbunds; to put it in the wording of Myers-Scotton (2002: 178): "there are no fences around the features defining many Sprachbund areas. That is, many of the features of a given Sprachbund are found elsewhere in the general areas." Accordingly, Campbell, Kaufman, and Smith-Stark conclude their assessment of the Balkans sprachbund thus:

In summary, few Balkan isoglosses bundle at the LA's (linguistic area's; a.n.) borders; some fail to reach all the Balkan languages, while others extend beyond. Of the strongest Balkan features, the postposed article is not in Greek [. . .] (1986: 561)[7]

Similarly, loss of the infinitive and its replacement by finite forms, another strong Balkanism, is not found in all Balkan languages; at the same time it also occurs in non-Balkan languages (e.g. in some dialects of Italian spoken in the south of Italy; Joseph 1983: 250).

Another problem relates to the question of whether all properties defining some sprachbund are in fact due to language contact. This problem does not exist in situations where we do not have any historical information: in such a case it is possible at least to hypothesize that that shared feature may be due to language contact. But a problem arises in those cases where a feature used to define a sprachbund can be demonstrated not to be the result of language contact. For example, loss of the infinitive and its replacement by finite verb forms is considered to be a strong candidate as a property of the Balkan sprachbund. But not always is this feature due to language contact. Joseph (1983: 250) observes that the retreat of the infinitive in literary Serbo-Croatian has taken place largely due to language-internal pressures, resulting from the language "going its own way" (Joseph 1983: 212), hence, it may well be unrelated historically to the loss of the infinitive in, say, Torlak Serbian or other Balkan languages.

Another problem with sprachbunds concerns the fact that, even if many or all of the languages defining a sprachbund have a particular property, this may not be fully diagnostic since there exist considerable differences in the degree to which that feature is grammaticalized (see Friedman 1994: 112 for discussion with regard to the Balkans). An areal property that appears as a full-fledged grammatical category in language A may simply constitute a minor use pattern in language B, and as such it may have more in common with an equivalent use pattern also lacking full categorial status in language C which is not a member of the relevant sprachbund.[8]

Conclusions

The preceding discussion is not meant to question the general validity of the notion "sprachbund." What it is meant to achieve is to contribute to a better understanding of what this notion exactly stands for, and what its significance is, or can be, for synchronic linguistics, historical linguistics, and for the history of the people speaking the languages concerned.

For most of the major sprachbunds it has not been possible to relate the linguistic findings uncontroversially to the overall external history of the areas concerned, e.g. to establish which historical processes exactly contributed to the rise of the area, which of the languages concerned provided the model and which replicated the model. Neither the growth of Ethiopia, South Asia, Meso-America, nor of the Balkans can be related to one specific historical event; rather, they all appear to be the result of various contact processes that took place at different periods in the history of the areas concerned. What this means is that for the historiography of these areas the presence of a sprachbund appears to be of limited significance.

The issue of sprachbunds will be taken up again in section 5.2.3.

5.1.2   *Metatypy*

An ideal linguistic area would be one having in particular the following characteristics:
(a) The languages making up the area share the same organization of semantic structure.
(b) They also share the same patterns in which morphemes are concatenated to form sentences, phrases, and words.
(c) The grammatical constructions are equivalent across the languages of the area.
(d) What distinguishes the languages is that each uses different forms but, on account of (a) and (b), each form has an exact structural equivalent in the other languages.

(e) Accordingly, the languages are intertranslatable to the extent that the task of the translator or language learner is confined to inserting the appropriate lexical and grammatical forms to move from one language of the area to another.

(f) The linguistic area is the result of language contact, that is, of a clearly definable historical process of linguistic assimilation.

In fact, ideal linguistic areas of this kind have been claimed to exist; they have been described under the label of metatypy (Ross 1996; 1997; 2001). In accordance with the descriptions provided by Ross, metatypy can be defined as the wholesale restructuring of a language's semantic and syntactic structures as a result of language contact, leading to a new typological profile in the replica language on the one hand, and to a large degree of direct intertranslatability between the model and the replica language on the other (see, for example, Ross 1996: 182). Metatypy can be viewed as constituting an extreme case of what in some models of language contact phenomena is referred to as "convergence" (see section 1.2) or isomorphism (see section 6.1).

A number of cases of metatypy have been reported. Ross (1997: 146) proposes a catalog of twelve linguistic communities that are said to have undergone metatypy, and almost all of them involve situations where one or more languages were restructured on the model of some other language or languages. At a closer look, however, none of these cases corresponds to the characteristics enumerated above in every respect; still they show approximations of varying degrees towards the ideal type of a linguistic area. Cases that are claimed to exhibit a fairly high degree of approximation include the Indian village Kupwar (Gumperz & Wilson 1971), Northwestern New Britain (Thurston 1987; 1982), the Gangou dialect of Chinese and the Mongolic language Minhe Monguor (Yongzhong, Chuluu, Slater & Stuart 1997), Arvanitika, the Albanian dialects spoken in central Greece, and Greek (Sasse 1985), or the Oceanic language Takia and the Papuan language Waskia of Papua New Guinea (Ross 1996; 2001).

Another case that would seem to qualify as an instance of metatypy concerns the Vaupés region of northwest Amazonia, involving in particular East Tucanoan languages and the Arawak language Tariana. While Aikhenvald (2002) does not use the term "metatypy," on account of the massive scale of grammatical replication that has taken place in this area, leading to a remarkable degree of immediate intertranslatability, this is arguably one of the best documented cases of metatypy (see section 5.2.4).[9]

In addition, a kind of metatypy situation is also reported for Modern Sri Lanka Malay, Modern Sri Lanka Portuguese, and Tamil, where the first two have been restructured on the model of Tamil. This development towards metatypy must have happened within a timespan of no more than sixty years; note that it involved massive grammatical but no lexical influence from Tamil

(Bakker 2000; see section 5.2.4 below). Furthermore, the situation of the Austronesian language Tigak and the lingua franca Tok Pisin on the island of New Ireland in Papua New Guinea might also qualify as an instance of metatypy – as far as the description by Jenkins (2002) suggests. This case is noteworthy insofar as there is evidence to the effect that replication was not unilateral but bilateral, leading both from Austronesian languages to this English-based pidgin/creole but also from the latter to the former (see section 5.2.4).

While it is hard to find cases that conform to all the properties characterizing ideal metatypy, it would seem that there are cases that come close to it. The North Russian Romani dialect appears to be suggestive of such a state (Rusakov 2001): its surface syntactic structure is identical to that of Russian, and the task of the speaker in translating from Russian into Romani is said to consist mainly in avoiding borrowed Russian lexemes (Rusakov 2001: 325–6). Still, even in North Russian Romani, or in other Romani varieties, there are numerous structures that make it difficult to achieve a description in terms of ideal metatypy. And in some way this also applies to the situation of Ma'a and Mbugu in northeastern Tanzania, which share the same grammar (basically that of the Bantu language Pare) but differ roughly in that the former has basically a Cushitic lexicon and the latter a Bantu lexicon (see, for example, Mous 1994; 2001).

It has been claimed that metatypy-like structures also exist in some of the sprachbunds, for example in the Balkans. More than a century before the Balkans came to be proposed as a sprachbund, already the general impression was that genetically distinct languages such as Albanian, Romanian, and Bulgarian are suggestive of one single *Sprachform* (linguistic form), distinguished only by the material used in the different languages (Kopitar 1829: 86; quoted from Friedman 1997: 23). In the same vein, Gołąb observes: "In many cases all a native speaker of one Balkan language has to do in speaking another Balkan language is to introduce different lexical material into the identical grammatical patterns" (1959: 417). In fact, a number of other authors have pointed out that "saying roughly the same thing in roughly the same way" in different languages of one and the same region is a definitional property of sprachbunds (see Becker 1948: 5). Even if such views are not shared by everybody, it seems that the boundary between metatypy and sprachbund is a fuzzy one and, conceivably, some of the sprachbunds that have been proposed can also be reanalyzed profitably with reference to metatypy, and vice versa.

But what distinguishes cases of metatypy typically from sprachbunds such as South Asia, Meso-America, Ethiopia, or the Balkans is, first, that they are characterized by a much more pervasive degree of structural isomorphism (see section 6.1). Second, they usually consist of a severely limited number of languages, sometimes no more than two (even though there is no theoretical limit as to how many languages are required). Third, there usually is fairly detailed information on the sociolinguistic and historical factors that contributed to the rise of metatypy. And fourth, while directionality of linguistic diffusion is frequently a controversial issue in the case of sprachbunds, in most cases of metatypy there is solid information on the patterns and directionality of linguistic transfer across languages.

We will return to metatypy in section 5.2.4.

5.2   Grammaticalization area

The contribution that the study of grammaticalization can make to defining areal relationship is a modest one. First, it is concerned with only a limited spectrum of linguistic phenomena; for example, phonological and lexical phenomena are not within its scope. Second, it is not concerned with borrowing, that is, with the transfer of sounds or form–meaning units (see section 1.1). Nevertheless, it can be of help in understanding certain areal patternings of linguistic properties, as we will argue in this section.

Our concern is confined to one particular question: Is contact-induced grammaticalization a factor that is relevant for understanding areal relationship? A survey of the relevant literature suggests that the answer is in the affirmative. Thus, Dahl observes:

In other words, while the chance that a certain morpheme or construction in a language will undergo a particular kind of grammaticalization is on the whole rather small, the probability increases dramatically if a neighbouring language undergoes the process in question. (Dahl 2001: 1469)

Like Myers-Scotton (2002: 178) we argue that linguistic areas (convergence areas in her terminology) should not be an exception to the principles characterizing other contact phenomena. We will try to demonstrate this in the following by looking in more detail at what we propose to call grammaticalization areas.

5.2.1   Definition

By grammaticalization area (see Heine 1994; Kuteva 1998; 2000; Stolz & Stolz 2001: 1549) we understand a group of geographically contiguous languages that have undergone the same grammaticalization process as a result of language contact. In order to identify a grammaticalization area it is therefore important to rule out factors other than language contact, such as genetic relationship, drift, and chance.

Theoretically, any case of contact-induced grammaticalization (see chapter 3) qualifies as a grammaticalization area. There is essentially no limit as to how many languages are required to make up a grammaticalization area; what matters is that a convincing case can be made that the languages concerned have undergone the same grammaticalization process as a result of language contact. While we do not wish to propose any specific number of languages that should be minimally present, we will assume that prototypically such an area consists of at least three languages, for the following reason: If there are only two languages then this is likely to be simply the result of a normal instance of contact-induced grammaticalization, whereby speakers have replicated a category in language R on the model of language M. A situation of a different nature arises if three (or more) languages are involved, in that the area must be the result of at least two instances of the same general grammaticalization process, which are of the following kind: (a) Either there is replication leading from the model language (M) to the replica language (R_1) which again serves as a model for another replica language (R_2), as sketched in (1a), or (b) the process leads from the model language to two different replica languages (R_1, R_2), cf. (1b). In both cases the result is a grammaticalization area consisting of three languages, namely M, R_1, and R_2.

(1) Patterns of transfer in grammaticalization areas

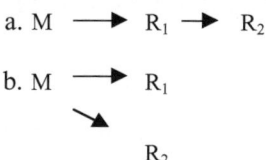

Unfortunately, most of the instances that have become known so far do not allow us to determine unambiguously which of the two developments was involved.

Not every geographically defined isogloss of a grammatical property is necessarily an instance of a grammaticalization area. As long as the presence of that property cannot be shown to be due to one and the same grammaticalization process shared by the languages concerned via language contact, we will not use the term grammaticalization area.

The notion grammaticalization area is similar to but must not be confused with that of *gram family* proposed by Dahl, referring to grammatical categories (grams) "with related functions and diachronic sources that show up in genetically and/or geographically related groups of languages" (Dahl 2000b: 317; 2001: 1469). What the two terms appear to have in common is that they refer to a grouping of languages that have undergone the same grammaticalization process; what distinguishes them is that "gram family" is a more extensive notion that includes grammaticalization areas as one of its subclasses. For example, the following cases, both concerning future tense marking in some European languages, would qualify as instances of a gram family but not of a grammaticalization area on the basis of the above characterization:

(a) A number of Romance languages, such as Portuguese, Spanish, Catalan, Occitan, French, and Romansh, have grammaticalized a use pattern consisting of an auxiliary 'have' plus an infinitival main verb to an obligative and eventually to a future tense category (see Dahl's Romance inflectional future gram family; Dahl 2001: 1469) – a process that can be traced back ultimately to Latin. Assuming that this grammaticalization is the result of a process that occurred, at least in part, prior to the split of some of these languages, the fact that these modern Romance languages share a grammatical category having related functions and diachronic sources would be suggestive of a gram family. However, it would not necessarily qualify as a grammaticalization area since this situation might – at least in part – be the result of common genetic inheritance.

(b) English and Greek have both developed a de-volitive future tense category, based on the grammaticalization of a use pattern involving a verb for 'want.' Since these are genetically related languages, this fact would fit the definition of a gram family. However, this case differs from the Romance one in that genetic relationship can essentially be ruled out as having been responsible for the fact that both English and Greek acquired a de-volitive future, nor is there any evidence to suggest that areal diffusion played a role. Accordingly, neither genetic relationship nor language contact can be invoked in the case of English and Greek; rather, the de-volitive futures must have evolved independently of one another in the two languages – in the same way that de-volitive futures also developed in many non-Indo-European languages (see Bybee, Pagliuca & Perkins 1991; see also below).

To conclude, neither the Romance nor the English/Greek case fit our definition of a grammaticalization area. What these cases are meant to emphasize is, first, that genetic relationship is entirely irrelevant for an understanding of such areas. Genetically unrelated languages can, and frequently do belong to the same grammaticalization area; this applies, for example, to the genetically unrelated languages Spanish and the Aztecan language Pipil, since they share a de-allative future as a result of contact-induced grammaticalization (see section 3.3). It is possible that areal diffusion is more likely to take place among genetically related than among genetically unrelated languages; our data suggest, however, that genetic boundaries in no way constitute boundaries to the diffusion of grammaticalization processes.

Second, universal principles of grammaticalization have to be ruled out as long as they do not involve language contact: related functions and diachronic sources may show up in genetically and/or geographically related groups of languages without necessarily involving language contact: English and Greek are genetically related and the fact that both languages have used the same grammaticalization process to develop a future tense is plausible on the basis of universal principles but is unlikely to be contact-related, hence it is irrelevant for defining grammaticalization areas.

As a matter of fact, however, Dahl's notion gram family corresponds closely to that of a grammaticalization area. That this is so is suggested, first, by Dahl's (2001: 1469) observation that gram families "can be assumed to be the result of one process of diffusion." Second, in spite of his definition, Dahl gives priority to areal over genetic factors, as is suggested, for example, by the fact that – in spite of his definition – he does not assign the English and Greek de-volitive futures to the same gram family (Dahl 2000b: 318; 2001: 1469). And third, most of the European future gram families proposed by Dahl (2000b: 317–25) are also likely candidates for grammaticalization areas.

Compared to sprachbunds, the study of grammaticalization areas has the following advantage in particular: rather than dealing with bundles of properties whose history and exact linguistic status remains opaque in many cases, the latter are concerned with the history of a single linguistic property and a clearly defined process whose general nature is predictable to some extent. Grammaticalization areas thus concern individual linguistic changes (or chains of changes), and they are based on hypotheses that are falsifiable – in this respect they differ from some sprachbunds whose historical significance is based on hypotheses which are neither easy to verify nor to falsify.

But in the same way as sprachbunds, grammaticalization areas are not without problems. First, it often remains unclear what exactly the historical forces were that can be held responsible for a grammaticalization area to arise. Second, there is frequently little reliable information on which the model languages and which the replica languages were in the diffusion of the process. And third, in a number of cases it also remains unclear which time depth was involved in the growth of the area. Still, we hope to demonstrate that grammaticalization area is a relevant notion that may also be of help in achieving a better understanding of linguistic areas in general and of the historical processes underlying them (see section 5.2.3 below).

5.2.2   Identifying grammaticalization areas

As we just noted, one problem that is notoriously associated with sprachbund-type situations is that there is no reliable information on which the ultimate model language or languages were (see section 5.2.1). It is nevertheless possible in some of these cases to argue that contact-induced grammaticalization must have taken place, as suggested by examples such as the following.

Passive markers in European languages commonly have 'be' or 'become' as auxiliaries, with the main verb being encoded as a perfect participle form or some equivalent of it. But Rhaeto-Romance, Italian, and the Bavarian dialect of German share a periphrastic passive construction where the passive auxiliary is historically derived from the lexical verb 'come', cf. (2).

(2) The Alpine 'come'-passive (Ramat 1998: 227–8)

    a. Ladin (Rhaeto-Romance)
       Cô   vain   fabricheda la scuola nouva.
       (here comes built   the school new)
       'Here the new school is constructed.'

    b. Italian
       Qui viene costruita la scuola nuova.
       (here comes built   the school new)
       'Here the new school is being constructed.'

    c. Bavarian (German)
       Då   kummt de nei(e) Schul gebaut.
       (here comes the new   school built)
        'Here the new school is constructed.'

Whichever language provided the model for this case of equivalence (see below), it is likely that a replication of a grammaticalization process from a construction ['come' + perfect participle] to a passive construction was involved in this case, for the following reasons: First, 'come'-passives do not appear to be common cross-linguistically[10] and it is therefore statistically unlikely that these three neighboring languages should have undergone such a rare process independently of one another. Second, common genetic inheritance can be ruled out as a contributing factor: the 'come'-passive cannot be traced back to earlier stages of Romance or Germanic languages. And third, the languages concerned can be shown to share a history of contact; thus, Ramat (1998: 227–8) notes that there have been centuries of contact between southern Germany and northeastern Italy and that it was the Romance type that "has influenced the geographically contiguous Bavarian passive." Accordingly, areal diffusion among these geographically adjacent communities appears to offer the most reasonable account, and we propose this Alpine 'come'-passive to be suggestive of a grammaticalization area.

Sometimes there is additional evidence for the presence of a grammaticalization area. Such evidence is provided, for example, when replication is not confined to a single grammaticalization process but involves polygrammaticalization (= several independent grammaticalizations of one source item, i.e. A > B; A > C; see Craig 1991) or repeated grammaticalization (= an item that is grammaticalized is itself further grammaticalized: A >B > C) can be identified in situations of language contact (see the model in (1) above). That

Southeast Asia somehow constitutes a sprachbund seems to be fairly uncontroversial, and grammaticalization provides one of the main parameters for defining this area (see Matisoff 1991; Bisang 1996a): Southeast Asia is characterized most of all by a bundle of grammaticalization areas, each characterized by a specific process of grammaticalization (see section 5.2.3.3). A case presumably involving both polygrammaticalization and repeated grammaticalization is provided by Bisang (1996a: 577–8): the verb for 'give' in Vietnamese (*cho*), Thai (*hâj*), and Cambodian (*ʔaoy*), has been grammaticalized not only to a dative-benefactive case marker (BEN; "coverb") but also to a causative auxiliary (CAU; "causative verb") and a complementizer (CONJ; "conjunctional verb") in all three languages (Bisang 1996a: 577). The following example from Cambodian illustrates all three gramaticalizations of the erstwhile verb *ʔaoy* 'give':[11]

(3) Cambodian (Bisang 1996a: 578)

> so: m ʔaoy lŏ: k ʔaoy yɔ: k kò: ʔaoy khɲom-ba: t vèɲ.
> ask   CONJ you CAU take cow BEN I   back
> 'I ask you [rich man] that you let me take the cows back for myself.'

As the work by Bisang suggests, this is not an isolated instance of replica polygrammaticalization and/or repeated replica grammaticalization. The verb 'get' offers another example of polygrammaticalization: In Hmong, Vietnamese, Thai, and Cambodian, the verb 'get' has developed into a modal marker of ability ("potential") on the one hand, and a past tense marker on the other. What makes this case of areal spread particularly compelling is the fact that that verb can occur in all these languages both in pre-verbal and post-verbal position (Bisang 1996a: 569). While it remains unclear which of these Southeast Asian languages provided the model, there can be hardly any doubt that the presence of a series of processes must have been due to replica grammaticalization in at least some of the languages concerned.

5.2.3   Sprachbunds

A survey of the patterns of areal relationship discussed in section 5.1 suggests that all major sprachbunds that have been proposed so far are based, at least to some extent, on the presence of grammaticalization areas. In the present section we will provide examples to substantiate this claim by looking at the major sprachbunds that have been distinguished.

5.2.3.1 The Balkans

The history of growth of the Balkan sprachbund is said to extend over a period of 1,500 years (Hinrichs 1999: 454), mainly between 800 and 1700 AD. Uncontroversial members of this area are Rumanian, Bulgarian, Macedonian,

Albanian, Modern Greek, perhaps also Balkan Romani and the southernmost varieties of Serbian/Croatian, while Turkish, though not considered a member, shares a number of Balkan properties.[12]

Of the ten-plus properties commonly associated with this sprachbund[13] (e.g. Sandfeld 1930; Schaller 1975; Solta 1980; Joseph 1992; van der Auwera 1998a; Hinrichs 1999; see also van der Auwera 1998c: 827–8), the majority are suggestive of contact-induced grammaticalization; accordingly, with respect to these properties, we can speak of distinct grammaticalization areas. We will demonstrate this with reference to the following properties:

(a) a periphrastic de-volitive future,

(b) pleonastic use of weak object pronominal forms in combination with full noun phrases,

(c) a superessive marker for numerals between '11' and '19,'

(d) infinitive loss and its replacement with a finite clause,

(e) replacement of synthetic adjectival comparative forms with analytic ones, and

(f) use of a quantifying interrogative 'how much?' in expressions for a degree marker ('inasmuch as, insofar as').

All of (a) through (e) are widely accepted to be salient Balkanisms, while (f) has more recently been proposed by Kortmann (1998b: 498–500) as an additional feature, to be found in all uncontroversial Balkan languages, that is, in Rumanian, Bulgarian, Macedonian, Albanian, and Modern Greek.

We will now look at each of these grammaticalization areas in turn. In doing so we will avoid dealing with the multitude of hypotheses that have been voiced concerning the historical diffusion processes leading to the rise of these areas; suffice it to note that most of these areas have been the subject of controversies on which language or language group was the ultimate source of a given transfer.

(a) The periphrastic de-volitive future   One of the most common ways in which new future tense categories arise is via the grammaticalization of a construction consisting of a verb of volition ('want') plus main verb – a process that is well documented (Bybee, Perkins & Pagliuca 1991); we referred to it earlier (section 3.3) as the de-volitive future.[14] At the same time, this is also one of the least controversial morphological properties of the Balkan sprachbund; it is described by Joseph thus: "A future tense based on a reduced, often invariant, form of the verb 'want' is found in Greek, Tosk Albanian, Rumanian, Macedonian, Bulgarian, Serbian/Croatian, and Romani" (Joseph 1992: 154, see map 5.1).[15]

It is widely accepted that this spread was contact-induced, and it involved all four mechanisms characterizing grammaticalization (see section 3.1): It entailed the "bleaching out" of the volition semantics in favor of a grammatical

Map 5.1 Approximate extension of the de-volitive future in southeastern Europe

function (desemanticization), the use of the erstwhile verbs of volition in new contexts that allow, for example, for inanimate subjects (extension), the loss of categorial properties, in that verbs meaning 'want' lost in morphosyntactic properties characteristic of lexical verbs and increasingly turned into invariable functional particles (decategorialization). And, finally, there also was erosion, in that the erstwhile verbs of volition lost in phonetic substance, frequently being reduced to monosyllabic clitics of the main verb (see Hinrichs 1999: 451 for examples).

A general description of the various stages of grammaticalization that can be distinguished in the Balkan languages has been presented by Fiedler

Table 5.1 *Grammaticalization chain of the Bulgarian future*

	Stage I OB	Stage II OB	Stage III Late OB	Stage IV 13th c.	Stage V 14th–15th c.	Stage VI 16th c.–
Meaning	Volition	Volition/ Intention	Future	Future	Future	Future
Subject	Animate	Animate	Animate	Animate	Animate/ Inanimate	Animate/ Inanimate
Form	*xotěti+NP*	*xotěti+inf.*	*xotěti+inf.*	*šta+inf.*	(i) *šta*+sh.inf. (ii) sh.inf.+*šta* (iii) *šta+da*+f.vb. (iv) *šta*+f.vb. (v) *šte+da*+f.vb.	*šte*+f.vb.

OB = Old Bulgarian.

(1999: 500–1). That we are in fact dealing with a contact-induced but neverthe-less universally observable process of grammaticalization can be demonstrated with an example concerning the positive future of Bulgarian, where the gram-maticalization in question concerns the development of the verb *xotěti* ('want') – its paradigm of grammatical forms in the present being *xošt* (1.SG), *xošteši* (2.SG), *xoštetŭ* (3.SG), *xoštemŭ* (1.PL), *xoštete* (2.PL), *xotětŭ* (3.PL) – into the auxiliary construction [*šte* (3.SG of *šta* 'want') + finite verb] for the future (positive). Drawing on the description of this development as given in Ivanova-Mirčeva (1962), Mirčev (1978), Damjanova and Grănčarov (1981), Maslov (1982), Zlatanova (1986: 193–4), and following Kuteva (1994; 2001: 125–8), we can distinguish between six stages in the *xotěti/šte* grammaticalization devel-opment (see table 5.1).

As can be seen from the progression of the stages in table 5.1, the modern Bulgarian future form (positive), i.e. Stage VI, turns out to be the final result of two successive conceptual-semantic shifts – from volition to intention and from intention to prediction/future – in the Old Bulgarian volitional structure *xotěti* + infinitive, i.e. 'want to do something,' leading to the Old Bulgarian future activity structure *xotěti* + infinitive, meaning 'will do something.' These two conceptual-semantic metamorphoses of the volitional meaning, ultimately leading to the prediction/future meaning, are paralleled by a series of mor-phosyntactic changes, which involve increasing phonological reduction in both the auxiliary component *xotěti* and the main verb form, the final result being a reduced form, *šte*, of the lexeme *xotěti* in the third-person singular present. The particulars of the formal morphosyntactic history of the structure are given in the bottom field of table 5.1.

Thus in Old Bulgarian the lexeme *xotěti* was used in its volitional meaning, in which it could be followed by either a noun phrase or an infinitive (cf. Stage

I and Stage II). In this period, futurity is expressed by the present tense. In late Old Bulgarian a number of forms come to function as futurity markers, one of these being [*xotěti* (conjugated in the present) + infinitive] (cf. Stage III). The structures most frequently employed for the expression of future activities, however, are those with the verbs *iměti* ('have') and *načati* ('begin') (see Mirčev 1978; see also Janakiev 1977, where it is argued that nearly all periphrastic forms for the expression of futurity in Old Bulgarian are borrowings from Greek). Later on, through Stages IV, V, and VI, the structure with *xotěti* gains priority as a form specialized for the expression of the future – though traces of the structure with *iměti* as a futurity marker still can be found in colloquial Modern Bulgarian:

(4) Bulgarian (Damjanova and Grănčarov 1981: 456)[16]

> Mnogo xljab ima   da   jade,
> (much   bread have.3SG.PRES CONJ.PTCP eat.3SG.PRES
> dokato se   izuči.
> until   REFL become.educated.3SG.PRES)
> 'A lot of time will pass before s/he gets his/her education.'

At Stage IV, due to phonological erosion, *xotěti* (1.SG *xoštǫ*) gets reduced to *šta*. At Stage V there are several morphosyntactic variants of the structure with *šta*:

> *šta* + shortened infinitive;
> shortened infinitive + *šta*
> *šta* + participle *da* + finite verb
> *šta* + finite verb
> *šte* + particle *da* + finite verb.

The last variant contains the form *šte*, which is a generalized and fossilized form of *šta* for third-person singular present.

In the period starting in the sixteenth century (cf. Stage VI), the structure [*šte* + main verb] in the present tense becomes a regular, highly grammaticalized future form. It would be an oversimplification, however, to assume that [*šte* + finite verb] is the only structure for the future at Stage VI:

a. particle *šte* + finite verb in the present
b. particle *šte* + conjunctive particle *da* + finite verb in the present
c. auxiliary verb *šta* in the present + finite verb in the present
d. shortened infinitive + auxiliary verb *šta* in the present.

In present-day Bulgarian, if dialectal and stylistic language variation is taken into account, it becomes clear that all variants from Stage V coexist with the structure *šte* + finite verb (see Maslov 1982). Moreover, the dialectal richness of Modern Bulgarian yields further variation: the form *šte* varies, depending on dialect, between *šte, ša, šă, še, ši, ce, ke, za, sa, să, š* and others (Stojkov 1960; Mladenov 1979; Calăkov 1974; Totev 1991; Georgiev 1985). Here one can observe the gradual but unmistakable process of phonological reduction, with the full lexical source form *xotěti* yielding *šte*, which is replaced by *ša/šă/še/ši/cě/ke/za/sa*, which in turn are superseded by *č, š*, e.g. *š să uprajš* (will-REFL-get.better.2.SG.PRES; 'you will get better' [a.n.]), until the form is lost completely in some dialectal uses, e.g. *să uprajš* (REFL-get.better.2.SG.PRES; 'you will get better' [a.n.]), see Totev (1991: 103ff.).

The degree to which the grammaticalization of a de-volitive future has proceeded in individual Balkan languages differs considerably. Decategorialization is less advanced in Rumanian (*voi*) and Serbian/Croatian (*ću, ćeš, će*), where the future marker is still an inflected auxiliary, while in Modern Greek (*tha* + subjunctive), Bulgariaň (*šte*), Macedonian (*ke*), and Albanian (*do* + subjunctive), decategorialization and erosion have given rise to an uninflected tense form (Dahl 2000b: 323); Solta (1980: 217) calls this the *eigentümlichen balkanischen Sprachzug* (= peculiar Balkanic language trait), where the frozen third-person singular of a verb for 'want' has turned into an invariable particle followed by the main verb inflected for person.

That we are dealing with an instance of areal diffusion affecting virtually all languages spoken in the Balkans may be illustrated with an example from the Indo-Aryan language Romani (see section 3.3): in varieties of this language that are spoken in the Balkans, the verb *kam-av* 'want, love' (e.g. *kamav te džav* 'I want to go'; Boretzky 1989: 368) has been grammaticalized to a future tense marker *ka(m)-* (e.g. *ka-džav* 'I will go'). With regard to Bulgarian varieties of Romani, Boretzky and Igla (1999: 719) argue that speakers of these varieties replicated the de-volitive future they found in Bulgarian, grammaticalizing their verb for 'want' to a future tense marker that is no longer inflected (see section 1.4.3 for examples).

(b) Object reduplication   This property, also called reduplicated object, object doubling, the pleonastic use of weak object pronominal forms, *Objektsverdopplung*, or *redoublement de l'objet*, is characterized by weak object markers used together with pronominal or nominal objects, and affecting both direct and indirect objects. This grammaticalization area includes Greek, Albanian, Rumanian, Bulgarian, and Macedonian, dialectally also Serbian/Croatian and to a limited extent Romani as spoken in the Balkans. Let us exemplify this grammaticalization area by means of object doubling in Bulgarian. The doubling of the object in this language involves two parallel developments:

(i) When used as direct and indirect objects, personal pronouns came to be followed by enclitic personal pronouns agreeing in gender, number, and case, cf.:

(7) Bulgarian

Neja ja
she.F.SG.COMMON.ACC she.F.SG.COMMON.ACC
nakarax da izmie poda.
make.1SG.AOR to wash floor.DEF
'I made her wash the floor.' *or* 'Her I made wash the floor.'

(ii) The nominal direct and indirect objects came to be followed by an enclitic personal pronoun agreeing in gender/number/case, cf.:

(8) Bulgarian

Na pacienta mu
to patient.M.SG COMMON.ACC(=DAT) he.M.SG.DAT
predpisaxa stroga dieta.
prescribe.3PL.AOR strict diet
'They prescribed to the patient a strict diet.' *or* 'To the patient they prescribed a strict diet.'

The earliest examples of object doubling in Bulgarian are attested in contexts with doubled pronouns (Mirčev 1963: 224). This phenomenon is avoided in literary Bulgarian; it is typical mostly of western Bulgarian dialects (Mirčev 1963: 224).

The overall process leading to the rise of object reduplication in the Balkans appears to be characterized by the following developments: It appears to have proceeded from definite to indefinite and from pragmatically marked to pragmatically unmarked participants, from indirect to direct objects, from human to inanimate participants, and from optional to obligatory/syntactically determined marking (see Hinrichs 1999: 448–50). Friedman (1994: 109) makes the important observation that object reduplication began with pragmatically conditioned constructions that became grammaticalized to varying degrees in different Balkan languages. These are developments that are commonly associated with grammaticalization, typically leading from free, pragmatically determined use patterns to fixed patterns of obligatory grammatical marking. And the rise of object reduplication can also be described with reference to the mechanisms characterizing grammaticalization, in particular desemanticization, whereby pronominal forms increasingly lose their association with both their deictic and pragmatic content, such as expressing deictic distinctions or thematic and focal/contrastive functions, and decategorialization, leading from pronouns to syntactically largely predictable agreement markers.

The degree of grammaticalization object reduplication exhibits differs considerably from one Balkan language to another. The construction is only weakly present in Greek, being associated particularly with definite objects, in Bulgarian it is for the most part not obligatory, being to some extent determined by pragmatic factors[17] (Hinrichs 1999: 448–50), and in Romani it is less fixed and less frequently used than in Macedonian or Rumanian (Boretzky & Igla 1999: 726). In Albanian, Macedonian, and Rumanian on the other hand it is strongly grammaticalized, being largely or fully syntacticized with indirect objects and definite direct objects.[18]

To conclude, object reduplication qualifies as another area that can be defined jointly with reference to language contact and grammaticalization.

(c) The superessive numeral marker   One way in which speakers may form numerals between 11 and 19 is via the grammaticalization of a location schema ['X on (top of) 10'], that is, by means of a conceptual structure ['1 on 10,' '2 on 10,' etc.], called the "superessive link" by Greenberg.[19] This grammaticalization[20] can be observed in a number of languages (Greenberg 1978b); still, its occurrence is cross-linguistically not very common. Accordingly, if we find that it has taken place in two neighboring languages then there is some probability that this is the result of contact-induced replication (provided that genetic inheritance can be ruled out as a contributing factor). There is thus reason to assume that we are dealing with a unidirectional process whereby a spatial construction involving a superessive marker is grammaticalized to a more abstract marker of the arithmetic operation of addition. For good reasons, this grammaticalization has been proposed as a Balkan feature: it occurs in the majority of Balkan languages: Tosk Albanian, Geg Albanian, Bulgarian, Serbian/Croatian, Macedonian, and Rumanian (see, for example, Reichenkron 1958; Schaller 1975: 150–2; van der Auwera 1998a: 262). Still, this grammaticalization is not confined to the Balkans: It is found in a contiguous area also including Hungarian, Latvian, as well as all Slavic languages (see map 5.2), and with the exception of Hungarian,[21] the unit number (digit) precedes the base number (decad) in all languages (Petrucci 1993). In the following example from Bulgarian, (9a) illustrates the source use of the superessive locative preposition *na*, while (9b) shows the use of the same item as a marker of the arithmetic operation of addition:

(9) Bulgarian

a. Naj- goljamata mu mečta v ži   vota beše
   most- big   his dream in life was
   da se   izkači na vrŭx   Everest.
   to REFL climb on mount Everest
   'His greatest dream in life was to climb up on Mount Everest.'

b. dva- na- deset
   two- on- ten
   'twelve'

Map 5.2 The superessive numeral marker in eastern Europe

While there are Balkanists who argue that Slavic languages played an insignificant role in the diffusion of Balkan properties,[22] such a view is in need of
modification. The present case of grammaticalization is attested already in Old
Church Slavonic, and it seems fairly uncontroversial that it was Slavic languages
which provided the model of transfer to the other European languages (see, for
example, Petrucci 1993; Hinrichs 1999: 43; Feuillet 2001: 1520). Irrespective of how exactly this grammaticalization diffused over a large east-central
European region stretching from the Baltic to the Mediterranean Sea, there are
reasons to assume that we are dealing with a solid grammaticalization area

originating in Slavic languages and replicated in non-Slavic languages of the Balkans, extending to adjacent languages such as Hungarian[23] and Latvian, but not Greek.[24]

(d) Infinitive loss and its replacement with a finite clause   A fairly common grammaticalization process concerns the evolution from nominal complement to complement having a non-finite (e.g. infinitival, participial, or gerundival) verb as its nucleus, and also to a finite subordinate clause. This evolution can be triggered by grammatical borrowing, whereby a subordinating conjunction is borrowed, a process subsequently leading to the transition from a non-finite complement to a finite subordinate clause (see Thomason 2001a: 1644–5; see also section 6.3.2). A similar example is provided by Turkish, a language where subordinated constructions generally have non-finite forms. Standard Turkish also has subordinate finite constructions, which are hypothesized to be a result of copying from Iranian languages, often introduced by a conjunction of Iranian origin (Johanson 1992: 259–64; see Matras 1998b: 91).

But such an evolution need not involve borrowing, it can happen as an instance of plain grammatical replication. There are two possible ways in which this may happen. One way concerns the reinterpretation of the non-finite marker on the verb as a marker of clause subordination – a canonical instance of grammaticalization whereby a marker reserved for presenting nominal participants, such as an adposition or a determiner, gradually turns into a marker used for presenting subordinate clauses. The second way is more difficult to locate with regard to principles of grammaticalization: it concerns the plain replacement of the non-finite construction with a finite construction. The development from nominal complement to clausal subordinate structure is a not uncommon result of grammaticalization; but the present case is not a canonical process of grammaticalization since it involves etymological discontinuity, in that the marking used for non-finiteness and for the finite subordinate construction are not etymologically identical (see section 4.4.3). It is the latter way that appears to have been at work in the development of Balkan languages.

One of the main characteristics of the Balkans as a linguistic area can be seen in a process whereby the infinitive is lost, being replaced with a finite clause (for detailed discussions, see Joseph 1983; Banfi 1990). There is wide agreement that this process was contact-induced, that is, that it spread from one Balkan language to another as a result of areal diffusion. But what appears to be suggestive of a discrete development from one morphosyntactic structure to another can perhaps more profitably be described as a gradual transition from a minor to a major use pattern (see section 2.2). Consider the following characterization of the process by Matras:

It is significant that all languages concerned displayed a finite option at least in some environments in the earlier system (i.e. prior to contact), and that the loss of the infinitive involves a gradual extension and ultimately a generalization of this option. (Matras 1998b: 90)

Thus, he argues that Balkan Turkish underwent a similar process to that of other Balkan languages, extending the distribution of a finite option to contexts where it was originally highly marked or even inadmissable (Matras 1998b: 93). Note also that Balkan Turkish provides another example of a transition from non-finite to finite subordination, although it is of a different kind from the preceding cases (Matras 1998b: 94–6). One of the functions of Standard Turkish converbs is expressing what corresponds to relative clauses in other languages, involving a non-finite attributive construction preceding the head noun. This construction is being replaced in Balkan Turkish with a finite-clause construction based on the grammaticalization of the interrogative *ne* 'what' referring back to the head noun. Replacement entails in particular the following changes. First, it introduces a new construction where the relative clause appears to be added to the main clause as a kind of afterthought. Accordingly, the new use pattern started out as a pragmatically marked structure rather than as a subordinating construction. Second, the interrogative-based relative use pattern entirely replaces the earlier non-finite gerundial or converbal relative construction in this Turkish dialect. Third, it also replaces Turkish converbs in adverbial clauses, drawing on the same semantic specifiers as the respective interrogatives, cf. (10). And fourth, it is in accordance with the general drift to be observed in Balkan languages leading from non-finite to finite constructions of clause subordination.

(10) Balkan Turkish (Matras 1998b: 94)

       eski konuşma ne   onlar   konuşurlar.
       old speech   REL 3.PL.NOM speak.HAB.3.PL
       'It is an old language that they speak.'

Like the other Balkanisms, infinitive loss is not confined to Balkan languages; as a grammaticalization area it includes, for example, some dialects of Italian spoken in the south of Italy (Joseph 1983: 250), where it is claimed to be due to Greek influence[25] (see Solta 1980: 214). What characterizes this area is a process that differs from most instances of grammaticalization discussed in this work in that, as observed above, we are confronted with etymological discontinuity rather than continuity. The relevant process has been described under the heading "renewal," whereby grammatical forms which have lost most of their semantic content tend to be replaced with forms having more concrete semantics, in this way starting a new cycle of grammatical evolution; for more details, see section 4.4.3.

(e) Replacement of synthetic adjectival comparative forms with analytic ones   As we observed in section 4.4.3, worn-out morphological categories may be subject to renewal, that is, they tend to be replaced with new lexical or grammatical forms, where "worn-out" refers to grammatical forms that have lost most of their earlier meaning, categorial distinctiveness, and/or phonetic substance. Renewal means, for example, that old tense or case affixes tend to be replaced with new periphrastic modes of expressing tense or case; it is usually described as a linguistic change leading from synthetic to analytic grammatical forms. But renewal may also concern suppletive grammatical forms that are replaced with less grammaticalized, morphologically transparent structures.

Renewal can be shaped or influenced by language contact, and it is widely agreed that this is what happened with the Balkan languages: there was a gradual transition from synthetic suppletive adjectival forms to analytic constructions by means of preposed markers in Bulgarian (*pó-*), Albanian (*më-*), Rumanian (*mai-*), and Modern Greek (πιό-), even if Greek has retained many of the earlier synthetic comparative structures (see Schaller 1975: 149; Solta 1980: 229). That this renewal is an instance of contact-induced replication is suggested, for example, by the fact that it introduced a less grammaticalized and morphologically more transparant structure, and that it affected languages of the Balkan sprachbund but not, or much less so, genetically related languages not belonging to the sprachbund, cf. Bulgarian *pó-dobσ r* 'better' vs. Russian *lučšij* (Solta 1980: 229). In addition to the Balkan languages, this grammaticalization appears to include Turkish (though not Serbian/Croatian; see van der Auwera 1998a: 260–3).

The replacement of synthetic comparative forms with analytic ones can be viewed as being part of a more general development characterizing the Balkan sprachbund whereby synthetic/inflectional forms of grammatical expression are replaced with analytic/periphrastic expressions. Such a development, leading to the rise of new cycles of grammaticalization (see section 4.4), is cross-linguistically common; the extent to which it has occurred in the Balkans, however, is unusual and can be accounted for meaningfully only by invoking language contact.

(f) Use of a quantifying interrogative in expressions for degree markers   In a monographic treatment of adverbial subordinators in the languages of Europe, Kortmann (1998b: 498–500) found, among others, that the languages of the Balkan sprachbund all employ a subordinator incorporating an interrogative quantifier 'how much?' for adverbial subordinators expressing degree ('inasmuch as, insofar as') as their exclusive or one of their primary meanings, e.g. Albanian *me sa* ('with how.much'), Bulgarian *do-kolko-to* ('until/up.to-how.much-REL'), Rumanian *după cît* ('according.to-how.much'). In addition to the uncontroversial Balkan languages, this structure is also found in Serbian/Croatian, Hungarian, Italian, Polish, Russian, and Latvian (but also in Udmurt and Armenian).

We hypothesize that this evidence is suggestive of another area of grammaticalization, for the following reasons. The geographical distribution of this property makes it plausible to assume that language contact was involved in its rise. And that we are dealing with a grammaticalization process is suggested by the fact that there is a more general development in the languages of Europe and a few other languages whereby interrogative pronouns grammaticalize to markers of clause subordination, including relative clause markers and complementizers; we have encountered this general process in previous chapters (especially sections 3.1.3 and 4.1.2). The present case, where a quantifying interrogative – typically in collocation with some adpositional or other element – assumes the function of a comparative subordinator, can be seen as a special instance of this conceptual transfer from interrogative to subordinating structures, arising and spreading in one specific region of Europe. But, like the other grammaticalization areas characterizing the Balkan sprachbund, this area is not restricted to Balkan languages.

5.2.3.2 Meso-America

The term Meso-America refers to a large part of Mexico, Guatemala, Belize, El Salvador, and to the southern parts of Honduras, Nicaragua, and Costa Rica and comprises some sixty languages belonging to a number of different genetic groupings. The analysis by Campbell, Kaufman, and Smith-Stark (1986) results in the claim that of thirty-one possible Meso-American properties, four provide solid evidence for a sprachbund, and another nine at least supporting evidence.[26] The four "uncontroversial" properties are (Campbell, Kaufman & Smith-Stark 1986: 555; see also van der Auwera 1998a: 263; Stolz & Stolz 2001: 1543–7):

(a) attributive possession of the type *his-dog the man*
(b) relational nouns
(c) vigesimal numeral systems
(d) non-verb-final basic word order, to which absence of switch-reference is correlated.

With the exception of (d), all of the uncontroversial Meso-American properties are suggestive of grammaticalization areas, as we will now try to establish.

(a) Attributive possession of the type *his-dog the man*   There is cross-linguistically only a limited number of diachronic sources that serve as conceptual templates for the grammaticalization of constructions of attributive/nominal possession (or genitive constructions), that is, for a schema of the type [Y *of* X]. One of these sources has been described as the Topic Schema, taking the form [(*As for*) X, X's Y], e.g. Afrikaans *die boer se huis* (the farmer his house) 'the farmer's house.' What characterizes this widespread source is that the possessor precedes the possessee and is cross-referenced, that is, repeated in the form of a pronominal modifier on the possessee (Heine 1997a: 144–9). But there are also languages where the reverse order is found, i.e. where the schema takes the form [X's Y, X], called the Anti-topic sub-schema, which is far less commonly encountered in the languages of the world. Most cases of it have been reported from Central America and – in fact – it constitutes one of the four uncontroversial properties of Meso-America; the following example illustrates this schema:

(11) Ch'ol (Mayan; Stolz & Stolz 2001: 1543)

i	tyaq'uin	i	yalobil	c-	amigo
POSS.3	money	POSS.3	son	POSS.1.SG-	friend

'the money of my friend's son'

In the languages of the Meso-America area, both the Topic and the Anti-topic sub-schema have been grammaticalized, but the latter appears to prevail. As the description by Campbell, Kaufman, and Smith-Stark (1986: 545) suggests, there is no doubt that this situation is the result of contact-induced transfer, and since we are dealing with an areally confined grammaticalization process cutting across genetically unrelated or remotely related languages, this appears to be an instance of an area of grammaticalization.

(b) Relational nouns   Perhaps one of the cross-linguistically most common processes of grammaticalization concerns the development of relational nouns including, but not being confined to, body-part terms to markers of locative, temporal, and other grammatical relations. This pathway of grammaticalization has led to the rise of prepositions and postpositions in many languages of the world (cf. English *in front of, in back of*), and it has also been at work in Meso-America. What makes the languages of this area a special case is the fact that the process has not been carried out to completion, that is, it has been arrested at some intermediate stage – with the effect that there is a construction halfway between nominal and adpositional structure, exhibiting some nominal properties such as using possessive pronominal affixes but expressing grammatical relations corresponding to locative and other prepositions in English or Spanish.[27]

Such a situation is in no way restricted to the Meso-America area; nevertheless, on account of its geographical density there is reason to assume that the situation is the result of areal diffusion. This suggests that in the present case it is not the selection of a specific process that defines a grammaticalization area but rather the fact that grammaticalization has not been carried through to completion in the languages of Meso-America, resulting in the emergence of a morphosyntactic category that combines both nominal and adpositional structures.

Further evidence for areal diffusion can be seen in the fact that, in addition to the morphosyntactic process just sketched, there are some conceptual developments characterizing this process (see, for example, Levinson 1994: 839), involving, for example, the grammaticalization of certain body parts to specific locative concepts that appear to be cross-linguistically uncommon (Stolz & Stolz 2001: 1544). For example, in many languages worldwide the spatial concept 'behind' is historically derived from the body part 'back' (cf. English *in back of*), less frequently from other body parts, such as 'buttock, anus.' Now, in Meso-American languages a fairly uncommon process can be observed, namely from 'shoulder' to 'behind': we gave examples of this unusual grammaticalization in section 1.4.2.

Perhaps more than morphological or syntactic replication, it seems that it is conceptual replication of the kind just sketched that accounts for grammaticalization areas in many parts of the world, whereby speakers select specific concepts on the model of some other language and grammaticalize them in the same way as speakers of the other language had done earlier.

(c) Vigesimal numeral systems   Worldwide, the most common conceptual template to structure the system of cardinal numerals is using the human body – this template has been referred to as the body-part model (Heine 1997b: 18–34). In accordance with this model, the human hand provides the most salient template for expressing '5,' two hands for '10,' and the numeral '20' tends to be expressed in terms of notions such as 'hands and feet' or 'the whole person.' While the grammaticalization from body-part terms to numerals is no longer transparent in many languages of the world, the presence of '5,' '10,' and '20' as a numerical base still bears witness to this pathway of grammaticalization leading to the rise of quinary, decimal, and vigesimal numeral systems, respectively. Of these three, decimal systems are cross-linguistically clearly predominant, while rigid quinary or vigesimal systems do occur but are less common in the languages of the world. Accordingly, if we find some region where all languages spoken in that region have a vigesimal system then this is unusual, and if some of these languages are genetically unrelated but are known to share a history of contact then areal diffusion is a plausible hypothesis to account for this situation.

This is exactly the situation found in Meso-America, which is characterized by the almost exceptionless presence of vigesimal numeral systems[28] – a situation that is described as "pan-Meso-American" by Campbell, Kaufman, and Smith-Stark (1986: 546). For example, the numeral for '20' in Tequistlatec is *anušans* (composed of *anu-* '1' and *-šans* 'man') and for '40' *oge?nušans* ('2 times 20'), and for '400' *anušans anušans* ('20 times 20'). Thus, there is good reason to assume that the grammaticalization of the vigesimal system is the result of diffusion throughout Meso-America in pre-Conquest times (Yasugi 1995: 89), giving rise to a solid grammaticalization area. Note, that the Meso-America sprachbund and the vigesimal grammaticalization area are not exactly co-extensive, in that the latter extends beyond the conventional borders of Meso-America, having also spread to other languages such as Coahuilteco, Cora, Mayo, and Northern Tepehuán to the north of Meso-America, and Sumu, Mískito, and Guaymí to the south (Campbell, Kaufman & Smith-Stark 1986: 546).

5.2.3.3 South Asia

Another well-known case of a sprachbund is what has variously been called the Indian Sprachbund, the Indosphere, or South Asia, which in addition to Indo-European and Dravidian languages also includes Tibeto-Burman and Munda languages, spoken in Pakistan, India, Nepal, Bhutan, Bangladesh, and Sri Lanka (Emeneau 1956; Masica 1976; for a review, see Ebert 2001). An important factor – though certainly not the only one (see Sridhar 1978: 197 for details) – leading to this sprachbund can be seen in the Indo-Aryanization of Dravidian languages, which has a history of nearly 3,500 years (for a reverse process, leading to the Dravidianization of Indo-Aryan languages, see section 4.3.3.4).

Like other sprachbunds such as the Balkans or Meso-America, the properties making up South Asia include a number of grammaticalization areas. One of these areas concerns an extended grammaticalization chain from a verb 'say' to a quotative, purpose, causal, or conditional marker, a complementizer, or an evidential particle, believed to have spread from Indic and Dravidian languages[29] (Saxena 1988a, 1988b; see also LaPolla 2001: 234ff.).

Another grammaticalization area within South Asia concerns a more general, cross-linguistically widespread auxiliation pattern involving a combination of two verbs, where the first (V1) is a non-finite content verb and the second (V2) a finite verb dubbed "vector verb," "verbal specificier," "aspectivizer," "explicator verb," etc. Within this pattern, V2 consists of a paradigm of lexical verbs meaning 'go,' 'come,' 'take,' 'sit,' 'throw,' etc., which assume grammatical functions such as expressing telicity, progressive, continuative, or inchoative aspect (Masica 1976: 146–7; Ebert 2001: 1531).

Finally, there is a possible grammaticalization area characterizing South Asia, being defined by the grammaticalization of a verb for 'say' to a comparative marker. Verbs meaning 'say' can give rise to a number of grammatical funtions, as we just observed; but their development to a comparative marker is cross-linguistically not really widespread. Accordingly, if this development is commonly found in a given area then this is suggestive of areally induced spread. Note, however, that so far only three South Asian languages (Newari,

Nepali, and Telugu) have been identified to have undergone this development (Ebert 2001: 1533).

5.2.3.4 Southeast Asia

That Southeast Asia somehow constitutes a sprachbund also seems to be fairly uncontroversial, and grammaticalization provides one of the main parameters for defining this area (see Matisoff 1991; Bisang 1996a): Southeast Asia is characterized most of all by a bundle of grammaticalization areas, each characterized by a specific process of grammaticalization, such processes being:
(a) the development from locative verb to progressive aspect
(b) the development from a verb meaning 'get' to an auxiliary of deontic modality ('have to,' 'be able to')
(c) the development from a verb 'give' to a causative or dative-benefactive auxiliary in Chinese, Hmong, Vietnamese, Thai, and Cambodian (Matisoff 1991; LaPolla 2001: 243; Bisang 1996a: 571)
(d) the development from a verb for 'replace, represent' to a replacive case marker ('instead') in Chinese, Hmong, Vietnamese, Thai, and Cambodian (Bisang 1996a: 571).

A case presumably involving both polygrammaticalization and repeated grammaticalization is provided by Bisang (1996a: 577–8): the verb for 'give' in Vietnamese (*cho*), Thai (*hâj*), and Cambodian (*ʔaoy*) has been grammaticalized not only to a dative-benefactive case marker but also to a causative auxiliary ("causative verb") and a complementizer ("conjunctional verb") in all three languages (Bisang 1996a: 577); we have discussed this grammaticalization area in section 5.2.2.

While these examples concern the grammaticalization of verbal structures, there are also instances involving nominal structures. For example, there is a process whereby nouns for 'thing,' 'object' figuring in what in Heine (1997a) is called the Topic Schema of the kind [possessee, *thing-of* possessor] is grammaticalized to a possessive marker (POSS), that is, a grammatical element linking the possessor and the possessee in a schema of nominal possession [possessee *of* possessor]. This grammaticalization process is not very common cross-linguistically, nevertheless it can be observed in languages of all major regions of the world (e.g. Haitian Creole, Kxoe, Maltese). In Southeast Asia, the process appears to have given rise to a grammaticalization area: in Vietnamese, Khmer, Thai, and Lao, a noun meaning 'thing(s), stuff' has been used in this schema, that is, the same grammaticalization process from 'thing' to possessive marker appears to have been transferred from one language to another (Matisoff 1991: 391; Enfield 2001: 260; Heine & Kuteva 2002: 296). However, no information is available on the directionality of diffusion within this grammaticalization area.

5.2.3.5 Ethiopia

Ethiopia, or more appropriately the Ethio-Eritrean area, is widely held to form a sprachbund since it had first been proposed by Ferguson (1976), although doubts have been raised concerning the validity of this classification (Tosco 2000). As in other instances of sprachbunds, in this area we also find grammaticalization areas. The following example may illustrate this. In many languages worldwide, verbs meaning 'say' have been grammaticalized to quotative markers, complementizers, and other subordination markers; we saw an example of the areal implications of a similar process in section 5.2.3.3. This kind of grammaticalization is also found in the present area, which includes all modern Ethiopic Semitic languages as well as Cushitic and Omotic languages. Tosco describes the situation thus:

> Generally, this trait involves an extension of direct speech, marked by a more or less desemanticized verb "to say", in order to link various subordinate sentences, as in Amharic *betun ṭäbbəqi bəla azzäzäččat* "she ordered her to watch the house" (lit. "the-house watch she-saying she-ordered-her"). Further desemanticization of "to say" may lead to its use in an auxiliary-like manner; for example, in order to express imminence, as in Amharic *baburu lihed sil därräsku* "I arrived when the train was about to leave" (roughly, "the train to-going when-saying I-arrived"). (Tosco 2000: 345)

While the presence of these grammaticalizations in Ethiopian languages is cross-linguistically not unusual, we nevertheless argue that this is a grammaticalization area, especially for the following reason: this is an instance of polygrammaticalization (see section 5.2.2) of a verb for 'say' that includes a cluster of individual processes, namely from 'say' to (a) quotative marker, (b) complementizer, (c) adverbial clause subordinator, and (d) marker introducing ideophones.

On the basis of the evidence available it would seem that this grammaticalization area evolved after the tenth century AD (Tosco 2000: 353) and that it is the result of the influence of Cushitic languages on Semitic languages, that is, Cushitic languages appear to have provided the model which was replicated in the Ethiopic Semitic languages (Tosco 2000: 346).

Concerning another possible grammaticalization area characterizing Ethiopia, see section 5.2.5.

5.2.3.6 Other areas

There are quite a number of regions in the world that have been suggested to exhibit sprachbund properties; not all of them however have so far been generally recognized as "legitimate" cases of sprachbunds. But what is common to all of them is that they include one or more grammaticalization areas. In the present section we will look at some of these regions in turn.

East Anatolia   As a more recent description by Haig (2001) suggests, East Anatolia corresponds to our general characterization of a sprachbund in section 5.1.1. The area is genetically highly heterogeneous, it includes languages from four different families: Turkish (Turkic), Laz (Kartvelian), Zazaki and Kurmanjî Kurdish (Iranian), and Aramaic and Arabic (Semitic) (see map 4.2). There are a number of properties across these languages that are suggestive of areal diffusion, and some of them can be defined as grammaticalization areas.

One diachronic source for markers of consecutive clauses in narrative discourse is provided by temporal adverbs (e.g. 'then') and other markers of temporal reference (see Heine & Kuteva 2002), and such a grammaticalization has also happened in East Anatolia. Three languages of the area, Turkish, Laz, and Zazaki, each belonging to a different family, exhibit the same type of linking sequences of clauses temporally, where a form meaning 'after' appears to have been grammaticalized to something like a consecutive clause marker added to the first clause (Haig 2001: 203–4). Accordingly, what in English would be expressed with [X happened then Y happened] takes the structure [[X happened]-after [Y happened]] in these languages. The fact that in all languages the same temporal concept and the same syntactic arrangement is used suggests strongly that language contact was a contributing factor, and Turkish appears to have provided the model for the rise of this grammaticalization area (see section 4.3.2).

Another case concerns the development of what appears to be a concessive clause marker ('nevertheless,' 'although,' 'but') in Turkish, Laz, Zazaki, and Kurmanjî via the grammaticalization of a word for 'again' in conjunction with the enclitic topic-switch marker to a marker introducing the second of two clauses (Haig 2001: 204–5). Once again, the specific meaning and structure involved in this process make this a likely case of areal diffusion, and adverbials expressing repetition ('again') are attested sources for concessive and adversative clause conjunctions. There is no information on the directionality of replication in this grammaticalization area, which unites four languages of three different families (see section 4.3.2).

The Balto-Finnic contact area   Multiple contacts across the genetic boundary separating Indo-European and Finno-Ugric languages have yielded a wide range of transfers between Baltic and Finnic languages. The Baltic language Latvian and the Finnic language Estonian in particular share a number of contact-related structures – to the extent that the possibility of a sprachbund has been discussed in a number of works (see especially Stolz 1991). While there is no conclusive evidence as to whether a legitimate claim for a Latvian-Estonian sprachbund can be made, there appears to be little doubt that these two languages participate in a number of grammaticalization areas. We have discussed some of these areas in different parts of this work (for more possible areas, see Stolz 1991), namely:

(a) The grammaticalization of a verb for 'come' to an auxiliary for the deontic modality of necessity ('must,' 'have to'), where the agent is presented as a participant in some oblique case (Stolz 1991: 65–8; see section 1.3).
(b) The grammaticalization via context extension of a polar complementizer ('whether,' 'if') to a sentence-initial word marking polar (yes–no) questions (Stolz 1991: 65–8; see section 2.2.3).
(c) The grammaticalization of a use pattern of high frequency to an analytic superlative of the type 'better than all,' which is found not only in Latvian and Estonian but also in the neighboring Finnic language Livonian (Koptjevskaja-Tamm & Wälchli 2001: 626–7; see also section 2.5).
(d) The introduction of productive compounding structures and of compound prepositions (where the first constituent is a noun) in Latvian on the model of neighboring Finnic languages (Forssman 2000; see section 4.3.2).
(e) The grammaticalization of verbal negation in Estonian on the model of Latvian (Stolz 1991: 70–2; see section 4.4.1).

The Balto-Slavic contact area   Another possible linguistic area in northeastern Europe concerns the contact zone of Baltic- and Slavic-speaking populations, where at least the following grammaticalization areas can be identified.

The 'behind'-area of comparison (see map 5.3). Among the various grammaticalization strategies used to present the standard of comparison in comparative constructions of inequality there is one based on the Location Schema. In accordance with this schema, the standard of comparison is introduced by means of a marker of static location, be that an inflection, a clitic, or an adposition. The source structure is [X *is* Y *at* Z], giving rise to a comparative construction taking the form [X *is* Y-*er than* Z]. The location marker typically denotes any of the functions 'at,' 'on,' 'above,' 'in,' or 'by' (Stassen 1985: 41–2; Heine 1997b: 112–5). In a number of languages of northeastern Europe, however, there is a fairly unusual source structure: rather than a general marker of static location, the locative marker is 'behind' (Koptjevskaja-Tamm & Wälchli 2001: 684). These languages include the Baltic languages Lithuanian (*už*) and Latvian (*aiz*) as well as a number of neighboring Slavic varieties, in particular the following: (a) at least part of Belorussian, (b) northeastern Polish dialects, that is, the "Prussian" dialects of Mazowsze close to Lithuania, (c) some western dialects of Ukrainian, and (d) the northwestern periphery of Russian, especially the Pskov dialect (see map 5.3).

On account of the fact that 'behind' as a conceptual source for standard markers of comparative constructions of inequality appears to be cross-linguistically rare, and that this grammaticalization process is shared by languages belonging to different branches of Indo-European, we conclude that this is a relevant instance of a grammaticalization area. No reliable information on the directionality of replication is available, but Koptjevskaja-Tamm

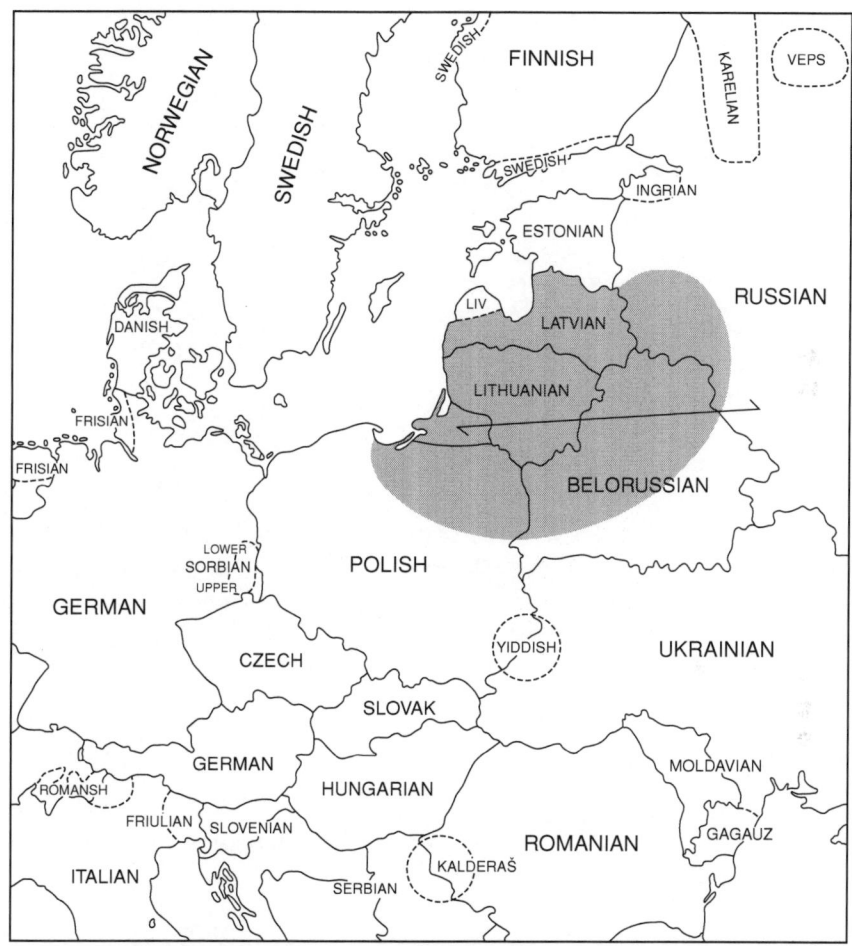

Map 5.3 Approximate extension of the "behind" area of comparison in northeastern Europe

and Wälchli (2001: 684) argue that we are dealing with a Baltic encoding
strategy which was replicated by some Slavic dialects.

From 'or' to question marker (see map 5.4). One common strategy of developing new markers for polar questions is by grammaticalizing an alternative
conjunction 'or' to a question marker (Heine & Kuteva 2001: 226–7); we drew
attention to it in section 2.2.2. This appears to have happened in northeastern
Europe in a number of geographically continuous languages, including Baltic
languages like Lithuanian and Latvian, and Slavic languages like Belorussian,
Ukrainian, and adjacent varieties of Russian (see map 5.4). What we find in

Fig. 5.4 Approximate extension of the "or"-to-interrogative area in northeastern Europe.

all these languages is a question particle that is identical or almost identical to the conjunction 'or' (Koptjevskaja-Tamm & Wälchli 2001: 714). While this grammaticalization is cross-linguistically widespread, its clustering across the Balto-Slavic boundary suggests that this may well be an area shaped by contact-induced grammaticalization.

The Daly River area   This area of northern Australia consists of five smaller language groups which are only distantly genetically related and have even been claimed to be genetically unrelated. Dixon (2002: 276–8) lists among others nine special features involving grammatical categories where the forms used for these categories are different across language groups. While none of these features is restricted to the languages of the Daly River area, combined they constitute robust evidence supporting a sprachbund hypothesis in accordance with our characterization in section 5.1.1.[30] One of these features concerns grammaticalization: there is a small set of stance and motion verbs added to another verb in a serial-type construction, whereby they specify the physical orientation of the subject and/or add aspectual information. In this way, verbs for 'sit' assume the function of continuous markers, and 'lie' of markers for permanent activities or states (Dixon 2002: 677). What this suggests is that there is a grammaticalization area characterized by a more general development from verbal to specific spatial and aspectual functions. This area is not co-extensive with the Daly River languages; rather, it also includes Miriwung and possibly other languages.

The Pacific Northwest Coast   Beck (2000) defines the Amerindian Pacific Northwest Coast as a sprachbund ranging from northern California up to the panhandle of Alaska, which includes "Mosan" and unites Salishan, Wakashan, and Chimakuan, being "one of the most geographically extensive and genetically diverse *Sprachbünde* in the world" (Beck 2000: 154). One example may suffice to illustrate that this sprachbund also includes groupings that can be defined as grammaticalization areas. There is a not uncommon process of grammaticalization whereby the use of certain linguistic markers associated with the noun phrase is extended to subordinate clauses. In this way, markers of nominalization, determiners, and adpositions can be grammaticalized to clause-subordinating conjunctions (see, for example, Heine, Claudi & Hünnemeyer 1991: 153, 183ff.). This general process appears also to have contributed to the rise of the Pacific Northwest Coast sprachbund. This sprachbund includes Bella Coola, a Salishan outlier surrounded on three sides by languages of the Wakashan family (Beck 2000: 168), being regarded as the most divergent member of the Salishan family. One of the features Bella Coola appears to have replicated from Northern Wakashan languages is the use of nominalization to form subordinate clauses (Beck 2000: 171).

5.2.3.7 Conclusions

Our discussion in the preceding paragraphs was not meant to be an exhaustive treatment of grammaticalization areas as a salient component of sprachbunds. We were confined to a few sprachbunds and a few isoglosses that can be defined as grammaticalization areas. Similar findings can be made in other regions of the world that have been proposed to constitute sprachbunds.

What we observed on the various sprachbunds that we surveyed in this section can be summarized as follows. First, quite a number of the properties that have been proposed as providing crucial evidence for the presence of sprachbunds can perhaps more profitably be reanalyzed as being suggestive of grammaticalization areas. Second, the latter are frequently not co-extensive with the respective sprachbunds. A paradigm case can be seen in the superessive numeral marker, one of the properties of the Balkan sprachbund: it is found not only in the Balkans but also, for example, in all Slavic languages, and its presence is not restricted to languages that are contiguous with the Balkan region, as its presence in Latvian shows (see section 5.2.3.1 (c); map 5.2). At the same time, the superessive numeral marker is not a general property of the sprachbund, being absent in Greek. Third, while sprachbunds are defined on the basis of clusters of isoglosses, with borders that are notoriously messy and controversial, the boundaries of grammaticalization areas can be defined fairly unambiguously on the basis of the geographical extension that the relevant grammaticalization process has experienced. And finally, while sprachbunds tend to rest on amalgamations of various historical processes that happened at different times in the past, involving a time depth of centuries or more, each grammaticalization area is more likely to be the result of a unique historical process or chain of processes.

5.2.4   Metatypy

What all the cases discussed in section 5.2.3 have in common is that they involve instances of contact-induced grammaticalization. But grammaticalization areas are not only an essential component of sprachbunds, they are in the same way a constituent part of metatypy situations. In the present section we will look at five cases of what appear to be cases of metatypy, that is, that come close to corresponding to the criteria set up at the beginning of section 5.1.2.

Kupwar   The Indian village of Kupwar offers a rich laboratory for contact-induced assimilation of languages. Located in the Sangli District of Maharashtra Province of India, Kupwar has been described as an extreme case of mutual assimilation of languages or "convergence," leading to a high degree of inter-translatability (Gumperz & Wilson 1971), and to what Ross (1996; 2001) describes as a metatypy situation. The languages involved belong to two genetic stocks, namely Indo-European (Urdu, Marathi) and Dravidian (Kannada, Telugu); Marathi and Kannada have been spoken in Kupwar for more than six centuries, and Urdu for at least three centuries. While Marathi was the language of a less prestigious group, being the language of the untouchable caste, it was perhaps the most influential component in achieving metatypy. As the description by Gumperz and Wilson (1971) suggests, the linguistic situation of Kupwar is characterized by a number of grammaticalization areas.

While Kupwar has been discussed in quite a number of works dealing with language contact, no mention is made in these works that grammaticalization was involved. In the following paragraphs we will discuss a few cases which are meant to demonstrate that what makes this area a fairly credible case of metatypy is in fact the role played by grammaticalization. One example is provided by the structure of markers for polar (yes–no) questions. As far as the description by Gumperz and Wilson (1971: 160) shows, the Indo-European languages Standard Hindi-Urdu and Marathi provided the model for the rise of this situation: these two languages appear to have grammaticalized the interrogative for 'what?' (*dii* in Standard Hindi-Urdu) to a polar question particle, while Kannada has a verbal suffix -*a* instead. Now, all languages spoken in Kupwar have used this grammaticalization as a model, replicating the Indo-European pattern in general and the Marathi one in particular: they use the interrogative for 'what?' as a clause-final marker for polar questions (Kupwar Urdu *kya*, Kupwar Marathi *kay*, Kupwar Kannada *yan*), and Kannada speakers in Kupwar reject the suffix -*a*. This suggests that the Dravidian language Kannada as used in Kupwar has undergone the same grammaticalization process from an interrogative pronoun for 'what?' to a polar question marker as the two Indo-European languages had done earlier.

A second grammaticalization area concerns case marking in Kupwar, this time involving Urdu as a replica language. Cross-linguistically, there is a grammaticalization process whereby benefactive (or dative) case markers give rise to purpose markers when instead of a human participant there is an inanimate participant (cf. English *for*; see Heine & Kuteva 2002: 55–7). Standard Urdu uses the marker *ke liye* in purpose constructions, but Urdu speakers of Kupwar (= R) follow the pattern used in the other two languages spoken in Kupwar, namely that of the Indo-European language Marathi and the Dravidian language Kannada (= M), according to which purpose clauses are encoded by means of a construction [verb + oblique + dative] (Gumperz & Wilson 1971: 160). This situation suggests that Kupwar Urdu has extended the use of its dative marker (= Ry) to also express purpose (= Rx). In doing so, it appears to have replicated a grammaticalization process that Marathi and Kannada had undergone earlier.

Kupwar provides yet another example of case syncretism resulting in a grammaticalization area. There is a fairly common grammaticalization process whereby allative/dative case markers are also used to mark patient participants, i.e. direct objects. The first stage in this process is characterized by a situation where the allative/dative marker is confined to human and definite object referents (see section 4.3.1). Such a process also appears to have occurred in Kupwar (Gumperz & Wilson 1971). Standard Kannada, a Dravidian language, distinguishes accusative and dative participants by means of postpositions. But in Kupwar, Kannada speakers have been in contact with speakers of the

Indo-European languages Urdu and Marathi (= M), which both have only a dative postposition for human objects (My = Mx). As a result of these contacts, lasting for more than three centuries, Kannada speakers (R) appear to have replicated the situation found in the two Indo-European languages by grammaticalizing the dative postposition (= Ry) to mark human direct objects (= Rx) in addition (Gumperz & Wilson 1971: 158).

To conclude, the situation of Kupwar can be described as crucially involving a bundle of grammaticalization areas. Note that these areas are not all co-extensive, that is, they are not restricted to that village; for example, Kannada or Urdu (spoken outside Kupwar) are part of some grammatialization areas but not of others.

Northwestern New Britain   The languages of northwestern New Britain (NWNB) of Papua New Guinea belong to two different genetic stocks. Most are Austronesian but belonging to different branches of the family, like Bibling (Mouk, Aria, Tourai, and Lamogi), Siasi (Lusi, Kove, and Kabana), and Whiteman (Amara), and one appears to be a genetic isolate (Anêm). NWNB is described by Thurston (1987; see also Thurston 1982) as a sprachbund; but it would seem that there is reason to consider it to be a candidate for the status of metatypy, as is suggested by the following description:

> It is possible to translate word by word among languages that belong to three different branches of AN [Austronesian; a.n.] and a NAN [non-Austronesian; a.n.] isolate. In view of the extensive multilingualism and dual-lingualism in NWNB, the implication is that all of these languages share a single semantic and syntactic structure, differing only in the forms encoding items of their lexics. That is, regardless of one's own vernacular, the way in which one's thoughts and ideas are construed in language operates with the same sets of categories arranged according to the same sets of rules [. . .] Learning a neighbouring vernacular, then, is mostly a matter of learning a new set of words to substitute for semantic and grammatical slots that are already known from one's own language. (Thurston 1987: 74)

The only major structural difference that Thurston found among these languages was that some languages are more complex than others. Some salient grammatical properties shared by all languages are a rigid verb-medial (SVO) word order, absence of grammaticalized tense distinctions, a focus particle denoting both 'not yet' and 'still,' a marker, glossed 'first,' indicating that the event described in a dependent clause occurs before some other event, and a marker denoting simultaneously 'too,' 'again,' 'also,' and 'another' (Thurston 1987: 74–80).

Thurston does not elaborate on the dynamics underlying the emergence and development of this linguistic area. The data given by him suggest, however, that grammaticalization processes constitute a not unimportant component of the area. For example, in all languages of the NWNB area, 'accompany' and 'with' are polysemous, that is, the two meanings are expressed by one and the same form (Thurston 1987: 147). Now, a grammaticalization process from a lexical verb meaning 'accompany' or 'meet' to a comitative adposition ('with') is cross-linguistically attested; we may therefore be dealing with a grammaticalization area, being the result of this process from lexical verb to grammatical marker and its diffusion across all languages of NWNB.

Another instance of a possible grammaticalization area can be seen in the polysemy between 'enter' and 'in,' to be found in all languages of NWNB – considering the fact that lexical verbs meaning 'enter' often acquire grammatical uses as inessive adpositions. A third case that presumably qualifies as an instance of a grammaticalization area concerns a verb for 'sit' which appears to have been grammaticalized in a number of languages of NWNB to an existential and/or locative copula (Thurston 1987: 67, 138).

The Waskia-Takia contact region   We have already provided examples from this case of metatypy on Karkar Island off the north coast of Papua New Guinea in previous chapters (see Ross 1996; 2001).[31] Note that this region consists of only two genetically unrelated languages: the Papuan language Waskia and the Western Austronesian language Takia. There are at least two grammaticalization areas characterizing this region. One concerns the development of postpositions in Takia on the model of Waskia postpositions (section 3.1.2). The second grammaticalization area is the result of a process whereby the replica language Takia developed postposed determiners using its own material but replicating the structure found in the model language Waskia (section 4.3.3.1).

The East Tucanoan–Tariana contact region   As we argued for in section 5.1.2, this area of northwest Amazonia can also be considered a case of metatypy on the basis of the description proposed by Aikhenvald (2002). This area is most of all the result of language contact between East Tucanoan languages and the North Arawak language Tariana, whereby Tariana has undergone a large number of contact-induced grammaticalizations, in addition to large-scale restructuring.[32] Consequently, East Tucanoan and Arawak, which are presumably genetically unrelated, are united by a range of grammaticalization areas.[33] Many of these areas were pointed out in previous chapters; in the present section we will restrict discussion to areas that have not been discussed earlier.

One cross-linguistically not uncommon pathway of grammaticalization concerns verbs for 'say' which develop into complementizers and may finally turn into markers of reason and purpose clauses (Heine & Kuteva 2002: 261–5); we observed that this line of grammaticalization has also contributed to other grammaticalization areas (sections 5.2.3.3, 5.2.3.5). This is a process that also characterizes the Vaupés region: it has given rise to purpose ('so that') clauses in

East Tucanoan languages, and from there it was replicated in Tariana, where the complementizer consists of the nominalized verb 'say' and the complement is a secondhand imperative. Accordingly, a sentence like 'I cut the parrot's wings so that it won't escape' is expressed both in Tucano and Tariana as 'I cut the parrot's wings saying let him not escape on someone else's order' (Aikhenvald 2002: 164–5).

Another grammaticalization area of the Vaupés region concerns the development from interrogative pronouns to complement or relative clause markers. Aikhenvald (2002: 165) observes that there is a pattern in East Tucanoan languages whereby interrogative pronouns, such as Tucano *noó* 'where?' are used in relative clauses with an indefinite meaning (similar to English 'wherever'); see Heine and Kutva (forthc.) for discussion. Tariana speakers have replicated this grammaticalization, using their own interrogative pronoun *kani* 'where?'. Accordingly, the sentence 'He follows me wherever I go' is rendered in both East Tucanoan languages and Tariana as 'Where my going [is] he follows me.'

Finally, there is a grammaticalization area characterized by the diffusion of an imperative category that Aikhenvald (2002: 130) calls the secondhand imperative, used to convey the meaning 'Do this because someone else told you to!' and used for second- and third-person referents. Once again, diffusion proceeded from East Tucanoan languages such as Tucano to Tariana; the following examples illustrate the category.

(12) Tucano (East Tucanoan; Aikhenvald 2002: 130)

      a'ti-   ato.
      come- IMP.SEC
      'Come (on his order)!'

(13) Tariana (North Arawak; Aikhenvald 2002: 130)

      pi-   nu-   pida.
      2.SG- come- IMP.SEC
      'Come (on his order)!'

Tariana speakers replicated this category from East Tucanoan by extending the use of one of their four evidential categories, the reported evidential, grammaticalizing the reported marker *-pida* to an imperative form that is equivalent to the corresponding categories of the model languages.

Sri Lanka   Another example of a metatypy-like situation that we mentioned in section 5.1.2 concerns three languages in Sri Lanka, namely Modern Sri Lanka Malay, Modern Sri Lanka Portuguese, and Tamil. Malay and Portuguese have been spoken on the island for at least three or four centuries, and both developed into creoles with an SVO word order. More recently, the two have

Table 5.2 *Some idiomatic collocations involving body parts shared by Waskia and Takia speakers*

Literal meaning	Idiomatic meaning
'man-woman'	'person'
'pig-dog'	'animal'
'my hand's liver'	'the palm of my hand'
'my eyes go round'	'I am dizzy'
'I am putting my eye'	'I am waiting for someone'
'his eye – his eye'	(do something) first'
'I hear his mouth'	'I obey him'
'I cut his mouth'	'I disobey him'

Source: Ross 1996: 190.

been Tamilized to the extent that they are now rigidly verb-final languages, and exhibit roughly the same case system, evidentials, quotative markers, semantics of verb markers, etc. (Bakker 2000). Grammaticalization played an important role in the Tamilization process. In an attempt to replicate the case system of Tamil, speakers of the erstwhile creoles used a universal process of grammaticalization in developing adpositional, adverbial, and other independent forms into case suffixes. Thus, Portuguese *pera/para* 'for' was grammaticalized to an accusative/dative case suffix *-pə*, Portuguese *junto* 'together' to a locative case suffix *-(u)nto*, or Portuguese *sua, seu* 'his, her, its' to a genitive suffix *-su(wə)* in Modern Sri Lanka Portuguese, thereby matching the corresponding Tamil case markers (Bakker 2000: 32).

Conclusions   The cases looked at above are simply meant to demonstrate that metatypy centrally involves contact-induced grammaticalization and, consequently, cases of metatypy can be expected to include grammaticalization areas.[34] But the diffusion of grammaticalization processes constitutes only a small part of the processes leading to metatypy, whereby speakers of the replica languages increasingly come to construe the world around them in the same way as speakers of the model language. Perhaps more common are processes leading to fixed collocations such as proverbial and idiomatic expressions. An impression of the kind of collocations involved is given by Ross (1996), where Waskia provided the model for Takia speakers, cf. table 5.2. Such replication patterns are characteristic of metatypy situations, even if they are not confined to them. Unfortunately, we cannot do justice to them here since they do not normally give rise to productive grammatical use patterns, which is the subject of the present work.

Table 5.3 *The main event schemas used for encoding comparative constructions*

Form of schema	Label of schema
X *is* Y *surpasses* Z	Action
X *is* Y *at* Z	Location
X *is* Y *from* Z	Source
X *is* Y *to* X	Goal
X *is* Y, Z *is not* Y	Polarity

See Heine 1997b: 112.

5.2.6   Africa as a macro-area: the comparative

The observations made in the previous section show that even in the case of proposed linguistic areas which have not been generally accepted to constitute areally defined units, grammaticalization areas are involved in some way or other. This also applies to some of the world's macro-regions, as can be demonstrated in this section with an example from Africa.

There are a number of linguistic properties that are widespread in Africa but uncommon outside Africa (see Greenberg 1959; 1983; Meeussen 1975; Gilman 1986); still, any attempt to define Africa as a linguistic area has been unsuccessful so far. Nevertheless, it is possible to argue that the African continent constitutes a grammaticalization area, as we will now try to show. Our concern here is with comparative constructions, more narrowly with the way the standard of comparison is encoded in comparative constructions of inequality (also called superior comparatives; see Stassen 1985; Heine 1997b). Cross-linguistically, there is only a small set of conceptual schemas that tend to be recruited to grammaticalize comparative constructions; these schemas are summarized in table 5.3. For exemplification of these event schemas, see Heine (1997b: 112–20). In principle, speakers of a given language may select any of these schemas to develop a new comparative construction, and in many languages, more than one schema has been grammaticalized. It would seem, however, that neighboring peoples are more likely to draw on the same schema than peoples living at some distance from one another. The result is that there are geographically defined regions where a preference for a specific kind of schema is preferred. Table 5.4 summarizes the results of a cross-linguistic survey of these constructions. Our interest here is with Africa as a macro-area, which exhibits a clear preference pattern: more than half of all African sample languages (56 percent) have grammaticalized the Action Schema to comparative constructions. But perhaps more significantly, almost two-thirds (65 percent) of all languages of the worldwide sample in table 5.4 having made use of this

Table 5.4 *Event schemas serving as sources for the grammaticalization of
comparatives of inequality*

Source Schema	Europe	Asia	Africa	The Americas	Indian/Pacific Ocean	Total
Action	0	4	13	1	2	20
Location	0	4	3	4	1	12
Source	0	18	4	9	1	32
Goal	1	0	3	3	0	7
Polarity	0	0	0	10	10	20
Total	14	26	23	28	18	109

Sample: 109 languages of worldwide distribution; Stassen 1985; Heine 1997b: 128.
This table differs slightly from that presented in Heine (1997b: 128) in that Classical Arabic and
Biblical Hebrew are treated here as "Asian languages," which means that, instead of a category
"Africa and Middle East" we now have a category "Africa," which includes only languages that
have been spoken natively in Africa for at least one millennium.

schema are spoken in Africa. There is some variation in the exact shape this
schema may take, the main ones being either [X *is* Y *surpasses* Z], as in (14a),
or [X *surpasses* Z (*at*) Y-*ness*], illustrated in (14b). What is common to all of
them is that the standard of comparison is presented by means of a verb meaning
'surpass,' 'defeat,' 'exceed,' 'pass,' and the like.

(14) Swahili and Hausa comparatives

    a. Swahili (Bantu, Niger-Congo)
      Nyumba yako ni kubwa kushinda yangu.
      house   your be big   to.defeat mine
      'your house is bigger than mine'

    b. Hausa (Chadic, Afroasiatic; Wolff 1993: 221)
      naa fi   Muusaa wàayoo.
      I   surpass Moses   cleverness
      'I am smarter than Moses.'

This areal distribution sets the African continent apart from the rest of the
world – to the extent that one can predict with a certain degree of probability
that if one finds any language that has a conventionalized comparative construction of inequality built on the Action Schema then that will be an African
language and, conversely, given any sub-Saharan African language, most likely
that language will use the Action Schema as its main, or one of its main,
comparative constructions. Note that genetic relationship can be ruled out as a
contributing factor since this grammaticalization area includes languages of all
four genetic stocks or phyla to be found in Africa.

To conclude, while grammaticalization areas may consist of less than a handful of languages, they may as well include more than one thousand languages, as in the present example. The hypothesis that sub-Saharan Africa constitutes a grammaticalization area is supported by the following facts:

(a) Nearly all of these languages have undergone the same grammaticalization process whereby a source schema of the form [X *is* Y *surpasses* Z] has been recruited to develop a comparative construction of inequality.
(b) This grammaticalization is rarely found outside Africa.
(c) Since it cuts across genetically unrelated languages, being found in all four African language families, the only reasonable explanation is that it is due to areal diffusion.

5.3   Conclusions

Discussion in this chapter was meant to show that sprachbund, metatypy, and grammaticalization area are related notions: all three are the result of contact among languages and they can be described in terms of areal-linguistic isoglosses. There are differences, however. First, compared to sprachbunds, the scope of grammaticalization areas is severely limited, being restricted to grammatical replication (see section 5.1). Second, all sprachbunds that we are familiar with are based at least to some extent on the presence of grammaticalization areas while the opposite does not apply: there are many grammaticalization areas that do not involve sprachbunds. And third, the two differ also with regard to the potential they offer for historical reconstruction. While sprachbunds tend to be the result of an amalgamation of different historical processes, usually involving multilateral processes of transfer, grammaticalization areas are more likely to be due to one specific historical cause; hence, they are more readily accessible for historical analysis.

But perhaps the main difference is the following: Whereas sprachbunds tend to be defined without reference to regularities of linguistic change, grammaticalization areas are essentially the result of unidirectional processes based on cognitive principles underlying grammaticalization. Accordingly, neither their development nor their synchronic structure is the arbitrary result of areal forces of some kind or other; rather, it can be described and understood with reference to these principles.

6   Limits of replication

Grammatical replication has been described in this book as an essentially uniform process, being shaped by universal processes of grammaticalization. However, this description ignores the fact that this process is constrained by a number of additional factors generally characterizing situations of language contact. In the present chapter we will deal with these factors, and we will adopt a wider perspective with a view to defining the environment in which replication takes place and to pointing out constraints characterizing the process. To this end, we deal in section 6.1 with equivalence – a notion that is widely held to be a major outcome of contact-induced language change, and we will show that this notion is more complex than has hitherto been assumed. In section 6.2 we will discuss a wide range of factors that have been said to constrain or enhance replication, and section 6.3 will be concerned with the question of how the transfer of forms or form–meaning units interacts with replication, and what the role of written discourse is in this process. Another possible limit of grammatical replication is the subject of section 6.4, which is devoted to the question of how replication relates to situations of language obsolescence. Finally, the distinction between internal and external constraints will be looked into in section 6.5, where we will relate contact-related change to language change not affected by language contact.

6.1   On equivalence

Equivalence is a central notion in most works on language contact.[1] In section 3.1.2 we raised the question of what exactly the nature of the categories is for which equivalence is sought by speakers in situations of language contact or, in more general terms, what constrains contact-induced language use. Grammatical replication means essentially that speakers aim at establishing some kind of equivalence relation between use patterns and categories of different languages. We proposed in chapter 1 (section 1.1) to use the term equivalence (or isomorphism) in a fairly unspecific way for corresponding structures of different languages (or dialects) that are conceived and/or described as being the same. This definition raises a number of problems which are the subject of the present section.

Theoretically, an equivalence relation can be the result of a number of different factors, but the cases that we are concerned with here relate exclusively to equivalence as resulting from established cases of grammatical replication. Accordingly, we apply the term equivalence to situations where a use pattern or category in one language is conceived or described as being the same as a corresponding use pattern or category in another language (see section 4.1.4).

A paradigm example of equivalence can be seen in the fact that in situations of language contact, speakers tend to treat infinitive markers in one language as being equivalent to markers of nominalization in another language. For example, Johanson (1998: 332) observes that combinatorial properties of the Persian infinitive are often copied onto the Southern Azerbaijanian verbal noun in -*mAK*. Similarly, speakers of Basque used their nominalizer -*tze* as an equivalent of the Gascon infinitive marker in developing a progressive aspect on the model of Gascon (Haase 1992: 92–3), and van Hamel (1912: 279) observes that the verbal noun in Irish is part of the verb, corresponding to the infinitive and gerund in Irish English. More examples of equivalence were given throughout this book, in particular in section 4.1.4, showing that speakers restructured the grammatical categories of the replica language to be semantically and morphosytactically equivalent to corresponding categories of the model language.

However, things are more complex. What we call equivalence relation has been described in a number of different ways, variously referred to with terms such as "connection," "correspondence," "isogrammatism," "mutual isomorphism," or "similarity." As these terms suggest, the term equivalence or equivalence relation may refer to a range of different things.

6.1.1   Structural isomorphism vs. translational equivalence

A question that is central to the present work is the following: How can instances of equivalence be identified or defined, that is, how is it possible to determine whether category Mx of the model language M is equivalent to category Rx of the replica language R? On the basis of observations made in the preceding chapters there are two main ways in which equivalence across languages has been defined (see section 1.1), and we will now look at each of them in more detail.

6.1.1.1 Structural isomorphism

One way concerns the linguist's theoretical construct of categories and their cross-linguistic compatibility. This is, for example, what Gołab refers to with the term "isogrammatism," which he defines thus:

An isogrammatism may be defined as the occurrence in two or more languages of an identical structural pattern according to which the morphological material of each language is united to form [. . .] words, word groups, and sentences. (Gołab 1959: 415)

Isogrammatism does not necessarily presuppose language contact, even though Gołab (1959) uses it to determine contact-induced equivalences between Arumanian and Macedonian in particular and across Balkan languages in general. Following Aikhenvald (2002: 59), we call this (structural) isomorphism, the outcome of areal diffusion, where there is a one-to-one correspondence in the morphosyntactic and/or semantic structure of a category between two languages in contact.

The following example from Spanish as spoken in Ecuador illustrates that structural isomorphism is not restricted to morphosyntax and meaning (Hurley 1995: 48–9). Quichua of Ecuador has grammaticalized its verb *carana* 'give' to a modal auxiliary with the main verb encoded in the gerund form, the function of the modal being to soften requests (translatable in English by *do me the favor of*); cf. (1). This grammaticalization has been replicated in Spanish spoken in the Ecuadorian Sierra, as illustrated in (2). Isomorphism in this case extends beyond the morphosyntactic and semantic structure: it also concerns the lexical cooccurrence restrictions characterizing both the model and the replica languages, in that, for example, the main verb must be transitive and the construction is rarely used when the transitive verb indicates benefit for the speaker.

(1) Ecuadorian Quichua (Quechuan; Hurley 1995: 48)

        Papa- cu-   ta   randi- shpa cara- hua- y.
        potato- DIM- ACC buy- ing give- me- IMP
        'Do me the favor of buying me some potatoes.'

(2) Spanish of the Ecuadorian Sierra (Hurley 1995: 48)

        Déme   haciendo un sanduche.
        (give.me making   a   sandwich)
        'Do me the favor of making me a sandwich.'

Whether structural isomorphism is a useful notion to describe equivalence relations depends on the criteria used to define it and on the purpose the term is meant to serve. In either case, there is the following problem inherently associated with this term. As we observed throughout this work, equivalence is achieved typically by replication, which again tends to be based on grammaticalization. The complexity that this strategy entails was apparent in our depiction of it in section 3.1.2 (2). It suggests that, rather than establishing equivalence between two languages by equating a category x of language M (= Mx) with a similar category of language R (= Rx), speakers tend to create an equivalent category by grammaticalizing category y of language R. This means that, rather than relating two categories to one another, speakers relate a category (Mx) in one language to a process (Ry > Rx) in another language – the result being the asymmetric formula of (3).

(3) Mx = [Ry > Rx].

The complexity inherently associated with this strategy is further aggravated by the fact that grammaticalization entails a development that extends over a long time; accordingly, structural isomorphism will refer to different things at different stages of the development.

We may illustrate this complexity with an example (for a second example, see further down). Some of the cases of replication that we have discussed concern adpositions in the model language, that is, functional categories. Now, the most common way to replicate an adposition (preposition or postposition) is by way of grammaticalizing a lexical category, using a body-part term or some other relational noun in possessive construction (cf. English *in back of, in front of*). As with other grammaticalization processes, the development from noun phrase to adposition takes generations, if not centuries, to be accomplished. This means that the speakers who initiate this development can achieve hardly more than establishing some kind of equivalence between a functional category, an adposition, in the model language (= Mx) and a lexical category of the replica language (Ry) that in some of its uses serves as an equivalent of Mx. It also means that for these speakers, and presumably also for subsequent generations of speakers, replication is unlikely to achieve structural isomorphism – that is, a situation where the model and the replica categories are in any way morphosyntactically alike (see below).

6.1.1.2 Translational equivalence

But there is an alternative way of describing equivalence relations – one that is not associated with the kind of problems that structural isomorphism is. This is what we call translational equivalence, which is defined on the basis of speakers' behavior, that is, with reference to what speakers in situations of contact conceive of and treat as equivalent use patterns or categories. The most obvious procedure to reconstruct such behavior is by studying translational work. Accordingly, if we find that speakers regularly translate category Mx of language M by using category Rx in language R, then we will say that this is an instance of translational equivalence between Mx and Rx – irrespective of the grammatical structure of the categories concerned. While the exact role of translational equivalence as a motivating force for grammatical change in situations of language contact is still not well understood, there is evidence to suggest that it provides one of the primary motivations in situations of communicative stress, where people readily accept that there are distinct advantages in adapting the use patterns of one language to those of another.

Accordingly, translational equivalence can be determined with reference to translational conventions obtaining between the model and the replica language. Clearest instances of translational equivalence can be expected to be found in cases of metatypy (see section 5.1.2). But unfortunately, in none of the metatypic or other kinds of contact areas that we have discussed, is more substantial information on translational habits or conventions available, and we therefore had to rely on casual observations made by the authors concerned. Two examples, both involving language contact between Irish English (Anglo-Irish or Hiberno-English) and the Celtic language Irish (Gaelic), may illustrate the kind of evidence that is used to determine translational equivalence. The first case concerns correspondence between an English auxiliary verb and an Irish suffix, which Bliss describes thus:

It is a striking fact that there is an almost complete correspondence between the uses of the dependent ending *-(e)ann* in early Modern Irish and the uses of the auxiliary *do* in English: every use of the auxiliary *do* in English requires the use of the dependent form in early Modern Irish [. . .] It seems inevitable that, during the formative period of Hiberno-English, an Irish-speaker learning English would establish, no doubt unconsciously, a connection between the Irish ending *-(e)ann* and the English auxiliary *does* [. . .] Similarly, when the ending *-(e)ann* was extended into the consuetudinal present of the substantive verb, the auxiliary *does* would naturally be extended into the English substantive verb [. . .]. (Bliss 1972: 78–9)

The second case relates to clause subordination. That speakers of the replica language may equate their dependent finite clauses with verbal nouns of the model language is suggested by the following observations made by van Hamel on equivalence strategies employed by speakers of Irish English on the model of Irish:

Any dependent clause in English may be translated into Gaelic by a verbal noun. The verbal noun is a part of the verb, corresponding with the English infinitive and gerund; still it has more of a substantive than of a verb, as its object is always put in the genitive. In idiomatic Anglo-Irish we find the infinitive, where in Gaelic the verbal noun would have been used, and therefore an infinitive is frequently met with instead of a dependent clause. (van Hamel 1912: 279)

With regard to the second example, van Hamel discusses the following case, where Irish English speakers use an infinitival construction as an equivalent of what would be expressed by means of a finite complement clause in English varieties not affected by contact with Irish:

(4) Irish English (van Hamel 1912: 279)

      It's a pity you not to have left him where he was lying.

Note also that Aikhenvald (2002: 250) observes with reference to the Vaupés region of northwest Amazonia that grammatical replication is "due to a need to achieve 'quick and ready' full intertranslatability between Tariana and Tucano." Extreme cases of translational equivalence can be expected in situations which Matras (1998a: 298) refers to as fusion, where speakers no longer clearly differentiate between operations in their L1 and their L2, that is, where there is "a nonseparation of the two systems" (see also Nadkarni 1975).

That the notions structural isomorphism and translational equivalence may refer to different phenomena can be illustrated with the following case of inter-translatability, involving language contact between East Tucanoan languages on the one hand and the North Arawak language Tariana on the other:

Thus, categories which are expressed within one grammatical word in East Tucanoan languages tend to develop a functionally equivalent grammatical morpheme in Tariana – it often happens that where East Tucanoan languages use a suffix, Tariana uses a clitic recently developed from an independent item. And categories that are expressed with several grammatical words in East Tucanoan tend to acquire an analytic expression in Tariana (which originally expressed them morphologically). (Aikhenvald 2002: 60)

Accordingly, whereas structural isomorphism relates primarily to the correspondences between morphosyntactic or semantic structures, e.g. tense prefixes in language M corresponding to tense prefixes in language R, translational equivalence may concern quite different structures, such as an East Tucanoan suffix correponding to a clitic in Tariana, an English auxiliary verb being equivalent to an Irish suffix, or an English dependent clause to a verbal noun in Irish. Both notions, structural isomorphism and translational equivalence, are used in the relevant literature but, unfortunately, in many of the cases analyzed in this work there is no conclusive evidence as to which of the two was involved.

In concluding, mention should be made that grammatical replication does not necessarily lead to a one-to-one translational equivalence between the model and the replica language. There are examples to suggest that speakers may replicate a category from another language but not necessarily the internal structure of that category. In the course of nearly a millennium of contact with German, speakers of the Slavic language Sorbian have acquired incipient categories of definite and indefinite articles on the model of German by grammaticalizing, respectively, a demonstrative and the numeral 'one' (see section 2.4.1). While there can be hardly any doubt that the emergence of these articles in Sorbian was influenced by contact with German, the way theses articles are used in Sorbian is different from that characterizing article use in German, that is, the former cannot be described as being a literal translation from German (see Nau 1995: 121).

Translational equivalence as a process?   As we would predict on the basis of the mechanism characterizing contact-induced grammaticalization sketched in section 3.1.2 (2), establishing translational equivalence can involve a fairly complex procedure. Consider the following case involving translations from German into Estonian. German has fully conventionalized indefinite and definite articles while the Finnic language Estonian has no articles. Looking at six translations of the ode *An die Freude* by the German poet Friedrich Schiller into Estonian, Lehiste (1999) found that the translators tended to use the Estonian numeral *üks* 'one' as an equivalent for the German indefinite article *ein*, and the Estonian demonstrative *see* as an equivalent for the German definite articles *der/die/das* – fully in accordance with universal principles determining the grammaticalization of articles[2] (Heine & Kuteva 2002). In the case of the indefinite article, German provided a convenient model for replication in that the German article is historically derived from and synchronically identical with the numeral *ein* 'one' – hence, this case might be suggestive of replica grammaticalization[3] (see section 3.1.3) or polysemy copying (section 3.2).

The situation is more complex in the case of the definite article. While the German definite article has a few uses as a demonstrative, it is unlikely that these uses provided a sufficient model for replication by a demonstrative in Estonian; more likely therefore we are dealing with a case of (incipient) ordinary grammaticalization from demonstrative to article uses (section 3.1.2). Assuming that this interpretation is correct, this would mean that translational equivalence did not concern equating a category of the model with a category of the replica language but rather a category of the model (= the German definite article) with a grammaticalization process in the replica language (= from demonstrative to article uses of Estonian *see*).

This Estonian example may also illustrate a problem that arises due to the asymmetry inherent in the formula $Mx = [Ry > Rx]$ of (3). Note that not all of the translators did make use of the grammaticalization strategy in order to establish equivalence between German and Estonian: one of them (Sepp) left the German indefinite article untranslated. This suggests that that translator differed in his conceptualization of German–Estonian equivalences, presumably maintaining that leaving indefiniteness unexpressed is more in accordance with the meaning of the Estonian text than taking a weakly grammaticalized equivalent that is more likely to be associated by Estonian speakers with its non-grammaticalized meaning as a numeral than with indefiniteness.

6.1.2   *Structural isomorphism as a diagnostic for reconstruction?*

Structural isomorphism between neighboring but genetically unrelated (or only remotely related) languages is a factor that is suggestive of areal, i.e. contact-induced relationship, and in some way we have used it as a diagnostic for reconstructing areal relationship (see section 1.4). However, as the preceding observations suggest, isomorphism is not really a foolproof parameter for reconstruction. We noted above that equivalence between languages in contact is frequently not a matter of structurally identical or similar categories; rather, it tends to be based on an asymmetric formula $Mx = [Ry > Rx]$, in that the model language provides a category Mx which is replicated by drawing on a process whereby speakers grammaticalize category Ry to Rx. Accordingly, genuine structural isomorphism between languages in contact is not necessarily the expected case; more likely, there is a full-fledged category in the model language corresponding to a less grammaticalized structure in the replica language (see section 3.4.5).

The following example, relating to the possessive perfect in Bulgarian, illustrates what this observation means with reference to the reconstruction of language change. A number of authors have pointed out that one of the most interesting issues regarding this category is why it arose in a language that already had a perfect (i.e. a 'be-perfect; see Georgiev 1957 [1976], Lindstedt 1994). On the traditional account, this question has been related to both language-external and language-internal factors. When it comes to the language-external factor, it has been observed that the possessive perfect of Bulgarian has analogues in neighboring, or geographically near languages, e.g. Macedonian, Romanian, Greek, Albanian (Georgiev 1957 [1976]). Even though the geographical presence of possessive perfect structures is so dense all around the Bulgarian perfect, on the traditional view, the areal/geographical factor for the genesis and evolution of the Bulgarian perfect has been discarded. Thus in his seminal study of the possessive perfect in Bulgarian, Georgiev (1957: 46) recognizes language contact only as a factor with a "certain (weak) influence." In the same work, he hastens to add that actually it would be very implausible to assume that the Bulgarian possessive perfect has evolved under the influence of some other language. The solution he comes up with is that this grammatical category is the result of a purely language-internal process. What is most arresting in his argumentation is the reason why he proposes a language-internal rather than a language-external explanation: the difference in degree of grammaticalization between the possessive perfect in Bulgarian and that found in the languages with which Bulgarian is in contact. Thus Georgiev excludes language contact with Macedonian as a factor for the development of the Bulgarian possessive perfect due to the fact that there are substantial differences between the two: the Macedonian perfect can be freely used with both transitive and intransitive verbs whereas the Bulgarian possessive perfect is not typically associated with intransitives. With respect to the language contact between Bulgarian on the one hand, and Greek and Rumanian on the other, he writes this off as an explanation, too, arguing that if the Bulgarian possessive perfect "were borrowed ready-made from Greek or Romanian, then it would have had the meaning of the Greek one or the Romanian one, and as we saw, the meaning of a tense [i.e. the perfect;

a.n.] of this syntagm is only in the process of appearing/emerging" (Georgiev 1957: 46).

Georgiev thus takes the fact that the Bulgarian possessive perfect is less grammaticalized than the possessive perfect in Macedonian, Greek, or Rumanian as evidence to rule out a hypothesis in terms of contact-induced relationship. The logic behind this argumentation is this: if it is not possible to observe a wholesale transfer of a grammatical category from one language M to another language R, then language contact should be ruled out as the explanation for the genesis of this category in R. The consequence of this kind of reasoning is the conclusion that if it is not language contact then it has got to be independent language-internal development that can explain the appearance of the Bulgarian possessive perfect. On the basis of our findings on grammatical replication, and in particular on the basis of the replication formula Mx = [Ry > Rx], however, the Bulgarian possessive perfect would qualify as a paradigm candidate of a replicated category (see especially section 3.4.5). This example suggests that the reconstruction of contact-related language change needs to be based on findings of grammaticalization, and some of these findings are likely to be at variance with commonly held assumptions on linguistic transfer across languages.

6.1.3   Evolutional equivalence

Equivalence has been described both as a product and as a process. To distinguish the two, we refer to the former as (synchronic) equivalence and to the latter as evolutional equivalence. This distinction corresponds fairly closely to that made by Gołab (1959: 415, 416) between isogrammatism (or calquing) and historically determined isogrammatism (see below). Evolutional equivalence means that two (or more) languages have undergone the same process as a result of language contact, leading to the rise of the same use pattern or grammatical category in the languages concerned. It relates to but is not identical to what Matras (1998b) calls mutual isomorphism, which he defines in the following way:

We [. . .] suggest the term *mutual isomorphism* to describe the process by which languages in contact stimulate one another to generalize iconic structures, thereby promoting structural compatibility among them. (Matras 1998b: 90)

A paradigm case of evolutional equivalence can be seen in what we described in section 3.1.3 as replica grammaticalization: speakers of the replica language (R) initiate a grammaticalization process, developing an existing category (Ry) into a grammatical category (Rx), in the same way as speakers of the model language (M) are assumed to have done earlier (My > Mx), as depicted in (5).

(5) The structure of replica grammaticalization (where ">" = develops
    into, and "≫" = is replicated as)

$$My > Mx \gg Ry > Rx$$

Thus, evolutional equivalence has two components: it includes at the same time
a process (y > x) and the synchronic product (Rx = Mx) of that process. The
following example, based on Johanson (1992: 251), illustrates the mechanism
concerned. Turkish (= M) has a construction of predicative possession [X has
Y] (= Mx) derived from what is technically known as the Genitive Schema [X's
Y exists] (Heine 1997a), that is, an existential construction having a genitival
phrase as its subject noun phrase (= My). Speakers of the Iranian language Tajik
(= R) appear to have replicated the grammaticalization process from Genitive
Schema to predicative possession of Turkish, e.g. Tajik *puläm häy* (money.my
is) = Turkish *param var* 'I have money.' Thus, Tajik and Turkish exhibit evolutional equivalence in that they have undergone the same grammaticalization
process (= y > x), resulting in what is portrayed by Johanson as synchronically
equivalent possessive constructions (= x), that is, in structural isomorphism.
The reader is referred to section 3.1.3 for more examples of this general process.

The process is more complex when speakers of the replica language choose
a channel of grammaticalization other than the one they observe in the model
language, or when the latter does not provide a model for grammaticalization
(see section 3.1.2). In this case there is synchronic equivalence but no evolutional equivalence. The following example illustrates such a situation. Italian
has a kind of progressive construction of the type *sta arrivando* 'is arriving'
corresponding to, but being less grammaticalized than, the English progressive construction. Breu (1992: 117) argues that speakers of Molise Croatian
in Molise, southeastern Italy, are trying to replicate this construction by using
their adverb *sa* 'now' frequently whenever Italian speakers use the progressive
construction, equating (6a) with (6b) of their Slavic language:

(6) (Breu 1992: 117)

    a. Italian   sta arrivando 'he is coming'
    b. Molisean Croatian sa gre   'he is coming' (lit.: 'now he comes')

Temporal adverbs for 'now' occasionally give rise to progressive aspects
(Bybee, Perkins & Pagliuca 1994), but the grammaticalization process leading to the Molise Croatian use pattern[4] is clearly different from the one that
gave rise to the Italian progressive construction. Thus, according to the description proposed by Breu (1992), we are dealing with an instance of evolutional
non-equivalence but synchronic, translational equivalence, in that the meanings
of the two constructions are treated as equivalent.

This example from Molise Croatian is suggestive of what we described in
section 3.1.2 as ordinary grammaticalization since Italian did not provide a

model for replication.[5] But it is not always possible to establish whether evolutional equivalence (or replica grammaticalization) or ordinary grammaticalization is involved (for ways of distinguishing the two, see section 3.1; see also our discussion in section 3.3 on the future tense in varieties of Pennsylvania German and Yiddish).

6.1.4   Semantic vs. morphosyntactic eqivalence

The data we surveyed in the preceding chapters suggest that virtually any semantic, morphosyntactic, or morphophonological structure can serve as a model for establishing equivalence relations. Nevertheless, these data also suggest that there is a preference: in establishing equivalences across languages, speakers appear to draw preferably (though not always) on semantic/functional rather than on syntactic or other structural parameters. That this is so has been pointed out by a number of students of language contact, who have come up with observations such as the following, made by Boretzky in his work on transfers from substrate languages to creoles: "Im Transfer wird dabei in der Regel die Funktion recht genau kopiert, während sich die formale Realisierung eher lose an die Substratstruktur anschließt." [In the transfer, the function is copied very precisely while the formal realization follows that of the substrate structure fairly loosely.] (Boretzky 1986: 24). We have seen a number of examples in the preceding chapters to substantiate this point. A perhaps somewhat unusual example is provided by Hurch (1989: 14ff.) relating to Spanish-Basque contacts, where it was the extension of the function rather than the structure of Spanish prepositions that was replicated in Basque (see section 4.3.1). The replication of the instrumental function by Basque speakers led to a transfer from three Spanish prepositions to three Basque case suffixes – a change that contributed to semantic equivalence between the two languages but did not affect the morphosyntax of the replica language (except for the decline of the instrumental case suffix).

The following examples also demonstrate that grammatical replication serves primarily the establishment of semantic rather than morphosyntactic equivalence. As is described in detail in Heine and Kuteva (forthc.), western and central European languages have developed a possessive perfect (or 'have'-perfect), by grammaticalizing a possession schema [X has Y]) to one expressing a verbal aspect ([X has done Y]). The evidence available suggests that the Celtic language Breton has replicated this construction by using the French possession schema ([X has Y]) as a model. But the Celtic equivalent of a possession schema differs drastically from that of French – it involves what is referred to by Heine (1997b) as the Dative Schema, which takes the form [Y is to/for X]. Now, rather than translating the French schema element by element into Breton, Breton speakers relied on their own possession schema as a whole in

230 Limits of replication

developing a periphrastic perfect. In this way, a Breton possessive structure of the kind *am euz* ('is to me') 'I have' gave rise to a perfect construction, as in *gwelet am euz* 'I have seen' (Vendryes 1937: 87, 88).

These are not isolated instances, as is suggested by the situation in some languages located at the eastern periphery of the Standard Average European area, e.g. in Slavic languages (see Heine & Kuteva forthc.). Unlike Breton, Standard Russian has not grammaticalized a possession schema to a 'have'- perfect; still, there appear to be occasional replications of this process. Now, the predominant schema used in Russian for predicative possession is what is technically referred to as the Location Schema ([Y is at X]; Heine 1997a); an example is provided in (7a). Accordingly, in such replications it is not the Standard Average European schema [X has Y] that is used for replication; rather, it is the Location Schema that is recruited, with peculiar results for participant marking; cf. (7b).

(7) Russian (Timberlake 1976; Jacob 1994: 49)

    a. U menja   mašina.
      at me.GEN car.NOM
      'I have a car.'

    b. Primus ne u menja   potuš-en,   ješče u babuški.
      Primus not   atmy.GEN switched.off rather at grandmother.GEN
      'It is not I who has switched off "Primus", rather (it is) grandmother.'

While Standard Russian is still at an incipient stage of grammaticalization, northern Russian has gone a considerable step further: possibly under the influence of northern Germanic languages (Breu 1996: 31),[6] it has used the Location Schema as a conceptual equivalent to grammaticalize its possessive construction to a fairly "mature" perfect not unlike that found in languages of the Standard Average European type. Characteristics of such a perfect are that its use is not restricted to transitive main verbs and animate agents, that is, it can also be used with intransitive verbs and inanimate agents – characteristics that are also found in northern Russian, as the following examples suggest.

(8) Northern Russian (Timberlake 1976)

    a. U   menja   odna zima   xožena.
      PREP me.GEN one   winter.NOM.F.SG walked.PART.F.SG
      'By me one winter was walked (to school).'[7]

    b. U   menja   zabyto,   a Stepanida pomnit.
      PREP me.GEN forgotten   remembers
      'By me it's been forgotten, but Stepanida remembers.'[8]

Like the Breton example just looked at, the present example suggests that contact-induced replication of grammatical categories (assuming that this northern Russian example is an instance of it) involves neither literal semantic translation nor morphosyntactic equivalence; rather, it is the overall conceptual schema that appears to have been replicated – in the present case a possession schema.

In fact conceptual schemas tend to be used to establish equivalence between languages in contact, as can also be illustrated with the following example from Pipil, an Aztecan language of El Salvador. Pipil has been strongly influenced by Spanish, and one effect of this influence is that Pipil developed a new future tense category on the model of Spanish (Campbell 1987: 267–8; Harris and Campbell 1995: 148–9). Pipil has future suffixes but they are extremely rare today, unused and almost unknown for the most part. Instead, Pipil speakers tend to use a 'go-to'-future which these authors attribute to the influence of the local Spanish de-allative future (*lo voy a hacer* 'I'm going to do it'). However, while Pipil speakers have established an equivalence relation with Spanish by replicating the concept of a schema of directed motion [X goes to Y], they have not adopted the Spanish morphosyntax, where the main verb is presented in a non-finite form as an allative/locative complement of the auxiliary; rather, they use a serial schema of the form [X goes X does Y] (see Heine 1993: 37–9), where both the main verb and the auxiliary are inflected for and agree in person, cf. (9).

(9) Pipil (Aztecan, Uto-Aztecan; Campbell 1987: 268)

    ti- yu- t ti- yawi- t   ti- pa: xa: lua- t   ne: pa ka ku: htan.
    we- go- PL we- go-   PL we- walk-   PL there in woods
    'We are going to go take a walk there in (the) woods.'

Overall we appear to be dealing with instances of evolutional equivalence between conceptual structures, while morphosyntactic change is an epiphenomenal result of this process. Still, this process can have substantial morphosyntactic consequences. For example, the contact-induced grammaticalization of concrete, referential nouns to adpositions may have the effect that new morphosyntactic classes evolve; the reader is referred to our examples from Pipil and Takia (see section 3.1.2), where new paradigms of prepositions (in Pipil) or postpositions (in Takia) emerged.

To conclude, it is semantic equivalence that appears to be the primary goal of speakers replicating material from another language. As we pointed out above, however, there may be other goals as well, such as replicating morphological or syntactic patterns characterizing the model language.

6.1.5   *Replicating polysemous categories*

A special problem of grammatical replication concerns cases where the model category has a range of different meanings but where there is no category in the replica language exhibiting a corresponding kind of grammatical polysemy. The following example, relating to language contact in western Kenya and discussed in more detail in section 3.1.2 (see Dimmendaal 2001b), appears to present such a case. Bantu languages are known for their rich paradigms of verbal derivational extensions marked by suffixes. There is nothing comparable in the Nilotic language Luo or its closest relatives, the Southern Lwoo languages of Uganda and the Sudan: verbal derivation is limited, mainly involving internal morphology in the verb root. One particularly productive Bantu derivational extension, commonly called the applied suffix *-id-, expresses a wide range of functions, such as benefactive, directional, and instrumental, but has no semantic equivalent in Luo. Now, apparently on the model of neighboring Bantu languages, Luo speakers have developed a set of what look like verbal enclitics or suffixes, expressing functions typically encoded by the Bantu applied suffix *-id- ('for, to, with reference to, on behalf of'). Luo speakers used the prepositions ne (or ni) benefactive, e locative, and gi instrumental to develop verbal enclitics or suffixes. What this would seem to suggest is that in order to establish an equivalence relation with the polysemous category of the Bantu model languages, Luo speakers grammaticalized three different forms in the same direction, namely from prepositions to verbal clitics or affixes, jointly corresponding to the main meanings of the Bantu category.

6.1.6   From equivalence to non-equivalence?

Establishing equivalence has the effect that structures become more readily compatible between languages in contact. This, however, is not always the case, as we will now demonstrate. Underlying contact-induced grammaticalization there is an attempt by speakers of the replica language to establish equivalence with a use pattern or grammatical category they find in the model language (see section 3.1.2). Not always, however, does this indeed lead to the establishment of equivalence. For example, in an attempt to replicate the second-person distinction of their Romance model languages between an informal/familiar (tu) and a formal/polite form (vos), Basque speakers eventually ended up with a situation where a distinction arose in the replica language that has no direct equivalent in the model languages (Haase 1992: 134).

An example of a different nature can be found in Molise Croatian, which has been strongly influenced by Italian (Breu 1996; see above). Molise Croatian has developed a progressive aspect by grammaticalizing the temporal adverb sa(d) 'now' to a progressive marker sa, e.g. sa gre 'he is coming' (see (6)). In doing so, Molisean speakers replicated a common Southern Italian use pattern consisting of the adverb mo 'now, instantly' plus finite verb, which has developed into a construction denoting a near future or an actual present situation (Breu 1996: 30, 36). But rather than being an exact semantic replica of the model construction, the Molisean construction has its semantic equivalent in the Standard Italian construction [*stare* + gerund], e.g. *sta arrivando* '(he) is coming.' The outcome of this process is that Molisean acquired a new aspect category for which it had no equivalent prior to language contact, but the strategy used was actually not designed for this purpose (see above).

Conceivably, such cases of equivalence mismatch are due to idiosyncratic historical developments. For example, the Basque development may be due to changes subsequent to grammaticalization (see Haase 1992: 134), and the Molise Croatian development can be related to a change in the contact situation whereby Molisean speakers gradually replaced Southern Italian by Standard Italian use patterns as a model. On the basis of the scanty information available, however, no reasonable generalization seems possible.

But it is also possible that grammatical replication, meant to achieve equivalence in a certain domain of grammar, can lead to non-equivalence in another domain. The following example, that we discussed earlier in section 4.1.4, suggests that such a situation could have arisen in the Vaupés region of northwest Amazonia. In East Tucanoan languages, inalienable (kinship) possession is expressed simply by juxtaposition, where the possessor precedes the possessee, e.g. Desano *igo pa-go* (she parent-F) 'her mother'. In the North Arawak language Tariana it is alienable possession that is marked by juxtaposition, e.g. *nuha tʃìinu* (I dog) 'my dog,' while inalienably possessed nouns require the indefinite prefix *i-* with non-pronominal possessors, e.g. *João i-ka: pi* (John INDF-hand) 'John's hand.' Intense contact between East Tucanoan languages and Tariana has the effect that there is now an ongoing process whereby younger and innovative Tariana speakers occasionally omit the indefinite prefix (e.g. *João ka: pi* 'John's hand'), thereby replicating the East Tucanoan inalienability pattern of juxtaposition and extending their pattern of alienable possession to inalienably possessed nouns (Aikhenvald 2002: 80–3). While this process is still in its initial stages, it could lead to a loss of the alienable–inalienable distinction in Tariana – a distinction that is consistently marked in both traditional Tariana and its East Tucanoan model languages. In other words, what is aimed at creating morphophonological isomorphism may well have the opposite effect, namely that of eliminating categorial isomorphism.

6.1.7   Conclusions

In the present section we have looked at a number of cases to illustrate the nature of equivalence. Our discussion suggests that this is a complex notion. We were confined to some kinds of equivalence that are commonly observed in grammatical replication or its products; they are summarized in (10).

(10) Kinds of equivalence (where M = model language, R = replica
language; x, y = use patterns or grammatical categories; ">" =
develops into, "≫" = is replicated as)

    a. Mx   = Rx   Structural or translational isomorphism
    b. Mx   = Ry > Rx Ordinary grammaticalization (see (3))
    c. My > Mx ≫ Ry > Rx Replica grammaticalization (see (5))

6.2   Some salient constraints

Grammatical replication does not take place in a vacuum, it is shaped by a
number of factors, and in the present section we will review the main factors
that influence, or have been claimed to influence, this process.

6.2.1   Possible typological constraints

A number of works have claimed that the particular structure of the languages
engaged in contact plays some role in establishing equivalence. Thus, it has been
argued that the grammaticalization of expressions for predicative possession
(e.g. *He has problems*) to possessive perfects (*He has gone*) mostly affected
languages disposing of a transitive (or quasi-transitive) lexical item for 'have'
and a morphological category of a past participle marked for gender, number,
and case – in fact, as a rule the possessive perfect has attained the highest
degree of grammaticalization in these languages (Dahl 1990: 7; Haspelmath
1998: 275; 2001: 1495). In a similar fashion, Haig (2001: 210–17) found in
his study of East Anatolia as a linguistic area that the official language Turkish
has influenced the minority languages of this area in different ways, where
structural compatibility played some role, contributing to a stronger influence
on the Kartvelian language Laz as opposed to a more limited influence on the
Iranian languages Kurmanjî and Zazaki (but see below).

This would suggest that typological dissimilarity between languages in contact is, or can be, an obstacle for contact-induced grammaticalization to happen. Thus, Vachek (1962) maintained that languages can borrow what is "in
harmony" with their "wants" and "needs" – whatever exactly these may be (see
Danchev 1988: 39) – and, in this tradition, Winford (2003: 98) concludes that
"the greater the congruence between syntactic structures in two languages in
contact, the greater the likelihood that one will replace the other." Danylenko
(2001: 260) goes one step further in arguing that typological similiarity is more
central in language contact than sociolinguistic parameters, that is, that "unless
the language is typologically ready for a particular change," social factors
cannot take effect (see also Aikhenvald 2002: 3).

The data that we were able to access do not allow for any generalizations
on this issue and we will leave it open to further research. But on the basis of

what we observed in chapters 3 and 4 it would seem that the views summarized above may be in need of qualification. For example, we saw that large-scale grammatical replication has taken place in spite of the fact that the languages involved in the relevant contact situations can be described as being clearly typologically distinct – the Basque-Spanish/Gascon and the Pipil-Spanish situations being cases in point. Furthermore, as we saw above, speakers of Breton and Northern Russian developed possessive perfects although they used morphosyntactic constructions that differ remarkably from those found in Standard Average European languages.

Haig's (2001: 212, 217) findings on contact-induced replication in the languages of East Anatolia suggest that these observations are not incompatible with one another. He observes that Turkish structural influence has been much stronger on the Kartvelian language Laz than on the Iranian languages Kurmanjî Kurdish and Zazaki, and he attributes this difference to the fact that Turkish shares a greater degree of structural compatibility with Laz than with the two Iranian languages. He admits, however, that structural incompatibility is no absolute obstacle for contact-induced change to happen since elsewhere Iranian languages (Tajik in particular) have moved structurally further towards Turkish, and he suggests that this could be due to "longer and more intense contact than has yet been the case in East Anatolia" (Haig 2001: 212).

A generalization of a different kind was proposed by Weinreich ([1953] 1964: 41). He argued that it is possible within limits to define which of the languages in contact will act as the model: it is the one that uses relatively free and invariant forms in its paradigm that serves as the model for imitation. On the basis of the data that we were able to access there is no clear evidence in support of this hypothesis, and the same conclusion was reached by Soper (1987: 410–12) when testing this hypothesis with data from language contact between Turkic and Iranian languages. For example, in the preceding chapters we were confronted with a number of cases where inflectional forms provided the model, replicated by means of other inflections or else by means of free forms (see, for example, section 4.3.1).

Nevertheless, there appear to be some linguistic factors that constrain what is replicated and how it is replicated. For example, which particular pathway is chosen for creating a grammatical category may be determined by what is available, that is, by the discourse-pragmatic use patterns and the morphosyntax that the replica language offers. As we saw in more detail in section 4.2, the Southern Nilotic language Kalenjin of Kenya has developed a set of tense markers on the model of neighboring Bantu languages; note that Bantu languages are well known for their richness in tense distinctions. To this end, Kalenjin has recruited temporal adverbs and grammaticalized them to verbal tense (proclitics and) prefixes (Dimmendaal 2001b). Now, adverbs are cross-linguistically not a very common source for the grammaticalization of tense categories (see Bybee, Perkins & Pagliuca 1994); that Kalenjin speakers nevertheless recruited them for this purpose appears to be due to the fact that this language commonly expresses distinctions of deictic time by placing adverbs of time before the verb phrase (or clause-finally). On the basis of this use pattern, grammaticalizing some of these adverbs to pre-verbal tense markers was presumably the most readily accessible means available to Kalenjin speakers to replicate the tense paradigms of the Bantu languages they were in contact with.

6.2.2   Drift

Another possible constraint of grammatical replication concerns the question of whether there are genetically motivated forces that delimit the kind of changes that may happen in situations of language contact. For example, if genetically related languages share the same grammatical structures then this may be due to a number of different factors, in particular to common inheritance, language contact, or chance. LaPolla (1994) argues that there is yet another factor – one that Sapir (1921: 150–5) referred to as drift. Languages of the same genetic stock, LaPolla maintains, may retain a similar worldview, leading to parallel grammaticalizations and metaphorical extensions of existing morphology, with the result that genetically related languages become structurally more similar. In Tibeto-Burman languages, LaPolla observes the same semantically based concept of grammatical relations, where the organization of discourse involves only semantic and pragmatic relations. This concept appears to channel what can be grammaticalized and what cannot; accordingly, he finds no grammaticalization of syntactic functions such as subject or direct object in these languages.

LaPolla (1994) discusses five kinds of parallel grammaticalization (not to be confused with paired grammaticalization; see section 1.4.3), that is, processes that appear to be uncommon or less common in other parts of the world but have occurred time and again in Tibeto-Burman languages, where none of these processes can be reconstructed back to Proto-Tibeto- Burman, the hypothetical ancestor language. For example, many of these languages distinguish what he calls the anti-ergative, an animate case role that might otherwise be interpreted as an actor but is something other than an actor. The anti-ergative markers cannot be reconstructed back to Proto-Tibeto-Burman; rather, they evolved more recently and independently as non-agent markers in different languages or groups of languages, frequently via the grammaticalization of allative or locative constructions.

Another possible instance of drift can be seen in the grammaticalization of interrogative sentences as relative clauses (see section 3.1.3). Worldwide, this process appears to be rare; in Indo-European languages, however, it is fairly widespread, to be found not only in Europe but also in other regions of the Indo-European world (as well as in languages that were in close contact with

Indo-European languages). While a number of these cases can be accounted for with reference to grammatical replication, as we saw in preceding chapters (e.g. section 3.1.3), areal diffusion is not a plausible hypothesis to explain why this process occurred, e.g. in Romance, Slavic, and Germanic languages on the one hand, and in Indo-Aryan languages of India and Pakistan on the other.

Aikhenvald observes that drift may also have contributed to the structural similarity characterizing East Tucanoan languages in northwestern Brazil, and her observations are presumably also relevant to a number of other contact areas in the world:

But since the East Tucanoan languages continue to be in contact, it is hard – if not impossible – to distinguish language convergence due to drift from convergence due to contact-induced isomorphism in morphosyntactic structures. (Aikhenvald 2002: 61)

Conceivably, Sapirian drift phenomena have also contributed to some other developments described in this book. In the absence of any more detailed information, however, the remarks made in this section are conjectural to some extent and we are not able to do justice to the phenomenon; what we may conclude with some degree of certainty, however, is that drift phenomena possibly do enhance grammatical replication but are in no way a prerequisite for it.

6.2.3   Sociolinguistic factors

Rather than linguistic characteristics, it has been argued, it is more likely that it is the particular sociolinguistic setting in which language contact takes place that determines the directionality of contact-induced linguistic transfer (see Thomason & Kaufman 1988; but see Aikhenvald 2002: 3). This raises the question of whether it is possible to predict on sociolinguistic grounds, for example, which will be the model and which the replica language in a given case.

A larger number of the cases we were concerned with are not very helpful in addressing this question, simply because there is no reliable information on the directionality of transfer or on the relevant sociolinguistic background. This applies in particular, but not only, to sprachbund-type situations such as the Balkans, where discussions on directionality have been notoriously controversial.[9] But there remain quite a number of cases where we know which direction replication took. Grossly speaking, there are two main types of settings characterizing contact-induced grammaticalization; we may refer to them, respectively, as L2>L1-replication and L1>L2-replication[10] – a distinction roughly corresponding to that proposed by Johanson (1992; 2000: 165–6; 2002a: 3) between adoption and imposition.

L2>L1-replication concerns in particular what Johanson refers to as dominated codes, not infrequently minority languages, acting as replica languages, while the models are major languages, or lingua francas, frequently but not necessarily being the official languages of the countries concerned (commonly referred to as "superstrate" languages) – that is, what Johanson calls dominant codes. Examples of this type of setting are provided, for example, by the following cases we discussed: Gascon/French/Spanish > Basque; Italian > Molisean Croatian; French > Breton; German > Sorbian, Kashubian, and Slovincian; Spanish > Pipil; Turkish > Laz; Persian > Irano-Turkic languages; or Tamil > Sri Lanka Portuguese and Sri Lanka Malay.

Another kind of L2>L1-replication concerns cases where there is no lingua-franca type of situation, but where there exists a situation of extensive asymmetrical bilingualism, with speakers of language R being fluent in language M, while the opposite does not apply, with the result that there is pronounced replication from M to R. An example is provided by Kannada – Konkani bilingualism in the coastal districts of North and South Kanara in the Indian State of Karnataka, where the Konkani-speaking Saraswat Brahmins are generally bilingual in Kannada but Kannada speakers hardly ever learn Konkani, the result being unilateral replication from Kannada to Konkani (Nadkarni 1975). Another example can be seen in the contact situation of the Vaupés region of northwest Amazonia, especially with reference to grammatical replication in the North Arawak language Tariana on the model of East Tucanoan languages in general and Tucano in particular. There was essentially no relationship of dominance diglossia between these languages, even though more recently Tucano, being spoken by a larger population and being promoted by outside agencies, is expanding at the expense of other languages of the Vaupés region, leading to a gradual obsolescence of these languages (Aikhenvald 2002: 265).

What these cases appear to have in common is that language contact has been going on for an extended period of time (see below), and the model language is widely used as the L2 by speakers of the replica language. Contact of this kind may lead to language shift from L1 to L2, as appears to be the case in the Vaupés example, though more often it does not.

In L1>L2-replication, languages that were acquired as second languages (L2) act as replica languages, while the first languages (L1), frequently referred to as "substrate" languages, serve as models for replication – see Johanson's notion imposition. The replica languages we were dealing with concern lingua francas, including pidgins and creoles such as Tok Pisin, Solomons Pijin, Bislama, Tayo and Sranan. The model languages are or were spoken natively; they are Austronesian, Papuan, West African Niger-Congo, and other languages.

Another case concerns Portuguese (L2) as a lingua franca in the Vaupés region of northwest Brazil, where the L2 Portuguese is the target of replication on the model of local Indian languages such as Tucano and Tariana (L1), leading to the emergence of new grammatical use patterns in the lingua franca. Aikhenvald summarizes the process thus: "The main characteristic of spontaneously produced discourse in Portuguese is an attempt to find an equivalent for grammatical distinctions found in the languages of the Vaupés. This makes the Indians' Portuguese in some ways richer than the standard language [. . .]" (Aikhenvald 2002: 313). But instances of L1>L2-replication do not appear to be confined to lingua francas, pidgins, and creoles; they can also be found in other kinds of situations where people use their first language to model new grammatical structures in their second language. The history of Irish English offers a number of examples. A frequently discussed case was presented in section 2.2, involving the "hot-news" perfect of Irish English, which can be assumed to be a replica of the corresponding Irish construction; another example concerns the cleft construction of Irish English, which appears to have been remodeled on the use patterns of Irish – to the extent, that the constructions in these two varieties are essentially identical but differ from those found in other varieties of English including Standard English (Harris 1991: 196–201).

From what we know about the history of the relevant cases of language contact it appears, first, that both kinds of replication involve gradual rather than abrupt, discontinuous processes (see also Mufwene 2001) but, second, that overall in L1>L2-replication contact-induced grammaticalization needs less time to evolve than in the case of L2>L1-replication. The boundary between the two types is, however, far from clear, especially since there are cases where one and the same language can act simultaneously as a model and a replica language. As we just saw, for example, Tariana acts both as replica language vis-à-vis East Tucanoan languages and as a model language vis-à-vis Portuguese, and Austronesian languages such as Tigak appear to have provided a model for replication in the lingua franca Tok Pisin, but Tok Pisin also served as a model for Tigak (Jenkins 2002). Furthermore, Basque has served as a replica language vis-à-vis its Romance neighbors Spanish, French, and Gascon (see, for example, Hurch 1989; Haase 1992; 1997) but, conversely, it has also acted as a model language for Spanish speakers in the Basque Country (Cárdenas 1995); see also Soper (1987) for similar observations on language contact between Turkic and Iranian languages.

While the distinction just described may be useful in determining the directionality of replication on the basis of sociolinguistic variables, we have not been able to discern any differences in the nature of the grammaticalization processes resulting from the two different settings: the same kinds of processes characterizing L2>L1-replication can also be found in L1>L2-replication, and vice versa.

6.2.4   Length of contact

It would seem that an ideal situation for grammatical replication, at least of the L2>L1 type (see above), is one that Nadkarni (1975: 681) characterizes as "intensive and extensive bilingualism with a certain time-depth," where "extensive" means that bilingualism is co-extensive with the entire speech community involved, while "intensive" means that that community uses both the model and the replica languages for a wide range of purposes in the course of normal, everyday interaction. However, such ideal situations do not appear to be extremely common.

Language contact of the kind looked at here relates as a rule to situations typically involving large-scale bilingualism among the linguistic communities concerned, or at least in one of the linguistic communities. And it also tends to involve a larger timespan, not infrequently extending over three to five centuries. For example, Molisean, a variety of the Slavic Croatian minority in Molise, southern Italy, has been strongly influenced by Italian (Breu 1996: 26–7) as a result of five centuries of language contact. The Slavic language Sorbian is spoken in Germany and has been affected by nearly a millennium of contact with German (Lötzsch 1969; 1996), and an equally extended timespan characterizes the history of language contact between Basque and Romance languages. In a similar fashion, contact between the Dravidian language Kannada and the Saraswat Brahmin dialect of the Indo-Aryan language Konkani, resulting in intensive grammatical replication, had a duration of at least four hundred years (Nadkarni 1975). Furthermore, language contact in Kupwar, located in the Sangli District of Maharashtra Province of India, has been described as an extreme case of mutual assimilation of languages, that is, of metatypy (see section 5.2.4; Gumperz & Wilson 1971). The languages involved belong to two genetic stocks, namely Indo-European (Urdu, Marathi) and Dravidian (Kannada, Telugu); Marathi and Kannada have been spoken in Kupwar for more than six centuries, and Urdu for at least three centuries. And as in the other cases just mentioned, contact-induced grammaticalization has played a not insignificant role.

Still, there are cases of long-term and intense language contact where grammatical replication appears to have played only a minor role. For example, the Daiso people of northeastern Tanzania originate from the central Kenyan highlands and appear to have reached their present territory early in the seventeenth century, and they now have a history of nearly four centuries of contact with the Tanzanian Bantu languages Shamba(l)a, Bondei, Swahili, and Digo in the course of which their language has been influenced in a number of ways by these languages. But on the basis of the description by Nurse (2000) it would seem that there are hardly any cases of contact-induced grammaticalization resulting from this contact situation.

Other examples are not hard to come by. For example, of the several thousand members of Montana Salish, an ethnic group of northwestern Montana, USA, fewer than seventy are fluent speakers of this Salishan language, and all of them have native fluency in English; still, apart from a few loanwords, some dating back to the nineteenth century, there is no detectable grammatical influence of English of any kind (Thomason 2003: 689). What this appears to suggest is that long-term language contact may but need not lead to massive grammatical replication.

There is also evidence to suggest that length of contact is not a decisive factor in inducing massive structural change in language-contact situations. That new typological profiles may evolve within a few generations of speakers can be shown with reference to situations of pidginization. A number of African-based pidgins, such as Sango, Lingala, Kituba, and some varieties of Swahili, are cases in point: as the evidence available suggests, they changed from "natural" languages to pidgins within a few decades. But, as the evidence provided by Bakker (2000) shows, new typological profiles, including contact-induced grammaticalization, can also arise in other kinds of situation within a fairly short period of time. A paradigm case is provided by the metatypy situation in Sri Lanka mentioned in section 5.1.2, where Sri Lanka Malay and Sri Lanka Portuguese were drastically restructured on the model of the Dravidian language Tamil within a timespan of no more than sixty years. What this suggests is that length of contact is a common but not a necessary factor in inducing grammatical replication.

6.2.5   Pidgins and creoles

Grammatical replication as described in this book appears to be a universal phenomenon, and the question arises whether there are any kinds of languages that would be a challenge to this assumption. Pidgins and creole languages are to quite some extent the product of language contact and it comes as no surprise that the study of these languages has served as a basis for generalizations on mechanisms of contact-induced language change and for proposing models to account for this change. We have discussed a number of examples from pidgins and creoles in the preceding chapters; still, it may seem surprising that these languages did not figure more prominently in the present work. While research on these languages has received considerable attention especially in the course of the last two decades, resulting in an enormous body of both sociolinguistic and linguistic data, there is only a limited number of documented cases of language change that allow for an uncontroversial reconstruction of grammatical replication; most of the data available concern cases that are open to multiple diachronic interpretations and have been the subject of not infrequently mutually exclusive interpretations. This applies in particular to creole genesis, which has received a number of highly contrasting interpretations.

The question that needs to be addressed here is the following: How do the findings made in the analysis of pidgins and creoles relate to the substance of the present work? It would seem that the overall answer is that these languages do not behave essentially differently from any other languages – that is, that grammatical replication in general and contact-induced grammaticalization in particular are the same – irrespective of whether pidgins, creoles, or any other languages are concerned.

A number of recent works have established that contact-induced grammaticalization is a major driving force in the grammatical development of pidgins and creoles (see, for example, Sankoff & Brown 1976; Sankoff 1979; Arends 1986; Plag 1992, 1993; Romaine 1995; Bruyn 1995, 1996; Baker & Syea 1996; Huber 1996; Mufwene 1996; Poplack & Tagliamonte 1996; Bruyn 1997; Romaine 1999; Tagliamonte 2000; Plag forthc.). A salient pattern, though not the only one, to be observed in these languages is that the model is provided by "substrate" languages to be replicated in the linguistic varieties commonly described as pidgins and creoles. One not uncommon stance taken in this research can be illustrated with an example from Melanesian Pidgin, which is described by Keesing in the following:

Where the substrate languages whose speakers play the main part in the development of a pidgin are sufficiently closely related to have a common basic grammatical pattern (as is the case with the Eastern Oceanic Austronesian languages), lexical items (or stylistic variants, such as resumptive pronouns) in the lexifying superstrate language can be equated directly with grammatical elements common to a substrate language. (Keesing 1991: 317)

As is to be expected, not all cases of grammatical change to be observed in pidgins and creoles conform to the unidirectionality principle. For example, while the grammaticalization of verbs as prepositions is well documented (cf. English *except*), a reversed directionality is hard to find. Still, in at least one creole there is an example: what are prepositions in Dutch and English (e.g. Dutch *door* 'through') end up as items having verbal uses in the English-based creole Sranan (e.g. Sranan *doro* 'put through, go through'; Bruyn 1997). Note further that in Australian Pidgin English, and later also in Melanesian Pidgin English varieties, the English phrase *first time* gave rise to a temporal marker *fastaem* 'before' and eventually to a spatial marker '(in) front (of)' (Keesing 1991; Bruyn 1996: 31) – a development that contradicts the otherwise fairly well attested unidirectional development from spatial to temporal grammatical forms (see also section 3.4.1).[11]

On the basis of such cases it has been argued that pidgins and creoles differ in their grammaticalization behavior from other languages and that they can therefore be of help for understanding why there are exceptions to the unidirectionality principle (Bruyn 1996; Plag forthc.). While this argument is well taken, more data are required to substantiate it. Our own research suggests that, on the whole, pidgins and creoles do not behave any differently from other languages in the way they have developed new grammatical categories. Of the roughly two hundred cases of grammatical development that we have been able to identify so far in pidgins and creoles (see Heine &

Kuteva 2002), hardly a handful are at variance with canonical pathways of grammaticalization.

A problem surrounding discussions on this issue relates to the fact that some authors are overly concerned about the distinction between contact-induced change, more specifically change resulting from substrate influence in pidgins and creoles on the one hand, and language-internal and/or universally induced change on the other. For example, it has been argued that the development of English *by-and-by* to a future tense marker (*baimbai* >) *bai* in Tok Pisin would not have proceeded the way it did without the model offered by substrate languages (Sankoff & Laberge 1973). While this argument is supported by good evidence, this development is nevertheless a canonical instance of unidirectional change: the development of temporal adverbs to future tense markers constitutes a cross-linguistically well-established path of grammaticalization (see Heine 1993: 77–8; Heine & Kuteva 2002). One is led to conclude from such observations that, rather than being shaped by either universal tendencies of language development or contact-induced transfer, the evolution of Tok Pisin *bai* is likely to be the result of what Plag (forthc.: 6) calls "a conspiracy of both factors" and Corne (1999) and Mufwene (2001) refer to as "congruence."

To conclude, pidgin and creole studies are a wide, and a well-documented field of language contact research. These studies appear to suggest that grammatical replication does not differ essentially from what can be observed in other languages.

Creole studies have been shaped to quite some extent by contrasting hypotheses. One set of hypotheses is based on the assumption that the particular grammatical form creoles take is shaped by universal aspects of human linguistic behavior, while another kind of hypotheses assumes that creole genesis is the result of a specific type of contact situation where one type of language involved provided the substrate for the resulting creole. It is beyond the scope of this work to establish what the findings made here can contribute to our understanding of the genesis and development of creole languages. But assuming that the processes characterizing the history of creoles are not fundamentally different from those that can be observed elsewhere in situations of language contact, then we are led to conclude that the two sets of hypotheses just mentioned are in no way mutually incompatible – as has in fact been argued for by some creolists (see especially Mufwene 1986; 2001).

6.3   The role of borrowing and written discourse

Grammatical replication is a complex process involving multiple causation. We are confined in this work to only one causal factor; with the following remarks we wish to draw attention to other variables that may delimit the behavior of use patterns and grammatical categories in some way or other.

6.3.1   Competing motivations: phonological similarity

Contact-induced grammaticalization does not happen in a vacuum. Not infrequently, it goes hand in hand with other factors relating to either the model or the replica language, or both. For example, in order to establish an equivalence relation with a model category, speakers may draw on additional structures other than the morphosyntactic ones determining grammaticalization. The outcome then is a kind of blend resulting from competing motivations.

That it can be language-specific properties in addition to universal pathways that influence the particular way grammaticalization takes can be illustrated with the following examples involving phonological similarity between words of the replica and the model language. Aikhenvald (2002: 5, 239; 2003: 2–3) refers to this process as grammatical accommodation. In the Malaita Oceanic languages there is a post-verbal particle to mark the perfect aspect, illustrated in (11). Apparently in an attempt to replicate this category, speakers of the English-based Solomons Pijin drew on the adverb *nao* (< English *now*) and grammaticalized it to a perfect particle in the same post-verbal slot of the verb phrase as in the Malaita model languages, cf. (12), and the existing pidgin marker *bin*, used for completed actions, virtually disappeared from Solomons Pijin.

(11) Kwaio (Eastern Oceanic; Keesing 1991: 330)

     (ngai) e   leka no'o.
     him   he go   PERF
     'He has gone.'

(12) Solomons Pijin (English-based pidgin; Keesing 1991: 330)

     hem- i   go nao.
     (him- he go PERF)[12]
     'He has gone.'

As far as we are aware, a grammaticalization from a temporal adverb to a perfect marker is not commonly found.[13] What appears to have influenced this choice of grammaticalization is, at least to some extent, the fact that *nao* resembles phonologically the corresponding Oceanic perfect particles (Kwaio, 'Are'are *no'o*, Lau *na*, Kwara'ae *na'a*; Keesing 1991: 329–30) – a case described by Weinreich ([1953] 1964: 39–40) as interlingual equivalence based on formal similarity.

As a rule, however, contact-induced grammaticalization influenced by formal similarity is in accordance with commonly observed patterns of grammatical evolution. Swedish speakers in the United States have grammaticalized their transitive verb *bekomma* 'obtain, do somebody good or bad, make an impression on somebody' to an inchoative auxiliary 'become' (Ureland 1984: 308). In doing so, they have drawn, on the one hand, on a universal strategy whereby lexical verbs tend to be recruited for the expression of tense-aspect meanings and develop into verbal auxiliaries. On the other hand, they appear to have replicated the structure of the English auxiliary *become* presumably on account of the formal similarity it shares with the Swedish verb *bekomma*.

In a similar fashion, speakers of Pennsylvania German may use the locative preposition *bei* 'at' to present agents in passive constructions (see section 4.1.6), cf. (13):

(13) Pennsylvania German (Costello 1985: 117)

> Der Pitscher iss verbroche bei der/die Anna.
> (the pitcher is broken   at the   Anna)
> 'The pitcher is (being) broken by Anna.'

The canonical marker for agents in passive constructions in German is the ablative preposition *von* 'from, of,' but cross-linguistically a much more common strategy is to grammaticalize a locative marker to an agent marker (Heine & Kuteva 2002: 199–200). Pennsylvania German speakers' adoption of the latter strategy was most likely influenced by the fact that their second language, English, uses the phonologically (and etymologically) corresponding preposition *by* in its equivalent passive construction. Conceivably, we are dealing with an instance of replica grammaticalization, where the English model structure was interpreted as an instance of a locative adverbial phrase [*by* NP] which was replicated by means of the corresponding German locative phrase [*bei* NP].

Molisean, a variety of the Croatian minority in Molise, southern Italy, has been strongly influenced by Italian (Breu 1996: 26–7) as a result of five centuries of language contact. As we observed in section 4.4.3, this influence caused the Slavic case inflections to be "strengthened" in specific contexts by prepositions, on the model of the Italian use of prepositions for marking case distinctions. In attributive possession, a new construction [possessee *do* possessor] was created on the pattern of Italian [possessee *di* possessor], where the Croatian allative preposition *do* 'to, toward' (governing the genitive case) was selected as an equivalent of the Italian possessive marker *di*, cf. (14):

(14) Italian vs. Molisean Croatian (Breu 1996: 26)

> a. Italian   la   casa di quella donna
> b. Molisean Slavic hiža   do one   žene
>   (the   house of that   woman)[14]
>   'the house of that woman'

The result is what is known technically as the Goal Schema [Y for/to X], according to which a possessive relation is established by using either a benfactive/dative or an allative marker linking the possessee and the possessor, cf. English *Secretary to the President* (Heine 1997a). The Molise Croatian speakers thus acted in accordance with universal principles of grammaticalization in choosing one of the major conceptual schemas available in order to create a new construction of attributive possession. In choosing this particular schema, Molise Croatian speakers may have been influenced by the phonological similarity between the markers *di* of the model language and *do* of the replica language, especially since the former is pronounced locally as [də]. But there may have been an additional, or perhaps an alternative, phonological motivation: the Slavic speakers possibly took their ablative preposition *od 'from' to be a morphophonological equivalent of Italian *di* – a hypothesis that would be supported by the fact that *od was subsequently lost (Breu 1996: 27). On the basis of the evidence available it is hard to decide which of these alternatives was involved, or to what extent they were involved; overall it would seem that there were both conceptual and phonological forces conspiring in the evolution of this Slavic construction.

Two final examples illustrating the relevance of phonological considerations in grammatical replication were provided earlier. One concerns the development of the relational noun *-pal* 'possession' of Pipil, an endangered Aztecan language of El Salvador, to a subordinating conjunction of purpose *pal* 'in order to, so that' on the model of Spanish *para* 'for, in order to.' Very likely, this particular path of grammaticalization was influenced by the phonological similarity of the two items; note that there is no *r* in native Pipil words (Campbell 1987: 263–4).

Pipil provides yet another example suggesting that phonological factors have contributed to shaping contact-induced grammaticalization. On the model of Spanish *sólo* 'alone, only,' Pipil has grammaticalized its relational noun *se:l* 'alone' to an adverb *se:l* 'alone, only.' While this development is an instance of a fairly widespread process of grammaticalization from 'alone' to 'only' (Heine & Kuteva 2002: 41–3), Campbell (1987: 264) hypothesizes that this instance was presumably influenced by the phonological similarity between the two items.

On the basis of observations made in the Vaupés contact region of northwest Amazonia, Aikhenvald (2002: 239) concludes that cases of grammatical accommodation, that is, combinations of borrowing and replication (direct and indirect diffusion in her terminology), are treated on a par with borrowing, and that they "are condemned as indicative of language mixing" by the speakers concerned.

Grammatical accommodation of this kind constitutes a salient force in shaping contact-induced transfer in general and grammatical replication in particular. In their detailed study of contact between the Aztecan language Mexicano

(Nahuatl) as spoken in the Malinche Volcano towns of Central Mexico and Spanish, Hill and Hill discuss the following situation that in some way or other also surfaces in other cases of language contact:

The Spanish particles *de* and *que* have been incorporated into Malinche Mexicano usage in so many environments, and are used at such a high frequency, that they are important contributors in their own right to syntactic convergence with Spanish. Apparently, these elements have been assimilated into Mexicano by first equating them with indigenous elements with which they have some semantic or formal overlap. Then they are extended into new environments, which were appropriate for the indigenous forms, but were not part of the original overlap. Finally, they may become dominant, expanding at the expense of the indigenous forms in the usage of many speakers. During this process, syntactic innovations may take place which have no precedent in either Spanish or Mexicano. (Hill & Hill 1986: 293)

To conclude, while all cases discussed in the present section are compatible with universal principles of grammatical evolution, it would seem that the particular path of grammaticalization that speakers of the replica languages in question chose was influenced by morphophonological considerations – in other words, what one may call the concept-cum-phonology conspiracy appears to constitute a not uncommon factor contributing to grammatical replication.

6.3.2 Replication vs. borrowing

Another possible constraint on replication can be seen in borrowing. Contact-induced grammaticalization is not the only means whereby a language may acquire a new grammatical category via language contact – a much better-known way is by borrowing a grammatical form–meaning unit from another language, that is, by using (1c) as a strategy (see section 1.1). The question that arises then is how the two relate to one another: (a) Are grammatical replication and borrowing two mutually exclusive strategies? (b) Are they equivalent alternative options that speakers have in contact situations? (c) And if (b) is to be answered in the affirmative: which of the two is more common in grammatical transfer?

It would seem that question (a) can be answered in the negative. There are attested cases where one and the same grammatical category arose via borrowing in one language but via replication – more precisely via contact-induced grammaticalization – in another language. For example, Chamorro, an Austronesian language of the Mariana Islands, has been in close contact with Spanish between 1665 and 1899, and as a result of this contact it has borrowed the Spanish indefinite article *un* and uses it in a manner similar to Spanish, both with nouns borrowed from Spanish and with Austronesian nouns, even if it is not inflected for gender or number (Stolz 2003). But indefinite articles may as well arise via contact-induced grammaticalization. One case is discussed by Haase (1992: 59–61, 71; see also Heine & Kuteva 2003: 556–7): Basque has acquired an indefinite article via contact-induced grammaticalization from

Gascon and/or Spanish, replicating the article *un(e)* of their Romance-speaking neighbors by grammaticalizing the Basque numeral *bat* 'one' to an indefinite article.

But this Basque example is not an isolated case. Another example is provided by Romani, which under the influence of European languages has grammaticalized its numeral for 'one,' inherited from its Indic past, to an indefinite article (Matras 1996: 60). Note also that the Slavic language Sorbian, which has been in contact with German for nearly a millennium, has replicated the German indefinite article by also developing its numeral for 'one' (Upper Sorbian *jedyn*, Lower Sorbian *jaden*) into a weakly grammaticalized indefinite article (Upper Sorbian *jen*, Lower Sorbian *jan*; Lötzsch 1996: 53).

This suggests that question (b) can essentially be answered in the affirmative, that is, speakers in contact situations can equally draw on both options, replication or borrowing, and not seldom they simultaneously draw on both; for example, speakers of the Aztecan language Pipil of El Salvador have borrowed the Spanish relative marker *que* as *ke*; at the same time, they have also grammaticalized their own constructions and forms to relative clause markers on the model of Spanish. What is in need of further research is the circumstances under which one is preferred over the other.

The following observations suggest that there might be some temporal sequencing relating to borrowing and contact-induced grammaticalization. A fairly common, though still not well understood, grammaticalization process concerns the evolution from nominal complements to complements having a non-finite (e.g. infinitival, participial, or gerundival) verb as their nucleus, to finite subordinate clauses – a number of Balkanic languages appear to have experienced this evolution. This evolution can be triggered by grammatical borrowing, whereby a subordinating conjunction is borrowed, a process subsequently leading to the transition from a non-finite complement to a finite subordinate clause, and it is not confined to the Balkans:

One typical set of changes took place in ASIATIC ESKIMO. The initial change, a direct influence from CHUKCHI, was the borrowing of conjunctions into ESKIMO [. . .]. Function words are frequently borrowed, and the conjunctions themselves would not disrupt the typology of clause combining. Later, however, as a result of this initial change, ESKIMO replaced native gerund and other non-finite verbal constructions with constructions of conjunction + finite clause. Similar change processes led to the development of finite subordinate clauses in BRAHUI, starting with a subordinating conjunction *ki* borrowed from BALOCHI [. . .], and in Azerbaidzhani, in which inherited Turkic participial or gerund constructions were replaced by subordinating conjunctions and finite verbs [. . .]. (Thomason 2001a: 1644–5)

There is no conclusive answer to question (c). To our knowledge, the only works that deal with this question in some detail is Heath (1978: 119–38), analyzing language contact among four Australian languages in Arnhem Land of northern Australia, and Aikhenvald's (2002) study of language contact in

Amazonia. Heath distinguishes between direct morphemic diffusion, that is, the borrowing of form–meaning units, and indirect morphosyntactic diffusion, that is replication not involving a transfer of form–meaning units.[15] He concludes that in all linguistic areas examined by him (the Balkans, South Asia, and Arnhem Land) indirect morphosyntactic diffusion has been extensive, especially in South Asia, but in Arnhem Land direct morphemic diffusion has also been extensive. (Note that many, though not all, instances of indirect morphosyntactic diffusion discussed by Heath relate to contact-induced grammaticalization.)

In her study of contact between East Tucanoan languages and the Arawak language Tariana in the Vaupés area of northwestern Amazonia, Aikhenvald (1996: 83; 2002) concludes that in this area there is a greater degree of indirect diffusion (replication) than direct diffusion (borrowing), and, in more general terms, Aikhenvald and Dixon conclude:

There are two kinds of grammatical diffusion. The most common is diffusion of a category; less common is diffusion of grammatical forms. For example, if a language moves into a linguistic area characterised by each language having a system of noun classes (genders) then it is likely to innovate a noun class system. But it will do this by developing noun class markers from its own internal resources (e.g. by grammaticalising classifiers to be affixes marking noun class) rather than by borrowing the actual forms from a neighbouring language. (Aikhenvald & Dixon 2001: 251)

While there are a few borrowed morphemes, they "fit into the previously calqued patterns" (Aikhenvald 2002: 59). Aikhenvald's work suggests that indirect and direct diffusion have different effects on the structure of the languages concerned, that is, the languages of the Vaupés region in northwestern Amazonia:

[. . .] indirect diffusion results in the emergence of new categories through reanalysis of existing grammatical patterns and through grammaticalization processes. The existing (albeit very limited) direct diffusion results just in adding another term to an already existing category. (Aikhenvald 2002: 12)

In terms of the distinctions that we proposed in chapter 4, it would seem that in the Vaupés region of Amazonia, indirect diffusion is more likely to lead to "gap filling" (section 4.1.1) while direct diffusion tends to give rise to what appears to be coexistence (section 4.1.2). Furthermore, also with reference to the Vaupés region, Aikhenvald (2002: 13) found that indirect diffusion preceded direct diffusion in time, and while most cases of the former are completed changes, the majority of the latter are ongoing and marginalized.

To conclude, while borrowing of grammatical forms is fairly well documented (see, for example, Thomason & Kaufman 1988), there is much less information available on the replication of grammatical use patterns and categories – in spite of the fact that the latter is presumably equally widespread. There is an obvious reason for this situation: grammatical replication is far more difficult to identify than the borrowing of form–meaning units.

6.3.3   Oral vs. written discourse

Grammatical change in general and grammaticalization in particular tend to arise first in the spoken use of a language, and usually it takes some time before they are also adopted in the written norm of the language concerned. While this also seems to apply to most instances of contact-induced grammaticalization, there are some notable exceptions. In some contact situations, the model language is accessible primarily as a written medium only while the replica language has no, or no commonly accepted, written norm. Now, in an attempt to translate texts from the former into the latter language, translators tend to conform to the structure provided by the model language, in particular if the latter is considered to represent a more attractive religion and/or a more powerful civilization. Such situations may have the effect that, at least in the initial stages, the replication of grammatical categories starts out with written discourse before it extends to spoken discourse, and it may result in a situation where the written register of a replica language is characterized by more transfers than the spoken registers. For example, what tends to be called the Indo-Aryanization of Dravidian languages – a complex process having a history of nearly 3,500 years – has had more pervasive effects in written than in spoken communication, in that Dravidian languages show more Indo-Aryan features in written style than in speech (Sridhar 1978: 200).

Examples such as the following suggest that such situations may affect the rise and spread of contact-induced grammaticalization. We observed in section 4.1.2 that Basque speakers used their question marker *zein* 'which?' as an equivalent of the Spanish interrogative pronouns and grammaticalized it to a relative clause marker on the model of Spanish. In spoken Basque this appears to be a fairly recent phenomenon, while in translated written texts it is documented since the seventeenth century (Hurch 1989: 21).

A number of cases showing how contact-induced grammaticalization is triggered or enhanced by written communication can be found in Nau (1995). For example, in German and other European languages, path prepositions ('through,' 'via') have been grammaticalized to prepositions expressing means, instruments, and/or cause. This process from locative to more abstract non-locative case functions has been replicated to some extent in peripheral languages of northeastern Europe. In this way, the Finnish postposition *kautta* and the Latvian preposition *caur*, both locative path markers meaning 'through, via,' have developed use patterns as instrumental/means/cause markers presumably through the influence of Bible and other translations from languages such as German and Swedish. Accordingly, it comes as no surprise that the use of Latvian *caur* as a means or cause preposition, being interpreted by Nau (1995: 145) as a replication of the uses of the German path preposition *durch* 'through,' is almost entirely restricted to the written language, even if this use pattern is not accepted as conforming to the standard language.

During the period of early writing in Finnish (appr. 1540–1820), Bible translators developed weakly grammaticalized futures based on the modal verbs *pitää* 'should, must' and *tahtoa* 'want, intend' – a process that is said to have been influenced by German and Swedish modals serving as models. These grammaticalizations, which were discontinued around or after 1820, do not appear to have affected spoken varieties of Finnish (Nau 1995: 99–104).

Another case is provided by the Slavic language Sorbian, having a history of nearly one thousand years of language contact with German. As we saw in section 2.4.1, Sorbian has acquired a definite article on the model of German by grammaticalizing a demonstrative to a definite marker. By the end of the sixteenth century, this grammaticalization was nearly complete in the written language (texts were then largely confined to church literature translated from German), while the definite article of modern spoken Sorbian is far less grammaticalized, its use being subject to contextual and situational variation (Lötzsch 1996: 52). Note further that the areal spread of infinitive replacement by finite subordinate clauses in the Balkans is attributed by some to the church environment provided by Byzantine-Medieval Greek (Banfi 1990: 179; see section 5.2.3.1 (d)).

Note further that among the Arawak-speaking Tariana of northwestern Brazil, translations from the official language Portuguese into Tariana are characterized by a relatively high degree of grammatical replication ("calquing"): "In their translations (just like on any other occasion of rendering or retelling other people's speech) the Tariana try to be as accurate and literal as possible" (Aikhenvald 2002: 184). For example, younger Tariana speakers replicated the Portuguese polysemy involving interrogative and relative clause uses of items such as *que* by extending the use of their interrogative pronoun *kwana* to relative clauses. This instance of replica grammaticalization (see section 3.4.3), restricted in spoken discourse to the younger and more innovative generation, is extremely widespread in texts translated into Tariana for Roman Catholic church services, as in the following example (15a), presumably modeled on the corresponding Portuguese sentence in (15b).

(15) Tariana (Arawak) and Portuguese (Aikhenvald 2002: 184)

    a. Tariana
      [kwana Maria- nuku   ka-   mesa] puhwi.
      who   Maria- TOP.NON.A/S REL- love   glad
      'Who loves Mary will become happy.'

    b. Portuguese
      Quem gosta da Maria será feliz.

It goes without saying that, typically, contact-induced grammaticalization arises first in oral forms of discourse, and it usually takes some time before the new use patterns and categories find their way into written discourse. Nevertheless, in situations where language contact is largely shaped by written communication, we may not be surprised to find this temporal sequencing reversed, and in some cases, as in the case of the early history of writing, e.g. in Estonian and Lithuanian, which was shaped to quite some extent by German and German writers, replication via written translation work was at times exceedingly strong – to the extent that Nau (1995: 122) proposes to call it *Zwangsgrammatikalisierung* (forced grammaticalization).

6.4   On attrition

Language contact reaches an extreme point when people give up one language in favor of another. One possible linguistic aspect of this general sociolinguistic process has been described under the label of language attrition, and the question that arises here is how attrition relates to grammatical replication. To start with, attrition must not be confused with language loss or language shift. Myers-Scotton (2002: 179) defines the latter as "a community phenomenon and a result arising from gradual loss of a language (usually an L1) over time," while attrition is "a phenomenon of individuals, referring to what happens to an individual's production of a language (usually an L1), *and* the state of any loss at a point of time." Not everybody would subscribe to these definitions in every detail. For example, shift has not always been described exclusively as a community phenomenon; it may as well relate to individuals giving up their first language (L1) in favor of some other language; and conversely, attrition may be, and has been, understood as referring not only to individual language production but also to the general development of a language. Furthermore, shift is not infrequently used as a sociolinguistic label, relating to the choice between languages as social institutions, while attrition is perhaps more commonly perceived as a linguistic phenomenon, associated with distinctions in grammatical expression within a given language. The definitions proposed by Myers-Scotton are in fact not shared by all students of language contact. For Thomason (2003: 704), for example, attrition is "the overall simplification and reduction of a language's linguistic structures, without concomitant complication elsewhere in the system."

A number of the grammatical changes discussed in the preceding chapters involve language-shift situations, while other changes do not; accordingly, contact-induced grammaticalization is confined neither to shift nor to non-shift situations. We have therefore avoided describing language change with reference to terms such as shift or language replacement. The situation is different in the case of attrition. Since we were not concerned with individual language production but rather with clearly defined segments of speech communities as populations, and frequently with entire speech communities, attrition was not a relevant notion in our discussions. Nevertheless, the question arises as to whether or how grammaticalization and attrition are related to one another. A number of authors have observed that the processes characterizing language loss, or language death, differ from other contact-induced processes; for example, Thomason observes that "non-convergent simplifying innovations in a dying language are certainly contact-induced, though they are not interference features" (Thomason 2003: 688). Nevertheless, language death does not necessarily entail attrition. Attrition is a wide field of study, and we will not attempt any balanced coverage of it (see, for example, Campbell & Muntzel 1989; Dorian 1989; Sasse 1992). Our interest is simply with aspects of attrition that immediately have a bearing on our general subject matter, more specifically on the question of how attrition relates to principles of contact-induced grammaticalization. What the latter has in common with attrition phenomena is, first, that both can be described in terms of the interaction between a model and a replica language, second, that they lead to linguistic changes in the latter as a result of this interaction, and, third, that these changes appear to be governed by more general, presumably universal, principles of grammatical development.

In addition, there are a few other characteristics shared by attrition and contact-induced grammaticalization. A paradigm case of attrition concerns the neutralization of contrasts, whereby speakers give up lexical and grammatical distinctions made in the language concerned, typically their L1 (see Myers-Scotton 2002: 198ff.). Neutralization of contrasts as observed in attrition is in accordance with principles of grammaticalization in that it can be described in terms of parameters of grammaticalization, namely extension (or context generalization) and desemanticization (see section 1.3): It has the effect that one linguistic structure S_1 is generalized at the expense of another structure S_2, with the effect that the contrast between the two is neutralized: S_1 comes to be used in contexts previously reserved for S_2. Context generalization entails desemanticization, i.e. loss in semantic specificity in that, as a result of its use in new contexts, S_1 tends to acquire a more general meaning, combining the semantics of both S_1 and S_2.

Another phenomenon that has been claimed to characterize attrition concerns the tendency to replace morphologically complex constructions with analytic constructions (see, for example, Thomason 2001b: 230). This tendency is by no means restricted to attrition; rather, it constitutes a salient stage in the rise of new grammatical structures – that is, it marks the initial stage of many grammaticalization processes, as we observed in section 4.4.3.

Finally, a number of cases that have been related to attrition can at the same time also be reanalyzed as instances of contact-induced grammaticalization. As we observed in section 2.2, the latter process generally starts out with existing use patterns acquiring a higher frequency of use and being extended to new contexts. In her treatment of attrition hypotheses, Myers-Scotton (2002: 201) discusses the development of pronominal subject marking based on findings made by Schmitt (2000; 2001) on five Russian boys living in the United States for whom English is or is becoming the dominant language. She concludes that this development is characterized by "the decline in the Standard Russian use of the pro-drop parameter."

We contend, however, that attrition is only one half of the story. The other half involves a complementary perspective to this same development. Myers-Scotton continues to observe that pronouns used as subjects are optional in Standard Russian and expected only for emphasis. Now, under English influence, the Russian boys appear to have changed this optional use pattern by using pronouns more frequently. It would seem that this is not an isolated case of incipient contact-induced grammaticalization (see sections 2.3.2, 3.1.3). There is substantial evidence to show that immigrants in the USA are likely to activate use patterns that are marginal in their respective L1 by using them more frequently in cases where their L2, English, provides a convenient model. A pro-drop language, for example, is likely to have a marginal use pattern where personal pronouns may be used optionally for pragmatic purposes such as marking topic or focus. Among immigrants speaking pro-drop languages, such as Russian, Serbian, or Hungarian, this marginal use pattern tends to gain in frequency of use on the model of English.

To conclude, contact-induced grammaticalization does for the most part not seem to be incompatible with the structural changes to be observed in attrition. This is also suggested by the observations made by Aikhenvald (2002: 250) on contact-induced change in the Vaupés region of northwest Amazonia, according to which "most processes triggered by language attrition point in a similar direction as that of diffusion without attrition."

But there are also differences. The following examples, all relating to case inflection, illustrate some differences between attrition and grammaticalization. Quite a number of studies on attrition are concerned with the neutralization of case distinctions in European languages in contact, and this appears to involve some overall directionality, of the kind summarized in (16).

(16) Neutralization of constrasts in case inflections in language attrition

    a. Nominative/subject markers tend to replace accusative/direct object markers.

    b. Accusative/direct object markers tend to replace dative/indirect object markers.

    c. Markers for core participants (subject, object) tend to replace markers for peripheral case functions, such as locatives or instrumentals.

This directionality can be linked to the frequently made observation that speakers of dying languages tend to overgeneralize unmarked features at the expense of marked ones (Anderson 1982; Campbell & Muntzel 1989: 187). A few examples may illustrate this line of directionality (see Myers-Scotton 2002: 227 for details; see also Savić 1995). Among young adult second-generation Croatian immigrants in Australia there is a tendency to replace the locative case by the accusative and, in a similar fashion, Croatian immigrant children in Sweden were found to use the accusative as the default replacement for locative. That the accusative frequently replaces the dative case has been recorded in the northern German city of Flensburg, and Polinsky's (1995) study on attrition among Russian immigrants to the USA suggests that there is a systematic replacement of the dative with the accusative, and of the accusative with the nominative. Further, Schmitt's (2000; 2001) findings on Russian children in the USA also exhibit a replacement of the instrument case with the nominative, and German immigrants in the USA have been found to show overgeneralization of the nominative case, which suggests that this case is extended at the expense of other case forms. Van Ness (1992: 189) observes that among the New Order Amish of Ohio using German as their L1, "a continuing convergence toward English has effectively eliminated the dative case from active use by informants under age forty-five."

Conceivably, such generalizations will require modification once a larger body of data on language attrition becomes available. Overall, however, these generalizations suggest that, in spite of all the similarities outlined above, attrition and contact-induced grammaticalization need to be kept apart. In the course of this work we discussed a number of pathways that case markers follow as a result of contact-induced grammaticalization, most of all the following (see section 4.3.1):

(17) Contact-induced grammaticalization pathways of case markers

       a. from comitative to instrumental
       b. from allative to indirect object marker
       c. from indirect object to direct object marker
       d. from peripheral to core participant marker

Note that these pathways apply irrespective of whether inflectional or any other forms of case marking are concerned. These findings would seem to suggest that certain context extensions that are possible in situations of attrition are less likely to occur in contact-induced grammaticalization. For example, in situations of attrition, nominatives and accusatives tend to replace other cases (Myers-Scotton 2002: 225), and, more generally, case inflections for peripheral participants are likely to be replaced by inflections for core participants. In contact-induced grammaticalization, as generally in grammaticalization (see Heine & Kuteva 2002), an opposite development can be observed: markers for peripheral participants may develop into markers for complements, that is, into core participants, while the opposite is unlikely to happen, as is suggested by the generalizations proposed in (17). Thus, case markers for dative/indirect objects are more likely to be treated as peripheral participants than direct objects, and markers introducing allative/directional participants are more likely to be encoded as peripheral participants than dative/indirect object markers.

These observations appear to suggest that both attrition and contact-induced grammaticalization are based on mechanisms generally characteristic of grammaticalization, but the two differ in the way categories of the model language are conceptualized and grammaticalized. While the latter leads to an enrichment of the language concerned, in that new use patterns and grammatical categories are created on the model of another language, new categories are far less likely to arise in the case of attrition; rather, existing categories are simplified, merge with other categories, or are simply abandoned. Note, however, that this is only one aspect of grammatical change in dying languages (see e.g. Dorian 1993 on a contracting Scottish Gaelic dialect); there is a plethora of examples to show that even in cases of advanced language death, new grammatical categories may evolve via contact-induced grammaticalization; we discussed a range of examples, e.g. from the moribund Aztecan language Pipil (Campbell 1987; see also Campbell and Muntzel 1989: 192–4).

To conclude, both attrition and contact-induced grammaticalization appear to be based on universal principles of language change, but these principles are not exactly the same in the two cases. They relate to what tends to be referred to as "simplification" and universal markedness (Thomason 2003: 705) in the case of attrition but to regularities underlying the creation of new linguistic structures in the case of grammaticalization (see section 1.5).

6.5   Natural vs. unnatural change

The discussion in the preceding chapters suggests that contact-related language change is not fundamentally different from language change as it can be observed in situations where contact can be ruled out as a contributing factor. This, however, is not the position maintained in many works on this general subject matter. A final issue to be addressed in this book therefore concerns the question of whether in fact language contact imposes specific constraints on what can and what cannot be replicated. This issue is a complex one and no attempt is made here to do justice to it; we simply want to examine whether the processes underlying grammaticalization are in any significant way different from those to be observed in situations of language change not involving language contact.

A survey of the literature on language change and language contact shows that for some sociolinguists – who by default put the emphasis on language-contact phenomena – the traditional assumption has been that the canonical case is for a particular language to be viewed as a closed system, with universal, perpetual processes of change triggered and actualized within that system. The changes due to language contact have tacitly been given the ranking of some sort of second-order processes, as processes which are not as "natural" as the language-internal ones. This fact is reflected in the very terminology used to refer to contact-induced change. In this tradition, Trudgill proposes to distinguish between what he calls natural and non-natural change in the following way:

linguistic changes may come in two rather different types. Some forms of linguistic change may be relatively "natural", in the sense that they are liable to occur in all linguistic systems, at all times, without external stimulus, because of the inherent nature of linguistic systems themselves – and it is here of course that the stability of the nature of human beings is relevant. Other types of linguistic change, on the other hand, may be relatively "non-natural", in the sense that they take place mainly as the result of language contact. They are, that is, not due to the inherent nature of language systems, but to processes that take place in particular sociolinguistic situations. (Trudgill 1983: 102)

In other words, language-internal changes are "natural" or "proper changes," contact-induced changes are "non-natural," "unnatural," or "improper" language changes (Danchev 1988: 39).[16] A number of further, more specific assumptions related to the above proposition have been made, in particular the following (Trudgill 1983: 103–5):
 (i) Language contact speeds up the rate at which language change proceeds.
 (ii) Other things being equal (such as attitudinal factors, for instance), varieties whose speakers have frequent contact with speakers of other varieties will change more than varieties whose speakers have infrequent external contact.
(iii) By far the most interesting assumption, however, concerns the issue of what type of linguistic change counts as a "natural" (that is, language-internal) change and what type counts as a "non-natural" (that is, contact-induced) one. In addition to sound changes such as phonological assimilation, Trudgill (1983: 103–5) classifies as natural linguistic changes the development from analytic to synthetic structure (e.g. the development of case endings or of personal inflections on verbs out of cliticization and morphologization processes) as well as increase in redundancy whereby a grammatical category gets marked several times. Non-natural linguistic changes, on the other hand, are assumed to involve a movement from synthetic to analytic (reduction in cases and an increase in prepositional usage, reduction in conjugations, declensions, and inflected forms, increase in periphrastic verb forms).

(iv) Yet another assumption highly relevant to the present study is that where varieties in contact are related and similar, they may retain what they have in common and lose what is different. In order to exemplify this, Trudgill (1983: 105) follows Bailey and Maroldt (1977), pointing to contact between English and Scandinavian as a factor in changes in English grammatical structure.

The observations made in this book do not contradict the assumptions in (i) and (ii); note, however, that we lack appropriate quantitative data to test these assumptions in any detail. But the standpoint we have taken here is clearly different from the assumptions in (iii) and (iv). On the basis of what we observe within the area of conceptual transfer – which underlies contact-induced morphosyntactic change – there is no meaningful way in which we could say that language-internal change is natural and contact-induced change non-natural. The reason is that contact-induced grammatical change involves, typically, grammaticalization *processes* (rather than the static end-results of such processes), which follow universal principles of grammaticalization. These are the same principles as the ones observed in language-internal grammaticalization (less-grammatical-to-more grammatical directionality of development, desemanticization, extension, decategorialization, and erosion). In other words, transfer of grammatical structures is unlikely to take place if it is not in accordance with universal principles of grammaticalization, which have been established already primarily on the basis of language-internal developments (Heine, Claudi & Hünnemeyer 1991; Hopper & Traugott 1993; Bybee, Perkins & Pagliuca 1994; Lehmann [1982]1995; Heine & Kuteva 2002).

As for (iv) above, on the basis of the contact-induced grammaticalization situations studied in this book, we conclude that contact situations, except for cases of attrition (see section 6.4), tend to lead not to the reduction and loss of existing grammatical categories, but rather to diversification and to the creation of new grammatical categories in one language on the model of another language. For example, if a language M has a definite article while a language R has not, then it is more likely that a new article will be created in R on the model of M rather than the lack of definite article in R being replicated in M.

This is closely related to the following observation spelled out in Trudgill (1983: 107), according to which "[I]ncreased geographical mobility, and increased world population, have probably led to an increase in contact situations, and thus perhaps to an increase in non-natural changes and relatively more analytic linguistic structures." For Trudgill, the increase in analytic structures is to be seen as the manifestation of increase in "non-natural" changes taking place in creoloid languages,[17] which are the result of an ever-increasing language contact. On the basis of the present approach, the analysis of this same observation involves absolutely natural transfer of grammaticalization processes, which, typically, exemplify analytic structures in their incipient and intermediate stages – as opposed to the end-results of grammaticalization developments, that is, synthetically expressed grammatical morphemes such as suffixes.

Yet another way in which our standpoint runs counter to the common practice in the literature concerns the way double marking is interpreted. Trudgill (1983: 105) views redundancy in marking (double marking) as a diagnostic for "natural" – that is, language-internal – change. In the above chapters we have shown that this same phenomenon can be clearly identified as the result of language contact; see, for instance, the discussion on double subject marking in Sauris German (section 2.1), on the double marking of relative clauses (sections 1.1, 3.1.3), or on object reduplication (section 5.2.3.1).

Nevertheless, the interpretations offered in the preceding chapters are not always unproblematic. There are a number of controversies surrounding some of these interpretations, typically of the kind where one author argues for a universal and/or language-internal hypothesis while another author proposes an external hypothesis. The following example illustrates such cases. The Aztecan language Nahuatl has a set of particles (*tlen* 'which', *aquin* 'who', and *canin* 'where') that serve both as interrogatives and as relative clause markers. While some authors claim that this case of polysemy is a manifestation of linguistic universals (e.g. Rosenthal 1972), others argue that it is the result of Nahuatl-Spanish contacts, whereby interrogative particles serving as indefinite pronouns of main clauses came to be identified with the interrogative-looking relative pronouns of Spanish and reanalyzed into the subordinate clause (Langacker 1975; Karttunen 1976: 151–2; see section 4.1.2).

Rather than being problematic, such alternative accounts are to be expected on the basis of the situations concerned: We concur with Johanson that contact-induced grammaticalization has both a universal/language-internal and an external/contact-related component: "External, extra-linguistic and internal factors may thus be reconciled – as it were, as options and triggers – in a single explanatory framework" (Johanson 2002b: 286). For a way of accounting for this fact, see Mufwene (2001; see also Mufwene 1986). Depending on the kind of model a given author recruits to account for the relevant facts, he or she will highlight one of these components and ignore or reject the other component, especially since models that simultaneously take care of both components are not readily available.

7   Conclusions

In the course of the preceding chapters a number of findings on the nature of grammatical replication were presented. First, the reader may be surprised that we have had fairly little to say about the sociolinguistic environment and its contribution to language change. Contact-related linguistic change is the result of interaction between people speaking different languages and, as has been demonstrated in much of the recent research, it tends to be shaped by the particular sociolinguistic situation in which it arose. One rather unexpected outcome of our work is, however, that grammatical replication is fairly independent of the particular sociolinguistic factors that may exist in a given situation of language contact. It occurs in all kinds of social, political, cultural, and demographical settings and the form it takes does not seem to be influenced dramatically by these factors.

This is suggested among other things by the fact that replication can be reciprocal. We had numerous examples where speakers replicated a grammatical category of their L2 in their L1, or of a dominant/majority language in a minority language; but there were also many examples exhibiting an opposite directionality, that is, where a category of an L1, or of a minority language, was replicated in an L2, or a dominant language, respectively. We found examples where a given language can at the same time replicate grammatical structures and provide a model for replication. Speakers of the North Arawak language Tariana in northwest Amazonia have developed a wide range of new grammatical structures on the model of East Tucanoan languages; at the same time, they have used Tariana, which is an endangered language, as a model for creating new categories in their L2 Portuguese (Aikhenvald 2002). In a comparable fashion, speakers of the Austronesian language Tigak of New Ireland in Papua New Guinea replicated grammatical structures from their L2 Tok Pisin, but Tigak and other Austronesian languages also provided a model for their major L2 Tok Pisin (Jenkins 2002), and language contact between Turkish and Macedonian also led to grammatical replications in both directions (see Friedman 2003 for examples).

Second, we saw that transfer of grammatical structures from one language to another without involving any linguistic form is perhaps more widespread than has previously been thought. In a recent textbook of contact linguistics, the following generalization is proposed: "Even when there is intimate inter-community contact leading to massive lexical diffusion, structure seems to resist externally motivated change" (Winford 2003: 74). The observations made in this book tend to contradict this generalization. In some cases where we have a more comprehensive knowledge of language contact, grammatical replication turns out to be hardly less common than lexical borrowing. What accounts for the fact that we know so little about this process is on the one hand that it is hard to identify: unlike borrowing, where formal similarity between items of the source language and the recipient language provides convenient clues for identification, there are no such clues in replication. This suggests that the cases of grammatical replication that have so far become known, presumably constitute no more than the tip of the iceberg of what actually has happened in language contact. Another reason for our limited knowledge on this subject concerns the fact that grammatical replication is the joint product of contact, of universal processes of grammaticalization, and of internal development, and frequently it turns out to be hard to determine the relative contribution made by each of these factors. It therefore comes as no surprise that the study of grammatical replication is rife with controversies on how a given instance of it is to be interpreted. The history of Balkan linguistics is a case in point: each of the features that have been proposed as characterizing the Balkans as a linguistic area has been the subject of conflicting, and frequently mutually contradicting, hypotheses.

Third, grammatical replication can involve virtually any domain of language structure and language use. As we saw perhaps most clearly in chapter 3, grammatical replication may in the same way affect morphological, syntactic, and pragmatic structures, the noun phrase and the verb phrase in the same way as the organization of clauses and clause combining. The outcome can be that the typological profile of the languages concerned undergoes noticeable changes, in some cases leading to metatypy, where the languages involved achieve a high degree of mutual intertranslatability (see chapter 5). At the same time, we have found no cases where this process had the effect that the languages concerned acquired an identical typological profile, that is, where there exists total one-to-one correspondence in the grammatical categorization of the languages concerned.

Fourth, there are a number of notions proposed in contact linguistics that turned out to be of limited relevance to our study. One of them concerns simplification. It has frequently been argued that one major effect of contact-induced language change is that it leads to a simplification in the typological outfit of the languages concerned. This is the conclusion reached, for example, by Gumperz and Wilson (1971) in their seminal study on language contact in the Indian village Kupwar – a study that, as we saw above, yielded a number of instances of contact-induced grammaticalization. These authors argue that almost all changes in Kupwar "can be interpreted as reductions or generalizations that simplify surface structure in relation to underlying categories and relationships" (Gumperz & Wilson 1971: 164). But this interpretation has not been corroborated by subsequent research – nor is it really corroborated by their own findings. With reference to the language-contact situation of Arnhem Land, northern Australia, that he studied in some detail, Heath (1978: 125) concludes that "no significant simplification has resulted from indirect diffusion." For example, the fact that, as a rule, contact-induced grammaticalization simply leads to the addition of new grammatical structures in the replica language suggests that simplification – however one may wish to define it – is not an appropriate notion. The result is that the grammar of that language is enriched but certainly not, or not necessarily, simplified (see Johanson 1992: 201).

Our findings on this issue are in line with those made by Heath (1978), in that none of the various definitions that have been proposed for "simplification" of language structure appears to be relevant to understanding the nature of contact-induced grammaticalization. It may happen that when a new grammatical category is acquired on the model of another language, a corresponding old category is given up, or that speakers eliminate a grammatical category in the replica language because the model language lacks this category – the loss of modal (or focus) particles among German–English bilinguals in the USA (Salmons 1990: 461ff.; see section 4.1.6) being a case in point. Such cases, however, are not very common, and they constitute but one of the many possible kinds of changes that can be observed. As we saw in chapter 4, there are other equally likely changes, e.g. where both the old and the new categories survive, or where the two categories merge into one more complex category, or where the old category is redefined, etc. (see especially section 4.1). Furthermore, what leads to structural similarity in one domain of grammar can result in increasing differentiation in other parts of grammar. Overall, replication has the effect that the structure of grammatical categorization in the replica language tends to become more differentiated and complex, rather than undergoing simplification of any kind (see Aikhenvald 2002).

We also found no evidence to support the view according to which the grammars of languages in contact are or behave like structurally balanced, self-contained, or closed systems (see section 6.5). Grammatical replication takes place not between different systems but rather between different ways of saying things, of structuring discourses, and of expressing grammatical concepts. While replication may, and frequently does, lead, for example, to a reorganization of grammatical paradigms, as a rule this has no noticeable effects on the structure of grammar as a whole.

Furthermore, we found little evidence to the effect that structural compatibility between the grammars affected by contact plays any significant role in making replication possible or impossible. There are examples to suggest that replication is most pronounced among structurally similar and/or genetically closely related languages; at the same time, there are also examples, such as Basque vis-à-vis Gascon (Haase 1992), Pipil vis-à-vis Spanish (Campbell 1987), Sri Lanka Portuguese vis-à-vis Tamil (Bakker 2000), or Tariana vis-à-vis East Tucanoan languages (Aikhenvald 2002), that show that neither structural nor genetic divergence form any serious obstacle to massive grammatical replication.

In connection with this issue there is another widely held assumption that is in need of qualification. It is almost a commonplace in contact linguistics to say that structures shared between languages in contact tend to be favored in replication whereas structures in one language without parallels in the other language tend to be less favored (see, for example, Salmons 1990: 467–8). While our data do not generally contradict this assumption, they suggest that with regard to grammatical replication the situation is more complex. Most of what happens in grammatical replication does not concern full-fledged grammatical categories but rather more subtle discourse structures. We were dealing in chapter 2 with the role played by use patterns in language contact, and we observed that one of the most ubiquitous phenomena characterizing grammatical replication concerns minor use patterns, that is, pieces of discourse that are of low frequency of use and confined to use in highly restricted contexts. Such minor use patterns can be activated and gradually develop into major use patterns, being used more often and in novel contexts, and becoming functionally equivalent to some major use pattern or category of the model language. This example may suffice to show that structural parallelism need not be, and frequently is not, a relevant factor in grammatical replication.

But there is yet another observation that shows that structural parallelism does not play a central role in grammatical replication. We have dealt with a number of examples where adpositions in the model language were replicated by grammaticalizing relational nouns in the replica language, or tense markers by grammaticalizing constructions involving lexical verbs (see especially chapter 3). Rather than being suggestive of structural parallelism, such cases could more appropriately be termed "structurally non-parallel," in that speakers relate functional categories such as adpositions and tense markers of the model languages to lexical structures of the replica languages (see section 6.1). To conclude, notions such as structural parallelism do not appear to be very helpful in understanding grammatical replication.

The way replication proceeds and the extent to which it is successful depends on a number of variables, each associated with a spectrum of different manifestations, extending, for example, from individual to communal activity, from occasional to regular use, or from merely copying features to creating new structures on the model of another language (see Johanson 1992, 2002a for detailed discussion). Our main interest in this work was with the last of these manifestations, that is, with communally shared, regular, and creative behavior. But we had little to say on what exactly motivates this behavior. Many of the works available are in fact silent on this issue or else offer interpretations that are not always fully convincing. What surfaces from these works is that there are not necessarily clearly definable goals that motivate people to replicate – other than speaking one language as they speak another language. Still, in doing so, they may be induced, for example by the fact that the other language offers a particularly useful way of saying certain things, or that expressing things the way they are expressed in the other language may be advantageous – socially, communicatively, or otherwise – or that replication reduces the cognitive load that the simultaneous handling of two or more different languages entails.

The main concern in this book was with conceptual and structural replication rather than with the borrowing of linguistic substance. The claim we made is a strong one, namely that grammatical replication is essentially unidirectional, being shaped by principles of grammaticalization. With the qualifier "essentially" we refer to two kinds of phenomena that are not accounted for by the unidirectionality principle. One of them concerns counterexamples to the principle (see section 3.4.1): In the same way as with grammaticalization not affected by language contact, contact-induced grammaticalization offers examples that are at variance with the principle; but in both cases these examples, referred to as "degrammaticalization" in the relevant literature, constitute a small minority, accounting at best for one tenth of all instances of grammatical evolution (see Heine 2003b). The second kind of phenomena, discussed in section 3.4.3 under the heading "restructuring," concerns grammatical replication, e.g. of linear arrangements or of grammatical constituents and paradigms, leading straight to structural changes without involving grammaticalization. Restructuring is non-directional, having simply the effect that categorization of one language is adapted to that of another language. There is no reliable information on the quantitative magnitude of restructuring; but on the basis of the data that we have been able to access, it appears to be far less common than contact-induced grammaticalization.[1] To conclude, grammaticalizaton is statistically the most common mechanism shaping replication.

With reference to this mechanism we were able to propose a number of generalizations on the nature of replication, such as the following: If speakers of language R replicate a grammatical category on the model of language M then they are likely to develop a less grammatical construction into a more grammatical construction, while a development in the opposite direction is unlikely to happen. For example, R speakers may use M as a model to create new adpositions by grammaticalizing head nouns in possessive construction to prepositions or postpositions, to create new categories of tense or aspect by grammaticalizing, e.g. lexical verbs to auxiliaries or verbal clitics (see especially chapter 3), to create new articles by grammaticalizing demonstratives and the numeral 'one,' or to create new structures of clause subordination via the grammaticalization of interrogative sentences. We have not found any examples in the literature on language contact contradicting such generalizations, that is, examples that would suggest, for example, that replication had the effect that R speakers used language M as a model to develop nouns from adpositions, full verbs from tense/aspect categories, demonstratives from definite articles, a numeral for 'one' from indefinite articles, or interrogative clauses from relative clauses.

Fifth, there is another generalization that can be proposed on the basis of our discussion, relating to the nature of grammatical categories emerging as a result of replication. A comparison between replicated categories and their respective models suggests that the former differ overall from their respective model categories in being less grammaticalized, being used less frequently and in fewer contexts than their respective models, being optional rather than obligatory, not seldom taking the form of incipient categories (see section 2.4.1) that tend to go unnoticed in linguistic descriptions, their use being discouraged by conservative grammarians. On the basis of this observation it seems possible with a certain degree of probability to predict that in situations involving replication, the replica category will exhibit a less advanced stage of grammaticalization than the model category. There is, however, one caveat with regard to this generalization: given enough time, replica categories can develop in the same way as their models – with the result that the two become structurally similar (see section 3.4.5).

Our survey does not offer conclusive evidence on whether there are linguistic structures that are more likely to be replicated than others or, in Johanson's (2002a: 2, 43–8) words, whether there are relative degrees of structural attractiveness. To be sure, certain grammaticalization processes are more likely to take place than others. For example, new future tenses are more likely to be created by speakers of replica languages than past tenses (see section 3.3), the grammaticalization from interrogative to relative clause markers no doubt provided an attractive model to speakers in contact with European languages, and languages lacking articles or evidentials are likely to develop article-like and evidential use patterns when in intense contact with model languages having conventionalized article and evidential categories, respectively; overall, however, there is no substantial quantitative data to allow for meaningful generalizations.

Sixth, when embarking on the work leading to this book we were assuming that grammatical change taking place as a result of language contact is fundamentally different from purely language-internal change. With regard to replication, which is the central theme of the present work, this assumption turned out to be unfounded: there is no decisive difference between the two. Language contact can and frequently does trigger or influence the development of grammar in a number of ways; overall, however, the same kind of processes and directionality can be observed in both. Still, there is reason to assume that language contact in general and grammatical replication in particular may accelerate grammatical change, and in fact quite a number of the examples that we reviewed might have occurred independently of language contact but took place presumably more rapidly as a result of contact (see Danchev 1988: 40).

Grammaticalization theory has up to now been applied essentially only to problems concerning the internal structure of languages. There is a wealth of studies showing that the theory can also be applied in much the same way to pidgins and creoles (see section 6.2), but with few exceptions (Haase 1992; Nau 1995), grammaticalization theory was not confronted with a larger body of data on contact-induced linguistic transfers. Exactly this was the purpose of the present work, and the outcome is obvious. Contact can affect all components of language structure, from semantics to phonology, and from discourse-pragmatic organization to syntactic structure; but – as already pointed out by Nau (1995: 121) – the general mechanism shaping the development of grammatical categories appears to be the same, irrespective of whether or not language contact was involved.

This suggests on the one hand that grammaticalization theory is applicable in much the same way to contact-induced change as it is to other kinds of grammatical change. On the other hand, it also suggests that the boundary between the two is not as clear-cut as one is led to believe on the basis of what has been written on this subject matter. There is an abundance of works devoted to the question of whether a given grammatical change was internally or externally motivated – a number of cases discussed in the preceding chapters were of this nature. On the basis of our findings it would seem that this question has received more scholarly attention than it actually deserves; the history of work on language contact is rich in studies that have established that this general discussion is in some ways an academic non-issue (see, for example, Danchev 1989; Thomason & Kaufman 1988: 61; Dorian 1993). A question that we consider to be more relevant for understanding linguistic change is not whether one or the other was responsible but rather in which way and to what extent each of the two contributed to shaping grammatical change. This is an issue that has not been tackled in the present book.

Notes

1. THE FRAMEWORK

1. Accordingly, we will not be concerned with what Johanson (1992) calls *Globalkopieren* but rather with one specific kind of what he calls *Teilstrukturkopieren*.
2. Thomason (2003: 688) uses the terms "contact-induced change" and "(linguistic) interference" interchangeably; we will use the former term roughly in the sense proposed by Thomason but avoid the latter term since it has been used in a number of different ways and therefore might give rise to misunderstandings.
3. There would be reason for rejecting terms such as "transfer" and "borrowing" since these terms suggest that the receiving language takes something away from the donor language. Johanson (1992: 175) therefore proposes the term "copying" instead.
4. Thomason and Kaufman (1988) distinguish two basic types of mechanisms of contact-induced change, which they call borrowing and shift-induced interference, with each type involving a different kind of sociolinguistic profile. As we will see below, both types may be associated with grammatical replication.
5. For a critical appraisal of this term, see Bunte and Kendall (1981).
6. On the other hand, the development from impersonal pronoun to first-person plural pronoun is well documented (see Heine & Kuteva 2002).
7. A slightly different definition was proposed by her earlier, according to which convergence is "the use of morphemes from a single linguistic variety, but with parts of their lexical structure coming from another source" (Myers-Scotton 1998: 290).
8. See Mufwene (2001) for a way of accounting for this fact.
9. The only sociolinguistic factor that Aikhenvald (2002: 240) found to account for directionality in transfer patterns between East Tucanoan languages and the Arawak language Tariana is the relative number of speakers of the languages concerned.
10. A number of examples will be provided in the following chapters to substantiate this point. A perhaps striking example can be found in the language-contact situation of the Indian village Kupwar, where Marathi, the language of the untouchable caste, was perhaps the most vital component in influencing other languages (Gumperz & Wilson 1971; see chapter 5 below); for a similar example and an elaborate discussion, see Nadkarni (1975).
11. Following Nadkarni (1975: 681) we will say that extensive bilingualism exists when bilingualism is co-extensive with the entire speech community, while intensive bilingualism refers to situations where an L2 is used for a wide range of purposes in the course of normal, everyday interaction.

12. For example, the fact that in many European and other languages of the Old World there is a striking similarity between possessive constructions (e.g. *He has a dog.*) and perfect constructions (*He has gone.*) has given rise to controversies on whether this similarity is due to historical/conctact-induced or to universal cognitive factors (see, e.g., Jacob 1998: 106).

13. In a number of schools of contemporary linguistics, "reanalysis" has turned out to be a useful term (with reference to theories of language change, see, for example, Harris & Campbell 1995); in grammaticalization studies, however, it has been applied in many and often conflicting ways – to the extent that its use has given rise to largely vacuous controversies; we will therefore avoid it in the present work (see Heine & Kuteva 2002).

14. There is one exception: The evidence for the historical processes underlying the development of Romani modal complements and purpose clauses (Matras 1998b: 96–7) is not entirely unambiguous; this case will therefore be ignored in following discussions.

15. But there is at least one more possibility for a contact explanation of this particular case, not mentioned by Stolz. According to this possibility, the model language is Russian, while Finnish, Estonian, and Latvian are the replica languages. The arguments in support of such a hypothesis would be: First, Russian has a pattern equivalent to the one that Latvian has for expressing the deontic modality of necessity, e.g.

Russian

    Mne   prišlo-   s'   ždat'   dolgo.
    I.DAT come.PRET.3- REFL wait.INF long
    'I had to wait for a long time.'

Second, Russian is geographically contiguous with Finnish, Estonian and Latvian, but not with Lithuanian.

16. For another example, also involving the Tariana language, see section 2.2.2.

17. English is only a secondary L2 of Tigak speakers, the primary L2 being the English-based pidgin/creole Tok Pisin (Jenkins 2002).

18. Kuteva (2000) uses the Nandi dialect to demonstrate areal relationship; even closer contacts have been identified between speakers of Gusii and the Kipsiikis dialect of Kalenjin.

19. Glosses in parentheses are ours; the author does not provide glosses.

20. But see Dorian (1993) on this general issue.

21. As we will see in chapter 6, however, grammatical replication in pidgins and creoles does not differ essentially from what can be observed in other languages.

22. A problem associated with that definition is that it excludes possible areas where all languages belong to the same language family. Such a problem does not exist if one takes Emeneau's predication not as a definition but as a convenient tool for identifying linguistic areas or, in our case, instances of contact-induced transfer.

23. The influence of Uzbek on Tajik has been massive, to the extent that it has been argued (Doerfer 1967: 57) that Tajik is developing into a Turkic language.

24. On the basis of the description provided by Bunte and Kendall (1981), it would seem that the present example is suggestive of a process from minor to major use pattern

(see section 2.2), rather than of a process resulting in an entirely new grammatical category.

25. The term "restructuring" has been associated with a number of different uses. It is employed here as a technical term for but one of the many phenomena that have been subsumed under it (see section 3.4.3).

2. ON REPLICATING USE PATTERNS

1. The author does not provide interlinear glosses. We are using parentheses to indicate that the glosses are ours.
2. Glosses placed in parentheses are ours; no glosses are provided by the author.
3. Glosses placed in parentheses are ours; no glosses are provided by the author.
4. In the Atzecan language Nahuatl, agreement between nouns and their numeral modifiers is traditionally optional, while in Spanish, the main model language of Nahuatl speakers, it is obligatory. The increase and generalization of numeral agreement marking in Nahuatl is a complex process, depending on a number of variables, in particular on speakers' attitudes vis-à-vis the model language (Hill & Hill 1980; see also Hill & Hill 1986: 266–76).
5. To our knowledge, the exact role played by English has not been determined for any of these use patterns of American German; for a critical account, see Dorian (1993).
6. But see Dorian (1993: 136–7).
7. Kostov (1973: 110–11) refers to the process as verbal compounding rather than derivation.
8. "Aber die ungarische Sprache, deren sich die Lovāri-Zigeuner in Ungarn als zweiter Muttersprache bedienen, hat dazu beigetragen, daß die Lovāri-Mundart über ein herausgebildetes, völlig selbständiges System der Verbalkomposition verfügt" (Kostov 1973: 111).
9. We are not concerned here with the permissive meaning of this use pattern; but see Heine and Kuteva (2002: 193).
10. As we will see in section 3.1.2, this is a canonical instance of ordinary grammaticalization.
11. To our knowledge, this process is so far not well documented; the directionality proposed therefore needs to be corroborated by further evidence.
12. For further similarities, see Stolz (1991: 66–8).
13. Grammaticalization frequently involves narrowing, in that out of a range of lexical or grammatical items forming a paradigm, one is further grammaticalized. For example, the evolution of definite articles is likely to be characterized by a process where there is a paradigm of demonstrative attributes and where one of these attributes is selected to serve as a definite marker. But narrowing need not be due to grammaticalization, it can simply be an instance of grammatical replication that we propose to call restructuring (see 3.4.3).
14. In Thomason (2003: 700) there is a slightly different rendering of this situation. She observes that bilingual Kadiwéu speakers usually use SVO order when translating sentences from Portuguese.
15. We are ignoring here the role of intonation, which contrasts sharply between the two languages (see, for example, Cotter 1994).

16. But see also Enninger (1980: 346–7).
17. No glosses are provided by the authors.
18. No glosses are provided by the authors.
19. Conversely, non-pro-drop languages may also have minor use patterns where no pronoun is used.
20. Note that these examples differ from the kinds of processes that we are commonly concerned with in this book. First, they concern language use of individuals or small groups of individuals rather than speech communities or distinct segments of speech communities and, second, they concern variation in language use rather than linguistic categorization and, accordingly, they involve actual language behavior rather than documented language change.
21. "It comes as no surprise that the question of article use was already treated controversially in the oldest grammars of Sorbian, and that in the end the purist tradition won out, which viewed the article as a detestable Germanism."
22. Two Slavic languages, Southwestern Macedonian and North Russian, have gone one step further, developing the possessive perfect into full-fledged grammatical categories (see Heine & Kuteva forthc.).
23. Concerning the meaning of "Standard Average European," see Haspelmath (1998; 2001).
24. Lars Johanson (p.c.) draws attention to the fact that 'man' in Standard Swedish is not a good example here since it can be used in its singular form for counting soldiers, sailors, athletes, etc.

3. GRAMMATICALIZATION

1. For a similar use of this term, see Bruyn (1995).
2. The parameters proposed here differ slightly from those considered in our earlier work (see, e.g., Heine & Kuteva 2002), in that it includes a discourse-pragmatic notion, that is, (1a).
3. Bislama *stap* is historically derived from English *stop*.
4. Our interpretation of this case rests on Keesing (1988). The grammaticalization of verbs meaning 'stay, be present, exist' as durative or progressive markers is cross-linguistically widespread (see Heine & Kuteva 2002). Note further that this grammaticalization is not confined to Bislama, it can also be observed in Tok Pisin and Solomons Pijin, and it remains unclear whether the process looked at here took place independently of these other cases.
5. The dual and trial markers of Proto-Oceanic appear to be grammaticalized forms of the numerals **dua* 'two' and **tolu* 'three,' respectively, and in modern Oceanic languages, the dual and plural markers tend to exhibit a form similar to that of the respective numerals (see Keesing 1988: 71ff.).
6. This does not necessarily mean that Tigak was the only model language of the Tok Pisin system.
7. For another Western Oceanic language (Maisin) that has also undergone metatypic developments as a result of contact with Papuan languages, see Ross (1996: 192–9).
8. The evidence for this reconstruction is confined to two of the eight Takia postpositions presented by Ross (2001: 143).
9. Concerning word-order change in Takia, see section 2.2.

10. The following analysis is not based on Ross (1996; 2001) but rather on cross-linguistic observations on grammaticalization.

11. There are some exceptions, for which see our example in section 5.2.3.2 from the Mayan language Ch'ol.

12. The abbreviation "PWOc" stands for Proto Western Oceanic (a.n.).

13. Instead of languages, the strategy may as well be applied between different dialects of the same language.

14. Note that Matras also uses the following slightly different characterization for this term: "We [. . .] suggest the term *mutual isomorphism* to describe the process by which languages in contact stimulate one another to generalize iconic structures, thereby promoting structural compatibility among them." (Matras 1998b: 90).

15. What this aspectual category expresses is an event that is located at a point that is separated from but temporally close to the moment of speaking, for example *John has just arrived* (see Harris 1991: 201ff.).

16. While the Indo-Aryan language Konkani thus has replicated a construction from the Dravidian language Kannada, that very construction was replicated earlier by Kannada speakers from Indo-Aryan languages (Nadkarni 1975: 675; Sridhar 1978: 204).

17. Nor was there any remarkable sociolinguistic motivation; note that the Saraswat Brahmins have always tended to regard themselves in many ways superior to the Kannada-speaking communities among whom they live (Nadkarni 1975: 680); see section 7.2.

18. We are grateful to Martin Haspelmath for having drawn our attention to this fact.

19. Note, however, that this case of polysemy copying is not confined to Epi-Bislama contacts but appears to be of wider distribution in English-based pidgin/creoles varieties of the southwestern Indian Ocean region.

20. It goes without saying that, given enough time, the replica construction may also develop into a fully grammaticalized category.

21. Other European languages are English (*will*), Danish (*vil*), Norwegian Bokmål (*vil*), Faroese (*vil*), and Frisian *wal* (Dahl 2000b: 322).

22. With regard to their relative degree of grammaticalization, two types of Balkan languages can be distinguished: one where there is still an inflected auxiliary (Romanian, Serbian, and Croatian), and another one where the resulting future marker ends up as an uninflected particle (Modern Greek, Bulgarian, Macedonian, and Albanian; see Dahl 2000b: 323).

23. German has a conventionalized future category, the *werden*-future, but it is rarely used in colloquial discourse.

24. In the course of grammaticalization, this verb has experienced a number of erosion processes; accordingly, the future tense marker is, for example, *kan-* in a Krim dialect, *am-* in northwestern Bulgaria, *ka-* in a number of other dialects, and perhaps *-ma/mə* in central Balkan dialects (Boretzky & Igla 1999: 718).

25. Boretzky (1989: 369) concludes that on their way to Europe, Romani speakers did not have a future tense in their language.

26. Note that historically English *to* of *be going to* is not an infinitive but rather an allative or goal marker, in accordance with the universal pattern. Allative markers may on the one hand give rise to purpose markers; on the other hand, they may develop into intention markers, which again can give rise to future tense markers

'erkins & Perkins 1991). In the present case, we are concerned with the
ɔlution.

ɔasis of the translations provided by Keesing it would seem that the "topi-
caᵤ ̣ g particles" are perhaps more appropriately described as focus markers.

28. Phonological similarity may have contributed to the equation of the Oceanic perfect
markers (e.g. *no'o, na'a, na*) with Solomons Pijin *nao* (Keesing 1991: 329; see
section 2.1).

29. We are using parentheses here since the interlinear glosses are ours; there are no
glosses in the original.

30. We are grateful to Salikoko Mufwene for having drawn our attention to this fact.

31. In this process, Tariana has lost all other locative case morphemes (Aikhenvald
2003: 10).

32. Thus, Aikhenvald (2003: 11) argues that no grammaticalization is involved in this
case. Note, however, that Aikhenvald uses a fairly narrow definition of grammaticalization, which she views "as a path from a lexical item to a grammatical
morpheme" (Aikhenvald 2003: 4). Perhaps the majority of cases that make up
grammaticalization do not involve lexical items but rather grammatical forms and
structures that develop into even more grammatical structures (see our definition in
section 1.3).

33. While this process is confined to younger Tariana speakers, it appears to be gradually
spreading to traditional speakers, who increasingly use *alia* for identity/equation
clauses (Aikhenvald 2002: 154).

34. See Mufwene (1986) for a similar view concerning pidgins and creoles.

4. TYPOLOGICAL CHANGE

1. For a taxonomy of mechanisms leading to grammatical change, see Aikhenvald
(2003: 2–4), where she distinguishes between reanalysis, reinterpretation, grammatical accommodation, and grammaticalization (see also Harris & Campbell 1995:
66–7, 97).

2. By lingua franca we understand a language that is used habitually between people
whose mother tongues are different.

3. Note that there is some disagreement among the authors concerned on whether,
or to what extent, language contact can in fact be held responsible in a number of
the cases concerned, especially in the case of Balkan languages such as Bulgarian,
Macedonian, or Albanian.

4. This construction is, however, not restricted to use in the imperfective aspect
(Bernard Comrie, p.c.).

5. This reconstruction is, however, not uncontroversial: while some attribute this
change in Nahuatl to universal/internal developments, others maintain that it can
be interpreted meaningfully if one assumes language contact (see Karttunen 1976:
152).

6. These forms are taken from Upper Sorbian; Lower Sorbian has slightly different
forms for the demonstrative (see Lötzsch 1996: 52).

7. To be sure, nouns in generic use may take the singular form in certain contexts of
Standard English; but in contexts such as the present ones, a plural form would be
required in Standard English.

8. In this process, Tariana has lost all other locative case morphemes (Aikhenvald 2003: 10).
9. The marker -*naku* presumably represents the earlier form of the case marker. In addition to being the one found in Baniwa, it is also the one used by older-generation Tariana speakers, while -*nuku* is characteristic of younger people (Aikhenvald 2002: 103).
10. The problem with replication in Melanesian Pidgin varieties is that in most cases it remains unclear which language or languages exactly provided the model.
11. Note, however, that Pennsylvania German-speaking Mennonite Anabaptists of Ontario, Canada, have developed a new discourse particle via grammaticalization of the habitual aspect marker *als*, originally an adverb meaning 'always.' As a discourse particle, *als* seems to function much like an evaluator or intensifier not unlike *nur* 'just' in Standard German (Burridge 1992: 217).
12. For a different view, see Trask (1998).
13. Note that the influence of Gascon on Basque was not unilateral; rather, it appears that Basque has also acted as a model language for Gascon (see Haase 1997).
14. Concerning the grammaticalization comitative > instrumental, see Luraghi (2001), Heine and Kuteva (2002).
15. Kostov (1973: 110–11) refers to the process as verbal compounding rather than derivation.
16. "Aber die ungarische Sprache, deren sich die Lovāri-Zigeuner in Ungarn als zweiter Muttersprache bedienen, hat dazu beigetragen, daß die Lovāri-Mundart über ein herausgebildetes, völlig selbständiges System der Verbalkomposition verfügt" (Kostov 1973: 111). At the same time, Kostov (1973: 113) mentions that verbal composition was not unknown to Lovāri speakers; what they did under Hungarian influence is to increase the frequency of use of a rare type of expression, and expand and elaborate it – that is, we appear to be dealing with a transition from a minor to a major use pattern in accordance with the model proposed in chapter 2.
17. In accordance with the contrasting linear arrangement patterns of the languages concerned, grammaticalization led to the rise of prepositions in Latvian but to postpositions in the Finnic languages (Forssman 2000: 129–30).
18. As the data presented by Aikhenvald (2002: 138–9) suggest, this process can more appropriately be described as grammaticalization rather than as calquing or loan translation.
19. It goes without saying that this is not the only way in which contact-induced word order change may take place (Bernard Comrie; p.c.); our interest here is confined to changes resulting from grammaticalization.
20. Ternes (1999: 238) describes the particle *a* as a "verbal particle" (VP). We follow Harris and Campbell (1995: 155–6) in glossing it as a relative clause marker (see below).
21. There is an alternative hypothesis according to which the grammaticalization that Breton underwent is not the result of transfer from Romance languages but can be traced back to an earlier Celtic structure (Jost Gippert; p.c.). While such a possibility cannot entirely be ruled out, the evidence available suggests that the Breton structure cannot be traced back to earlier Celtic; rather, it is the result of processes that happened more recently, that is, within the last millennium after the split of Breton from its insular Celtic relatives. Nevertheless, assuming that that hypothesis is correct, this would not change the basic fact that there was a transfer of a

grammaticalization process from one language to another – be it from Romance to Celtic or the other way round.

22. There is yet another – more specific – possibility, which is beyond the scope of this investigation: worn-out forms are not lost; rather, they are kept as forms but their grammatical function is changed (exaptation).

23. Glosses are ours; no glosses are provided by the author.

24. Glosses are ours; no interlinear glosses are provided by the author.

5. ON LINGUISTIC AREAS

1. In a number of works discussing linguistic areas, Joseph (1983) is cited as the primary reference work, or at least as one of the primary works on the Balkan sprachbund. However, while this work constitutes the most detailed study on the sprachbund, it deals essentially with only one linguistic property characterizing this area, namely infinitive loss.

2. The Sri Lanka sprachbund consists of languages belonging to at least four different families: Singhalese (Indo-Aryan), Tamil (Dravidian), Sri Lanka Malay (Austronesian), Sri Lanka Portuguese, and Vedda, the aboriginal language which appears to be a genetic isolate. Bakker (2000: 31) regards Sri Lanka as a sprachbund which itself is part of the wider South Asian sprachbund.

3. Cf. also the following statement according to which areal linguistics "deals with the results of the diffusion of structural features across linguistic boundaries" (Campbell, Kaufman & Smith-Stark 1986: 530).

4. "This term 'linguistic area' may be defined as meaning an area which includes languages belonging to more than one family but showing traits in common which are found not to belong to the other members of (at least) one of the families" (Emeneau 1956: 16, n. 28).

5. Note, however, that Campbell, Kaufman & Smith-Stark (1986: 535) have a more extended notion of areal linguistics: "We conclude then [. . .] that our goal should be to determine the historical facts which explain similarities among languages, regardless of whether they result from common heritage from some proto-language, or from diffusion."

6. Kazazis (1965) restricted his analysis to the following Balkan languages: Tosk Albanian, Bulgarian, Greek, and Rumanian.

7. Furthermore, these authors note:

   That is, typical LA's [linguistic areas; a.n.] such as South Asia and the Balkans [. . .] are characterized by different sorts of diffusion. Some are restricted locally, and do not extend throughout the area; some reach beyond the borders of the area; some overlap, or show criss-crossing isoglosses from other LA's. (Campbell, Kaufman & Smith-Stark 1986: 558)

8. Friedman (1994: 109) notes that classic Balkanisms such as object reduplication began with pragmatically conditioned constructions that became grammaticalized to varying degrees in different Balkan languages.

9. Comparing the situation of the Vaupés region with the one described by Gumperz and Wilson (1971) for Kupwar, Aikhenvald concludes: "The end-result of diffusion seems to be very much like that of the diffusion in the Vaupés – whereby an almost full intertranslatability is achieved" (2002: 240).

10. The only other case we are aware of is found in Maltese.
11. Note that our glosses differ slightly from those given by Walter Bisang.
12. The area includes all Indo-European languages of Europe spoken south of Slovene, Hungarian, and Ukrainian (Fiedler 1999: 487), although there is some disagreement as to its exact delimitation.
13. For possible additional properties, see Joseph 1992.
14. This is presumably the most salient grammaticalization pathway for future tenses arising in the Balkans, but it is certainly not the only one characterizing this sprachbund (see, for example, Schaller 1975: 152–5).
15. The rise of this grammaticalization area is said to date back to the "imperial sprachbund" of around 300 AD (Hinrichs 1999: 454).
16. Glosses and translation of this example are provided by the present authors.
17. In Bulgarian, object reduplication is documented at least since the thirteenth century, and the earliest examples involved reduplicated pronouns, that is, objects expressed by personal pronouns (Asenova 1999: 224–5).
18. This difference in grammaticalization is reflected in the frequency of use of object reduplication: while in Bulgarian literary texts the number of reduplicated objects in comparison with the total number of objects used is not greater than 10 percent, in Macedonian it is around 50 percent (Asenova 1999: 226).
19. Greenberg accounts for this schema in the following way: "If we add three items to ten, then the three are put on the heap of ten and not vice versa" (1978b: 265).
20. That this is an instance of a canonical grammaticalization process is suggested, for example, by the observation that locative and comitative adpositions commonly give rise to linking elements of noun phrases (see Heine & Kuteva 2002 for examples).
21. For an explanation of the situation in Hungarian, see Petrucci (1993: 297–8).
22. For example, Gołab (1959: 419) concludes bluntly: "In short, a 'Balkanism' of Slavic origin is very difficult to find."
23. For example, Schaller (1975: 151) argues that the Hungarian structure of numerals has been influenced by the Slavic pattern.
24. There are traces of the construction in Greek around 400 AD, but it was never conventionalized (Hinrichs 1999: 44). For a more detailed reconstruction of this grammaticalization, see Reichenkron (1958).
25. Note that among the many hypotheses that have been proposed to account for the directionality of infinitive loss in the Balkans, the one proposed by Sandfeld (1930: 19, 173–9) and propagated by Banfi (1990) appears to be based on the strongest kind of evidence. According to this hypothesis, the process started in the church environment of Byzantine-Medieval Greek.
26. For a critical review of the Meso-America hypothesis, see Stolz and Stolz (2001: 1547–50).
27. We are restricted here to the main characteristics of the construction; for a number of differences in individual languages, see Campbell, Kaufman & Smith-Stark (1986: 546), Stolz and Stolz (2001: 1544–5).
28. Note, however, that not uncommonly there are quinary and/or decimal structures in addition to the vigesimal system (see Stolz & Stolz 2001: 1545–6).
29. Note that this is also a widespread grammaticalization in Sinitic languages; see Chappell (2001: 347–50).

30. In addition to the Daly River area, Dixon (2002: 668–86) proposes three other areas in Australia, which he calls the Lower Murray, the Arandic, and the North Kimberley small linguistic areas. However, in these three areas there appears to be a distinct possibility that some of the shared linguistic features are the result of genetic rather than of contact-induced relationship.
31. Another Western Oceanic language, Maisin, has also undergone metatypic developments as a result of contact with Papuan languages (see Ross 1996: 192–9).
32. Concerning the term restructuring, see section 3.4.3.
33. Note, that these areas concern only one replica language, Tariana.
34. There is one possible exception: in the case of the metatypy-like situation of Ma'a and Mbugu in northeastern Tanzania (see section 5.1.2), no grammaticalization processes have been identified so far.

6. LIMITS OF REPLICATION

1. See e.g. Poplack's (1981: 174) notion Equivalent Constraint relating to the linear arrangement of grammatical constituents in code-switching.
2. Note, however, that translators were not consistent in their behavior, and some would prefer to leave German articles untranslated.
3. This grammaticalization could have been enhanced by the fact that there "is a certain shade of indefiniteness in the use of *üks* in Estonian" (Lehiste 1999: 41).
4. Note that the Molise Croatian progressive constitutes a recurrent use pattern which has not developed into a conventionalized construction.
5. As we will see later in this section, there are further problems associated with this example.
6. This view is not shared by all authors who have dealt with this issue.
7. Translation as provided by Timberlake (1976).
8. Translation as provided by Timberlake (1976).
9. The Balkan sprachbund, for example, is fairly uncontroversial as a linguistic area; but when it comes to determining how this area arose or which the ultimate model language was, one is faced with a plethora of hypotheses some of which are hard to reconcile with one another (see, for example, Joseph 1992: 155).
10. With this distinction we do not wish to add to the many already existing typologies of language-contact situations (see, for example, Thomason & Kaufmann 1988); we are simply concerned with the question of whether it is possible to predict which kinds of languages provide the model for contact-induced grammaticalization.
11. Not all cases that have been claimed to violate the universality principle, however, are really convincing; see Plag (forthc.) for details.
12. The glosses are ours; there are no glosses in the original.
13. Rather than perfect markers, adverbs meaning 'now' are more likely to give rise to aspectual constructions denoting that an action is still going on (Heine & Kuteva 2002: 218).
14. Glosses are ours; no interlinear glosses are provided by the author.
15. "Indirect diffusion thus involves patterns, while direct diffusion involves actual morphemes" (Heath 1978: 119).

16. Concerning problems of separating internal from external/contact-induced motivation, see Dorian (1993).
17. Trudgill (1983: 106–7) suggests that Afrikaans (relative to Dutch), Norwegian (relative to Old Norse) and Middle English (relative to Old English, see also Bailey & Maroldt 1977) may be considered as creoloids.

7. CONCLUSIONS

1. Note that in the relevant literature on this issue, contact-induced replication has been referred to summarily as "calquing," "reanalysis," "indirect diffusion," etc. But, as we saw in the preceding chapters, most of the cases discussed in such works concern grammaticalization rather than restructuring.

References

Abbi, Anvita. 1992. *Reduplication in South Asian languages: an areal, typological, and historical study*. New Delhi: Allied Publishers.

Aikhenvald, Alexandra Y. 1996. Areal diffusion in northwest Amazonia: the case of Tariana. *Anthropological Linguistics* 38: 73–116.

2002. *Language contact in Amazonia*. New York: Oxford University Press.

2003. Language contact and language change in Amazonia. In Blake and Burridge (eds.), pp. 1–20.

Aikhenvald, Alexandra Y. and Robert M. W. Dixon. 1998. Evidentials and areal typology: a case study from Amazonia. *Language Sciences* 20, 3: 241–57.

(eds.). 2001. *Areal diffusion and genetic inheritance: Problems in comparative linguistics*. Oxford: Oxford University Press.

(eds.). 2003. *Studies in evidentiality*. (Typological Studies in Language, 54.) Amsterdam, Philadelphia: John Benjamins.

Alanne, Eero. 1972. Zur Rolle der syntaktischen Interferenz der verwandten und unverwandten Sprachen. *Neuphilologische Mitteilungen* 73: 568–74.

Allard, F. X. 1975. *A structural and semantic analysis of the German modal "mögen."* (Stanford German Studies, 6.) Berne, Frankfurt.

Andersen, Henning (ed.). 1995. *Historical linguistics 1993: Selected papers from the 11th International Conference on Historical Linguistics, Los Angeles, 16–20 August 1993.* (Amsterdam Studies in the Theory and History of Linguistic Science, 124.) Amsterdam, Philadelphia: John Benjamins.

Anderson, John M. 1997. Remarks on the structure and development of the *have* perfect. *Folia Linguistica Historica* 18, 1–2: 3–23.

Anderson, Roger W. 1982. Determining the linguistic attributes of language attrition. In Lambert and Freed (eds.), pp. 83–118.

Arends, Jacques. 1986. Genesis and development of the equative copula in Sranan. In Muysken and Smith (eds.), pp. 103–27.

Asenova, Petja. 1999. Bulgarian. In Hinrichs and Büttner (eds.), pp. 211–37.

Bailey, C.-J. N. and K. Maroldt. 1977. The French lineage of English. In Meisel (ed.), pp. 21–53.

Baker, Philip (ed.). 1995. *From contact to creole and beyond*. London: University of Westminster Press.

Baker, Philip and Anand Syea (eds.). 1996. *Changing meanings, changing functions: Papers relating to grammaticalization in contact languages*. (Westminster Creolistics Series, 2.) London: University of Westminster Press.

Bakker, Peter. 2000. Convergence intertwining: an alternative way towards the genesis of mixed languages. In Gilbers, Nerbonne, and Schaeken (eds.), pp. 29–35.

Bakker, Peter and Maarten Mous (eds.). 1994. *Mixed languages: 15 case studies in language intertwining*. (Studies in Language and Language Use, 13.) Amsterdam: Institute for Functional Research into Language and Language Use (IFOTT).

Banfi, Emanuele. 1990. The infinitive in south-east European languages. In Bechert, Bernini, and Buridant (eds.), pp. 165–83.

Bascom, William R. and Melville J. Herskovits (eds.). 1959. *Continuity and change in African cultures*. Chicago: University of Chicago Press.

Bechert, Johannes, Giuliano Bernini, and Claude Buridant (eds.). 1990. *Toward a typology of European languages*. (Empirical Approaches to Language Typology, 8.) Berlin: Mouton: De Gruyter.

Beck, David. 2000. Grammatical convergence and the genesis of diversity in the Northwest Coast *Sprachbund*. *Anthropological Linguistics* 42, 2: 147–213.

Becker, Henrick. 1948. *Der Sprachbund*. Leipzig: Humboldt Bücherei Gerhard Mindt.

Bender, Marvin L., J. D. Bowen, R. L. Cooper, and Charles A. Ferguson (eds.). 1976. *Language in Ethiopia*. London: Oxford University Press.

Berger, T. n.d. Das System der tschechischen Demonstrativpronomina: Textgrammatische und stilspezifische Gebrauchsbedingungen. Unpublished Habilitationsschrift, Munich.

Bernini, Giuliano and Paulo Ramat. 1996. *Negative sentences in the languages of Europe: A typological approach*. (Empirical Approaches to Language Typology, 16.) Berlin: Mouton de Gruyter.

Bickerton, Derek. 1981. *Roots of language*. Ann Arbor, Mich.: Karoma.

Bisang, Walter. 1996a. Areal typology and grammaticalization: Processes of grammaticalization based on nouns and verbs in East and Mainland South East Asian languages. *Studies in Language* 20, 3: 519–97.

   1996b. Sprachliche Areale in Asien am Beispiel der Satzverknüpfung. In Boretzky (ed.), pp. 24–50.

   1998. Grammaticalization and language contact, constructions and positions. In Giacalone Ramat and Hopper (eds.), pp. 13–58.

   (ed.). 2001a. *Aspects of typology and universals*. (Studia typologica, 1.) Berlin: Akademie-Verlag.

   2001b. Areality, grammaticalization and language typology: on the explanatory power of functional criteria and the status of Universal Grammar. In Bisang (ed.), pp. 175–223.

Blake, Barry J. and Kate Burridge (eds.). 2003. *Historial linguistics 2001: Selected papers from the 15th International Conference on Historical Linguistics, Melbourne, 13–17 August 2001*. (Amsterdam Studies in the Theory and History of Linguistic Science, 237.) Amsterdam, Philadelphia: John Benjamins.

Blench, R. and Spriggs, M. (eds.). 1997. *Archaeology and language*. Vol. I: *Theoretical and methodological orientations*. London: Routlege.

Bliss, A. J. 1972. Languages in contact: Some problems of Hiberno-English. *Proceedings of the Royal Irish Academy* 72, Section C: 63–82.

Boeder, Winfried, Christoph Schroeder, Karl Heinz Wagner, and Wolfgang Wildgen (eds.). 1998. *Sprache in Raum und Zeit: In memoriam Johannes Bechert*. Vol. II: *Beiträge zur empirischen Sprachwissenschaft*. Tübingen: Gunter Narr.

Boeschoten, Hendrik E. and Lars Johanson (eds.). In press. *Turkic language contacts.* Amsterdam, Philadelphia: John Benjamins.

Bolonyai, Agnes. 2000. "Elective affinities": Language contact in the Abstract Lexicon and its structural consequences. *International Journal of Bilingualism* 4, 1: 81–106.

Borg, Albert and Manwel Mifsud. 2002. Maltese object marking in a Mediterranean context. In Ramat and Stolz (eds.), pp. 33–46.

Boretzky, Norbert. 1975. *Der türkische Einfluss auf das Albanische.* Part 1: *Phonologie und Morphologie der albanischen Turzismen.* (Albanische Forschungen, 11.) Wiesbaden: Otto Harrassowitz.

  1983. *Kreolsprachen, Substrate und Sprachwandel.* Wiesbaden: Otto Harrassowitz.

  1986. Regelentlehnung und Substrateinfluss in Kreolsprachen. In Boretzky, Enninger and Stolz (eds.), pp. 9–39.

  (ed.) 1996. *Areale, Kontakte, Dialekte, Sprachen und ihre Dynamik in mehrsprachigen Situationen.* (Bochum-Essener Beiträge zur Sprachwandelforschung, 24.) Bochum: N. Brockmeyer.

Boretzky, Norbert, Werner Enninger, and Thomas Stolz (eds.). 1986. *Beiträge zum 2. Essener Kolloquium über "Kreolsprachen und Sprachkontakte."* (Essener Beiträge zur Sprachwandelforschung, 2.) Bochum: N. Brockmeyer.

  1989. Zum Interferenzverhalten des Romani. *Zeitschrift für Phonetik, Sprachwissenschaft und Kommunikationsforschung* 42, 3: 357–74.

  (eds.). 1989. *Beiträge zum 5. Essener Kolloquium über "Grammatikalisierung: Natürlichkeit und Systemökonomie."* Vol. I. (Essener Beiträge zur Sprachwandelforschung, 7.) Bochum: N. Brockmeyer.

Boretzky, Norbert and Birgit Igla. 1994. Romani mixed dialects. In Bakker and Mous (eds.), pp. 35–68.

  1999. Balkanische (südosteuropäische) Einflüsse im Romani. In Hinrichs and Büttner (eds.), pp. 709–31.

Brendemoen, Berndt, Elizabeth Lanza, and Else Ryen (eds.). 1999. *Language encounters across time and space: Studies in language contact.* Oslo: Novus Forlag.

Brenzinger, Matthias (ed.). 1992. *Language death: Factual and theoretical explorations with special reference to East Africa.* Berlin: Mouton de Gruyter.

Breu, Walter (ed.). 1990a. *Slavistische Linguistik 1989.* Munich: Otto Sagner.

  1990b. Sprache und Sprachverhalten in den slavischen Dörfern des Molise (Süditalien). In Breu (ed.) 1990a, pp. 35–65.

  1992. Das italokroatische Verbsystem zwischen slavischem Erbe und kontaktbedingter Entwicklung. In Reuther (ed.), pp. 93–122.

  1994. Der Faktor Sprachkontakt in einer dynamischen Typologie des Slavischen. In Mehlig (ed.), pp. 41–64.

  1996. Überlegungen zu einer Klassifizierung des grammatischen Wandels im Sprachkontakt (am Beispiel slavischer Kontaktfälle). *Sprachtypologie und Universalienforschung* 49, 1: 21–38.

Bright, William (ed.). 1992a. *International encyclopedia of linguistics.* Volume 1. New York, Oxford: Oxford University Press. [See under Areal linguistics, Balkan languages].

  (ed.) 1992b. *International encyclopedia of linguistics.* Vol. II. New York, Oxford: Oxford University Press.

Bruyn, Adrienne. 1995. *Grammaticalization in creoles: The development of determiners and relative clauses in Sranan*. Amsterdam: IFOTT.
  1996. On identifying instances of grammaticalization in Creole languages. In Baker and Syea (eds.), pp. 29–46.
  1997. The history of locative verbs in Sranan. Paper presented at the 1997 annual meeting of the Society for Pidgin and Creole Linguistics. London.
Bunte, Pamela A. and Martha B. Kendall. 1981. When is an error not an error? Notes on language contact and the question of interference. *Anthropological Linguistics* 23, 1: 1–7.
Burridge, Kate. 1992. Creating grammar: Examples from Pennsylvania German, Ontario. In Burridge and Enninger (eds.), pp. 199–241.
  1995. Evidence of grammaticalization in Pennsylvania German. In Andersen (ed.), pp. 59–75.
Burridge, Kate and Werner Enninger (eds.). 1992. *Diachronic studies on the languages of the Anabaptists*. (Bochum-Essener Beiträge zur Sprachwandelforschung, 17.) Bochum: N. Brockmeyer.
Bybee, Joan L. 2003. Mechanisms of change in grammaticization: The role of frequency. In Joseph and Janda (eds.), pp. 602–23.
Bybee, Joan L. and Suzanne Fleischman (eds.). 1995. *Modality in grammar and discourse*. Amsterdam, Philadelphia: John Benjamins.
Bybee, Joan L. and Paul Hopper (eds.). 2001. *Frequency and the emergence of linguistic structure*. (Typological Studies in Language, 45.) Amsterdam, Philadelphia: John Benjamins.
Bybee, Joan L., William Pagliuca, and Revere D. Perkins. 1991. Back to the future. In Traugott and Heine (eds.) 1991b, pp. 17–58.
Bybee, Joan L., Revere D. Perkins, and William Pagliuca. 1994. *The evolution of grammar: tense, aspect and modality in the languages of the World*. Chicago: University of Chicago Press.
Calăkov, M. 1974. Casticite za badešte vreme *za* i *sa* v balgarskite govori'. In *V pamet na Prof. St. Stojkov. Ezikovedski izsledvanija*. Sofia.
Campbell, Lyle. 1985. *The Pipil language of El Salvador*. (Mouton Grammar Library, 1.) Berlin, New York, Amsterdam: Mouton.
  1987. Syntactic change in Pipil. *International Journal of American Linguistics* 53, 3: 253–80.
  1993. On proposed universals of grammatical borrowing. In Jeffers (ed.), pp. 91–109.
  2001. What's wrong with grammaticalization? *Language Sciences* 23, 2–3: 113–61.
Campbell, Lyle and Richard Janda. 2001. Introduction: Conceptions of grammaticalization and their problems. *Language Sciences* 23, 2–3: 93–112.
Campbell, Lyle, Terrence Kaufman, and Thomas C. Smith-Stark. 1986. Meso-America as a linguistic area. *Language* 62, 3: 530–70.
Campbell, Lyle and Marianne Mithun (eds.). 1979. *The language of Native America: Historical and comparative assessment*. Austin: University of Texas Press.
Campbell, Lyle and Martha C. Muntzel. 1989. The structural consequences of language death. In Dorian (ed.), pp. 181–96.
Cárdenas, Hernán Urrutia 1995. Morphosyntactic features in the Spanish of the Basque country. In Silva-Corvalán (ed.), pp. 243–59.

Chappell, Hilary. 2001. Language contact and areal diffusion in Sinitic languages. In Aikhenvald and Dixon (eds.), pp. 328–57.

Clyne, Michael. 1972. *Perspectives on language contact based on a study of German in Australia.* New York: W. S. Heinman.

Comrie, Bernard. 1981. *The languages of the Soviet Union.* Cambridge: Cambridge University Press.

Corne, Chris. 1995. A contact-induced and vernacularized language: How Melanesian is Tayo? In Baker (ed.), pp. 121–48.

 1999. *From French to Creole: The development of new vernaculars in the French colonial world.* London: University of Westminster Press.

Costello, John R. 1985. Pennsylvania German and English: Languages in contact. In Kloss (ed.), pp. 111–20.

 1992. The periphrastic *duh* construction in Anabaptist and nonsectarian Pennsylvania German: Synchronic and diachronic perspectives. In Burridge and Enninger (eds.), pp. 242–63.

Cotter, Colleen. 1994. Focus in Irish and English: Contrast and contact. *Berkeley Linguistics Society* 20: 134–44.

Craig, Colette G. 1991. Ways to go in Rama: A case study in polygrammaticalization. In Traugott and Heine (eds.) 1991b, pp. 455–92.

Croft, William. 1990. *Typology and universals.* Cambridge: Cambridge University Press.

Csató, Éva Ágnes. 1996. Some typological properties of North-Western Karaim in areal perspectives. In Boretzky (ed.), pp. 68–83.

 2001. Syntactic code-copying in Karaim. In Dahl and Koptjevskaja-Tamm (eds.), 2001a, pp. 271–83.

 2002. Karaim: A high-copying language. In Jones and Esch (eds.), pp. 315–27.

Csató, Eva A., Bo Isaksson, and Carina Jahani (eds.). In press. *Linguistic convergence and areal diffusion: Case studies from Iranian, Semitic and Turkic.* Routledge Curzon.

Cyffer, Norbert. 2000. Areale Merkmale im TAM-System und in der Syntax der saharanischen Sprachen. In Vossen, Mietzner and Meissner (eds.), pp. 159–82.

Dahl, Östen. 1990. Standard Average European as an exotic language. In Bechert, Bernini, and Buridant (eds.), pp. 3–8.

 1996. Das Tempussystem des Deutschen im typologischen Vergleich. In Lang and Zifonun (eds.), pp. 359–68.

 (ed.). 2000a. *Tense and aspect in the languages of Europe.* (Empirical Approaches to Language Typology, Eurotyp, 20–6.) Berlin, New York: Mouton de Gruyter.

 2000b. The grammar of future time reference in European languages. In Dahl (ed.), 2000a, pp. 309–28.

 2000c. Verbs of becoming as future copulas. In Dahl (ed.), 2000a, pp. 351–61.

 2001. Principles of areal typology. In Haspelmath et al. (eds.), pp. 1456–70.

Dahl, Östen and Maria Koptjevskaja-Tamm (eds.) 2001a. *Circum-Baltic languages: Typology and contact.* Vol. I: *Past and present.* (Studies in Language and Companion Series, 54.) Amsterdam, Philadelphia: John Benjamins.

 (eds.) 2001b. *Circum-Baltic languages: Typology and contact.* Vol. II: *Grammar and typology.* (Studies in Language and Companion Series, 55.) Amsterdam, Philadelphia: John Benjamins.

Damjanova, M. and Ch. Grănčarov. 1981. Analogični momenti v razvoja na badešte vreme v balgarski i anglijski ezik¹. *Balgarski Ezik* 33, No. 5.

Danchev, Andrei. 1984. Translation and syntactic change. In Fišiak (ed.), pp. 47–60.

1988. Language contact and language change. *Folia Linguistica* 22: 37–53.

1989. Language change typology and adjectival comparison in contact situations. *Folia Linguistica Historica* 9, 2: 161–74.

Danchev, Andrei and Merja Kytö. 1994. The construction *be going to + infinitive* in Early Modern English. In Kastovsky (ed.), pp. 59–77.

Danylenko, Andrii. 2000. The genitive of agent and the instrumental of means in Old Ukranian: An old idea worth revising? *General Linguistics* 37, 1: pp. 41–70.

Danylenko, Andrii. 2001a. Russian *čto za*, Ukrainian *ščo za*, Polish *co za* "was für ein": A case of contact-induced or parallel change? *Diachronica* 18, 2: 241–65.

2001b. The verb "have" in East Slavic. In *The Proceedings of the 13th UCLA Indo-European Conference*. Los Angeles.

Danylenko, Andrii and Serhii Vakulenko. 1995. *Ukranian*. Munich and Newcastle: Lincom Europa.

DeLancey, Scott and Russel Tomlin (eds.). 1988. *Papers from the 3rd Pacific Linguistics Conference*. Eugene: University of Oregon.

Demiraj, Shaban. 1985. About the origin of the possessive perfect in Albanian and in some other languages. In Ölberg, Schmidt, and Bothien (eds.) 1985, pp. 81–5.

Denison, N. 1968. Sauris: A trilingual community in diatypic perspective. *Man*, n.s., 3: 578–92.

1988. Language contact and language norm. *Folia Linguistica* 22: 11–35.

Diessel, Holger. 1999. *Demonstratives: Form, function, and grammaticalization*. (Typological Studies in Language, 42.) Amsterdam, Philadelphia: John Benjamins.

Dihoff, Ivan R. (ed.). 1983. *Current approaches to African linguistics*. Vol. I. Dordrecht: Foris Publications.

Dil, Anwar (ed.). 1980. *Language and linguistic area*. Stanford: Stanford University Press.

Dimmendaal, Gerrit J. 1995. The emergence of tense marking in the Nilotic-Bantu borderland as an instance of areal adaptation. In Zima (ed.) 1995, pp. 29–43.

2001a. Areal diffusion versus genetic inheritance: An African perspective. In Aikhenvald and Dixon (eds.), pp. 358–92.

2001b. Language shift and morphological convergence in the Nilotic area. *SUGIA* 16–17: 83–124.

Dixon, Robert M. W. 2002. *Australian languages: Their origin and development*. Cambridge: Cambridge University Press.

Doerfer, Gerhard. 1967. *Türkische Lehnwörter im Tadschikischen*. (Abhandlungen für die Kunde des Morgenlandes, 37, 3.) Wiesbaden: Steiner.

Dorian, Nancy C. (ed.). 1989. *Investigating obsolescence: Studies in language contraction and death*. Cambridge: Cambridge University Press.

1993. Internally and externally motivated change in language contact settings: Doubts about dichotomy. In Jones (ed.), pp. 131–55. ← not in lib

Drewes, A. J. 1994. Borrowing in Maltese. In Bakker and Mous (eds.), pp. 83–111.

Drinka, Bridget. 1998. The evolution of grammar. In Schmid, Austin and Stein (eds.), pp. 117–33.

Forthc. Areal factors in the development of the European periphrastic perfect. *Word*.

Dryer, Matthew S. 1992. The Greenbergian word order correlations. *Language* 68: 81–138.

DuBois, John W. 1987. The discourse basis of ergativity. *Language* 63: 805–55.

Durán, Richard P. (ed.). 1981. *Latino language and communicative behavior*. Norwood, NJ: Ablex.

Durie, Mark and Malcolm D. Ross, M. (eds.). 1996. *The comparative method reviewed: Regularity and irregularity in language change*. New York: Oxford University Press.

Ebert, Karen. 2001. Südasien als Sprachbund. In Haspelmath et al. (eds.), pp. 1529–39.

Eichhoff, J. 1971. German in Wisconsin. In Gilbert (ed.), pp. 43–57.

Emeneau, Murray B. 1956. India as a linguistic area. *Language* 32, 1: 3–16.
    1980. Bilingualism and structural borrowing. In Dil (ed.), pp. 38–65.

Enfield, Nick J. 2001. On genetic and areal linguistics in mainland south-east Asia: Parallel polyfunctionality of "acquire." In Aikhenvald and Dixon (eds.), pp. 255–90.

Enninger, Werner. 1980. Syntactic convergence in a stable triglossia plus trilingualism situation in Kent County, Delaware, USA. In Nelde (ed.), pp. 343–50.

Epstein, R. 1993. The definite article: Early stages of development. In van Marle (ed.), pp. 111–34.

Ferguson, Charles A. 1976. The Ethiopian language area. In Bender et al. (eds.), pp. 63–76.

Feuillet, Jack. 2001. Aire linguistique balkanique. In Haspelmath et al. (eds.), pp. 1510–28.

Fiedler, Wilfried. 1999. Tempus, Modus und Aspekt in den Sprachen Südosteuropas. In Hinrichs and Büttner (eds.), pp. 487–517.

Filin, F. P. 1972. *Proisxoždenie russkogo, ukrainskogo i belorusskogo jazykov*. Leningrad: Naouka.

Filppula, Markku. 1986. *Some aspects of Hiberno-English in a functional sentence perspective*. (University of Joensuu Publications in the Humanities, 7.) Joensuu: University of Joensuu.

Fišiak, Jaček (ed.). 1984. *Trends in linguistics: Historical syntax*. Berlin: Mouton de Gruyter.

Fleischman, Suzanne. 1982a. *The future in thought and language: Diachronic evidence from Romance*. (Cambridge Studies in Linguistics, 36.) Cambridge: Cambridge University Press.
    1982b. The past and the future: Are they *coming* or *going*? *Berkeley Linguistics Society* 8: 322–34.
    1983. From pragmatics to grammar. Diachronic reflections on complex pasts and futures in Romance. *Lingua* 60: 183–214.

Forssman, Berthold. 2000. Baltisch-finnische Sprachkontakte am Beispiel der Adposition. In Ofitsch and Zinko (eds.), pp. 125–32.

Foulet, Lucien. 1920. La disparition du prétérite. *Romania* 46: 271–313.

Frajzyngier, Zygmunt and Traci S. Curl (eds.). 2000. *Reflexives: Forms and functions*. (Typological Studies in Language, 40.) Amsterdam, Philadelphia: John Benjamins.

Friedman, Victor A. 1976. Dialectal synchrony and diachronic syntax: The Macedonian perfect. *Chicago Linguistic Society, Papers from the Parasession on Diachronic Syntax* (1976): 96–104.

    1994. Variation and grammaticalization in the development of Balkanisms. *Chicago Linguistic Society* 30, 2: 101–15.

    1997. One grammar, three lexicons: Ideological overtones and underpinnings in the Balkan *Sprachbund*. *Chicago Linguistic Society* 33: 23–44.

    2003. *Turkish in Macedonia and beyond: Studies in contact, typology and other phenomena in the Balkans and the Caucasus*. (Turcologica, 52.) Wiesbaden: Otto Harrassowitz.

Fuller, Janet M. 1996. When cultural maintenance means linguistic convergence: Pennsylvania German evidence for the Matrix Language Turnover hypothesis. *Language in Society* 25: 493–514.

Garza Cuarón, Beatriz and Paulette Levy (eds.). 1990. *Homenaje a Jorge A. Suárez: Lingüística indoamericana e hispánica*. (Estudios de lingüística y literatura, 18.) Mexico: El Colegio de México.

Geisler, Hans and Daniel Jacob (eds.). 1998. *Transitivität und Diathese in romanischen Sprachen*. (Linguistische Arbeiten, 392.) Tübingen: Max Niemeyer.

Georgiev, V. D. 1957 [1976]. Văznikvane na novi složni glagolni formi săs spomagatelen glagol "imam." *Izvestija na Instituta za bălgarski ezik* 5, Sofia.

    1985. Văznikvane na časticata za bădešte vreme kešte. In *Problemi na balgarskija ezik*. Sofia: BAN Press.

Georgiev, V., D. Ivanova-Mirčeva, I. Kočev, M. Dejanova, and St. Stojanova (eds.). 1986. *Uvod v izucavaneto na juznoslavjanskite ezici*. Sofia: BAN Press.

Gerhardt, Dietrich (ed.). 1971. *Hugo Schuchardt, Slawo-deutsches und Slawo-italienisches. Mit Schuchardts übrigen Arbeiten zur Slavistik und mit neuen Registern*. (Slavische Propyläen, 66.) Munich: Wilhelm Fink.

Giacolone Ramat, Anna and Paul J. Hopper (eds.). 1998. *The limits of grammaticalization*. Amsterdam, Philadelphia: John Benjamins.

Gilbers, D. G., J. Nerbonne, and J. Schaeken (eds.). 2000. *Languages in contact*. (Studies in Slavic and General Linguistics, 28.) Amsterdam, Atlanta, Ga: Rodopi.

Gilbert, Glenn G. (ed.). 1971. *The German language in America: A symposium*. Austin, London: University of Texas Press.

    (ed.) forthc. *Pidgin and creole linguistics in the 21st century*. New York: Lang.

Giles, Howard, Justine Coupland, and Nikolas Coupland (eds.) 1991. *Contexts of accommodation: developments in applied sociolinguistics*. Cambridge: Cambridge University Press.

Giles, Howard, A. Mulac, J. J. Bradac, and P. Johnson. 1987. Speech accommodation theory: The next decade and beyond. In Mclaughlin (ed.), pp. 13–48.

Giles, Howard, Donald M. Taylor, Richard Bourhis. 1973. Towards a theory of interpersonal accommodation through language: Some Canadian data. *Language in Society* 2: 177–92.

Gilman, Charles. 1986. African areal characteristics: Sprachbund, not substrate? *Journal of Pidgin and Creole Languages* 1, 1: 33–50.

Givón, Talmy. 1971. Historical syntax and synchronic morphology: An archaeologist's field trip. *Chicago Linguistic Society* 7: 394–415.

1981. On the development of the numeral "one" as an indefinite marker. *Folia Linguistica Historica* 2, 1: 35–53.

Gołąb, Zbigniew. 1959. Some Arumanian-Macedonian isogrammatisms and the social background of their development. *Word* 15: 415–35.

1960. The influence of Turkish upon the Macedonian Slavonic dialects. *Folia Orientalia* (Cracow) 1: 26–45.

Goldberg, Adele E. 1995. *Constructions: A construction grammar approach to argument structure*. Chicago, London: University of Chicago Press.

Greenberg, Joseph H. 1959. Africa as a linguistic area. In Bascom & Herskovits (eds.), pp. 15–27.

1978a. How does a language acquire gender markers? In Greenberg, Ferguson, and Moravcsik (eds.), pp. 47–82.

1978b. Generalizations about numeral systems. In Greenberg, Ferguson, and Moravcsik (eds.), pp. 249–95.

1983. Some areal characteristics of African languages. In Dihoff (ed.), pp. 3–21.

Greenberg, Joseph H., Charles A. Ferguson, and Edith Moravcsik (eds.). 1978. *Universals of human language*. Vol. III: *Word structure*. Stanford: Stanford University Press.

Grenoble, Leonore and Lindsay Whaley (eds.). 1998. *Endangered language: language loss and community response*. Cambridge: Cambridge University Press.

Güldemann, Tom. 1997. *The Kalahari Basin as an object of areal typology: a first approach*. (Khoisan Forum, 3.) Cologne: Institut für Afrikanistik.

Gumperz, John J. and Robert Wilson. 1971. Convergence and creolization: A case from the Indo-Aryan/Dravidian border in India. In Hymes (ed.), pp. 151–67.

Haase, Martin. 1992. *Sprachkontakt und Sprachwandel im Baskenland: die Einflüsse des Gaskognischen und Französischen auf das Baskische*. Hamburg: Buske.

1997. Gascon et basque: bilinguisme et substrat. *Sprachtypologie und Universalienforschung* 50, 3: 189–228.

Haase, Martin and Nicole Nau (eds.). 1996. *Sprachkontakt und Grammatikalisierung*. *Sprachtypologie und Universalienforschung*. (Special issue, 49, 1.) Berlin: Akademie-Verlag.

Hagège, Claude. 1993. *The language builder: An essay on the human signature in linguistic morphogenesis*. (Amsterdam Studies in the Theory and History of Linguistic Science, 94.) Amsterdam, Philadelphia: John Benjamins.

Haig, Geoffrey. 2001. Linguistic diffusion in present-day East Anatolia: From top to bottom. In Aikhenvald and Dixon (eds.), pp. 195–224.

Hammond, Michael and Michael Noonan (eds.). 1988. *Theoretical morphology: Approaches in modern linguistics*. New York: Academic Press.

Hamp, Eric. 1977. On some questions of areal linguistics. *Berkeley Linguistics Society* 3: 279–82.

1979. A glance from here on. In Campbell and Mithun (eds.), pp. 1001–15.

Harris, Alice. 2003. Cross-linguistic perspectives on syntactic change. In Joseph and Janda (eds.), pp. 529–51.

Harris, Alice C. and Lyle Campbell. 1995. *Historical syntax in cross-linguistic perspective*. Cambridge: Cambridge University Press.

Harris, John. 1984. Syntactic variation and dialect divergence. *Journal of Linguistics* 20: 303–27.

1991. Conservatism versus substratal transfer in Irish English. In Trudgill and Chambers (eds.), pp. 191–212.

Harris, Martin and Paolo Ramat (eds.). 1987. *Historical development of auxiliaries.* (Trends in Linguistics, 35.) Berlin, New York: Mouton de Gruyter.

Haspelmath, Martin. 1989. From purposive to infinitive – a universal path of grammaticization. *Folia Linguistica Historica* 10, 1–2: 287–310.

1998. How young is Standard Average European? *Language Sciences* 20, 3: 271–87.

1999. Why is grammaticalization irreversible? *Linguistics* 37, 6: 1043–68.

2001. The European linguistic area: Standard Average European. In Haspelmath et al. (eds.), pp. 1492–510.

Haspelmath, Martin, Ekkehard König, Wulf Oesterreicher, and Wolfgang Raible (eds.). 2001. *Language typology and language universals: An international handbook.* Vol. II. (Handbücher zur Sprach- und Kommunikationswissenschaft, 20.2.) New York: Walter de Gruyter.

Haugen, Einar 1950a. Problems of bilingualism. *Lingua* 2: 271–90.

1950b. The analysis of linguistic borrowing. *Language* 26: 210–31.

1953. *The Norwegian language in America: A study in bilingual behavior.* Philadelphia: University of Pennsylvania Press.

1989. The rise and fall of an immigrant language: Norwegian in America. In Dorian (ed.), pp. 61–73.

1992. Borrowing: an overview. In Bright (ed.), 1992a, pp. 197–200.

Head, Brian F. 1978. Respect degrees in pronominal reference. In Greenberg, Ferguson, and Moravcsik (eds.), pp. 151–211.

Heath, Jeffrey. 1978. *Linguistic diffusion in Arnhem Land.* (Australian Aboriginal Studies Research and Regional Studies, 13.) Canberra: Australian Institute of Aboriginal Studies.

1981. A case of intensive lexical diffusion. *Language* 57: 335–67.

Heine, Bernd. 1992. Grammaticalization chains. *Studies in Language* 16, 2: 335–68.

1993. *Auxiliaries: Cognitive forces and grammaticalization.* New York, Oxford: Oxford University Press.

1994. Areal influence on grammaticalization. In Pütz (ed.), pp. 56–68.

1997a. *Possession: Sources, forces, and grammaticalization.* Cambridge: Cambridge University Press.

1997b. *Cognitive foundations of grammar.* Oxford, New York: Oxford University Press.

2003a. Grammaticalization. In Joseph and Janda (eds.), pp. 575–601.

2003b. On degrammaticalization. In Blake and Burridge (eds.), pp. 163–79.

Heine, Bernd, Ulrike Claudi, and Friederike Hünnemeyer. 1991. *Grammaticalization: A conceptual framework.* Chicago: University of Chicago Press.

Heine, Bernd and Tania Kuteva. 2001. Convergence and divergence in the development of African languages. In Aikhenvald and Dixon (eds.), pp. 393–411.

2002. *World lexicon of grammaticalization.* Cambridge: Cambridge University Press.

2003. On contact-induced grammaticalization. *Studies in Language* 27, 3: 529–72.

Heine, Bernd and Tania Kuteva. Forthc. *Towards a European sprachbund.* Cologne/Düsseldorf.

Heine, Bernd and Mechthild Reh. 1984. *Grammaticalization and reanalysis in African languages.* Hamburg: Buske.

Heine, Bernd and Derek Nurse (eds.). 2000. *African languages: An introduction.* Cambridge: Cambridge University Press.

Henderson, Eugenia J. A. 1965. The topography of certain phonetic and morphological characteristics of South East Asian languages. *Lingua* 15: 400–34.

Hill, Jane H. and Kenneth C. Hill. 1980. Mixed grammar, purist grammar, and language attitudes in Modern Nahuatl. *Language in Society* 9: 321–48.

1986. *Speaking Mexicano: Dynamics of syncretic language in Central Mexico.* Tuscon: University of Arizona Press.

Hill, Kenneth C. (ed.). 1979. *The genesis of language.* (The First Michigan Colloquium, 1979.) Ann Arbor, Mich.: Karoma Publishers.

Hinrichs, Uwe. 1999. Die sogenannten "Balkanismen" als Problem der Südosteuropa-Linguistik und der allgemeinen Sprachwissenschaft. In Hinrichs and Büttner (eds.), pp. 429–62.

Hinrichs, Uwe and Uwe Büttner (eds.). 1999. *Handbuch der Südosteuropa-Linguistik.* (Slavistische Studienbücher, Neue Folge.) Wiesbaden: Otto Harrassowitz.

Hinze, Friedhelm. 1969. Die Wiedergabe des deutschen Substantiv-Verbalabstrakt-Kompositums im Slovinzischen. In Krauss et al. (eds.), pp. 63–8.

Hock, Hans Heinrich. 1986. *Principles of historical linguistics.* Berlin: Mouton de Gruyter.

Hodge, Carleton T. 1970. The linguistic cycle. *Language Sciences* 13: 1–7.

Hollenbach, Barbara E. 1990. Semantic and syntactic extensions of Copala Trique body-part nouns. In Garza Cuarón and Levy (eds.), pp. 275–96.

1991. On some principles of grammaticization. In Traugott and Heine (eds.), 1991a, pp. 17–35.

Hopper, Paul J. and Elizabeth C. Traugott. 1993. *Grammaticalization.* Cambridge: Cambridge University Press.

Huber, Dieter and Erika Worbs (eds.). 1997. *Ars transferendi: Sprache, Übersetzung, Interkulturalität: Festschrift für Nikolai Salnikow zum 65. Geburtstag.* Wuppertal: Peter Lang.

Huber, Magnus. 1996. The grammaticalization of aspect markers in Ghanaian Pidgin English. In Baker and Syea (eds.), pp. 53–70.

Huffines, Marion Lois. 1986. The function of aspect in Pennsylvania German and the impact of English. *Yearbook of German–American Studies* 21: 137–54.

1988. Building progressives: Evidence from cognate structures. *Journal of English Linguistics* 21, 2: 137–48.

1991. Pennsylvania German: Convergence and change as strategies of discourse. In Seliger and Vago (eds.), pp. 125–37.

Hurch, Bernhard. 1989. Hispanisierung im Baskischen. In Boretzky, Enninger, and Stolz (eds.), pp. 11–35.

Hurley, Joni Kay. 1995. The impact of Quichua on verb forms used in Spanish requests in Otavalo, Ecuador. In Silva-Corvalán (ed.), pp. 39–51.

Hymes, Dell (ed.). 1971. *Pidginization and creolization of languages: Proceedings of a conference held at the University of the West Indies, Mona, Jamaica, April 1968.* Cambridge: Cambridge University Press.

Ivanova-Mirčeva, D. 1962. *Razvoj na badešte vreme (Futurum) v bălgarskija ezik ot X do XVIII vek.* Sofia.

Jacob, Daniel. 1994. *Die Auxiliarisierung von* habere *und die Entstehung des romanischen periphrastischen Perfekts, dargestellt an der Entwicklung vom Latein zum Spanischen.* Habilitationsschrift, University of Freiburg.

1998. Transitivität, Diathese und Perfekt: zur Entstehnung der romanischen *haben-*Periphrasen. In Geisler and Jacob (eds.), pp. 105–26.

Jacobs, Melville. 1954. The areal spread of sound features in the languages north of California. In *Papers from the Symposium on American Indian Languages*, pp. 46–56.

Janakiev, M. 1977. Za gramemite, naričani v balgarskata gramatika "segašno vreme" i "badeste vreme". In Pašov and Nicolova (eds.).

Jeffers, Robert (ed.). 1993. *Selected papers of the Ninth International Conference on Historical Linguistics.* Amsterstam, Philadelphia: John Benjamins.

Jeffers, Robert and Ilse Lehiste. 1979. *Principles and methods for historical linguistics.* Cambridge, Mass.: MIT Press.

Jenkins, Rebecca Sue. 2002. *Language contact and Composite Structures in New Ireland, Papua New Guinea.* Ann Arbor, Mich.: UMI Dissertation Services.

Johanson, Lars. 1992. Strukturelle Faktoren in türkischen Sprachkontakten. (Sitzungsberichte der Wissenschaftlichen Gesellschaft an der Johann Wolfgang Goethe-Universität Frankfurt am Main, volume 29, 5, pp. 169–299.) Stuttgart: Franz Steiner.

1996b. Kopierte Satzjunktoren im Türkischen. *Sprachtypologie und Universalienforschung* 49, 1: 39–49.

Kopien russischer Konjunktionen in türkischen Sprachen. In Huber and Worbs (eds.), pp. 115–21.

1998. Code-copying in Irano-Turkic. *Language Sciences* 20, 3: 325–37.

1999. The dynamics of code-copying in language encounters. In Brendemoen, Lanza, and Ryen (eds.), pp. 37–62.

2000. Linguistic convergence in the Volga area. In Gilbers, Nerbonne, and Schaeken (eds.), pp. 165–78.

2002a. *Structural factors in Turkic language contacts.* London: Curzon.

2002b. Contact-induced linguistic change in a code-copying framework. In Jones and Esch (eds.), pp. 285–313.

In press. On copying grammatical meaning. *Sprachtypologie und Universalienforschung* in print.

Jones, Charles (ed.). 1993. *Historical linguistics: Problems and perspectives.* London, New York: Longman.

Jones, Mari C. and Edith Esch (eds.). 2002. *Language change: The interplay of internal, external and extra-linguistic factors.* (Contributions to the Sociology of Language, 86.) Berlin: Mouton de Gruyter.

Joseph, Brian D. 1983. *The synchrony and diachrony of the Balkan infinitive: A study in areal, general, and historical linguistics.* (Cambridge Studies in Linguistics, Supplementary Volume.) Cambridge: Cambridge University Press.

1992. The Balkan languages. In Bright (ed.) 1992a, pp. 153–5.

Joseph, Brian D. and Richard D. Janda (eds.). 2003. *The handbook of historical linguistics.* Oxford: Blackwell.

Karttunen, Frances. 1976. Uto-Aztecan and Spanish-type dependent clauses in Nahuatl. (Papers from the Parasession on Diachronic Syntax.) *Chicago Linguistic Society* 1976: 150–8.

Karskij, E. F. 1956. *Belorusy: Jazyk belorusskogo naroda.* Moscow: Academy of Sciences Press.

Kastovsky, Dieter (ed.). 1994. *Studies in Early Modern English.* Berlin, New York: Mouton de Gruyter.

Kazazis, Kostas. 1965. Some Balkan constructions corresponding to Western European infinitives. PhD dissertation, Indiana University.

   1967. On a generative grammar of the Balkan languages. *Foundations of Language* 3: 117–23.

Keesing, Roger M. 1988. *Melanesian Pidgin and the Oceanic substrate.* Stanford: Stanford University Press.

   1991. Substrates, calquing and grammaticalization in Melanesian Pidgin. In Traugott and Heine (eds.), 1991a, pp. 315–42.

King, Ruth. 2000. *The lexical basis of grammatical borrowing: A Prince Edward Island case study.* Amsterdam, Philadelphia: John Benjamins.

Klee, Carol A. and Alicia M. Ocampo. 1995. The expression of past reference in Spanish narratives of Spanish-Quechua bilingual speakers. In Silva-Corvalán (ed.), pp. 52–70.

Kloss, Heinz (ed.). 1985. *Deutsch als Muttersprache in den Vereinigten Staaten.* Part 2. (Deutsche Sprache in Europa und Übersee, Berichte und Forschungen, 10.) Stuttgart: Franz Steiner.

Koneski, Blaže. 1965. *Istorija na makedonskiot jazik.* Skopie: Kočo Racin/Belgrad: Prosveta.

König, Ekkehard and Martin Haspelmath. 1999. Der europäische Sprachbund. In Reiter (ed.), pp. 111–27.

König, Ekkehard and Peter Siemund. 2000. Intensifiers and reflexives: A typological perspective. In Frajzyngier and Curl (eds.), pp. 41–74.

Kopitar, Jernej. 1829. Albanische, walachische und bulgarische Sprache. *Jahrbücher der Literatur* 46: 59–106.

Koptjevskaja-Tamm, Maria and Bernhard Wälchli. 2001. The Circum-Baltic languages: an areal-typological approach. In Dahl and Koptjevskaja-Tamm (eds.) 2001b, pp. 615–750.

Kortmann, Bernd. 1998a. The evolution of adverbial subordinators in Europe. In Schmid, Austin, and Stein (eds.), pp. 213–27.

   1998b. Adverbial subordinators in the languages of Europe. In van der Auwera (ed.) 1998b, pp. 457–561.

Koschmieder, Erwin and Maximilian Braun (eds.). 1968. *Slavistische Studien zum VI. Internationalen Slavistenkongress in Prag 1968.* Munich: Rudolf Trofenik.

Kostov, Kiril. 1973. Zur Bedeutung des Zigeunerischen für die Erforschung grammatischer Interferenzerscheinungen. *Linguistique Balkanique* 16, 2: 99–113.

Krauss, W., Z. Stieber, J. Bělič, and V. I. Borkovskij (eds.). 1969. *Slawisch-deutsche Wechselbeziehungen in Sprache, Literatur und Kultur.* (Veröffentlichungen des Instituts für Slawistik, 44.) Berlin: Akademie-Verlag.

Kuteva, Tania. 1994. Iconicity and auxiliation. *Journal of Pragmatics* 22: 71–81.

1998. Large linguistic areas in grammaticalization: Auxiliation in Europe. *Language Sciences* 20, 3: 289–311.

2000. Areal grammaticalization: The case of the Bantu-Nilotic borderland. *Folia Linguistica* 34, 3–4: 267–83.

2001. *Auxiliation: An enquiry into the nature of grammaticalization.* Oxford: Oxford University Press.

Lambert, Richard D. and Barbara F. Freed (eds.). 1982. *The loss of language skills.* Rowley, Mass.: Newbury House Publishers.

Lang, Ewald and G. Zifonun (eds.). 1996. *Deutsch – Typologisch.* Berlin: Mouton de Gruyter.

Langacker, Ronald W. 1975. Relative clauses in Classical Nahuatl. *International Journal of American Linguistics* 41, 1: 46–68.

LaPolla, Randy J. 1994. Parallel grammaticalizations in Tibeto-Burman languages: Evidence of Sapir's "drift." *Linguistics of the Tibeto-Burman Area* 17, 1: 61–80.

2001. The role of migration and language contact in the development Sino-Tibetan language family. In Aikhenvald and Dixon (eds.), pp. 225–54.

Larsson, Lars-Gunnar. 2001. Baltic influence on Finnic languages. In Dahl and Koptjevskaja-Tamm (eds.) 2001a, pp. 237–53.

Lehiste, Ilse. 1999. Successive translations as source of evidence for linguistic change. *International Journal of the Sociology of Language* 139: 39–48.

Lehmann, Christian. [1982]1995. *Thoughts on grammaticalization.* Munich: Lincom Europa.

Leirbukt, Oddleif. 1981. "Passivähnliche" Konstruktionen mit *haben* + Partizip II im heutigen Deutsch. *Deutsche Sprache* 9: 119–46.

Levinson, Stephen C. 1994. Vision, shape, and linguistic description: Tzeltal body-part terminology and object description. *Linguistics* 32, 4–5: 791–855.

Li, Charles N. (ed.). 1976. *Subject and topic.* New York, San Francisco, London: Academic Press.

1983. Languages in contact in western China. *Papers in East Asian Languages* 1: 31–51.

Lindstedt, Jouko. 1994. On the development of the South Slavonic perfect. *EUROTYP Working Papers*, Series VI, No. 5.

Lord, Carol Diane. 1993. *Historical change in serial verb constructions.* (Typological Studies in Language, 26.) Amsterdam, Philadelphia: John Benjamins.

Lorimer, D. L. R. 1937. Burushaski and its alien neighbors: Problems in linguistic contagion. *Transactions of the Philological Society* 1937: 63–98.

Lötzsch, Ronald. 1969. Zum indirekten Passiv im Deutschen und Slawischen. In Krauss et al. (eds.), pp. 102–9.

1996. Interferenzbedingte grammatische Konvergenzen und Divergenzen zwischen Sorbisch und Jiddisch. *Sprachtypologie und Universalienforschung* 49, 1: 50–9.

Luraghi, Silvia. 2001. Some remarks on instrument, comitative, and agent in Indo-European. *Sprachtypologie und Universalienforschung* 54, 4: 385–401.

Masala, Carlo (ed.). 2002. *Der Mittelmeerraum – Brücke oder Grenze?* (Schriften für Europäische Integrationsforschung, 48.) Baden-Baden: Nomos.

Masica, Colin P. 1976. *Defining a linguistic area: South Asia.* Chicago, London: University of Chicago Press.

1992. Areal linguistics. In Bright (ed.) 1992a, pp. 108–12.

Maslov, J. S. 1949. K voprosu o proischoždenii possessivnogo perfekta. (*Učenye Zapiski LGU*, 97.) *Serija filologičeskich nauk* 14: 76–104.

Maslov, J. 1982. *Gramatika na bălgarskija ezik*. Sofia: Nauka i Izkustvo.

Matisoff, James A. 1991. Areal and universal dimensions of grammaticalization in Lahu. In Traugott and Heine (eds.) 1991b, pp. 383–453.

Matras, Yaron. 1996. Prozedurale Fusion: Grammatische Interferenzschichten im Romanes. *Sprachtypologie und Universalienforschung* 49, 1: 60–78.

  1998a. Utterance modifiers and universals of grammatical borrowing. *Linguistics* 36, 1: 281–331.

  1998b. Convergent development, grammaticalization, and the problem of "mutual isomorphism." In Boeder et al. (eds.), pp. 89–103.

Matras, Yaron and Peter Bakker (eds.). 2003. *The mixed language debate: Theoretical and empirical advances*. (Trends in Linguistics, Studies and Monographs, 145.) Berlin, New York: Mouton de Gruyter.

McWhorter, John H. (ed.). 2000. *Language change and language contact in pidgins and creoles*. (Creole Language Library, 21.) Amsterdam, Philadelphia: John Benjamins.

Meeussen, A. E. 1975. *Possible linguistic Africanisms*. Fifth Hans Wolff Memorial Lecture. *Language Sciences* (Bloomington, Indiana) 35.

Mehlig, Hans Robert (ed.). 1994. *Slavistische Linguistik 1993*. Munich: Otto Sagner.

Meisel, J. M. (ed.). 1977. *Langues en contact*. Tübingen: Narr.

  1937. *Mélanges de linguistique et de philologie offerts à Jacq. van Ginneken à l'occasion du soixantième anniversaire de sa naissance*. Paris: Librairie C. Klincksieck.

Messner, Dieter (ed.). 1984. *Das Romanische in den Ostalpen*. (Veröffentlichungen der Kommision für Linguistik und Kommunikationsforschung, 15.) Vienna: Verlag der Österreichischen Akademie der Wissenschaften.

Mian-Lian, Ho and John T. Platt. 1993. *Dynamics of a contact continuum: Singaporean English*. (Oxford Studies in Language Contact.) Oxford: Clarendon Press.

Mirčev, K. 1978. *Istoriceska gramatika na balgarskija ezik*. Third edition. Sofia: Nauka i Izkustvo.

Mladenov, S. 1935. Prinos kăm izučavane na bălgarskite govori v iztočna i zapadna Trakija. *Trakijski cbornik* (Sofia) 6: 66–105.

  1979. *Istorija na bălgarskija ezik*. Sofia: BAN Press.

Moravcsik, Edith. 1978. Language contact. In Greenberg, Ferguson, and Moravcsik (eds.), pp. 93–123.

Morfill, W. R. [1885] 1971. Review of Schuchardt 1884. *The Academy, Edinburgh*, 11. IV, 1885, pp. 261f. Reprinted in Gerhardt 1971, pp. 266–71.

Moser, Michael. 1998. *Die polnische, ukrainische und weißrussische Interferenzschicht im russischen Satzbau des 16. und 17. Jahrhunderts*. Frankfurt am Main: Peter Lang.

Mous, Maarten. 1994. Ma'a or Mbugu. In Bakker and Mous (eds.), pp. 175–200.

  2001. Ma'a as an ethno-register of Mbugu. *Sprache und Geschichte in Afrika* (SUGIA) 16–17: 293–320.

Mufwene, Salikoko S. 1986. The universalist and substrate hypotheses complement one another. In Muysken and Smith (eds.), pp. 129–62.

  1996. Creolization and grammaticization: What creolistics could contribute to research on grammaticization. In Baker and Syea (eds.), pp. 5–28.

2000. La fonction et les formes réfléchies dans le mauricien et le haitien. In Véronique (ed.), pp. 114–23.

2001. *The ecology of language evolution.* (Cambridge Approaches to Language Contact.) Cambridge: Cambridge University Press.

Mühlhäusler, Peter and Rom Harré 1990. *Pronouns and people: The linguistic construction of social and personal identity.* (Language in Society, 15.) Oxford: Blackwell.

Muysken, Pieter and Norval Smith (eds.). 1986a. *Substrata versus universals in Creole genesis.* (Creole Language Library, 1.) Amsterdam, Philadelphia: John Benjamins.

1986b. Introduction: Problems in the identification of substratum features in the creole languages. In Muysken and Smith (eds.) 1986a, pp. 1–13.

Myers-Scotton, Carol. 1993. *Duelling languages.* Oxford, New York: Oxford University Press.

1998. A way to dusty death: the Matrix language Turnover hypothesis. In Grenoble and Whaley (eds.), pp. 289–316.

2002. *Contact linguistics: Bilingual encounters and grammatical outcomes.* Oxford: Oxford University Press.

bought

Nadkarni, Mangesh V. 1975. Bilingualism and syntactic change in Konkani. *Language* 51, 3: 672–83.

Nau, Nicole. 1992/3. Der ostseefinnische Superlativ im arealen Kontext. *Finnisch-Ugrische Mitteilungen* 16–17: 13–23.

1995. *Möglichkeiten und Mechanismen kontaktbewegten Sprachwandels unter besonderer Berücksichtigung des Finnischen.* (Edition Linguistik, 08.) Munich, Newcastle: LINCOM Europa.

1996. Ein Beitrag zur Arealtypologie der Ostseeanrainersprachen. In Boretzky (ed.), pp. 51–67.

Nelde, Peter Hans (ed.). 1980. *Sprachkontakt und Sprachkonflikt.* (Zeitschrift für Dialektologie, Beihefte, 32.) Wiesbaden: Franz Steiner.

Neumann-Holzschuh, Ingrid and Edgar W. Schneider (eds.). 2000. *Degrees of restructuring in creole languages.* (Creole Language Library, 22.) Amsterdam, Philadelphia: John Benjamins.

Newmeyer, Frederick J. 1998. *Language form and language function.* Cambridge, Mass.: MIT Press.

Nilsson, Torbjörn. 1988. Reflexive possessive pronouns in the East Baltic area. In *Ural-Altaische Johrbücher*, N.F. Weisbaden: Otto Harvassowitz, pp. 18–37.

Nurse, Derek. 1994. South meets north: Ilwana = Bantu + Cushitic on Kenya's Tana River. In Bakker and Mous (eds.), pp. 213–22.

2000. *Inheritance, contact, and change in two East African languages.* (Sprachkontakt in Afrika, 4.) Cologne: Köppe.

Ofitsch, Michaela and Christian Zinko (eds.). 2000. *125 Jahre Indogermanistik in Graz.* Graz: Leykam.

Ölberg, Herrmann M., Gernot Schmidt, and Heinz Bothien (eds.). 1985. *Sprachwissenschaftliche Forschungen: Festschrift für Johann Knobloch.* (Innsbrucker Beiträge zur Kulturwissenschaft, 23.) Innsbruck: Amoe.

Östmann, Jan Ola. 1981. *You know: A discourse-functional approach.* Amsterdam, Philadelphia: John Benjamins.

Papers from the Symposium on American Indian Languages. 1954. (University of California Publications in Linguistics, 10.) Berkeley, Los Angeles: University of California Press.

Pašov, P. and R. Nicolova (eds.). 1976. *Pomagalo po balgarska morfologija. Glagol.* Sofia: Nauka i Izkustvo.

Pawley, Andrew. 1992. Formulaic speech. In Bright (ed.) 1992b, pp. 22–5.

   1994. Beyond the grammar lexicon model: The central role of speech formulas in linguistic competence. Paper presented at the International Symposium on Phraseology, University of Leeds, 18–20 April.

Petrucci, Peter R. 1993. The areal distribution of a Slavic language shift feature. *Berkeley Linguistics Society* 9: 291–9.

Plag, Ingo. 1992. From speech act verb to conjunction: The grammaticalization of *taki* in Sranan. *Journal of Pidgin and Creole Languages* 7, 1: 55–73.

   1993. *Sentential complementation in Sranan: On the formation of an English-based creole language.* Tübingen: Niemeyer.

   Forthc. On the role of grammaticalization in creolization. In Gilbert (ed.), forthc.

Polinsky, Maria. 1995. Cross-linguistic parallels in language loss. *Southwest Journal of Linguistics* 14, 1–2: 87–123.

Poplack, Shana. 1981. Syntactic structure and the social function of codeswitching. In Durán (ed.), pp. 169–84.

Poplack, Shana and Sali Tagliamonte. 1996. Nothing in context: Variation, grammaticization and past time marking in Nigerian Pidgin English. In Baker and Syea (eds.), pp. 71–94.

Pütz, Martin (ed.). 1994. *Language contact and language conflict.* Amsterdam, Philadelphia: John Benjamins.

Putzu, Ignazio. 2002. Total/universal quantifiers and definite articles in the Mediterranean languages: A typological, diachronic, and areal point of view. In Ramat and Stolz (eds.), pp. 247–57.

Putzu, Ignazio and Paolo Ramat. 2001. Articles and quantifiers in the Mediterranean languages: A typological-diachronic analysis. In Bisang (ed.). 2001a, pp. 99–132.

Ramat, Paolo. 1990. Area influence versus typological drift in Western Europe: The case of negation. In Bechert, Bernini, and Buridant (eds.), pp. 25–46.

   1998. Typological comparison and linguistic areas: Some introductory remarks. *Language Sciences* 20, 3: 227–40.

Ramat, Paolo and Giuliano Bernini. 1990. Area influence versus typological drift in western Europe: The case of negation. In Bechert, Bernini, and Buridant (eds.), pp. 25–46.

Ramat, Paolo and Thomas Stolz (eds.). 2002. *Mediterranean languages: Papers from the MEDITYP workshop, Tirrenia, June 2000.* (Diversitas Linguarum, 1.) Bochum: N. Brockmeyer.

Rayfield, Joan Rachel. 1970. *The language of a bilingual community.* The Hague: Mouton.

Raz, Shlomo. 1989. Areal features as a further criterion in elucidating the term "Ethiopian Semitic." *African Languages and Cultures* 2, 1: 93–108.

Reed, Carroll E. 1947. The question of aspect in Pennsylvania German. *Germanic Review* 20: 5–12.

Reichenkron, G. 1958. Der lokativische Zähltypus für die Reihe 11 bis 19: "eins auf zehn." *Südost-Forschungen* 17, 1: 152–74.

Reis, Marga. 1985. Mona Lisa kriegt zuviel – vom sogenannten 'Rezipientenpassiv' im Deutschen. *Linguistische Berichte* 96: 140–55.

Reiter, Norbert (ed.). 1999. *Eurolinguistik*. Wiesbaden: Otto Harrassowitz.

Riehl, Claudia Maria. 1996. Deutsch-romanische Sprachkontakte: Gemeinsamkeiten der Kontaktphänomene am Beispiel des Deutschen. In Boretzky (ed.), pp. 189–206.

    2001. *Schreiben, Text und Mehrsprachigkeit: Zur Textproduktion in mehrsprachigen Gesellschaften am Beispiel der deutschsprachigen Minderheiten in Südtirol und Ostbelgien.* (Tertiärsprachen. Drei- und Mehrsprachigkeit, 4.) Tübingen: Stauffenberg.

Reuther, Tilmann (ed.). 1992. *Slavistische Linguistik 1991*. Munich: Otto Sagner.

Romaine, Suzanne. 1988. *Pidgin and creole languages*. London, New York: Longman.

    1989. *Bilingualism*. Oxford: Blackwell.

    1995. The grammaticalization of irrealis in Tok Pisin. In Bybee and Fleischman (eds.), pp. 1–39.

    1999. The grammaticalization of the proximative in Tok Pisin. *Language* 75, 2: 322–46.

Rosenthal, Jane M. 1972. On the relative clauses of Classical Nahuatl. (The Chicago Which Hunt, Papers from the Relative Clause Festival.) *Chicago Linguistic Society* (1972): 246–55.

Ross, Malcolm D. 1996. Contact-induced change and the comparative method: cases from Papua New Guinea. In Durie and Ross (eds.), pp. 180–217.

    1997. Social networks and kinds of speech-community event. In Blench and Spriggs (eds.), pp. 209–61.

    2001. Contact-induced change in Oceanic languages in North-West Melanesia. In Aikhenvald and Dixon (eds.), pp. 134–66.

Rusakov, Aleksandr Yu. 2001. The North Russian Romani dialect: Interference and code switching. In Dahl and Koptjevskaja-Tamm (eds.) 2001a, pp. 313–37.

Šafranov, S. 1852. *O vidax russkix glagolov v sintaksičeskom otnošenii*. Moscow.

Salmons, Joe. 1990. Bilingual discourse marking: Code-switching, borrowing and convergence in some German-American dialects. *Linguistics* 28: 453–80.

Sandfeld, Kristian. 1930. *Linguistique balkanique: problèmes et résultats*. (Collection Linguistique, 31.) Paris: Champion.

Sankoff, Gillian. 1979. The genesis of a language. In Hill (ed.), pp. 23–47.

Sankoff, Gillian and Penelope Brown. 1976. The origins of syntax in discourse. *Language* 52: 631–66.

Sankoff, Gillian and Suzanne Laberge. 1973. On the acquisition of native speakers by a language. *Kivung* 6: 32–47.

Sapir, Edward. 1921. *Language: An introduction to the study of speech*. New York: Harcourt Brace Jovanovich.

Sasse, Hans-Jürgen. 1985. Sprachkontakt und Sprachwandel: Die Gräzisierung der albanischen Mundarten Griechenlands. *Papiere zur Linguistik* 32: 37–95.

    1992. Language decay and contact-induced change: Similarities and differences. In Brenzinger (ed.), pp. 59–80.

Savić, Jelena M. 1995. Structural convergence and language change: Evidence from Serbian/English code-switching. *Language in Society* 24, 4: 475–92.

Saxena, Anju. 1988a. On syntactic convergence: The case of the verb "say" in Tibeto-Burman. *Berkeley Linguistics Society* 15: 375–88.

 1988b. On the grammaticalization of the verb "say": a typological and diachronic study. In Delancey and Tomlin (eds.).

Schaller, Helmut Wilhelm. 1975. *Die Balkansprachen: Eine Einführung in die Balkanphilologie.* Heidelberg: Carl Winter.

Schiffrin, Deborah. 1987. *Discourse markers.* Cambridge: Cambridge University Press.

Schmid, Monika S., Jennifer R. Austin, and Dieter Stein (eds.). 1998. *Historical Linguistics 1997: Selected papers from the 13th International Conference on Historical Linguistics, Düsseldorf, 10–17 August 1997.* (Amsterdam Studies in the Theory and History of Linguistic Science, 164.) Amsterdam, Philadelphia: John Benjamins.

Schmitt, Elena. 2000. Overt and covert codeswitching in immigrant children from Russia. *International Journal of Bilingualism* 4: 9–28.

 2001. Beneath the surface: Signs of language attrition in immigrant children from Russia. PhD dissertation, Columbia, SC: University of South Carolina.

Schourup, Lawrence. 1985. *Common discourse particles in English conversation.* New York: Garland.

Schuchardt, Hugo. 1884. *Slawo-deutsches und Slawo-italienisches.* Graz: Leuschner und Lubensky.

Sebeok, T. (ed.). 1973. *Current trends in linguistics.* Vol. X. The Hague: Mouton.

Seliger, Herbert W. and Robert M. Vago (eds.). 1991. *First language attrition.* Cambridge: Cambridge University Press.

Sherzer, J. 1973. Areal linguistics in North America. In Sebeok (ed.), pp. 749–95.

Shopen, Timothy (ed.). 1985. *Complex constructions.* (Language typology and syntactic description, 2.) Cambridge: Cambridge University Press.

Silva-Corvalán, Carmen. 1994. *Language contact and change: Spanish in Los Angeles.* (Oxford Studies in Language Contact.) Oxford: Clarendon Press.

 (ed.) 1995. *Spanish in four continents: Studies in language contact and bilingualism.* (Georgetown Studies in Romance Linguistics.) Washington, DC: Georgetown University Press.

Silverstein, Michael. 1974. Dialectal developments in Chinookan tense-aspect systems: An areal-historical analysis. *International Journal of American Linguistics,* Memoir 29.

Simon, Horst J. 1997. Die Diachronie der deutschen Anredepronomina aus Sicht der Universalienforschung. *Sprachtypologie und Universalienforschung* (STUF, Berlin) 50, 3: 267–81.

Simon-Vandenbergen, Anne-Marie, Kristin Davidse, and Dirk Noel (eds.) 1997. *Reconnecting language. Morphology and syntax in functional perspectives.* Amsterdam, Philadelphia: John Benjamins.

Smith, Norval S. H., Ian E. Robertson, and Kay Williamson. 1987. The Ijo element in Berbice Dutch. *Language in Society* 16: 49–90.

Solta, Georg Renatus. 1980. *Einführung in die Balkanlinguistik mit besonderer Berücksichtigung des Substrats und des Balkanlateinischen.* Darmstadt: Wissenschaftliche Buchgesellschaft.

Soper, John David. 1987. *Loan syntax in Turkic and Iranian: The verb systems of Tajik, Usbek, and Qashqay.* Ann Arbor, Mich.: UMI Dissertation Services.

Soper, John David. 1996. *Loan syntax in Turkic and Iranian*. Bloomington, Ind.: Eurolin-
     gua.
Spier, Leslie (ed.). 1941. *Language, culture, and personality: Essays in memory of
     Edward Sapir*. Menasha, Wisc.: Sapir Memorial Publication Fund.
Sridhar, S. N. 1978. Linguistic convergence: Indo-Aryanization of Dravidian languages.
     Studies in the Linguistic Sciences 8, 1: 197–215.
Stassen, Leon. 1985. *Comparison and universal grammar*. Oxford, New York: Black-
     well.
     2000. AND-languages and WITH-languages. *Typological Linguistics* 4, 1: 1–54.
Steinkrüger, Patrick Oliver. 1995. Grammatikalisierungen von Auxiliaren und Copulae
     im Katalanischen der Decadència. *Zeitschrift für Katalanistik* 8: 35–62.
Stimm, Helmut. 1984. Eigenheiten der Kausativkonstruktionen im Surselvischen. In
     Messner (ed.), pp. 329–50.
Stojkov, St. 1960. Obrazuvane na badeste vreme (futurum) v savremennija balgarski
     ezik. *Ezikovedsko-etnografski izsledvanija v pamet na Akademik St. Romanaski*.
     Sofia.
Stolz, Thomas. 1991. *Sprachbund im Baltikum? Estnisch und Lettisch im Zentrum einer
     sprachlichen Konvergenzlandschaft*. (Bochum-Essener Beiträge zur Sprachwan-
     delforschung, 13.) Bochum: N. Brockmeyer.
     1996a. Komitativ-Typologie: MIT- und OHNE-Relationen im crosslinguistischen
     Überblick. *Papiere zur Linguistik* 51, 1: 3–65.
     1996b. Some instruments are really good companions – some are not: on syncretism
     and the typology of instrumentals and comitatives. *Theoretical Linguistics* 23, 1–2:
     113–200.
     2001. On Circum-Baltic instrumentals and comitatives. In Dahl and Koptjevskaja-
     Tamm (eds.), pp. 591–612.
     2002a. No *Sprachbund* beyond this line! On the age-old discussion of how to define
     a linguistic area. In Ramat and Stolz (eds.), pp. 259–81.
     2002b. Crosscurrents – the Mediterranean region as a potential linguistic area. In
     Masala (ed.), pp. 52–73.
     2002c. Mediterraneanism vs. universal process: Word iteration in an areal perspective.
     Typescript, University of Bremen.
     2003. Not quite the right mixture: Chamorro and Malti as candidates for the status of
     mixed language. In Matras and Bakker (eds.), pp. 271–315.
Stolz, Christel and Thomas Stolz. 1996. Funktionswortentlehnung in Mesoamerika:
     Spanisch-amerindischer Sprachkontakt (Hispanoindiana II). *Sprachtypologie und
     Universalienforschung* 49, 1: 86–123.
     2001. Mesoamerica as a linguistic area. In Haspelmath et al. (eds.), pp. 1542–53.
Sullivan, James P. 1980. The validity of literary dialect: Evidence from the theatrical
     portrayal of Hiberno-English forms. *Language in Society* 9: 195–219.
Suttles, W. (ed.). 1990. *Northwest Coast*. (Handbook of North American Indians, 7.)
     Washington, DC: Smithsonian Institute.
Tagliamonte, Sali A. 2000. The story of *kom* in Nigerian Pidgin English. In McWhorter
     (ed.), pp. 253–82.
Ternes, Elmar. 1999. Ist Bretonisch SVO oder VSO? Typologische Überlegungen zu
     einer umstrittenen Frage. In Zimmer, Ködderitzsch, and Wigger (eds.), pp. 236–
     53.

Thomas, George. 1975. The calque – an international trend in the lexical development of the literary languages of eighteenth-century Europe. *Germano-Slavica* 6: 21–41.

Thomason, Sarah Grey (ed.). 2000. *Contact languages: An introduction*. Washington, DC: University Press.

2001a. Contact-induced typological change. In Haspelmath et al. (eds.), pp. 1640–8.

2001b. *Language contact*. Edinburgh: Edinburgh University Press.

2003. Contact as a source of language change. In Joseph and Janda (eds.), pp. 686–712.

Thomason, Sarah Grey and Terrence Kaufman. 1988. *Language contact, creolization, and genetic linguistics*. Berkeley, Los Angeles, London: University of California Press.

Thompson, L. C. and M. D. Kinkade. 1990. Languages. In Suttles (ed.), pp. 30–51.

Thompson, Sandra A. and Robert E. Longacre. 1985. Adverbial clauses. In Shopen (ed.), pp. 171–234.

Thurston, W. R. 1982. *A comparative study in Anêm and Lusi*. Pacific Linguistics B-83. Canberra: Australian National University.

Thurston, William R. 1987. *Processes of change in the languages of north-western New Britain*. Pacific Linguistics B-99. Canberra: Australian National University.

Timberlake, Alan. 1976. Subject properties in the North Russian passive. In Li (ed.), pp. 547–71.

Tommola, Hannu. 2000. On the perfect in North Slavic. In Dahl (ed.) 2000a, pp. 441–78.

Tosco, Mauro. 2000. Is there an "Ethiopian language area"? *Anthropological Linguistics* 42, 3: 329–65.

Totev, Ch. 1991. Formi na casticata za obrazuvane na badeste vreme v stolicnija razgovoren ezik. *Ezik i Literatura*, 1.

Toweett, Taitta. 1979. *Kalenjin linguistics*. Nairobi: Kenya Literature Bureau.

Trask, Robert L. 1998. The typological position of Basque: Then and now. *Language Sciences* 20, 3: 313–24.

Traugott, Elizabeth C. and Bernd Heine (eds.). 1991a. *Approaches to grammaticalization*. Vol. I. Amsterdam, Philadelphia: John Benjamins.

(eds.) 1991b. *Approaches to grammaticalization*. Vol. II. Amsterdam, Philadelphia: John Benjamins.

Trudgill, Peter. 1983. *On dialect. Social and geographical perspectives*. Oxford: Basil Blackwell.

Trudgill, Peter and J. K. Chambers (eds.). 1991. *Dialects of English: Studies in grammatical variation*. Revised edition. New York: Longman.

Tsitsipis, Lukas D. 1998. *A linguistic anthropology of praxis and language shift: Arvanítika (Albanian) and Greek in contact*. (Oxford Studies in Language Contact.) Oxford: Clarendon Press.

Tucker, Archibald N. 1994. *A grammar of Kenya Luo (Dholuo)*, edited by C. A. Creider. 2 vols. (Nilo-Saharan, 8.1, 8.2.) Cologne: Köppe.

Ureland, P. Sture and Iain Clarkson (eds.). 1984. *Scandinavian language contacts*. Cambridge: Cambridge University Press.

Vachek, Josef. 1962. On the interplay of external and internal factors in the development of language. *Lingua* 11: 433–48.

van der Auwera, Johan. 1998a. Revisiting the Balkan and Meso-American linguistic areas. *Language Sciences* 20, 3: 259–70.

(ed.) 1998b. *Adverbial constructions in the languages of Europe*. (Empirical Approaches to Language Typology-EUROTYP, 20-3.) Berlin: Mouton de Gruyter.

1998c. Conclusion. In van der Auwera (ed.) 1998b, pp. 813–36.

van Hamel, A. G. 1912. On Anglo-Irish syntax. *Englische Studien* 45: 272–92.

van Marle, Jaap (ed.). 1993. *Historical linguistics 1991*. Amsterdam, Philadelphia: John Benjamins.

Van Ness, Silke. 1992. The New Order Amish in Ohio: A grammatical change in progress. In Burridge and Enninger (eds.), pp. 182–98.

Vasilev, Christo. 1968. Der romanische Perfekttyp im Slavischen. In Koschmieder and Braun (eds.), pp. 215–30.

Veenker, Wolfgang. 1967. *Die Frage des finnougrischen Substrats in der russischen Sprache*. (Uralic and Altaic Series, 82.) Bloomington, The Hague: Mouton.

Vendryes, J. 1937. Sur l'emploi de l'auxiliaire "avoir" pour marquer le passé. In *Mélanges* (ed.), pp. 85–92.

Véronique, Daniel (ed.). 2000. *Syntaxe des langues créoles*. (Langages, 138.) Paris: Larousse.

Vossen, Rainer, Angelika Mietzner, and Antje Meissner (eds.). 2000. *"Mehr als nur Worte . . . ": afrikanistische Beiträge zum 65. Geburtstag von Franz Rottland*. Cologne: Köppe.

Wehr, Barbara. 1984. *Diskurs-Strategien im Romanischen: ein Beitrag zur romanischen Syntax*. Tübingen: Narr.

1998. Typologische Parallelen in der französischen und irischen Syntax. In Boeder et al. (eds.), pp. 335–54.

Weinreich, Uriel [1953] 1964. *Languages in contact*. London, The Hague, Paris: Mouton.

Winford, Donald. 2003. *An introduction to contact linguistics*. Oxford: Blackwell.

Wolff, Ekkehard 1993. *Referenzgrammatik des Hausa* (Hamburger Beiträge zur Afrikanistik, 2). Münster, Hamburg: Lit Verlag.

Yasugi, Yoshiho. 1995. *Native Middle American languages: An areal-typological perspective*. (Senri Ethological Studies, 39.) Osaka: National Museum of Ethnology.

Yongzhong, Zhu, Üjiyediin Chuluu, Keith Slater, and Kevin Stuart. 1997. Gangou Chinese dialect: A comparative study of a strongly altaicized Chinese dialect and its Mongolic neighbor. *Anthropos* 92: 433–50.

Ziegeler, Debra. 2000. *Hypothetical modality: Grammaticalization in an L2 dialect*. (Studies in Language Companion Series, 51.) Amsterdam, Philadelphia: John Benjamins.

Zima, Petr (ed.). 1995. *Time in languages*. Prague: Institute for Advanced Studies at Charles University and the Academy of Sciences of the Czech Republic.

Zimmer, Stefan, Rolf Ködderitzsch, and Arndt Wigger (eds.). 1999. *Akten des Zweiten Deutschen Keltologen-Symposiums*. Tübingen: Niemeyer.

Zlatanova, Rumjana. 1986. Istoričeski razvoj na bălgarskija ezik'. In Georgiev et al. (eds.).

Index of authors

Index of languages

Index of subjects

Action Schema 216–17
adoption 6, 13, 237
Aktionsart 157
article 23, 101, 116–17, 121, 132, 158, 159,
 178, 224, 247–8, 251, 258, 265
aspect 30, 82, 93, 102, 109, 110, 121, 125,
 126, 127, 129, 139, 140, 144, 147, 169,
 202, 203, 209, 220, 228, 229, 232, 244,
 245, 251, 264
attractiveness 12, 265

Balkans; Balkan Sprachbund 20, 26, 79, 104,
 105–6, 107, 117, 173, 176, 177, 178–9,
 181–2, 187–99, 202, 210, 237, 248, 249,
 261
bilingualism; stable 158
bleaching 80, 188
body-part model 201
borrowing xii, 3, 6, 7–8, 9, 12, 13, 30, 34, 54,
 79, 85, 90, 94, 142, 158, 175, 182, 196,
 211, 261, 264
 hierarchies of 8
 implications of 7

calquing xi, 18, 19, 31, 100, 101, 157, 227,
 249, 251
case syncretism 148–9, 153, 211
clefting; cleft construction 163, 239
cliticization 224, 257
code-copying 6–7, 11, 13, 35, 119
coexistence 17, 18, 124, 132, 137, 143, 153,
 249
communication; accomodation theory 12
compound preposition 154, 206
compounding 154, 156–7, 206
congruence 6, 234, 243
conjunction; coordinating 16, 94, 128, 160,
 207–8
conjunction; subordinating 91, 196, 205, 209,
 246, 248
context extension 45, 50–8, 89, 113, 115, 141,
 206, 255

context generalization 89, 99, 114, 253, 254
context-induced reinterpretation 15, 45, 80
convergence xi, xii, 6, 9–11, 12, 19, 79, 175,
 210, 237, 247, 255
coordination; clause 17, 110, 128, 159
copying 7, 12, 93, 100–3, 196, 225
Creole xi, 12, 32, 83, 111, 125, 134, 135, 181,
 203, 214, 229, 238, 239, 241–3, 266
cycle of grammaticalization 116, 197, 198

decategorialization 15, 17, 21, 80, 85, 86, 87,
 90–1, 99, 103, 104, 111, 146, 147, 159,
 162, 165, 167, 189, 192, 193, 258
deontic modality 23–4, 136, 206
desemanticization 15, 16, 36, 80, 85, 89–90,
 99, 115, 159, 162, 189, 193, 204, 253, 258
discourse marker 48, 82, 98, 100, 121, 143
dominance 12, 238
Dravidianization 96, 163, 164, 202
durative 82, 125, 127

erosion 15, 17, 18, 80, 85, 86, 87, 91–2, 98,
 99, 103, 104, 146, 147, 162, 189, 190,
 191, 192, 258
evidential 47, 125–6, 129, 147–8, 202, 214,
 215, 265
extension 15, 16, 50, 80, 89–90, 96, 99–100,
 110, 113, 115, 120, 124, 136, 137,
 138–41, 189, 236, 253, 258

focus particle 143, 212, 262
fusion 224

gap filling 124–30, 133, 138, 249
global copying 6
Goal Schema 31, 246

imperfect learning 34, 37
imposition 13, 237, 238
indirective 126
Indo-Aryanization 163, 202, 250
infinitive; loss of 178, 188, 196–7, 251

307

1411411R0

Printed in Great Britain by
Amazon.co.uk, Ltd.,
Marston Gate.